Postmodern Investment

Postmodern Investment

Facts and Fallacies of Growing Wealth in a Multi-Asset World

GARRY B. CROWDER
THOMAS SCHNEEWEIS
HOSSEIN KAZEMI

WILEY

John Wiley & Sons, Inc.

Cover Design: Leiva-Sposato
Cover Photograph: © Entienou / iStockphoto

Published by John Wiley & Sons, Inc., Hoboken, New Jersey.
Published simultaneously in Canada.

For general information on our other products and services or for technical support, please
contact our Customer Care Department within the United States at (800) 762-2974, outside
the United States at (317) 572-3993 or fax (317) 572-4002.

Wiley publishes in a variety of print and electronic formats and by print-on-demand. Some
material included with standard print versions of this book may not be included in e-books or
in print-on-demand. If this book refers to media such as a CD or DVD that is not included in
the version you purchased, you may download this material at http://booksupport.wiley.com.
For more information about Wiley products, visit www.wiley.com.

Library of Congress Cataloging-in-Publication Data:

Crowder, Garry B., 1954—
  Postmodern investment : facts and fallacies of growing wealth in a multi-asset world /
Garry B. Crowder, Thomas Schneeweis, Hossein Kazemi.
      p. cm.
  Includes bibliographical references and index.
  ISBN 978-1-118-43223-5 (cloth); ISBN 978-1-118-48383-1 (ebk);
  ISBN 978-1-118-48384-8 (cloth); ISBN 978-1-118-48385-5 (ebk)
  1. Investments. 2. Portfolio management. I. Schneeweis, Thomas. II. Kazemi, Hossein,
1954- III. Title.
  HG4521.C869 2013
  332.6—dc23

                                                        2012030608

Printed in the United States of America

10 9 8 7 6 5 4 3 2 1

To Jill
—*Garry B. Crowder*

To Alison
—*Thomas Schneeweis*

To Mahnaz and Maziar
—*Hossein Kazemi*

Contents

Preface

For the most part, significant individual wealth is built on the foundation of the single unadulterated bet with little regard given to risk. Examples abound in life and literature. This is the domain of the entrepreneur who focuses on the single product or idea, the oil wildcatter who sinks his or her last penny into the next well, or the investor who bets it all on the single stock or market trend. There is no risk-to-reward calculation in this model only the pure belief that there can be only one outcome and that loss and risk lie in not fully engaging with a given path. In contrast, institutional wealth is built by the steady analysis and implementation of risk and return models. This approach entails an understanding that preservation of the corpus against inflation is foremost in the accumulation of wealth. The institutional wealth model incorporates concepts such as time horizons, diversification, and asset allocation.

The two models converge when speaking to preservation of wealth with the single bet approach giving way to reasoned and sustained accumulation. Here, the goal of any large portfolio of assets held by individuals, pension plans, banks, insurance companies, or any other similar scheme is simply to earn a rate of return. Earning a rate of return is a relative enterprise. Its success depends on the financial obligations associated with the scheme as well as market variables such as inflation, regulatory policy, investment costs, and time horizons. Intrinsic to the concept of earning a rate of return is an understanding of the risks associated with the scheme's portfolio.

Recently, we authored a book on asset allocation and the use of alternative asset classes and made the argument that the inclusion of new financial assets such as hedge funds, private equity, structured products, and venture capital vehicles would significantly enhance risk management within large multi-asset portfolios. The starting point of *The New Science of Asset Allocation* (John Wiley & Sons, 2010) was that asset allocation is a risk-management tool and not, as popularly understood, a return-enhancement structure. Further, we argued that substantive risk management only exists in a world of transparency where both assets and managers are subject to an objective pricing mechanism. Within this argument we explored and concluded that with the exception of a rare few, active managers add little to the equation of making money.

Candidly, there is nothing monumental in this assessment. Investors in traditional assets came to this conclusion long ago. With the creation of meaningful benchmarks such as the Standard & Poor's (S&P) 500 and the Russell 2000, investors began to have sufficient market visibility to meaningfully evaluate the performance and contribution of their active equity managers. This evaluation exposed a number of key points. First, traditional equity asset managers are primarily index followers and often do not outperform their given benchmarks. Second, there are transformational managers—unicorns—managers who through their judgment and guile are able to add genuine value by understanding the absolute and relative valuations of markets, and thus profit on fundamental changes at the margin. Third, there are not enough transformational managers to offset the explicit and hidden costs of investing in those managers who are primary index followers. Thus, our argument continued, just as traditional asset management has moved in part from "active only" to replication or tracking investment products, in the alternative investment area, investors will increasingly come to realize that indexation or replication is an appropriate substitute for the broader universe of alternative managers.

The market disturbance of 2007 and 2008 and its immediate aftermath can only be characterized as a systemic structural failure of accepted financial models as well as their underlying assumptions and beliefs. The current European sovereign debt crisis is something completely different, yet akin. When coupled, these twin failures of market norms provide a telling opportunity to reexamine the purpose of the asset allocation decision in finance and the changing nature of risk as we strive to create, manage, and preserve wealth in an uncertain environment.

What was forgotten or overlooked by sovereigns, investment banks, and their regulatory oversight companions is that the changed and changing nature of risk is at the core of the asset allocation decision. Risk-based asset allocation presupposes the introduction of proven due diligence practices where equal type assets with less-than-perfect common sensitivity to informational changes lead to higher long-term returns than if those assets were held individually. Repeatedly, history has shown that many of the benefits of asset allocation have been lost because of oversimplified approaches and a less-than-rigorous understanding of the risks and sources of return of differing asset classes. While this is particularly true of "new" asset classes such as hedge funds, private equity, real estate, commodities, and structured products, it remains a constant within traditional asset classes as well.

THE CORE CONCEPTS IN MANAGING WEALTH

At its core, risk management and asset allocation require asset managers and their investors to jointly appreciate the fundamental concept that an asset's, or a portfolio of assets', expected return is based on expected risk; and that investors must actually confront and contemplate the concept of risk. That said, the concept of risk itself is an amorphous and intimidating beast that most investors, and unfortunately most asset managers, steadfastly refuse to embrace as an ordinary extension of a portfolio's returns—so the concept is never fully developed or defined. We know that an investor's definition of risk depends a great deal on the perceived stability of his or her environment. We also know that most academics describe risk in terms of standard deviation and beta; and practitioners who typically have little genuine insight into their individual investor's view of the world, and have virtually no understanding of academic principles, rely on past experience, mathematical models, and company practice in defining risk.

These differing approaches to embracing and understanding risk make a definitive approach to risk measurement and risk-based asset allocation elusive. In addition, since we monitor only what we can measure, most approaches to risk measurement within asset allocation continue to rely on simplified measures of security and market risk (alpha and beta) as the principal tools governing the determination of fundamental asset risk, as well as the ability of managers to create value. However, we have learned that both the simple world of single-factor risk models (e.g., standard deviation, skewness, market beta) as well as more complex models of risk and return determination, may impede or limit the understanding of fundamental risks (e.g., counterparty risk, liquidity). In short, there is risk in assuming that we can define risk and there is risk in the actual models used for risk estimation. Numerous examples exist of investors using historical data to approximate expected return and risk relationships between assets. This approach ignores the fact that the fundamental trading aspects of these assets have long changed and that the historical indices used to capture asset return distributions have little to do with the construction of current indices. The use of such data also dismisses the reality that historical data has little, if any, relationship to current expected returns (e.g., using historical fixed-income returns as a basis for future expected return rather than correctly using the expected return imbedded in current yield curves is but one example of faulty use of historical data).

Other examples include the use of historical asset returns reflected in various asset indices when the underlying investable portfolio that an investor holds does not fundamentally reflect the data used in portfolio risk or return estimation. Investors must come to appreciate that the expected risk and return of an asset simply reflects the informational sensitivity of the fundamental risk factors contained in a portfolio. Research has shown that hedge funds are not absolute investment vehicles in that they are not able to provide a positive expected return in all market environments. Results show that correlations of the various hedge fund strategies with traditional stock and bond investments often depend on the security markets in which hedge fund managers trade. The expected correlation relationships of various hedge fund strategies with a range of market factors simply reflect the expected relationships between equity and bond market factors and hedge fund returns. Investors now realize that hedge fund returns, or the performance of any asset, change over time, and as such, the benefits of the asset as a stand-alone investment or as an addition to traditional portfolios depend on the unique investment environment of that period. Thus, we can think of active asset management returns as a combination of manager skill and an underlying return to the strategy of the investment style itself.

The cascading financial crisis over the past five years has raised doubts as to the fundamental benefits of asset diversification. These doubts are misplaced. Most financial assets have actually performed as expected during this crisis. Given lending and regulatory pressures, equity hedge funds performed like low beta equity funds. Similarly, distressed debt funds performed like high duration-low liquidity bond funds and managed futures (e.g., commodity trading advisors [CTAs]) offered positive returns in 2008, as liquid futures contracts offered a means to benefit from the negative price momentum of many financial assets. Also, the negative returns to commodities reflected a fundamental reduction in global demand.

In summary, the performance of the assets themselves has not been surprising. The genuine surprise has been the lack of fundamental due diligence and care inherent in many portfolios and investment schemes. Investors have discovered that their hedge fund managers can only trade within the guidelines and terms offered by their lenders and that those lenders actually hold first priority to the ownership of all monies within the fund. Similarly, these investors discovered that the returns associated with their real estate, private equity, and venture capital investments had more to do with accounting assumptions and the sponsor fund's business model than with the actual value of the underlying financial assets. Finally, investors discovered that effective financial engineering presupposes that managers understand the logical stopping point of models, as well as the need for a transparent measurement of the risks associated with the underlying assets within such models. These are all things known, but learned again in retrospect. So once again, investors learned that there is no substitute for fundamental research and due diligence, and that the price of benign negligence is horrific.

POSTMODERN INVESTMENT

A key issue in the art of asset management is the degree to which we should rely on past data and relationships while making investment decisions. Beginning with the work of Markowitz, investment management has increasingly become more quantitative. To use these quantitative models, we need accurate estimates of economic relationships, which are typically estimated using historical data. How much weight we should assign to the past is most critical. In understanding our past, we move to the future. In so doing, we understand that it was the manner in which the assets were deployed, and not their intrinsic characteristics, that failed. If we accept this proposition, then the future course in understanding diversification as a risk-management tool is to fully comprehend the sources of return, correlations, and limitations of individual assets as well as how they function in tandem. Equally as important is to understand that the world has changed significantly since the introduction of the simple stock and bond portfolio as the primary example of adequate portfolio diversification. In an interdependent global market we cannot assume that historical relationships or sources of return remain static. In addition, the answer to the benefits of asset allocation in a multi-asset universe may simply be that "more is better than less." As sources of return evolve, so must nomenclature. Hedge funds are simply extensions of the proprietary trading desks of investment banks. Structured products are extensions of prepackaged convertible bonds and the initial public offerings (IPOs) of new enterprises. Many of the limitations of the current asset allocation approaches and models are that they concentrate primarily on investment in a limited number of assets and adhere to their historical definitions. Today, investment in a larger range of investable assets is being addressed through more active asset construction and more focus on the actual source of return and risk. The increase in potential investment opportunities increases the potential benefit of strategic asset allocation opportunities as well as tactical and dynamic approaches to asset allocation.

There are, of course, numerous approaches to asset allocation and risk management. At the core of asset allocation remain the fundamental set of decisions centered on what and how much to buy, given risk preferences. However, as in most questions of asset management, the details are key. For many portfolios, it is necessary to back into the asset allocation decision by first determining a reasonable set of investment vehicles with the desired liquidity and return characteristics. While fundamentally flawed, for most, traditional asset allocation remains the simple choice of mixing various asset classes to provide a mix of assets that offer increased expected return for a particular level of risk tolerance. However, as discussed previously, there is no one definition of risk. Before risk can be managed, the intrinsic risks impacting a particular investor must be understood as well as some common methods of managing them. In many books on asset allocation, the systematic model-driven approach is emphasized. The importance of manager discretion is emphasized. Most investors simply fail to take to heart the axiom that unusual returns can only be obtained from holding unusual risks or paying for means of managing that risk.

Asset allocation exists in an evolving marketplace. There will certainly be a series of choices, and each of those choices will have ripple consequences. Throughout the recent crisis, extreme events have occurred. If history is to instruct, we know that the future will provide additional crises, and despite the best efforts of regulatory bodies, investors will lose money. In the recent crisis many mutual fund investors lost 40 to 50 percent of their investment because many fund managers were forced by government regulation, market order, or contractual dictates to follow a prescribed market index. For example, many continued to track the Russell 2000 index for which returns fell as volatility increased from 20 to 40 percent. Managers could have, and perhaps should have, focused on keeping a constant risk profile (e.g., 20 percent) in line with original expectations rather than simply following a prospectus-bound representative index. Alternatively, they could have simply liquidated the portfolios and returned the cash to their investors, because no meaningful investments existed within the proscribed risk parameters. Interestingly, none of the managers we spoke with contemplated this latter scenario.

As we emerge from this drama, what have we learned? Hopefully, investors have been cautioned to be wary of historical data, historical thoughts, and historical performance. In other words, we must show little fear in puncturing myths and their companions. History rarely repeats itself in the same manner, and one of the failings of modern portfolio and risk-management design, as well as some of the recent academic and quantitative research, is the presumption that it will.

HOW THE CHAPTERS ARE STRUCTURED

As we begin this book's journey, we want to tell a simple story. Our goal is to provide both a fundamental understanding of the sources of risk and return for the primary investment classes and to raise concerns on many of the closely held assumptions that lead even the most sophisticated investors to erroneous asset allocation decisions. In so doing, in Chapter 1, we start with a brief historical overview of the financial markets. In Chapters 2 through 9, we turn our attention to the business models and risk and return characteristics of some of the more prevalent traditional and alternative asset classes and ask and answer questions regarding their true sources of return. We have devoted individual chapters to traditional equity and fixed income, hedge funds, private equity, managed futures, commodities, and real estate. Within these chapters, we also explore some of the myths and misconceptions that have developed over the years regarding the underlying economic behavior of these asset classes and their place in a multi-asset portfolio.

We elected not to comment on the derivatives market or to analyze structured products and replication scenarios. Replication scenarios was the underlying thesis of our previous book, *The New Science of Asset Allocation*, and the two remaining topics—structured products and derivatives—are vast enough to warrant their own book treatment. In any event, we did not believe we could do justice to both our analysis of the basic asset classes and these highly fluid structures in this setting. Finally, this book is designed to offer suggestions on how investors can protect themselves in this very fluid global market environment. As a precursor, we share some generalities.

AS YOU BEGIN

In our explorations, we have learned that financial myths contain enough plausibility to encourage intellectual laziness; enough truth to support the lie; enough pathos to snare the human condition; and, enough visceral appeal to be widely embraced. But, more importantly, myths and misconceptions are usually based on rigorously tested past truths. Behavioral science informs us that there is perhaps nothing more difficult to abandon than a tested past truth. We find this true in all aspects of life. At poker tournaments, the new players, those who have not been tested against the pressure of wagers made in a public setting, are called "dead money." They are called this because the probability of their winning in a world of professionals is not remote—it is nonexistent. Our goal is to provide the reader tools to be competitive.

Acknowledgments

Any individual who has gone through the process of writing a book realizes that its final success depends on those individuals who read and reread every chapter, who make sure that deadlines are met, and who constantly keep everyone on the same path. We would like to offer special thanks to just those individuals: our editor at John Wiley & Sons, Emilie Herman, and our internal editors, Edward Szado and Patricia Bonnett. Without them, this book would have remained an idea rather than a reality.

Postmodern Investment

CHAPTER 1

Investment Ideas

Evolution or Revolution?

The universe of investment opportunities can seem infinite. For most investors, modern investment is a complex minefield of multiple assets, multiple products, and multiple means of investment. Added to this mix are the vast numbers of firms competing for an investor's money and the myriad "stories" developed to provide credence to their particular approach.

On the surface, it would appear that modern investment should be a relatively straightforward exercise. At its essence, the process should entail (1) selecting securities that are expected to outperform other securities in an asset class, (2) selecting a group of asset classes that will outperform other asset classes, and (3) deciding on the allocations among asset classes and securities that meet an investor's risk tolerance. Beneath the surface calm of this investment process, however, lie riptides of incomplete information, changing expectations and circumstances, and evolving interrelationships. This state of flux exists both with the investor and the market (the composite investor). An investor's tolerance for or understanding of risks changes over time, as does his or her investment horizon and view of the future. The market's tolerance for an estimate of risks also changes over time, if for no other reason than the sources of returns and risk profiles of differing assets are not static. They change with new information, new interrelationships with the economy and other asset classes, and new modes of product delivery. Thus, it is not surprising that a vast asset management industry has grown to meet these changing expectations and processes.

The asset management industry is not monolithic. It consists of investment managers, marketers, consultants, accountants, lawyers, television or Internet personalities, journalists, and, of course, the pundit of the day. With so many sources of information and versions of the truth, the question is and remains, who is an investor to trust? In Lewis Carroll's *Alice in Wonderland*, Alice asks the Cheshire Cat which path she should take, and the cat answers by saying, "That depends a good deal on where you want to get to." Alice answers that she does not know, at which the cat answers, "Then it doesn't matter which way you go." Most investors share this hidden angst, wanting to reach an end that seems so reasonable yet defies specific definition. In short, all investors really want is a simple answer to the basic question, What do I invest in to make as much money as possible with as little risk as possible?

This chapter provides a brief history of how major advances in financial theory and investment practice have attempted to reduce the infinite opportunities of the marketplace into a manageable subset of investable choices and, in so doing, answer the question of how an investor can make as much money as possible with as little risk as possible. The chapter shows how investment processes and attitudes toward those processes have evolved to meet ever-increasing changes in the economy, regulations, and technological advancements. It offers a review of the range of current and past efforts to understand and rationalize the process of security selection, risk management, and asset allocation. We mentioned earlier that investment managers have a story. We, too, have a story. Throughout this chapter and the course of the book, we explore the premise that investing always entails known and unknown risks, and that, irrespective of its source, investors must always aggressively question information and the due diligence of others. For example, the first questions an investor should ask about a product are when will it make money and when will it lose money. Surprisingly, far too often the individual selling or advising on the product either does not know or refuses to discuss the potential risks of investing alongside the potential benefits.

In this vein, perhaps one of the greatest myths and misconceptions of the investment management industry is that an investor can fully rely on the advice and recommendations of professionals. In truth, not all professionals are professional, and even those who are, sometimes lack the resources or understanding to fully educate their audience. For the most part, these industry professionals are charged with selling a number of different ideas or products and may have limited knowledge, limited experiences, and conflicts of interest—all of which require intense examination prior to any reliance on their recommendations. The true professionals in this area have a striking willingness to investigate. When the right questions are asked, it is not unusual for these professionals to learn the particulars of an investment or investment process along with their clients. Investors should take advantage of the absolute, or comparative, advantage of these skilled professionals and try to avoid the others. How to distinguish between the two is difficult. Investors should understand the world in which these professionals exist and try to determine if an advisor has adequate knowledge and limited conflicts of interest.

As mentioned in the introduction, the authors have had a long history in the field, as both academics and practitioners. On average, we began our careers about 30 years ago. When we started, options and futures were more myth than substance, and private equity, hedge funds, and real estate investment products were still the domain of the privileged. What we did have were a few guiding principles of how to invest. Among those principles, we were taught that unless absolutely necessary, never give up complete control of the investment decision to others, and always know when an asset should either make money or lose money. These two principles have held up well over the years, especially in markets where the failure of bond ratings and the failure of multi-asset diversification have greatly tested investor reliance on investment professionals. A third principle, despite or perhaps because of the recent failure of investment advice, has singularly withstood a changing and complex world. That third principle is this: In the end, investors are and must be responsible for their own investment decisions. This is not to say that an investor should not look to the advice of others, only that it is imperative to seek transparent and objective validation of all advice.

The synopsis of our experiences is that in this modern world of investment, change is a constant, adaptation a necessity, and due diligence a given. This view has led the authors to seek transparency in, and an understanding of, the sources of returns of various asset classes and investment products and to objectively test both the implementation and the boundaries of professional investors' recommendations.

Given the changing dynamics of modern capital markets, much of modern investment is centered on the methods employed to estimate what may happen and alternative approaches to managing the risks surrounding these events. Our central thesis is that expected return is a function of the risks taken within any endeavor and that those risks may not be able to be measured or managed solely through complex systematic quantitative models. Thus, modern investment must focus on a broader context, including the benefit of an individual's discretionary oversight, and each investor is responsible for accepting the upside potential of an asset as well as its downside.

The story of the evolution of our understanding of that return-to-risk trade-off is one of the underlying themes of this book. The "evolution" part must be emphasized, as the expected return-to-risk relationship changes with new information. Exhibit 1.1 offers a summary of some of the major advancements in investment management over the past 60 years. Most of these advancements are in the areas of how we value investments and how

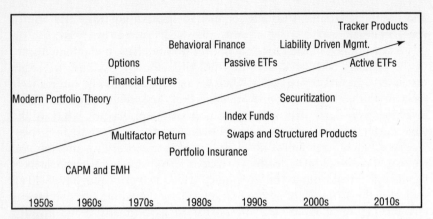

EXHIBIT 1.1 Evolution of Asset Management

new investment alternatives were created. We can only hypothesize what changes will happen in the future: but happen, they will.

Much of what we do in investment management is based on understanding the trade-offs between the risks and returns of various investable assets, as well as understanding various aspects of the asset allocation process, including alternative approaches to return estimation and risk management. These trade-offs are often conditioned by a belief system built within a historical context. Behavioral science has shown that most people have a great deal of difficulty moving beyond what has once been tested and learned. However, the world does change. Over time and as additional information is received, we learn that risk and its measurement are current snapshots rather than the never-changing map we once thought. Collectively, those snapshots describe a road that is bumpy at times but nevertheless reveals changing ideas and processes and enables an investor to find a workable solution. In this regard, there are no optimal solutions and no easy paths. Within our view, there are only those decisions taken with understanding and care and those that are not. This is the heart of modern investment.

IN THE BEGINNING

Maximizing return and reducing the role of chance in the investment and asset allocation decision have dominated the evolution of investment management. Knowing that it is difficult to forecast return and that all chance cannot be eliminated, investors, industry professionals, and academics have sought ways of understanding the independent elements of the investment decision process so as to measure their respective contributions and to predict outcomes. These elements include factors such as asset risk, sources of investment return, and the business models integral to determining and delivering an investment decision. As we begin this analysis, the first order is to examine the beginning of the market's attempt to structure and understand risk and value, and to trace those efforts to today's investment tools and practices. Along the way we will discuss the linkages between and among theories and models, such as modern portfolio theory, the efficient market hypothesis, and the capital asset pricing model. Although important tools, each has limitations, and in some instances, each has been distorted to reach fairly unsupportable ends. Finally, we conclude this chapter with an overview of the financial markets and the many ways they have implemented these models in creating new investment products and supporting due diligence efforts.

Modern Portfolio Theory and the Efficient Market Hypothesis

Our starting point is that there are two fundamental directives of security selection and asset allocation: (1) estimate what may happen, and (2) choose a course of action based on those estimates. These directives have been at the core of practitioner and academic debate since the early 1950s. What we describe today as the field of modern financial economics and investment management was created throughout the 1930s, 1940s, and 1950s with the publication of a handful of articles and books. Arguably, the most important were written by Irving Fisher, Benjamin Graham, and David Dodd; Franco Modigliani and Merton Miller, and, finally, Harry Markowitz. Each made important contributions to our understanding of financial markets, security selection, corporate financial decision making, and portfolio construction. The latter is known as *modern portfolio theory* (MPT), which for many is synonymous with Markowitz. Today MPT is now almost 60 years old, and there have been significant advances in thought and practice based on this work. The fundamental concept expressed in Markowitz's article is the ability to measure investment risk based on the comovement of investment returns (i.e., correlations). In other words, Markowitz attempted to provide a scientific foundation for the allocation of investment capital.

In the absence of such a foundation, an investor will have to follow a naïve strategy, in which available capital is allocated among available assets using a rather ad hoc rule (e.g., equally weighted or equal number of shares). The goal of naïve diversification is to create a portfolio that does not include the entire investment universe but could offer a risk-return profile close to that of the entire investment universe. Using the United States as an example, the performance of an equally weighted portfolio of 50 randomly selected exchange-listed stocks is likely to be very similar to that of a portfolio of all exchange-listed stocks. With the addition of more randomly selected securities to this 50-security portfolio, the risk-return profile of the portfolio will remain mostly unchanged (Exhibit 1.2). To achieve a better risk-return profile, the portfolio must be constructed using the framework set forth by Markowitz and other pioneers in the field of modern investment.

Markowitz formalized the security selection process to form optimal portfolios within the return-and-risk relationship between securities in what is known today as the *mathematics of diversification*. If standard deviations (volatility) and expected returns of available securities, as well as the correlations (comovement of securities) among them can be estimated, then the standard deviation and expected return of any portfolio consisting of those securities can be calculated. From those simple concepts, an industry was born with the sole purpose of constructing portfolios with desirable risk-return profiles. One particular set of such portfolios comprises the so-called mean-variance efficient portfolios—a set of portfolios, each with the highest expected rate of return for a given level of risk (standard deviation

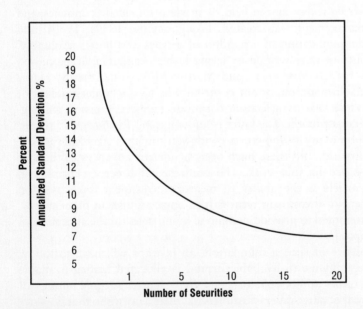

EXHIBIT 1.2 Naïve Diversification

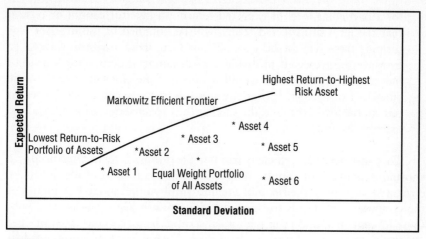

EXHIBIT 1.3 Efficient Frontier

or variance), leads to what is called the *mean-variance efficient frontier* (Exhibit 1.3).

This simple concept—the efficient frontier—has formed the basis of investment management for the past 60 years. It is found in textbooks, in marketing materials, and on the web, with more than 1,770,000 hits on Google (as of the date this chapter was written). However, despite becoming part of the lexicon, the true meaning of Markowitz's efficient frontier analysis has become confused and at times misused. And no wonder: a review of this "simple concept" reveals numerous complicating factors:

- The efficient frontier does not come with a single "one-size-fits-all" inclusive, efficient portfolio construction process. The measured efficient frontier depends on the set of securities analyzed. The efficient frontier for a set of equities differs from an efficient frontier for fixed-income securities, which differs from an efficient frontier for a set of stocks and bonds (Exhibit 1.4). In addition, the portfolios that fall on the frontier typically have weights that are not practical (e.g., large positive allocations for some securities and large negative allocations for others). Further, when the methodology is applied to individual securities, the resulting portfolios typically consist of a large number of securities, making them inefficient when transaction costs are taken into account.
- Between the minimum-risk portfolio and the highest-risk portfolio are a number of portfolios with a mix of assets that constantly change as one goes up and down the efficient frontier line. However, because each portfolio has by design its own level of risk (i.e., standard deviation)

for a particular level of expected return, an investor cannot be certain that the level of expected return will be obtained (if the investor was certain, there would be no risk). In fact, if an investor wanted to measure the expected probability of obtaining a return for a level of measured risk, the result would be more of the efficient cone than the efficient frontier (the higher the risk, the more uncertain the expected return; the lower the risk, the smaller the expected deviation around the expected return).

To construct these efficient frontier portfolios, a researcher needs an enormous amount of inputs. Risk and returns of all securities must be estimated, as well as their comovements. To obtain reasonable estimates of these inputs, there needs to be a fairly long return history associated with these investments; and even with a substantial history, the estimations are uncertain. Over time, firms simply change. Their capital structure, product mix, governance, and interrelationships with other firms and asset classes are in flux. As such, the estimates of needed inputs contain significant uncertainty. No one really knows what the true standard deviation of Exxon stock is now or will be in the future. And of course no one knows the true mean return distribution from which monthly returns on Exxon stock are drawn. Thus, depending on when or how those inputs are estimated, an investor would obtain a different set of efficient portfolios. This means the efficient frontier is really a band, or range, within which the true efficient frontier is likely to lie.

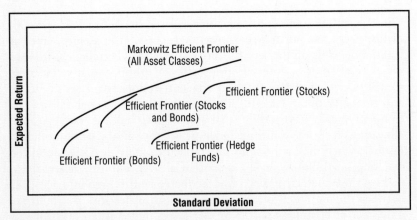

EXHIBIT 1.4 Efficient Frontiers for Multiple Asset Classes

Capital Asset Pricing Model

It is claimed that while reading Harry Markowitz's research, William Sharpe noticed a footnote in which Markowitz wondered about the implications of his prescriptions for investors. In other words, how would one measure the riskiness of individual securities if all investors followed his advice and invested only in portfolios that lie on the efficient frontier? Sharpe followed the logic of this footnote and came up with a model that described the relationship between risk and return of securities. The model, known as the *capital asset pricing model* (CAPM), provided a rather simple framework for measuring the riskiness of investments and established an intuitive relationship between risk and return: the higher the risk, the higher the expected return. The question remains how to measure that risk. In Sharpe's world, there exists a risk-free rate along with the efficient frontier. In such a world, there is a point—a portfolio—which when combined with the risk-free rate offers a set of portfolios that dominates all other portfolios on the efficient frontier. That line is called the *capital market line* (CML), and that portfolio is called the *market portfolio* (Exhibit 1.5). In this world, the risk of an individual security is measured not by its own standalone risk, such as volatility (e.g., standard deviation), but by its marginal contribution to the volatility (risk) of the market portfolio. This leads to the so-called CAPM, in which the expected return of a security is based on a combination of the risk-free rate and an asset's systematic sensitivity to the market portfolio (known as a security's *beta*).[1]

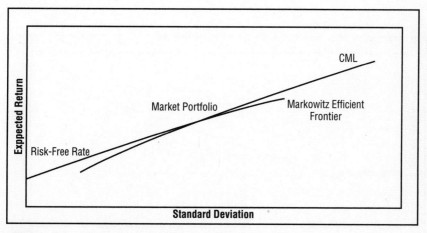

EXHIBIT 1.5 Capital Market Line

The required return of an individual security is therefore not directly related to its standard deviation but to its beta. Thus, in the world of CAPM, all assets are located on the same straight line that passes through the point representing the market portfolio (with beta equal to 1). That line, as shown in Exhibit 1.6, is called the *security market line* (SML). The basic difference between the CML and the SML is one of reference. In the CML, the risk measured is total risk (standard deviation); in the SML, the risk measured is a security's marginal risk to the market portfolio (beta).

Although CAPM has proven to be highly unreliable when subjected to empirical tests, two of its core messages are still true today. First, there are certain risks that can be diversified away rather inexpensively (e.g., by holding the market portfolio), and therefore investors should not expect to earn an additional return for bearing or holding additional risk that is separate from its relationship with the market portfolio. For example, individuals who invest their entire portfolio in the stock of their employer are creating an enormous amount of risk (just ask employees of Enron or Lehman Brothers). The investor should not expect an abnormally high return for bearing the risk of making such an investment. The arguments that risks that cannot be diversified easily and inexpensively (called *systematic risk*) are important determinants of expected returns on various investments and are the enduring legacy of CAPM.

The second basic message of MPT and CAPM is that the creation of efficient portfolios is rather straightforward. Only two investments are required: (1) a highly diversified portfolio of available securities (the market portfolio) and (2) a safe asset. Various combinations of these two

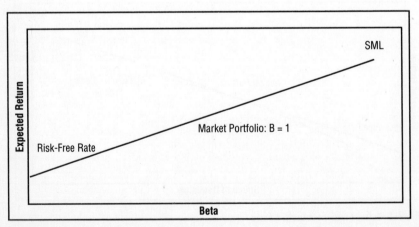

EXHIBIT 1.6 Security Market Line

investments can be used to create all efficient portfolios. If this essential message were accepted and practiced by the entire investment community, there would be no need for this and hundreds of other books written on the subject of alternative approaches to asset allocation and investment management. More important, the asset-management industry would need to shrink substantially and employ far fewer people at far smaller salaries.

Of course, there are many reasons to believe that the simple investment strategy just described would not be suitable for all investors. Most investors have liabilities that need to be funded through their investment portfolio. This means that the portfolio has to be managed in the context of those liabilities. A university endowment has no finite time horizon, and its implicit liability is to help fund the operations of a university. A pension fund has multiple objectives and varied beneficiaries with various time horizons. A family office has one client, but multiple objectives. Clearly, a strategy consisting of various combinations of a well-diversified portfolio and cash cannot possibly be optimal for all of these investors. The message we want to leave investors with is that modern asset allocation requires an investor to see the world the way an institution does: with knowledge of future liabilities; a known time horizon of investment; and a well-defined plan for holding assets, which will hopefully meet those future liabilities in the time frame stated. An additional message is that this asset allocation process is always evolving, and it rarely fits nicely into the one-size-fits-all asset allocation process currently recommended by many financial institutions and investment personnel.

A third message (or more of a practical implication) to be gained from CAPM is that if systematic risk can be measured by a security's beta and that beta can be estimated by the market model, then it stands to reason that an asset's expected return can be forecast using CAPM. Of even greater significance, as is discussed later, if an asset's expected return can be forecast based on its systematic risk, then any excess return greater than that may be attributed to the expertise of an individual manager (in short, the manager's *alpha*, or excess return, is caused by his or her unique skill).

THE BEGINNING OF INFORMATION TRANSPARENCY

As noted, modern investment theory and its implementation is a complex minefield. In negotiating this minefield, with time and disciplined analysis we have moved from the belief that financial markets are unbridled casinos to an understanding that they can be a reasoned risk-and-reward system. To be such, however, and to implement the models as well as test the theories we have examined in the preceding sections requires the support of a multifaceted industry willing to provide transparent and objective information at a price.

One of the basic results of the MPT and CAPM was that portfolios with efficient risk-return profiles could be constructed rather easily, that is, by combining a well-diversified portfolio of all available investments with safe assets. An important by-product of this result was that we now had an alternative against which other investment products—and, in particular, actively managed investments—could be evaluated. Benchmarking and return attribution form the cornerstone of the institutional asset-management industry, and investors have benefited greatly from having objective, if perhaps at times flawed, benchmarks to evaluate actively managed investment products.

The development of objective benchmarks led to the concept of *alpha*, or a measure of individual manager outperformance. According to CAPM, a portfolio's expected return is directly related to the level of systematic risk that the portfolio contains. Once the risk of the portfolio is estimated, that estimate can be used as a basis for determining whether the individual who manages the portfolio could consistently choose assets that were fundamentally underpriced and offer an ex post return greater than that consistent with its underlying risk. In sum, could the manager obtain an alpha (excess return above that consistent with the expected return of a similar risk-passive investable asset)? The search for managers who can generate alpha has become a major part of the investment process, especially for institutional investors. However, even in the context of the extremely simplified world of CAPM, a number of parameters have to be estimated (such as a security's beta) in order to implement the model. The net result is that depending on when or how the risk of a portfolio is estimated, the portfolio may display a positive, a negative, or no alpha. And just as important, even when a positive alpha is estimated, there is a high probability that the estimated alpha could be entirely caused by chance (the manager may just get lucky), and therefore the manager may not possess the skills needed to provide alpha in the future.

With the availability of objective benchmarks, we were, for the first time, able to measure an individual investor's performance against the returns of a verifiable financial market. This development not only spawned passive investments or index funds but also put into play one of the unending debates of an evolving industry: Can professional investors consistently outperform similarly mandated passive investments? The resounding answer has been no, especially after fees and taxes. As a collective, money managers have shown an appalling inability to consistently outperform passive benchmarks—no matter the asset class. A recent study showed that over 80 percent of the domestic equity funds managers underperformed their benchmark in 2011. Over longer historical time periods over 60 percent of active equity managers generally underperformed their benchmarks.[2] These empirical results (the underperformance of active equity managers relative to their passive benchmarks) helped give rise to the creation of a series of investable products and exchange-traded funds (ETFs) that capture the return-and-risk characteristics of these passive benchmarks. This is not to say, however, that money managers do not offer benefits outside of their stated ability to outperform a cited benchmark. In fact, it is the ability of managers to make investment decisions that move a portfolio away from the benchmark in unique market conditions (go to cash when the benchmark is falling) that forms one of the basic benefits of active money managers in contrast to a passive nonactively managed benchmark. Unfortunately, an investor may never know if his money manager has that ability, if for no other reason than that the time period of investment did not include any such events. The investor may wish to continue to use (and pay) the money manager in the hope that the manager will act correctly in some future market, and in the belief that the fees are worth the everyday accounting, managerial oversight, and compliance required for any investment process. (Just choose the manager with the best back office rather than the one with the biggest marketing budget).

While the new concepts of risk-to-return trade-off and benchmarking were being developed and refined by academics and practitioners, another central concept of modern finance was taking shape as well: the *efficient market hypothesis* (EMH). The underlying logic of the EMH is rather simple and entirely consistent with other aspects of modern economics: In a capitalist system, competition among economic entities drives down gross profits to these various economic activities. According to the EMH, competition among investors drives to zero the potential profits from gathering and using information about investment returns. In other words, most, if not all, available and relevant information about security prices gets incorporated into prices rather quickly. Therefore, the expected profit from gathering and using information is nearly zero. In this case, profit refers to earnings in excess of what is needed to pay for the resources employed in the investment process. This includes earning a fair rate of return on the capital employed.

The EMH does not imply that investors make no mistakes or that their expectations about future returns from various investments will not be realized. For example, many have argued that the financial crisis of 2007–2008 clearly shows that the EMH is not valid. After all, we saw many AAA-rated securities default within months of their issue, and stocks of several highly valued financial institutions were sold at a fraction of their pre-crisis prices. In addition, others have gone further and blamed the EMH for bringing about the financial crisis. Jeremy Grantham argued that the EMH was responsible for the financial crisis because of its role in the "chronic underestimation of the dangers of asset bubbles" by the financial community.[3] Of course, there were bubbles and financial crises long before the concept of the EMH came along. One of the most famous bubbles took place in 1637, when prices for Dutch tulips increased to unimaginable levels, and one of the worst financial crises started in 1929.

The events leading to the 2007–2008 financial crisis and what happened during the crisis are not necessarily inconsistent with the EMH. In fact, it can be argued that some of the losses experienced by homeowners and banks resulted from a lack of faith in the EMH.[4] Homeowners used significant leverage to purchase ever more expensive properties in the hope of earning significant returns from their investments; that is, they believed that the properties were undervalued. Trading desks of banks and other financial institutions poured significant amounts of capital into mortgage-backed securities, believing that they were mispriced. The EMH is a hypothesis that needs to be tested and, like other hypotheses (especially in the social sciences), has many limitations. However, the lack of faith that current prices reflect the best estimate of the true value of an asset is more often than not at the root of financial debacles and crisis. Against all reasoned advice, investors rush to invest in funds that recently outperformed their peers and believe promises made by money managers that there is no need to bear higher risk in order to earn higher returns (e.g., in the case of Bernie Madoff, in which he generated steady above-normal returns for many years). Pre-crisis prices reflect the information available at the time and the way that information was understood by a large majority of market participants. Only a few skilled (perhaps lucky) investors were able to gather and use relevant information about the potential mispricing of some of the assets that crashed in the aftermath of the crisis.

The EMH implies that investors can earn returns that will exceed what their level of risk predicts only if there is some violation of information efficiency (similar to a Monopoly game in which one individual has inside information on what number you will roll). However, if the EMH is true, most investors should not waste their time trying to pick stocks using well-known sources of public information but should concentrate on risk determination and the proper set of assets to capture that expected risk and corresponding return level (you win the game of Monopoly by diversifying across spaces and paying the right price for those spaces—that and a LOT of LUCK). More important, investors need to keep a level head in the game and remember to pick, from a bucket of overall risk choices, one that matches their genuine risk preferences and constraints.

Despite the reasoned purity of the EMH, many investors simply refuse to accept its conclusions. That is, if an investor wishes to obtain investment returns above the average for a particular level of risk, then he needs to bet on being lucky. Perhaps the most striking aspect of the rise of informational transparency is the extent to which it has become commoditized. Most information is increasingly free; however, investors should take heed: prices are available on the Internet for free with about a five-minute lag; if past prices had any value, you would have to pay for them. In short, you generally cannot use private information, and all the other information is worthless.

Like other hypotheses, the EMH has its own limitations. For example, to establish if a particular market is truly efficient, a determination needs to be made as to whether there exists a trading strategy that could generate abnormal returns. Clearly, such a test cannot possibly take place, as there are an infinite number of strategies that could be implemented. In addition, for each strategy, we must be able to measure its true risk. Precise estimates of risk are impossible. In fact, there is no agreed-on universal measure of risk. There are simply indicative estimates, and none of those estimates can determine if a strategy is earning an abnormally high return. Again, it is important to come to terms with what the EMH says and does not say. The EMH states that tomorrow's expected price is equal to today's price times the asset's expected return, where expected return is based on current information (risk assessment). Implicit in this analysis is that markets are subject to correction and that ex post tomorrow's actual price may not equal today's expected price for tomorrow. Further, the EMH says that some free lunches may exist for certain individuals with privileged information, but that such informational advantages do not persist and that profit opportunities that may accrue from that informational divide are quickly eliminated. Since asset prices quickly reflect new information and since no one individual has consistent access to unique information, the EMH says that the only way an investor can earn a higher rate of return is by assuming a higher level of risk. Stated a different way, there are no products with ex ante high rates of return without commensurate risk—and anyone who offers such a product is not telling the truth. History is full of examples, such as:

- High-rated bonds with high yields are in fact wolves in sheep's clothing—they are really low-rated bonds for which the rating companies have simply not gotten around to changing the rating (e.g., various highly rated money market funds before the financial crash in 2008).
- Collateralized debt obligations (CDOs) and collateralized loan obligations (CLOs) or any real estate-backed high-yield investment of the mid-2000s.

Unfortunately, despite warnings or historical facts, many investors do not have the time or discipline to understand the basic tenets of investing. If behavioral finance has anything to say, it is that individuals want to believe. Here, investors believe that somehow, somewhere, there must be someone who can provide the one thing they want: return without risk. We call this the hope over history (HOH) model of investment. At bottom, all we can say is that the EMH suggests that if a manager makes an excess return (e.g., because of access to better technology or information), the investor will be charged a fee equal to the excess return such that the investor's return will be similar to that of the passive index (i.e., manager returns − manager fee = return similar to passive index). The fee covers the cost of acquiring the technology or information, plus the investment made in time and effort to use that technology and information for the investor's benefit.

The emerging tools and theories of asset pricing—efficient market investing, mean-variance efficient frontiers, and CAPM—required knowledge and experience in financial markets. Who better than an investment professional to help the average investor navigate this new world? It should come as no surprise that the birth of today's popular Chartered Financial Analyst certification occurred in the same decade as that of CAPM and the efficient frontier. The place of the financial advisor was no longer based solely on his or her ability to find superior stocks or bonds but in helping investors find their true return-to-risk trade-off. How financial advisors do this—and whether they actually do this or not—is a question to be explored in later chapters, but the evolution of these models depends on the industry's ability to support the basic business model. The single-factor model worked. Once the industry evolved to find ways of selling products that met the requirements of a mean-variance efficient, CAPM, and efficient-market world, advisors did not find it in their interest to change their approach when these models simply reached their end point of applicability.

In short, the two cornerstones of modern finance, MPT/CAPM and EMH, do an excellent job of describing most market conditions for many asset classes. For the most part, markets work efficiently. Financial markets for which there is low-cost information and substantial visibility, and for which asset prices reflect current information—such as the U.S. Treasury bond market—are remarkably efficient. Other markets and assets (e.g., real estate, private equity) require extended risk-based factor models, which capture an enlarged set of underlying risks; therefore, sources of expected returns cannot be explained by these simple models. Small firms that have few analysts following them, less ability to raise capital, a less diversified client base, and less legal support may or may not be priced to reflect those risks. Many assets are simply not tradable or have high transaction costs (e.g., housing, employment contracts, and distressed debt).

NEW MARKETS, NEW PRODUCTS, AND THE EVOLUTION OF MODERN INVESTMENT

People spend a great deal of time focused on the equity markets for the simple reason that for most investors, this is the primary area of concern; it is also the one area in which most investors feel some level of comfort. The average investor understands the basic message of equity investment: It is something that brings in more money in the future. The average investor also has a rudimentary understanding of the bond market: High-rated bonds are good, and low-rated bonds are bad. However, since the beginning, to go beyond stocks and bonds was to go into a no-man's-land similar to those shown on maps of old—to venture into foreign lands meant passing through seas where monsters lived. Most people had friends and neighbors who owned stocks and bonds; no one owned futures, options, private equity, or commodities.

In the early 1970s, political and economic forces significantly changed the financial landscape of the investment-management industry and, in so doing, changed the way risk could be managed. Just as the simple dividend discount models for stocks, developed and expanded in the 1930s, were all that was needed to determine stock prices prior to the 1960s and 1970s, bond ratings and yields to maturity, also developed and expanded during the 1930s, were seemingly all that was needed to understand how to hold bonds. During the second half of the 1960s, spurred by regulatory change (ability to trade options, removal of fixed exchange rates) and market conditions, considerable research centered on direct arbitrage relationships between assets (pricing models for options and futures) as well as more efficient ways (e.g., duration) of pricing fixed-income securities.

In the early 1970s, Fischer Black and Myron Scholes (1972) and Robert Merton (1973) developed the option pricing model. Similar models had existed before, and in fact, Louis Bachelier, a French mathematician, had developed a rather similar model in 1900. The seminal contributions of Black, Scholes, and Merton was the concept of delta hedging, which meant that at least in theory, an investor could create a synthetic option through a trading strategy involving stocks and cash. This was of enormous value, because it showed market makers how to hedge their option books, making them more willing to take large positions in these derivative markets. Exchange-based trading floors soon came into existence, which helped to eventually develop a market for a wide range of option-based financial derivatives. Although a range of dynamic futures-based approaches should provide similar risk-management opportunities, options provided a direct and easily measured approach to fundamentally change the risk composition of an asset or a portfolio. Equally important, the model allowed an investor to estimate the insurance cost for modifying the risk of a portfolio. In the decades that followed, new forms of risk management would be advanced that would eventually offer investors a range of risk-management approaches, each with its own unique costs and benefits.

NEW OPPORTUNITIES CREATE NEW RISKS

By the early 1980s, a range of financial products and databases had come into existence that provided the ability to empirically test investment management decision rules. Options trading had grown, and financial futures markets had evolved (Standard & Poor's [S&P] 500 equity index futures contracts came into existence in the mid-1980s). Other changes had taken place regarding technology, regulation, and market structure to provide a set of conditions that supported further development of asset management within a risk-controlled environment. During this period, systemized approaches to tactical asset allocation were being developed and marketed. By the mid-1980s, concepts such as alpha transfer (e.g., taking an equity portfolio, removing its beta with the stock market, and selling the difference to someone who wants alpha with no market risk) and dynamic portfolio insurance were well understood. In addition, during the 1980s, advances in computer technology and software made available for the first time a series of self-serve portfolio management tools that enabled investors to directly manage and adjust their risk exposure. Not only did advances in technology and product development permit investors to manage and adjust risk exposure, but it also allowed investors to take existing assets, dissect their payment streams, and rearrange those payment streams into new assets. The process through which an issuer creates a financial instrument by repackaging financial instruments into a new asset or series of assets came to be known as *securitization*. The classic case in the 1980s was the growth of new mortgage-based products, in which a large pool of mortgages was divided into smaller pieces, which were then sold to investors. Investment firms were able to create entire series of new securities, each with its own unique return-and-risk characteristics that could better meet the risk and return goals of investors. Over the next decades, the securitization industry grew to manage and market an ever-increasing array of financial instruments based on a wide range of underlying securities and cash flows, including credit cards, accounts receivables, and credit spreads. Unfortunately, as many of these new "structured" forms of securities were created, the underlying risks and rewards became more difficult to determine. In short, the further one moved from the original single-security form (the tree) and concentrated on each new financial asset (the limbs), the more difficult it became to trace the stream of cash flows going to the security.

THE MARKET IS NOT EFFICIENT FOR EVERYONE

Looking back over the 1990s and through the early 2010s, the issues intrinsic to modern investment had less to do with the theoretical models underlying return determination than with the changes in market and trading structures. These changes have led to a rapid increase in the number of available investable alternatives and the growth of the financial advisor industry with associated asset allocation and security selection tools required to service all those individuals who require hand-holding to face the complex world of modern investments. Today, as shown in Exhibit 1.7, the number of investment choices has expanded beyond those available in traditional stock and bond investments to a wider range of alternative investments, including traditional alternatives, such as private equity, real estate, and commodities, as well as more modern alternatives, such as hedge funds and managed futures.

In the past 10 years, academics and practitioners have also come to appreciate that traditional stocks and bonds and the alternatives (real estate, commodities, private equity, hedge funds, and managed futures) have common risk factors that drive returns and that those risk factors are contingent on changing market conditions. Moreover, global and domestic regulatory forces as well as market forces have created a new list of investable products (both exchange traded and over the counter [OTC]). These products include more liquid and readily available forms of traditional

EXHIBIT 1.7 Investment Opportunities—Traditional and Alternative Asset Classes

stock and bond investments (e.g., ETFs and OTC forward and options contracts) as well as investable forms of alternative asset vehicles, such as hedge funds, real estate, and private equity.

The addition of new investment forms has permitted individuals to more readily access previously illiquid or less transparent asset classes and has increased the number of assets that provide the potential for risk diversification in various states of the world. In fact, risk itself has become a more tradable asset. Although options had always provided a means to directly manage risk, previous attempts to directly trade risk had not met with success. In the mid-2000s, various forms of VIX (the ticker symbol for the Chicago Board Options Exchange [CBOE] Volatility Index) began to be traded directly on central exchanges. In addition, advances in various forms of structuring along with algorithmic-based trading products have offered investors a broader set of domestic and international vehicles by which to manage asset portfolios. Finally, the growth of the Internet, along with the expansion of data and product availability and computer technology, has permitted the development of a wide set of new approaches to asset allocation and risk management.

At certain levels of the industry we know what we can reasonably expect from these new products as well as from the various risk-management and asset-allocation systems; however, there is evidence that many investment firms have not changed their current business model to reflect these known changes in market return-and-risk opportunities. The market is never efficient for everyone in that transaction costs differ, borrowing costs differ, and taxation differs such that the actual after-tax return across individuals and institutions varies greatly. In sum, the ability to process and understand information and its consequences differs. The unpredictable nature of risky asset pricing raises the issue of how best to manage that risk. Certainly Markowitz's model, based on estimates obtained from historical figures, continues as a primary means by which individuals attempt to estimate portfolio risk; however, the 2008 market collapse illustrated the fundamental flaw of the Markowitz diversification approach; that is, Murphy's Law of Diversification—assets and markets only offer diversification benefits when such benefits are not needed.

Investment management in its most basic form is the ability to manage the return-to-risk trade-off. For many investment firms, simple models of risk management are best met with simple approaches to asset allocation. For many of these firms, the investment decision still comes down to how much equity and how much debt is required to provide an investor with a conservative, a moderate, or an aggressive risk-return portfolio. What risk levels these three portfolios really provide is not detailed, nor is the fact that the risk of these portfolios is not split equally between the stock and bond investments but is often impacted primarily by the high-risk stock or bond included in the investment. The potential addition of a range of other investment classes should at least offer one answer to the stock–bond conundrum: Are more investment opportunities better than less? Additional assets may provide investors with greater access to return opportunities that may not exist in most states of the traditional stock and bond world.

A PERSONAL VIEW OF MODERN INVESTMENT

In previous sections, we cautioned against an overreliance on empirically based solutions and simple one-size-fits-all security selection and asset allocation approaches. Each month, financial firms offer a new array of financial products for the investment community. Cost containment and other business concerns generally result in a one-product-fits-all-investors approach. Equally important, the product that is offered is, not surprisingly, the one with the most recent higher return to risk performance. Results based on historical data are just that: results based on historical data. However, despite the often-given admission that past performance is not a forecast of future performance, most investors do not know where else to look. We also stressed the importance of estimation error in the returns as well as model error and estimation error in the parameters used in any individual model. Finally, we pointed out that there exists not only an efficient market in asset pricing but the potential for an efficient market in ideas, such that any "new" approach to investment management or asset allocation offering new advances often reflects marketing advances more than an asset-management advance. After all of those caveats, the following chapters present the analysis of various asset classes as if there exists a simple set of rules for determining the underlying risks and returns of each investment area. In short, for purposes of presentation, the following chapters emphasize well-known and often-used measures of risk and return. We use them not because they are the best, but because they are the most popular and the ones most individuals feel comfortable using. At some level we are all guilty of the same sin; we sell what we can, not what we should.

In the upcoming chapters we explore the risk, return, and operational approaches embedded in the major stock, bond, and alternative investment asset classes (e.g., hedge funds, managed futures, commodities, real estate, and private equity). Each chapter may be read as a self-contained unit in that it concentrates on a single asset class without overemphasizing its relationships with other asset classes. After the chapters on each individual asset class, we concentrate on presenting alternative methods of asset allocation and risk management. We point out that there are no universal solutions for how these asset classes should be combined to form investor portfolios or how the risk embedded in those portfolios should be managed. What is important is that the investor knows the return-and-risk characteristics of each asset class as well as the risks embedded in asset allocation and risk-management models used to create and evaluate the potential benefits of various asset groupings.

The touchstone of evolution is that an entity will adapt in order to survive. Understand that the operative word is *survive*, and survival does not carry an optimization requirement. Thus, we will not find the perfect theory or grouping of products as change comes to the corporate or investment world—or, for that matter, to academic research. Rather, we will find that we have a better understanding of risk and return relationships. Today's growth in off-exchange and screen-traded markets, in contrast to floor-traded markets, is only one example of such understanding and change. There can be, however, a gulf between reality and perception. A delay in an investor's (and here the term is used broadly to incorporate regulators and corporate boards) understanding or market awareness of new research or market relationships often results in a delay in an appreciation of these changes and leads to significant disadvantages in the marketplace.

Change comes from many sources. Modern investment products grew out of economic necessity, regulation, and technological innovations. Currency derivatives came into existence out of the failure of the United States to manage its own currency, and thus the market had to devise an approach to facilitate international trade in a world of uncertain currency values. Individual options grew in the early 1970s as risk-management tools, partly in response to the collapse of the stock markets of the late 1960s and the demand for new means of equity risk management. In the 1980s, the expansion of interest rate futures and the development of equity futures followed, in part, from the Employee Retirement Income Security Act (ERISA) of 1974, which required vesting of pension fund benefits and eventually led to pension fund asset increases to a size that required new means of managing risk. During the 1990s and into the current era, new product creations (e.g., swaps) were part of the changing world of technology and the resulting ability to manage and monitor an increasingly complex series of financial and nonfinancial products.

Although we know very few fundamental truths, one on which we can collectively agree is that the evolution of asset allocation draws on the aforementioned changes flowing from a dynamic world, in which new forms of assets and risk-management tools are constantly being created. Relative risks and returns, and the ability to monitor and manage the process by which these evolving assets fit into portfolios, will change and will be based on currently unknown relationships and information. Certainly today the challenge is greater, not only because we are working in a more dynamic market but also because the number of investment vehicles available to investors has increased. Hopefully, the following chapters will provide some guidance to meet this challenge.

WHAT EVERY INVESTOR SHOULD KNOW

For many, investments are viewed as an individual snapshot; that is, each investment approach stands on its own regardless of changes in investment models or investment theory. For others, investments can be more easily seen as a road map offering new ideas and approaches while rejecting some traditional investment approaches as old snapshots in an investor's photo album. Chapter 1 provided a brief summary of how some of the most basic approaches to investment came into existence and how some of them have evolved over time. Whatever your view, that is, investments as a snapshot or a road map, there are a number of simple concepts that every investor should know:

- **Know Your Risk Tolerance:** Most security and portfolio recommendations are based on models that remain focused on offering an investor a selection of asset choices based on a series of portfolios, each with a different expected return and risk. Unfortunately, many models use an asset's standard deviation as the proper measure for risk, and for most investors, standard deviation is a poor standalone measure of risk. Risk may be better viewed as a probability of large losses that one cannot recover from or the inability for the investments to match future cash flow needs. Investors should choose investments based on their view of risk tolerance and not the one embedded in a model for firm recommendation.
- **Know the Fatal Flaw in Every Investment Model and Idea:** Every model or investment theory has a logical and finite end point. Rigorously challenge the basic ideas behind investment models and recommendations. Is your advisor using historical returns and risks in creating a portfolio when those returns and risks have no relevance in today's world? Is your advisor recommending a product that does not permit you to easily change as your investment objectives change? Ask your advisor to give you the best case and the worst case scenarios based on the model or models he or she is using to recommend a particular portfolio. Investment advisors have varying degrees of skill and competence. Investors should openly challenge their level of knowledge, credentials, conflicts, and motivations.

- **Limit Your Investment Portfolio to What You Understand:** Every investor has investment limits based on their risk tolerance, knowledge, age, and investment horizon. Some investments are just not suited for some, while well suited for others. Risk-and-return relationships between and among both singular assets and asset classes can and do dramatically change over time. New forms of assets and risk-management tools are constantly being created. If you do not understand or if you feel uncomfortable with certain ideas, just say "no."

MYTHS AND MISCONCEPTIONS OF MODERN INVESTMENT

Change is a common part of the corporate or investment world as well as academic research. Research on the use of various investment processes and their effect on asset management as well as on corporate and financial risk management is an evolving area, not only because new theories come into existence that better explain risk-and-return relationships but also because changes in regulations and trading technology may result in changes in the underlying markets in which assets trade and in which corporate and financial firms operate. Today's growth in off-exchange and screen-traded markets, in contrast to floor-traded markets, is only one example of such change.

A delay in investors' understanding, or even market awareness, of new research or market relationships often results in a delay in investors', corporate officials', and government regulators' appreciation of these changes and the creation of a series of myths and misconceptions about how financial products perform, as well as their effects on financial markets, domestically and globally. That is, as markets change, misconceptions grow and myths (embedded in our experiences) become ways of coping with that change. In short, myths and misconceptions are a fixed part of the investment landscape.

Myth 1.1: Beta Is Dead

For years, academics and some practitioners have attempted to put beta in its grave. In theory, "true" beta is a number that supposedly measures the sensitivity of a security to the market portfolio (all assets) and that, in combination with CAPM, offers the investor a forecast of an asset's expected return relative to other assets. This last statement is important because CAPM does not forecast returns; it only makes a statement about relative returns. In truth, we never measure true beta; we measure "little" beta, a number that measures the sensitivity of a security to a preselected index (e.g., the S&P 500). As such, little beta is only an approximation for true beta. How close the approximation is depends on the time period used to estimate little beta, the investment interval used (daily, weekly), and the degree to which a firm changes character (holds more debt, hedges current risks). With all of these issues, one might think little beta should be dead. There have even been academics and others who have advocated for models (arbitrage pricing theory [APT], four-factor model) that have been shown to provide somewhat better estimates of relative returns. So why isn't little beta dead? First, it is a simple model that can be easily calculated (a simple Excel function does it for you). Second, it has been enshrined in educational material, marketing documents, and regulatory actions such that any change would require drastic and in some cases illegal actions. Finally, it actually does a fairly good job, especially when you know its limitations. Remember, before you kill something, you ought to have something significantly better to take its place; how else would you explain the change to others who would be resistant for all the aforementioned reasons? Little beta still exists; learn to live with it, but be careful in its use.

Myth 1.2: Mean-Variance Optimization Models Correctly Balance Risk and Return

Although MPT is almost 60 years old, it still forms the basis for much of investment analysis. Financial advisors invariably emphasize the importance of maximizing return while minimizing risk. The primary role of many financial advisors is to find a set of securities that provide excess return (greater than the benchmark) for a level of risk equal to the benchmark. Why hire an advisor if he cannot do better than the benchmark? In short, these advisors emphasize maximizing the mean return for a particular level of risk. This is all well and good, but it is the outcome that you have to worry about. Almost every model of mean-variance portfolio optimization (choosing those assets with the highest expected return for a given level of risk) is expected to be return sensitive. For example, the advisor can use an optimization model to find the optimal portfolio for a level of risk. In that portfolio, if there is one stock that outperforms all the other stocks of similar risk, even if that one stock is only, say, 5 basis points better, it is in and the others are out. Unfortunately, these models end up pointing to stocks that have done better in the past mostly because of pure luck. In the future, two stocks of the same risk should have the same return. In the next period, the stocks that did best in the past (the stocks that you picked) return to the same mean return as the other similar risk stocks, such that the expected return of your optimized portfolio overestimates its "true" expected return and you end up disappointed—you fail to outperform the benchmark as the model or your advisor forecast. So we know the optimization model has inherent flaws: Its perfection is a myth.

Myth 1.3: Yield to Maturity Is Dead

Some individuals believe the concept of *yield to maturity* (YTM) should be left for dead, except for zero-coupon bonds for which the YTM equals the *yield to duration* (YTD). It is well known—well, obviously not well known, or we would be using it—that two bonds of the same maturity but different coupons could be priced dramatically different. Why do we still concentrate on a bond's YTM? First, it is a simple model. Investors know what "maturity" means (old and wise). They also know what "yield" means (something you get back). Second, to go beyond that puts any financial advisor at risk for sounding too academic, especially when all the other firms continue to emphasize YTM. In truth, in board meetings and investment committee meetings, YTD—a kind of coupon-adjusted YTM—has started to replace YTM, just as some sort of multifactor return model has started to replace beta for stocks. It appears that until economic conditions change such that the difference in YTM and YTD is dramatic (widely different coupons on new and old bonds), YTM will dominate the discussions.

Myth 1.4: Investment Managers Matter

It has been pointed out that one of the investment evolutions over the past 60 years has been from "managers matter" to "benchmarks matter." In fact, both do, just not for the reasons most investors think. First, there are some great managers, although not enough to make a difference in a well-diversified portfolio (no one should risk all his or her money on a great manager—bad things happen to good people). Second, we do not know who the great managers are (as will be discussed later). As an example, let's say for period 1 you take 200 managers and split the sample in two (go long and go short). For period 2, you take the 100 managers who outperform and split the sample in two (go long and go short). For period 3, you take the 50 managers who outperformed and split the sample in two, and so on. After a number of periods, you are down to managers who were in the top group in every year by pure chance. Managers matter, if for no other reason than that someone has to turn the lights on in the morning. Managers matter but not for the reasons normally emphasized.

Myth 1.5: Structured Products Are Dead

In recent years, one of the worst things that could be said about an investment vehicle was that it was a structured product (a product designed from other products to have a unique return-to-risk trade-off). Structured products have existed for a long time and will continue to exist. Structured products allow investment firms to unbundle the risks of various products. For example, an investor in corporate securities may not want to bear the interest rate risk associated with U.S. Treasury securities. In this case, credit default swaps will allow the investor to participate in the credit risk of a corporate bond without participating in the interest rate risk of the same security.

What an investor really wants going forward is not fewer structured products, but more products designed to provide returns in unique risk environments. There are, of course, good structured products and bad ones. There is risk in choosing risky investments; if you cannot live with this, put your money in a bank and have them choose the risky structured products for you (although history proves this doesn't always work out so well, either). Ultimately, we embrace structured products when they work, and we blame others when they do not, but the belief that they are inherently evil does not reflect reality. Within this analysis, if there is a constant, be wary of structured products that are based on a bank's or investment bank's balance sheet. Here, there are a large number of unsystemic risks that are difficult to factor.

Myth 1.6: Behavioral Finance Is the New Normal

Over the past 20 years there has been a body of new work relating to financial theories on why individuals hold certain assets and portfolios of assets. The set of research in this area has fallen under the term *behavioral finance*. It is partially founded in the research of Daniel Kahneman and Amos Tversky, which illustrates that people act differently after wins than after losses. Behavioral finance attempts to explain that behavior and its potential effect on financial markets. While interesting on its own, this work does not have all the requisite market insights to replace other asset-pricing models. This behavioral research tends to work at the micro (individual) but not the macro (market) level and provides only a stopgap to a more complete model of asset pricing. Here, some researchers seem to ignore the fact that CAPM is at its essence a behavioral model of asset pricing (variance counts). More to the point, individuals have very little effect on the day-to-day operations or behavior of financial markets. Large institutional investors and traders dominate the terrain through high-frequency trades and other models used to immediately respond to changing risk-and-return scenarios. The individual as a dominant force in market behavior is a quaint anachronism.

Myth 1.7: Derivative Markets Promote Increased Market Volatility

We have all heard that it is better to be lucky than to be good. Many new financial ideas, which may have real long-term benefit to the markets, are simply launched at the wrong time and have no immediate market (e.g., volatility-based products in periods of low volatility) or come into existence at a time when their benefits are misunderstood. Most of present-day financial futures and option markets came into existence in the 1980s. When academics looked at the return volatility of the futures-based contracts, in many cases the volatility was greater than the associated cash instrument, or the volatility after the period the futures contracts were introduced was higher than it had been in prior periods. Many individuals cited these as examples of the negative impact of futures and options on market volatility. In fact, it was just the opposite. Futures contracts have lower transaction costs, so people trade a futures contract if prices go up or down just a little. The same price change exists in the cash, but the costs of trading are so high that no one trades there (the cash price remains the same and looks stable, but if you really tried to trade it, there'd be a big price change). More important, futures and option contracts are generally most successful if they are launched in a period of high volatility, as individuals use them to manage risk. In this way, successful futures and option contracts can be considered a type of backfill bias. There is currently a spirited debate over regulation in this area. However that debate turns, this market requires known transparency if it is to reach its full potential value.

Myth 1.8: Global Equity Markets and Bond Markets Act Differently Than U.S. Markets

In the 1970s, one of the most notable academic articles showed the benefits of global diversification. An associated article showed that when two countries start to trade financial assets, the historical pricing relationship and the historical correlation were meaningless until new pricing relationships were established. One of the reasons for the benefits of global diversification was simply that certain companies and industries were primarily traded on local exchanges within their national markets. With advancements in technology and uniform regulation, it is possible for investors to have direct access to geographically dispersed markets. For the most part, while acting separately, these markets have similar regulatory schemes that foster transparent pricing and the movement of monies on a cross-border basis. Today markets are more similar than different, and certain stocks and bonds trade on exchanges around the globe such that sometime in the future there may well be only one trading market on one big "cloud" in the sky.

Myth 1.9: An Asset's Price Never Changes

Each day, there is a mad scramble at 4:00 p.m. eastern standard time. It is at this time that many U.S. mutual funds and other financial holdings are priced for the day. For most individuals, that price is sacred; it is the price of their holdings until the end of the next day. Of course, by the time they receive that valuation on their smartphone, the actual value of that asset or portfolio of assets has changed (we see it referred to on TV as the "after-market market"). What's more, the price at 4:00 p.m. is not necessarily a traded price, as these prices are sometimes dealer estimates, benchmark-based algorithmic prices, or traded prices from markets long closed. Yet even some academic research is based on those prices actually being true. Investors need to realize that the valuation of their portfolio is only an estimate, and that if they traded that portfolio, its actual value could be dramatically different.

CHAPTER 2

Equity and Fixed Income

The Traditional Pair

For most investment firms, financial products reflect the opportunities of a given time and place. For example, in the 1970s and early 1980s, changes were taking place in how individuals viewed bond ratings and the pricing of fixed-income securities. During this period, Salomon Brothers took a 20-year government bond and split it into 41 individual bonds (i.e., 40 semiannual coupon payments and one principal payment). Salespeople then took each of the individual bonds (zero coupons) with a fixed maturity and sold it at a discount equal to the bonds' then-required return. Suddenly there existed a complete series of zero-coupon yield-to-maturity (YTM) or yield-to-duration (YTD) bonds (note that for zero-coupon bonds, YTM and YTD are the same thing), such that investors had access to a complete term structure for bonds (i.e., spot rates and forward rates). The creation and further development of a series of zero-coupon bonds forced a sea change in how fixed-income securities could be managed. For the first time, investors could easily single out, mix, or match bonds to meet a particular investment need, with little or no default or reinvestment risk.

Correspondingly, other changes were taking place in the fixed-income area. In the 1970s, research increasingly began to address the use of a bond's duration rather than a bond's maturity as the primary means to compare yields on bonds.[1] In addition, with the New York City credit crisis in the mid-1970s questions were raised as to the quality of traditional bond ratings. In addition, academics were addressing why high-rated (AAA) bonds reported less price volatility than supposedly more risky lower-rated (BAA) bonds.[2] In fact, the answer was relatively simple and related to the aforementioned concept of duration. Without getting into the mathematics of duration estimation, and all else being equal, a bond with the higher coupon (e.g., a lower-rated BAA bond) will have a lower duration than a similar maturity lower coupon bond (e.g., a higher-rated AAA bond).

Investors can view duration as a kind of coupon-adjusted maturity (all else being equal, a lower-rated, higher-coupon bond may pay back its purchase price quicker than the higher-rated, lower-coupon AAA bond). Moreover, as beta can be used to help measure the systematic risk of a stock, duration can be used similarly to measure the systematic risk of a bond to changes in interest rates. Again, without going into too much detail and all else being equal, the lower the duration of a bond, the lower its measured volatility. Bonds with lower ratings may in certain market conditions report a lower standard deviation. For many investors at that time, duration replaced both maturity and bond ratings as the basis for measuring a bond's risk. The financial market had created new financial products based on the knowledge of (1) understanding how bond prices moved, (2) the availability of bonds to meet structured product requirements, and (3) the ability to find customers who understood how these new products could enhance their portfolios.[3]

Despite all of the information on the relative benefits of YTD over YTM as well as concerns over the use of bond ratings, why did investment firms still emphasis the latter over the former? The answer is simple—ease and market acceptance. For most individuals who hold short-term bonds, the difference between duration and maturity is minor, and bond ratings provide a simple answer as to what is an acceptable investment. For most fixed-income practitioners, life is too short to try to educate the world.

The average individual bond risk-and-return measurement rarely went beyond reliance on a bond's YTM and rating. This fact provided a number of opportunities for some investors to arbitrage basic misunderstandings about how bonds were priced and risks were assessed. Opportunities for profit existed when one group of individuals priced bonds using model A and the trading firm knew that the proper pricing model was actually model B. The growth of futures markets in fixed-income securities during the 1980s also offered special pricing rules on what could be delivered. This soon produced a simple one-size-fits-all solution to how all deliverable government bonds would be priced (based on the most deliverable bonds). As noted, mathematical models could be derived to indicate when arbitrage profits were possible. This knowledge eventually led to the growth of a range of fixed-income arbitrage firms. These firms made money when their models worked and model A prices moved to model B prices (e.g., Long-Term Capital Management L.P. pre-1998) and of course lost a lot when they either did not move or moved too slowly (e.g., Long-Term Capital Management L.P. in 1998).

For purposes of this book, the primary point is that over the past 30 years of fixed-income research, much has changed and much has stayed the same. For many investors, at least retail investors, in the fixed-income world, bond ratings and YTM remain the rule. For others, fixed-income investment is founded in elaborate mathematical models that supposedly match the present value of expected cash flows of X with the price of Y and arbitrage the two. For still others, bond markets are just one of many asset classes, each with its own set of return expectations over a set of unknown future events.

Eventually, the knowledge derived from the advancements in how to price fixed-income securities and how to divide them and put them back together in new forms would provide the basis for the creation of marketable securitized structured products using assets such as credit card receivables, mortgages, and automobile loan receivables as their base. While these new products were based on the assumptions of expected cash flows, their values were based on the continuing assumption of transparency and verifiable information within the structures. So long as the market could properly value and ascertain changing risk patterns, both bankers and their clients could be comfortable with risk-and-reward decisions. October 2008 changed all that.

In October 2008, we rediscovered that risky fixed-income bonds (regardless of rating or maturity) could not be protected from all negative events despite all the duration matching, hedging, and advancements over the past 30 years. We also discovered the downside to global diversification. By enlarging the market to include more bonds, more traders, and more investors; by creating a world in which individuals traded daily; and by taking bonds and breaking them up into smaller pieces that were then put back together into new securities that traded daily, we were now dependent on the daily liquidity fix. When liquidity disappeared the market froze. In large part, the subprime mortgage market was the catalyst for the overall contagion. With subprime mortgages embedded into differing tranches of mortgage-related securities and without a clear picture as to the continued economic viability of those mortgages or which securities contained these toxic mortgages or which institution owned toxic mortgages, banks refused to lend to each other. And what started out as a crisis of confidence within a market segment spread to the entire global financial market. Moreover, counter to what its proponents espoused, global diversification was shown to lack its assumed risk-reduction benefits in periods of extraordinary market stress. The ability of government regulations and legal precedent to protect investors during periods of market stress also showed its weakness. Legally required rating completely vitiated the ability of fiduciaries to substitute independent analysis and judgment for letter ratings in meeting the time-tested reasonable person standard. And once again, markets learned that algorithmic-based models, as well as discretionary assessments of bond risk, when unsupported by transparent information, cannot often be relied on in periods of crisis. The current European sovereign debt crisis is illustrative of this latter point. For all practical purposes this is an economic crisis imbedded in the political uncertainty of whether there will be a united Europe.

The changing world of equities mirrored, in part, the changing world of fixed income. Many of the advancements in asset pricing and risk management have been centered on the valuation of equities. During the 1970s, when the revolution in bond valuation and fixed-income management was starting, similar changes were being experienced in equity investment management. Regulatory changes in the mid-1970s created the Employee Retirement and Income Security Act (ERISA) of 1974. By requiring that pension plans must provide for vesting of employees' pension benefits, the Act helped foster a new industry focused on building investment products for the pension fund industry. By the mid-1980s, public and private pension funds were holding large pools of capital, and new tools were created (e.g., equity futures contracts and options on equity futures) to help manage the equity risk of those pools of capital. The growth of pension funds and institutional money shifted the way investors viewed financial assets and their place in asset allocation. The hot product of the mid-1980s was known as portfolio insurance, a product that used futures contracts as a means to replicate an option position that would supposedly protect the downside valuation of equity-based portfolios. It did not, as the 1987 market crash proved.

The failure of futures-based portfolio insurance in 1987 did not stop the investment community from trying to find alternative solutions to portfolio risk management. In the mid-1980s changes in technology also drove changes in how investors viewed and managed equity portfolios. For the first time, portable computers were available as well as software that offered research and trading teams the ability to look inside portfolios as a way to determine underlying risks and market sensitivities. Also, in the 1980s additional forms of data became increasingly available, including daily prices for a range of exchange-traded assets and equities, futures, option contracts, and services that offered analyst estimates of a firm's expected earnings. All of this information created a new culture of equity research that no longer centered solely on measuring a firm's beta but also attempted to capture the wide range of market factors driving investor returns.

By the late 1980s, both practitioners and academics were concentrating on reviewing the principal tools (e.g., alpha and beta) by which we attempt to determine fundamental asset risk as well as the ability of managers to create value. The growth of these large pools of capital not only encouraged new ways of managing performance and risk, it also gave impetus to the active management business and its corollary segments. In addition to professional money managers, we also had the growth of investment consulting firms that declared their ability to manage the individual managers who manage this money. This new paradigm declared beta dead, and new multifactor models of return estimation came into existence. These equity-return estimation models look to firm size (large cap and small cap), investment strategy (value and growth), and price patterns (momentum) as additional factors to describe return movement.[4] The ability to determine the unique market or firm factors driving equity return as well as the ability of individual managers to offer special benefits remains at the center of equity valuation, risk management, and portfolio creation.

Throughout all of the changes there remains a constant—expected return is a function of risk (i.e., there are no solutions without return and/or risk impact), and an investor can fundamentally adjust the normal return and risk profile through a number of financial instruments, including futures, options or their synthetic alternatives.

A BRIEF REVIEW

Historically, equity and fixed-income investments have been the major part of an investor's asset-allocation decision. In recent years, the number of investable equity and fixed-income indices and structure investments (e.g., exchange-traded funds [ETFs]) has increased dramatically. Today, we have the ability to create almost any portfolio of equity or fixed-income securities, each based on a unique vision of the required return and risk characteristics (e.g., country based, industry based, fundamental-factor based, and so on). The question that remains is the degree to which each of these new equity and fixed-income products provides unique return and risk opportunities at the macro, asset-sector, or manager levels. For example, there exists a range of macroeconomic-based investment models that purport to show that equity valuation is related to gross domestic product (GDP) growth, and fixed-income valuation to the real rate of production plus inflation plus some risk premium. More micro firm-based investment models, which concentrate on elements such as earnings per share and dividends, also provide a basis for relative valuation; however, each investment product has differing strengths (increasing earnings per share and dividends are often signals of firm strength) and weaknesses (factor-specific portfolios are often very concentrated, and the historical track record may not reflect current risk-and-return opportunities).

Despite the common problem of uncertainty as to the quality of the valuation and selection models in both fixed-income and equity investment, there is common agreement that both stocks and bonds in an investment portfolio increase the investor's ability to manage expected return and expected risk. The question often raised by academics and practitioners has less to do with the potential benefits of stock and bond investments and more to do with whether passive investment in contrast to active management may provide similar benefits with less cost.

EQUITY AND FIXED-INCOME STYLES AND BENCHMARKS

Most traditional investment strategies are divided into the markets in which managers trade and the type of trading that takes place in those markets. For equities and fixed income, for example, investing has been divided into the markets (e.g., U.S. and non-U.S.), industrial sectors (e.g., energy, technology), and some of the unique approaches to trading (e.g., large cap, small cap, value, and growth). For each of these forms of trading and markets traded, investment benchmarks have been created.

In many investment reviews, the Standard & Poor's (S&P) 500 and the Russell 2000 indices are used as the primary representative U.S. equity indices. MSCI Europe, Australasia, Far East (EAFE) and Emerging Markets (EM) are used as the primary non-U.S. equity indices. BarCap U.S. Government, BarCap U.S. Aggregate, and BarCap U.S. Corporate High Yield Bond indices are used as the primary representative U.S. fixed-income indices. BarCap Global Government Bond Index, BarCap Global Aggregate Bond Index, and the J.P. Morgan Emerging Market Bond Index (EMBI) are the three primary non-U.S. fixed-income indices. Each index has its own unique return and risk characteristics. For example, the S&P 500 is an asset-weighted index, such that those firms with the highest stock price and the greatest number of shares outstanding have a greater effect on the valuation of the index. In fact, the S&P 500 has often been called a growth index of 50 stocks that matter and 450 stocks that do not. The methodology of a growth index is that as prices increase, the impact of individual stocks as measured by asset weight on the index increases. Investors should continuingly update their understanding of the current composition of each index and how it is expected to perform in the current market environment, not how it performed in a past market environment dissimilar to today's.

BASIC SOURCES OF RISK AND RETURN

The benefits of traditional stock and bond investments are almost a truism among most investors. As discussed in the previous section, there are a number of quantitative models that provide a basis for determining an expected individual stock (e.g., capital asset pricing model [CAPM]) or bond return (i.e., duration for U.S. Treasury bonds) or for determining the impact of changes in firm or macroeconomic events on actual stock market or bond returns. At its most basic, the value of either investment is a function primarily of its ability to generate cash flow and the risk associated with those cash flows in comparison to risk-returns provided by other investable assets or benchmarks.

Indicative of the difficulty for an average investor to determine which country or which sector or which security to invest in, major investment firms spend large amounts of money in an attempt to determine the importance of the various firm and macro factors that drive the valuation of equity securities. Over time, however, the importance of firm and macro factors change. Equally important, the relative domestic and global impact of these factors has also changed over time. One of the problems in focusing on the basic sources of return and risk is not that we are unfamiliar with the basic dynamics of what affects the valuation of a firm (e.g., cash flow and required return), but that once a firm invests millions of dollars on a particular approach, it is difficult for the firm to change directions in its asset-selection process unless the model completely falls apart. As a sidebar, academics are just as much at fault as practitioners. Despite considerable research[5] that has called into question CAPM and multifactor models, academics continue to reference and use these models as the basis for risk and performance analysis (all well and good) and in estimating expected returns (which is questionable, in that over the past 20 years there have been periods when the model has worked well and others when its value has been marginal).

Simple models of asset valuation may also work, as may more complicated versions. The day the first draft of this chapter was written, the markets were working as they should; the U.S. employment number was 115,000 compared to the expected 150,000, and all sectors in the U.S. stock market fell. If there is an unexpected decrease in new hiring, there may be an assumption that firms see a decline in economic activity and thereby an unexpected decrease in the level of future cash flows to firms; as a result, stock prices unexpectedly fall. Similarly, risky bonds that are paid from the excess earnings of firms may fall as the expected future earnings of firms fall, and the potential for bonds' future coupon payments is reduced. Bonds with little or no risk may increase in value as individuals think that in the future the government may reduce interest rates thereby increasing the value of low-risk government bonds.

If an investor cannot predict where the market is going, is there any evidence that U.S. equity mutual fund managers outperform simple passive benchmarks? In short, mutual funds may provide the risk-and-return benefits to individual investors, but questions still arise if certain managers of actively managed portfolios outperform a passive benchmark and their peers. To demonstrate their ability in generating excess returns (i.e., positive alphas), money managers have to rely on their past performance. Those who invest with managers and those who evaluate money managers also have to rely on past performance. The important question is, therefore, whether active mutual fund managers provide unique investment skills either in terms of their ability to time the market or in their ability to select undervalued securities. In addition, an investor may wish to determine whether past performance has any predictive power about future performance. If past performance can predict future performance, then a portfolio consisting of best-performing managers should outperform a randomly selected portfolio of money managers. Investors should be warned, however, that there is little if any evidence that past performance can predict future performance or that best-performing managers outperform a randomly selected portfolio of similar strategy-based money managers. If information enters the market in a random fashion, the strategy that benefits from unexpected good information is also hurt by unexpected bad information. For a period, any manager can get a series of good unexpected information, but that is luck, not skill, although from the numbers it is hard to tell the difference. In addition, as pointed out previously, although a manager may show historical outperformance, it is difficult to determine if that outperformance is skill or luck. This is not to say that skill does not exist—only that if there is a manager with extreme skill, that manager will probably charge higher fees than another manager, such that the after-fee returns of the two managers may well be similar. In sum, all of the available research shows that collectively, managers do not outperform passive indices, and the probability of choosing the unique manager who does is remote.

PERFORMANCE: FACT AND FICTION

As markets evolve there is a constant struggle to remain current as to what is fact and what is fiction within any one or number of asset classes. As we discussed in previous sections, over the past decades, our understanding of how equity and fixed-income securities are priced and how to evaluate their risks has changed. In the following sections, we provide evidence not only on the stand-alone risks of stock and bond investments, but on the interrelationships within and between equity and fixed-income markets. We examine these markets over a broad time period, as well as on shorter time intervals (e.g., annual) as well as their relative performance in extreme market conditions. Results show that as expected equity markets generally offer both high return as well as higher risk than comparison fixed-income investments, and equity markets generally have a relatively low correlation with certain fixed-income markets; combining equity and fixed income often results in a superior return-to-risk trade-off.

Results also show that some of what we espouse to investors may be regarded more toward fiction than fact. For example, results also show that

- There is a high correlation (e.g., low diversification benefits) between domestic and international equity as well as between domestic and international fixed income.
- Certain fixed-income investments (e.g., fixed-income high yield) may be regarded as equity return enhancers rather than equity risk reducers.
- Especially in periods of extreme equity market movements, both domestic and international equity have similar return patterns and provide little evidence of diversification benefit.

Results also show that in periods of extreme equity market movements, equity sectors within the S&P 500 also have similar return patterns and provide little evidence of diversification benefit, and investors should not take the return and risk performance from extended time frames as a basis for how equity and fixed income may perform over relative shorter time periods (e.g., annual). Also, evidence derived over long investment periods as to the benefits of certain investment strategies (e.g., value versus growth or small cap versus large cap) may not reflect the variability in relative performance when analyzed over shorter time intervals (e.g., annual).

RETURN AND RISK CHARACTERISTICS

Although we have argued against the use of historical data as the sole basis for describing the return and risk characteristics of either equity or fixed income, there are certain benefits in examining the historical risk and return characteristics of various asset classes. Exhibits 2.1 and 2.2 display this information for a wide range of equity and fixed-income indices covering the period 1994–2011. As shown in Exhibit 2.1, for this period the S&P 500 exhibited a lower annualized standard deviation (15.7 percent) than the comparison equity indices (i.e., Russell 2000 [20.3 percent], MSCI EAFE [17.0 percent], and MSCI EM [24.5 percent]). This is consistent with the expectations of most investors, who believe that U.S. large-cap indices (e.g., S&P 500) have lower volatility than small-cap U.S. equity indices (e.g., Russell 2000), developed non-U.S. indices (e.g., MSCI EAFE), and emerging markets indices (e.g., MSCI EM). Over the period of analysis, the S&P 500 also reported similar annualized total return (7.7 percent) to the Russell 2000 (7.5 percent) and higher annualized total return than the MSCI EAFE (4.2 percent) and the MSCI EM (3.0 percent). Moreover, stand-alone historical return and risk comparison may not reflect the potential for the benefits of the S&P 500 or other equity indices when combined with

EXHIBIT 2.1 Equity and Fixed-Income Index Performance

Stock and Bond Performance	S&P 500	Russell 2000	MSCI EAFE	MSCI EM
Annualized return	7.7%	7.5%	4.2%	3.0%
Annualized standard deviation	15.7%	20.3%	17.0%	24.5%
Information ratio	0.49	0.37	0.25	0.12
Maximum drawdown	−50.9%	−52.9%	−56.7%	−62.7%
Correlation with S&P 500	1.00	0.81	0.83	0.74
Correlation with BarCap U.S. Aggregate	0.06	−0.04	0.02	−0.02

Stock and Bond Performance	BarCap U.S. Government	BarCap U.S. Aggregate	BarCap U.S. Corporate High Yield	BarCap Global Aggregate
Annualized return	6.1%	6.3%	7.3%	6.2%
Annualized standard deviation	4.4%	3.8%	9.4%	5.7%
Information ratio	1.39	1.67	0.78	1.09
Maximum drawdown	−5.4%	−5.1%	−33.3%	−10.1%
Correlation with S&P 500	−0.14	0.06	0.62	0.17
Correlation with BarCap U.S. Aggregate	0.94	1.00	0.21	0.70

Period of analysis: 1994 to 2011.

EXHIBIT 2.2 Equity and Fixed-Income Portfolio Performance

Portfolios	A	B	C	D
Annualized return	7.8%	6.0%	7.4%	6.5%
Annualized standard deviation	17.1%	17.7%	8.8%	9.8%
Information ratio	0.45	0.34	0.85	0.66
Maximum drawdown	−51%	−56%	−27%	−32%
Portfolio A	Equal Weights S&P 500 and Russell 2000			
Portfolio B	50% Portfolio A and 50% (MSCI EW EAFE/EM)			
Portfolio C	50% Portfolio A and 50% BarCap U.S. Aggregate			
Portfolio D	50% Portfolio B and 50% BarCap Global Aggregate			

Period of analysis: 1994 to 2011.

other traditional assets, such as fixed-income indices. For example, for the period of analysis the S&P 500 had a relatively high correlation (0.74 and above) with the other U.S. and non-U.S. equity indices; however, it had low correlations with the BarCap U.S. Government (-0.14) and U.S. Aggregate (0.06) fixed-income indices. The relatively high correlation of the S&P 500 with the BarCap U.S. Corporate High Yield fixed-income index (0.62) may lead investors to question high-yield fixed income as a primary means of diversification for equity-dominated portfolios.

Modern portfolio theory (MPT), however, emphasizes that the benefits of individual assets should be evaluated on their performance alongside other assets in investors' portfolios. The diversification benefits of adding any individual investment to other assets or other asset portfolios depend on the comparison stand-alone investment. The relatively high correlation between the S&P 500 combined and a range of equity financial assets (e.g., MSCI EAFE, MSCI EM) may indicate that a portfolio of non-U.S. equities may provide only minimal reduction in the risk (i.e., standard deviation) to a U.S.-dominated equity portfolio. For the period of analysis (see Exhibit 2.2), adding an equal portion (50 percent) of non-U.S. equity to an equal-weighted (EW) U.S.-equity portfolio resulted in a somewhat lower annualized total return (6.0 percent) and a similar standard deviation (17.7 percent) as the pure U.S. stock, which had a return of 7.8 percent and a standard deviation of 17.1 percent.

In contrast, adding U.S. fixed income (i.e., BarCap U.S. Aggregate) to the portfolio of U.S. and international stocks resulted in a portfolio (see Portfolio C) that exhibits a somewhat higher return (7.4 percent) to Portfolio B (6.0 percent) but with a considerably lower standard deviation (8.8 percent versus 17.7 percent for Portfolio B). The addition of an international fixed-income portfolio (i.e., BarCap Global Aggregate) to Portfolio B likewise resulted in a portfolio (see Portfolio D) that did not have dramatically different return and risk characteristics in comparison to Portfolio C but did result in a portfolio with considerable lower risk than a stock-only portfolio.

The ability of fixed-income investments to provide risk reduction opportunities as additions to a sample equity portfolio is indicative of the potential ability of fixed income (when combined with equity) to provide a positive return-to-risk trade-off over a lengthy time period. Investors must be warned, however. First, as mentioned previously and expanded on later, performance in a single period is not indicative of relative performance in other periods. Second, the S&P 500 is only one of several equity indices; other equity indices may provide different performance results. Third, there is no requirement that investors invest in a single composite equity index. Exhibit 2.3 shows return and risk performance for S&P 500 equity sector indices over the 1994–2011 period as well as the relative performance

EXHIBIT 2.3 Standard & Poor's 500 and Equity Subindices Performance

U.S. Equity Index Performance

	S&P 500	Consumer Discretionary	Consumer Staples	Energy	Financials	Health Care	Industrials	Information Technology	Materials	Telecom Services	Utilities
Annualized return	7.7%	5.8%	7.3%	9.6%	2.8%	8.6%	5.9%	9.2%	4.4%	1.0%	2.3%
Annualized standard deviation	15.7%	18.7%	13.1%	19.6%	23.2%	15.7%	18.7%	28.2%	21.7%	20.9%	16.0%
Information ratio	0.49	0.31	0.56	0.49	0.12	0.55	0.31	0.33	0.20	0.05	0.15
Maximum drawdown	−50.9%	−56.2%	−31.2%	−49.8%	−80.0%	−39.9%	−60.2%	−80.4%	−57.9%	−76.1%	−58.6%
Correlation with S&P 500	1.00	0.89	0.61	0.62	0.84	0.64	0.90	0.81	0.78	0.66	0.44
Correlation with BarCap Aggregate	0.06	0.01	0.13	0.01	0.10	0.16	0.01	−0.03	−0.02	0.04	0.20

Equity Indices: Monthly Returns Ranked on S&P 500

	S&P 500	Consumer Discretionary	Consumer Staples	Energy	Financials	Health Care	Industrials	Information Technology	Materials	Telecom Services	Utilities
Average/Bottom third months	−4.3%	−4.6%	−2.0%	−3.2%	−5.3%	−2.6%	−4.7%	−6.2%	−5.0%	−4.5%	−2.2%
Average/Middle third months	1.2%	1.0%	1.0%	1.7%	0.5%	1.3%	1.0%	1.5%	1.0%	0.8%	0.7%
Average/Top third months	5.3%	5.4%	3.0%	4.3%	6.1%	3.7%	5.6%	7.9%	5.7%	4.5%	2.4%

of these indices in periods of extreme equity market returns. While these returns and standard deviations often differ from the composite S&P 500 index; most of the S&P 500 sector indices report a relatively high correlation with the S&P 500 (with the exception of utilities, all the other equity sectors had a correlation with the S&P 500 of more than 0.60). In contrast, most of the S&P 500 equity sector indices report a relatively low correlation with the BarCap U.S. Aggregate. (With the exception of utilities, all the other equity sector indices had a correlation with the BarCap U.S. Aggregate of less than 0.20.) Exhibit 2.3 shows that in periods of extreme equity returns, all of the S&P 500 sector indices report the same directional return as the S&P 500, that is, when the S&P 500 has its worst performance, none of the underlying equity sectors provided a positive return. Results in Exhibit 2.3 indicate that both the high correlation of equity sector indices with the S&P 500 as well as the evidence of comovement in periods of equity-market stress may call into question some of the diversification benefits often proscribed to investing in multiple equity sectors.

In summary, historical return for the period 1994–2011 provides valuable information about the benefits of some equity indices and subindices as suitable stand-alone investments and, more important, as part of a diversified equity and fixed-income portfolio. However, the relatively high correlation (0.62) of the BarCap U.S. Corporate High Yield index with the S&P 500 may make that fixed-income index be regarded as a return enhancer rather than a risk reducer to an equity portfolio. Investors should be certain to check how a particular equity or fixed-income security performs across a wide range of economic and financial markets and if the program they wish to invest in has a strategy for taking those changes into consideration. Investors should also be aware of the relative performance of individual equity sector or non-U.S. equity indices as well as various fixed-income benchmarks when stocks or bonds report extreme positive or negative returns.

THE MYTH OF AVERAGE: EQUITY AND FIXED-INCOME RETURN IN EXTREME MARKETS

The results in the previous section illustrate the performance of the S&P 500 index and comparison traditional investment indices over the entire 18-year period (1994–2011). The results indicate the return or risk benefits of other equity indices or fixed-income indices as stand-alone investments or as additions to an existing portfolio. However, that performance may differ in various subperiods in comparison to their performance over the entire period of analysis. This is especially true in periods of market stress, when certain equity or fixed-income strategies may experience dramatic return movement.

In Exhibit 2.3, we reported the performance of various S&P 500 sector indices when ranked on the S&P 500. Similarly, Exhibit 2.4 shows monthly U.S. and non-U.S. stock and bond indices returns ranked on the S&P 500 and grouped into three segments (bottom, middle, and top) of 72 months each, with average returns for each index presented. Results show that in the periods of the worst and best S&P 500 months both the comparison domestic and international equity indices had similar negative and positive returns to the S&P 500. In contrast, the comparison fixed-income indices had positive returns on average (with the exception of the BarCap U.S. Corporate High Yield Index) in the worst S&P 500 return months and also provided positive returns (although less than the S&P 500) in the best S&P 500 return months. The positive performance in up markets may be partially caused by the positive economic conditions (e.g., reduced credit risk) driving both stock and fixed-income prices higher.

The superior performance of the fixed-income index when the S&P 500 performs poorly may be driven by various factors. First, bonds have

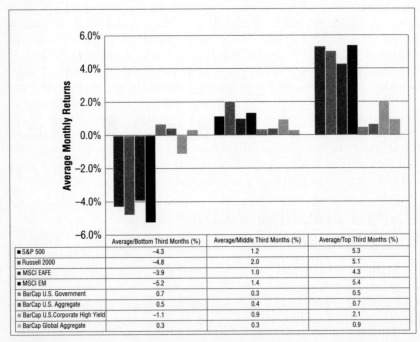

	Average/Bottom Third Months (%)	Average/Middle Third Months (%)	Average/Top Third Months (%)
■ S&P 500	−4.3	1.2	5.3
■ Russell 2000	−4.8	2.0	5.1
■ MSCI EAFE	−3.9	1.0	4.3
■ MSCI EM	−5.2	1.4	5.4
■ BarCap U.S. Government	0.7	0.3	0.5
■ BarCap U.S. Aggregate	0.5	0.4	0.7
■ BarCap U.S.Corporate High Yield	−1.1	0.9	2.1
■ BarCap Global Aggregate	0.3	0.3	0.9

EXHIBIT 2.4 Equity and Fixed-Income Indices: Monthly Return Ranked on the S&P 500
Period of analysis: 1994 to 2011.

a prior claim on corporate earnings and assets. Second, if the economy is slowing down, then equities would perform poorly because of lower expected corporate earnings, but bonds may perform well to the degree that real rates and nominal rates decline in a declining economy (e.g., a weaker economy may mean lower expected inflation). Third, high-quality fixed-income securities are more liquid than equities, and in periods of financial distress, some institutional investors would move into high-quality fixed-income instruments because of their liquidity—the so-called flight to quality. Results in Exhibit 2.5 show that when the returns are ranked on the BarCap U.S. Aggregate, the equity indices had a positive return in the worst BarCap U.S. Aggregate return months and generally provided positive returns (although less than the BarCap U.S. Aggregate) in the best BarCap U.S. Aggregate return months. The superior performance in down BarCap U.S. Aggregate months and the participation in up markets may be partially caused by the ability of equities to participate in positive return opportunities in periods of low fixed-income returns, as well as to obtain positive returns even in periods of positive fixed-income return conditions.

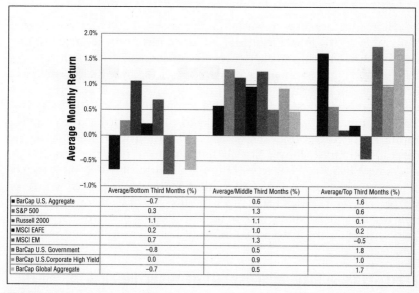

	Average/Bottom Third Months (%)	Average/Middle Third Months (%)	Average/Top Third Months (%)
■ BarCap U.S. Aggregate	−0.7	0.6	1.6
■ S&P 500	0.3	1.3	0.6
■ Russell 2000	1.1	1.1	0.1
■ MSCI EAFE	0.2	1.0	0.2
■ MSCI EM	0.7	1.3	−0.5
■ BarCap U.S. Government	−0.8	0.5	1.8
■ BarCap U.S.Corporate High Yield	0.0	0.9	1.0
■ BarCap Global Aggregate	−0.7	0.5	1.7

EXHIBIT 2.5 Equity and Fixed-Income Indices: Monthly Return Ranked on the BarCap U.S. Aggregate
Period of analysis: 1994 to 2011.

ANNUAL PERFORMANCE

In this section, we provide a review of the relative performances by year, of the primary equity and fixed-income indices. Results in Exhibit 2.6 show that over the entire period, the annual returns of the S&P 500, BarCap U.S. Aggregate, and the other equity and fixed-income indices varied in many years. However, in 6 of the 18 years, the BarCap U.S. Aggregate and the S&P 500 moved in opposite directions.

Similarly, Exhibits 2.7 through 2.9 show the relative volatility of the indices as well as the intra-year correlation of the various equity and fixed-income indices with the S&P 500 and the BarCap U.S. Aggregate. Results in Exhibit 2.7 also show that the relative volatility of the fixed-income indices has consistently remained below that of the S&P 500. However, Exhibits 2.8 through 2.9 show that the intra-year correlation of the various equity and fixed-income indices with the S&P 500 and the BarCap U.S. Aggregate varies over the years of analysis. In short, investors should be aware that results from longer time frames may not reflect results for individual years.

PERFORMANCE IN 2008

The relative performance of various asset classes in 2008 requires special emphasis. In 2008, global investment markets underwent a severe correction across most traditional and alternative investment markets. In that year, the S&P 500 and high-risk fixed income were impacted by the subprime crisis. For the first six months of the year, the S&P 500 had a negative return of −11.9 percent, while in the second six months, the S&P 500 Index had a negative return of −28.5 percent, as markets responded to the declining drop in expected corporate profitability associated with declining global demand. In contrast, for the first six months of the year, the BarCap U.S. Government Index had a positive return of 2.1 percent, while in the second six months, the BarCap U.S. Government Index had a positive return of 10.1 percent, as investors had a flight to safety. That is, there was not one 2008 but several 2008s in that some asset classes performed well while others reported extreme negative returns.

SPECIAL ISSUES: MAKING SENSE OUT OF TRADITIONAL STOCK AND BOND INDICES

Stock and bond indices have formed the basis for much of asset-allocation research. For example, in the 1960s, the introduction of the international

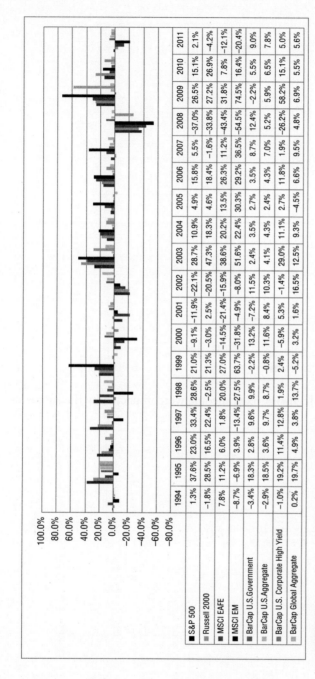

	1994	1995	1996	1997	1998	1999	2000	2001	2002	2003	2004	2005	2006	2007	2008	2009	2010	2011
S&P 500	1.3%	37.6%	23.0%	33.4%	28.6%	21.0%	-9.1%	-11.9%	-22.1%	28.7%	10.9%	4.9%	15.8%	5.5%	-37.0%	26.5%	15.1%	2.1%
Russell 2000	-1.8%	28.5%	16.5%	22.4%	-2.5%	21.3%	-3.0%	2.5%	-20.5%	47.3%	18.3%	4.6%	18.4%	-1.6%	-33.8%	27.2%	26.9%	-4.2%
MSCI EAFE	7.8%	11.2%	6.0%	1.8%	20.0%	27.0%	-14.5%	-21.4%	-15.9%	38.6%	20.2%	13.5%	26.3%	11.2%	-43.4%	31.8%	7.8%	-12.1%
MSCI EM	-8.7%	-6.9%	3.9%	-13.4%	-27.5%	63.7%	-31.8%	-4.9%	-8.0%	51.6%	22.4%	30.3%	29.2%	36.5%	-54.5%	74.5%	16.4%	-20.4%
BarCap U.S.Government	-3.4%	18.3%	2.8%	9.6%	9.9%	-2.2%	13.2%	-7.2%	11.5%	2.4%	3.5%	2.7%	3.5%	8.7%	12.4%	-2.2%	5.5%	9.0%
BarCap U.S.Aggregate	-2.9%	18.5%	3.6%	9.7%	8.7%	-0.8%	11.6%	8.4%	10.3%	4.1%	4.3%	2.4%	4.3%	7.0%	5.2%	5.9%	6.5%	7.8%
BarCap U.S. Corporate High Yield	-1.0%	19.2%	11.4%	12.8%	1.9%	2.4%	-5.9%	5.3%	-1.4%	29.0%	11.1%	2.7%	11.8%	1.9%	-26.2%	58.2%	15.1%	5.0%
BarCap Global Aggregate	0.2%	19.7%	4.9%	3.8%	13.7%	-5.2%	3.2%	1.6%	16.5%	12.5%	9.3%	-4.5%	6.6%	9.5%	4.8%	6.9%	5.5%	5.6%

EXHIBIT 2.6 Equity and Fixed-Income Indices: Annual Returns

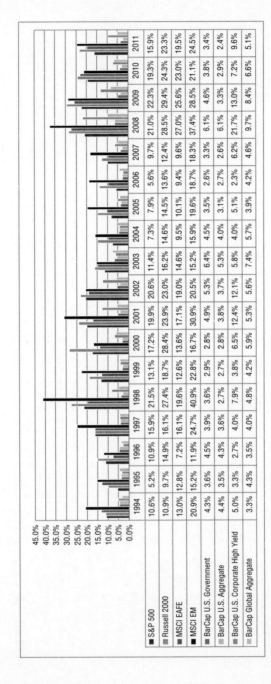

	1994	1995	1996	1997	1998	1999	2000	2001	2002	2003	2004	2005	2006	2007	2008	2009	2010	2011
S&P 500	10.6%	5.2%	10.9%	15.9%	21.5%	13.1%	17.2%	19.9%	20.6%	11.4%	7.3%	7.9%	5.6%	9.7%	21.0%	22.3%	19.3%	15.9%
Russell 2000	10.9%	9.7%	14.9%	16.1%	27.4%	18.7%	28.4%	23.9%	23.0%	16.2%	14.6%	14.5%	13.6%	12.4%	28.5%	29.4%	24.3%	23.3%
MSCI EAFE	13.0%	12.8%	7.2%	16.1%	19.6%	12.6%	13.6%	17.1%	19.0%	14.6%	9.5%	10.1%	9.4%	9.6%	27.0%	25.6%	23.0%	19.5%
MSCI EM	20.9%	15.2%	11.9%	24.7%	40.9%	22.8%	16.7%	30.9%	20.5%	15.2%	15.9%	19.6%	18.7%	18.3%	37.4%	28.5%	21.1%	24.5%
BarCap U.S. Government	4.3%	3.6%	4.5%	3.9%	3.6%	2.9%	2.8%	4.9%	5.3%	6.4%	4.5%	3.5%	2.6%	3.3%	6.1%	4.6%	3.8%	3.4%
BarCap U.S. Aggregate	4.4%	3.5%	4.3%	3.6%	2.7%	2.7%	2.8%	3.8%	3.7%	5.3%	4.0%	3.1%	2.7%	2.6%	6.1%	3.3%	2.9%	2.4%
BarCap U.S. Corporate High Yield	5.0%	3.3%	2.7%	4.0%	7.9%	3.8%	6.5%	12.4%	12.1%	5.8%	4.0%	5.1%	2.3%	6.2%	21.7%	13.0%	7.2%	9.6%
BarCap Global Aggregate	3.3%	4.3%	3.5%	4.0%	4.8%	4.2%	5.9%	5.3%	5.6%	7.4%	5.7%	3.9%	4.2%	4.6%	9.7%	8.4%	6.6%	5.1%

EXHIBIT 2.7 Equity and Fixed-Income Indices: Annual Standard Deviations

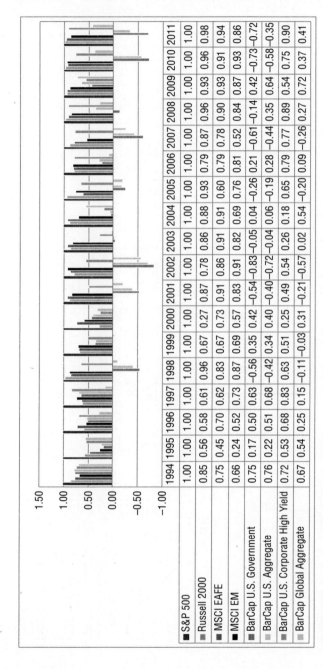

	1994	1995	1996	1997	1998	1999	2000	2001	2002	2003	2004	2005	2006	2007	2008	2009	2010	2011
■ S&P 500	1.00	1.00	1.00	1.00	1.00	1.00	1.00	1.00	1.00	1.00	1.00	1.00	1.00	1.00	1.00	1.00	1.00	1.00
■ Russell 2000	0.85	0.56	0.58	0.61	0.96	0.67	0.27	0.87	0.78	0.86	0.88	0.93	0.79	0.87	0.96	0.93	0.96	0.98
■ MSCI EAFE	0.75	0.45	0.70	0.62	0.83	0.67	0.73	0.91	0.86	0.91	0.91	0.60	0.79	0.78	0.90	0.93	0.91	0.94
■ MSCI EM	0.66	0.24	0.52	0.73	0.87	0.69	0.57	0.83	0.91	0.82	0.69	0.76	0.81	0.52	0.84	0.87	0.93	0.86
■ BarCap U.S. Government	0.75	0.17	0.50	0.63	−0.56	0.35	0.42	−0.54	−0.83	−0.05	0.04	−0.26	0.21	−0.61	−0.14	0.42	−0.73	−0.72
■ BarCap U.S. Aggregate	0.76	0.22	0.51	0.68	−0.42	0.34	0.40	−0.40	−0.72	−0.04	0.06	−0.19	0.28	−0.44	0.35	0.64	−0.58	−0.35
■ BarCap U.S. Corporate High Yield	0.72	0.53	0.68	0.83	0.63	0.51	0.25	0.49	0.54	0.26	0.18	0.65	0.79	0.77	0.89	0.54	0.75	0.90
■ BarCap Global Aggregate	0.67	0.54	0.25	0.15	−0.11	−0.03	0.31	−0.21	−0.57	0.02	0.54	−0.20	0.09	−0.26	0.27	0.72	0.37	0.41

EXHIBIT 2.8 Equity and Fixed-Income Indices: Annual Correlation with the S&P 500

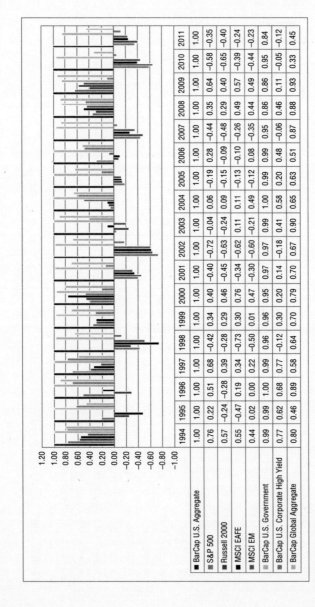

	1994	1995	1996	1997	1998	1999	2000	2001	2002	2003	2004	2005	2006	2007	2008	2009	2010	2011
■ BarCap U.S. Aggregate	1.00	1.00	1.00	1.00	1.00	1.00	1.00	1.00	1.00	1.00	1.00	1.00	1.00	1.00	1.00	1.00	1.00	1.00
■ S&P 500	0.76	0.22	0.51	0.68	-0.42	0.34	0.40	-0.40	-0.72	-0.04	0.06	-0.19	0.28	-0.44	0.35	0.64	-0.58	-0.35
■ Russell 2000	0.57	-0.24	-0.28	0.39	-0.28	0.29	0.46	-0.45	-0.63	-0.24	0.09	-0.15	-0.09	-0.48	0.29	0.40	-0.65	-0.40
■ MSCI EAFE	0.55	-0.47	0.19	0.34	-0.73	0.30	0.76	-0.34	-0.62	0.11	0.11	-0.13	-0.10	-0.26	0.49	0.57	-0.39	-0.24
■ MSCI EM	0.44	0.02	0.00	0.22	-0.50	0.01	0.47	-0.30	-0.60	-0.21	0.49	-0.12	0.08	-0.35	0.44	0.49	-0.44	-0.23
■ BarCap U.S. Government	0.99	0.99	1.00	0.99	0.96	0.96	0.95	0.97	0.99	0.99	1.00	0.99	0.99	0.95	0.86	0.86	0.95	0.84
■ BarCap U.S. Corporate High Yield	0.77	0.62	0.68	0.77	-0.12	0.30	0.20	0.14	-0.18	0.41	0.58	0.20	0.48	-0.06	0.46	0.11	-0.05	-0.12
■ BarCap Global Aggregate	0.80	0.46	0.89	0.58	0.64	0.70	0.79	0.70	0.67	0.90	0.65	0.63	0.51	0.87	0.88	0.93	0.33	0.45

EXHIBIT 2.9 Equity and Fixed-Income Indices: Annual Correlation with the BarCap U.S. Aggregate

stock indices provided a much-needed basis for testing the potential benefits of international equity investment. In the 1960s, Salomon Brothers bond indices were commonly used to offer historical performance information on a range of fixed-income benchmarks. Unfortunately, most of that data had a limited historical record. However, in the late 1970s, a historical series of U.S. stock and bond indices were created, with data going back to the 1920s. This data provided the ability to test the performance of the primary stock and bond markets over a wide range of economic periods. Although the availability of this data provided the groundwork for testing the potential benefits of various asset-allocation processes, asset allocators failed to emphasize some of the problems in the use of generic stock or bond benchmarks. Investors should note that both equity and fixed-income benchmarks have their own unique portfolio characteristics. For example, if certain equity subsectors have risen and fallen in value over time, their influence on the performance of the S&P 500 may also have risen and fallen, such that the risk characteristics of today's S&P 500 may have little in common with the risk characteristics of the index 10 to 15 years prior.

Analogous problems exist in the use of various bond indices. First, for many years, bond indices were created not from actual market prices but from what is commonly referred to as benchmark prices (i.e., computer-generated prices based on an assumed relative price movement to a benchmark bond). Second, many bond indices are based on maturity rather than duration. As a result, as coupon level moves, the underlying duration of some of the maturity-based bond indices may change, such that the sensitivity of the benchmark to changes in yield may change over time. Finally, as indicated for stocks, as the underlying bonds used to calculate the bond index change (e.g., industry component), the sensitivity of the portfolio to various developments in market subsectors may also change. For example, in recent years, the increase in government debt has adjusted the risk composition of the fixed-income BarCap U.S. Aggregate Bond Index to better reflect that of a less risky government bond index.

Other problems exist in the use of international indices. First, most asset-allocation programs use U.S.-dollar-based international stock indices. Over time, the returns to international stock indices may be dominated by currency returns and not the underlying returns (i.e., local returns) in each country. Even international equity indices that are represented as fully hedged against changes in the U.S. dollar assume a perfect hedge. Today, problems in benchmark creation have partially led to an entire industry of new investment products based on fundamental indices (e.g., GDP weighted), which attempt to capture more basic changes in market factors affecting stock prices.

The previous examples reflect potential concerns in the use of various stock and bond benchmarks in asset allocation. Moreover, stocks and bonds are often combined to create a set of conservative, moderate, and aggressive portfolios. A common weighting for a moderate portfolio may be 50 percent stocks and 50 percent bonds to create what is often called a *balanced portfolio*. Of course, the portfolio, although balanced in asset weightings, is not balanced in volatility weightings. To the degree that the stock component has a significantly higher volatility than the bond portfolio, it is the stock portion of the balanced fund that drives the return and the return volatility. Finally, most academic and practitioner research has emphasized the use of monthly data, if for no other reason than investors have become comfortable with the use of monthly reports. Investors should be aware that the performance of any individual manager, investment sector, and so on, can be impacted by the return interval used in the analysis. In brief, if a single day, a single week, or a single month normally in the analysis is modified or dropped, the results can change dramatically.

A PERSONAL VIEW OF EQUITY AND FIXED-INCOME ANALYSIS

Research has often addressed the benefits of equity and fixed income from the viewpoint of the changing value of assets, reflecting changing corporate supply and demand characteristics. Often research in this area has failed to consider the unique strategy emphasis of an individual asset and how that asset must be classified. Today, equity portfolios are often classified into four basic areas: (1) value, (2) growth, (3) small, and (4) large with value stocks often regarded as better values than growth and small stocks believed to outperform larger equities. The fact is that, as shown in Exhibits 2.10 and 2.11, analysis of the yearly returns to these equity indices indicates that firm segmentation does not have any major impact as to discerning the differential returns over time. Individual equities also require a more conditional analysis. As shown in Exhibit 2.12, when the monthly returns of the stocks in the Dow Jones Industrial Average 30 Index are ranked on the S&P 500, in periods of extreme monthly S&P 500 returns, virtually all the stocks in the Dow Jones Industrial 30 have the same directional movement as the S&P 500. In brief, the expected returns of equities must be conditioned on the general movement of the equity market. In addition, we remain locked into a world where new areas of equity investment (e.g., infrastructure) or commodity-related opportunities (e.g., water, agriculture, timber) are either not reviewed or reviewed from a totally domestic context.

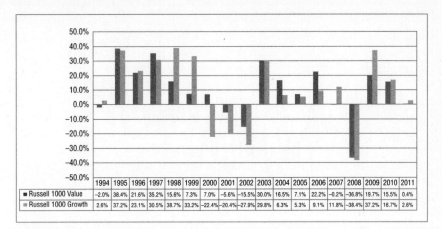

	1994	1995	1996	1997	1998	1999	2000	2001	2002	2003	2004	2005	2006	2007	2008	2009	2010	2011
■ Russell 1000 Value	-2.0%	38.4%	21.6%	35.2%	15.6%	7.3%	7.0%	-5.6%	-15.5%	30.0%	16.5%	7.1%	22.2%	-0.2%	-36.8%	19.7%	15.5%	0.4%
▨ Russell 1000 Growth	2.6%	37.2%	23.1%	30.5%	38.7%	33.2%	-22.4%	-20.4%	-27.9%	29.8%	6.3%	5.3%	9.1%	11.8%	-38.4%	37.2%	16.7%	2.6%

EXHIBIT 2.10 Russell 1000 Value and Growth: Annual Returns

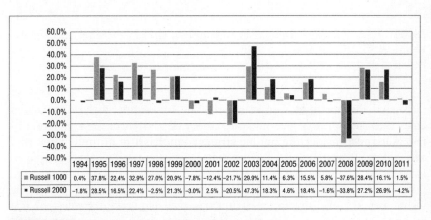

	1994	1995	1996	1997	1998	1999	2000	2001	2002	2003	2004	2005	2006	2007	2008	2009	2010	2011
▨ Russell 1000	0.4%	37.8%	22.4%	32.9%	27.0%	20.9%	-7.8%	-12.4%	-21.7%	29.9%	11.4%	6.3%	15.5%	5.8%	-37.6%	28.4%	16.1%	1.5%
■ Russell 2000	-1.8%	28.5%	16.5%	22.4%	-2.5%	21.3%	-3.0%	2.5%	-20.5%	47.3%	18.3%	4.6%	18.4%	-1.6%	-33.8%	27.2%	26.9%	-4.2%

EXHIBIT 2.11 Russell 1000 and 2000: Annual Returns

Distributional Characteristics

The primary reason for equity and fixed-income investment is the degree
to which an individual asset provides unique risk and return characteristics
not easily available in other investment vehicles. Various fixed-income and
equity vehicles trade in unique markets in unique forms. These vehicles
have a dynamic element such that the instrument does not track a particular long-only strategy. That having been said, the expected distributional
characteristics of an individual vehicle reflect the holdings of the underlying
product and the degree to which the asset adjusts to the underlying driving

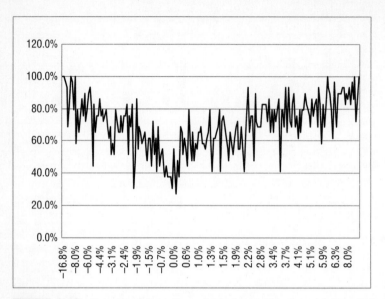

EXHIBIT 2.12   Percent of Dow Jones 30 Industrial Stocks with Same Directional
Return as S&P 500 (Ranked on S&P 500)
Period of analysis: 1994 to 2011.

factors of the portfolio. Unfortunately, the conditional nature of various
assets makes any cross-sectional or time-series analysis of the historical distributional nature of an equity or fixed-income product a simple "prisoner"
of the data. Researchers and reviewers are often enticed by the "more data
is better" syndrome; that is, five years of data is good, 10 years is better,
20 years is best. However, in a market partially driven by rapidly changing
technological and distribution channels as well as regulatory rules, what is
true of the 1980s may have little relevance for 2012. For example, many
products have dramatically different characteristics in a global production
market with low transportation costs. Many products are driven more by
changes in regulation than by changes in product investor consumption.

Governance and Micromarket Structure

The fundamental assumption of many academic analyses is that equity or
fixed-income products are just there and can be easily accessed by a number
of potential suppliers. Rarely is there a detailed description of the various
governance or structural elements associated with the product's delivery
as an investable program. There appears to be little understanding of the
fact that past and current business practices combined with new regulatory

concerns drive the manager selection and management process. There are few, if any, studies that truly understand the management or trading process of fund complexes.

WHAT EVERY INVESTOR SHOULD KNOW

Most investors' asset portfolios are made up exclusively of stocks and bonds. The reasons for this are varied but, of the major classes of investable assets, they are the most liquid, transparent, and most importantly, the most well-known and supposedly understood by both advisors and investors alike. As it often cited, no one has ever been sent to jail for investing in IBM or government bonds. The common rules of investing (e.g., diversification within and across asset classes, knowledge of inherent risks) seem to draw investors to the traditional pair of investments. However, common does not make it correct (or incorrect). What was once true may no longer represent current market understandings of the traditional pair. Despite their common use, there are a number of common misconceptions that every investor should know as well as a number of common rules of investment.

- **Know What You Own:** In all but the rare instance, investors are better off holding a large diversified portfolio of stocks or an index rather than attempting to hold a concentrated set of individual securities. However, investors should be aware of the unique risk characteristics of the portfolio or index they hold. For example, the S&P 500 diversifies across 500 stocks, but since it is asset weighted, it is really diversified across 50 stocks that count and 450 stocks that do not. Even EW portfolios are not truly diversified in that any one portfolio may have some stocks with high standard deviation and others with low standard deviations. In an EW portfolio, the stocks with the highest standard deviations may drive the return of the portfolio.
- **Diversification Does Not Eliminate Risk:** A number of investors seem to believe that diversifying across a number of stocks (domestically or internationally) reduces or eliminates risk. In fact it may increase risk. Diversification across equities (equal weights across multiple stocks) may reduce the impact of the business risk of individual firms, but by increasing exposure across multiple securities you are increasing your general exposure to conditions that affect all equities. You still have risk; you just know what that risk is.
- **A Stock's Beta or a Bond's Rating Is Not Sufficient:** Most equity financial reports contain a measure of an equity's beta (i.e., sensitivity

to a market index) or a bond's rating (i.e., potential for default). In the case of beta, if it is high, it is assumed risky. In the case of a bond rating, if it is high (AAA), it is assumed to not be risky. In both cases, the problem is that firms change quickly, such that most measures of historical beta may not reflect the current price risk, and it tells you little about all the other risks (i.e., liquidity). Similarly a bond's rating changes infrequently and tells little as to current risks (and it tells even less about current price sensitivity). If they are so limiting in terms of their risk assessment, why use them? The answer is that they are easy to get and regulation supports their use. However, remember the basic law of finance: If they are cheap and easy to get, the benefit may be limited. Use them, but be very careful—do not depend on them.

- **Returns Are Where the Risks Are**: Investments in small capitalization equity and emerging market equities have the capacity to provide meaningful returns, because in their markets, information asymmetries can exist that can lead to their superior performance. It is in these areas that managers that have significant research teams or insights can add value.

- **Do Not Trust Just Stocks or Just Bonds for the Long Run**: It can be expected that, on average, over a long enough time period, some stocks will have a higher return than some bonds. But some bonds are riskier than some stocks. In some (and in fact most) economic conditions, stocks are riskier than bonds, and in others, bonds are riskier than stocks. Economic conditions (and information uncertainty) may be viewed as a risk factor underlying the expected return process of a particular investment class sensitive to that information.

MYTHS AND MISCONCEPTIONS OF EQUITY AND FIXED INCOME

During the past decade, the investment-management industry has undergone numerous changes. New forms of traditional investment products, as well as alternative investment products (e.g., hedge funds, managed futures), have come into existence to meet the needs of changing financial regulation, information technology, and investor demands. Today, despite the existence of an increasing array of investment products, most investors concentrate on traditional investment vehicles such as stocks, bonds, and mutual funds. Although stock and bond investments may arguably be recommended as the primary investment vehicle for individual investors, many myths exist as to the actual basis for stock, bond, and mutual fund performance. In this short review, a series of myths and misconceptions on traditional stock and bond investments are presented.

Myth 2.1: Dividends Are Certain While Capital Gains Are Uncertain

One piece of advice heard loud and clear is to buy stocks with high dividend yield. This is a good advice, but not for the reason most people would believe. Dividends are not free. When a firm pays dividends, its stock price will decline by the amount of the dividend. That is, one cannot separate dividend income from capital gain income (ignoring taxes for now). However, it is often good advice to buy stocks with high dividend yields. First, most firms tend to do stupid things with their excess cash. Once upon a time, Kodak purchased a chain of drugstores with its excess cash. It is also often believed that firms that are committed to paying dividends tend to run more efficiently in terms of not using cash for any and all internal projects since you cannot pay dividends with accounting numbers.

Myth 2.2: Investor Attitudes, Not Economic Information, Drive Stock and Bond Values

Academic theory suggests, and empirical results support, that stocks and bonds should offer an expected return that is consistent with their underlying risk (i.e., variance in return in the assets not held in a market portfolio and beta [correlation] for assets held in an overall market portfolio). What investors must realize, however, is that an asset's own volatility or its correlation with a market portfolio is not the source of return. Asset volatility or market correlation merely reflects its sensitivity (i.e., movement) to new information entering the market or changes in how individuals interpret existing data. Thus, a security's expected return is conditional on the expected informational market. The sharpest gains and losses on stock and bond investments generally happen on a day on which there is a release of information that changes attitudes toward expected risk and required returns or expected cash flows. As informational uncertainty increases, so does expected volatility, and stock and bond prices fall in order to offer new investors an expected return consistent with the expected greater risk of holding the asset. In short, asset returns simply reflect changes in investors' reaction to information. By definition, it is impossible to forecast content of new information or investors' attitudes toward that new information.

While a large number of investors acting on faulty beliefs may in the short term affect market prices, assets will move to valuations that reflect the market consensus on information. Although behavioral implications on stock and bond movement remain a principal focus of recent research, stock market value remains linked to growth in earnings (e.g., productivity) and reduction in the required rate of return (e.g., interest rates [inflation] and risk premia).

Myth 2.3: Despite the Volatility of Stocks and Bonds in the Short Run, Time Diversification Reduces Their Volatilities in the Long Run

Although many investors would agree that both stocks and bonds must be priced such that assets that face greater price sensitivity (i.e., sensitivity to changes in information) offer greater expected returns, some believe that in the long run, traditional stock and bond investments can be viewed as almost riskless because U.S. stock and bond investments have always offered positive returns over long investment horizons (e.g., 20 years). Nothing could be further from the truth. Simply put, the two-year expected rate of return should be twice the one-year expected rate of return and, all else equal, the three-year expected rate of return is three times the one-year return. The same linear relationship exists for risk. The two-year expected variance is twice the one-year rate, and the three-year expected variance is three times the one-year variance. Summarizing, in the long run both the expected return and the expected risk increase—there is no free lunch. It is the linear relationship between expected return, risk, and investment horizon that makes reducing risk a prime goal for investors (e.g., the long-term rate of return is related to the annual return and volatility such that the lower the annual volatility, the greater the long-term rate of return). Managing risk remains a primary investor goal.

Myth 2.4: Diversification across Equity Issues or Countries Is Sufficient to Reduce Risk

MPT, advanced by Markowitz in the 1950s, centers on the correlation relationships and risk reduction opportunities of adding together securities that respond differently to changing economic conditions. In short, by combining securities, an investor can reduce a portfolio's variance. Equally important, the effect on expected return may be such that through judicious use of borrowing or lending, an investor can achieve higher returns with similar risk at the portfolio level than at the individual security level. However, Markowitz's theory is now 60 years old, and although it still forms the basis for many asset allocation models, it may be regarded as "ancient portfolio theory." The present primary concern is how to obtain the estimates of expected returns and correlations between assets. The past may not be a good reference for the future as firms change their risk and as countries become linked globally. Empirical market movements have shown that especially during periods of major market stress, the market effect on stocks domestically and globally dominates returns such that simple stock or international diversification may not reduce volatility in such risk-adverse market environments.

Myth 2.5: Historical Returns from Security Indices Provide the Most Important Information as to Expected Future Performance

When considering investment in equities or fixed income, most investors immediately look to a series of commonly used benchmarks (S&P 500, BarCap U.S. Aggregate) or even longer benchmark series to determine their historical performance. This is all well and good, the problem becomes that investors often tend to use the historical returns of those security indices as a basis for extrapolating expected returns. However, as discussed previously, because firms change financial structure, indices change composition, and past risk environments may differ from those of today, simple use of past data may not provide the best forecast of current economic factors. Historical equity returns in the United States may have come from periods when the average growth in GDP was more than 5 percent; going forward it may be closer to 3 percent. Government bond yields are closer to 2 percent, so how can any investor use a historical expected bond return near 6 percent? In the mid-2000s, the S&P 500 was heavily weighted toward the financial sector; today that sector's influence is marginal. Investors should be aware that historical data is just that—historical—it does not necessarily indicate current or future long-term expected returns for any asset class. They only provide a window into what factors drive stock returns and yields such that one can use those factors (e.g., GDP growth, inflation) as a basis for estimating future expected returns.

Myth 2.6: Recent Manager Fund Performance Forecasts Future Return

Managers' recent past performance is not necessarily the best forecast of how managers will perform in the near future. Many investors may respond that if one cannot use recent performance, what should be used? Each manager holds a unique portfolio. That portfolio will outperform in some market environments and underperform in others. In fact, most risk-management software provides an analyst with the exact market factor sensitivities of various portfolio managers, such that one knows when they will make money and lose money. Only if economic conditions favorable to a manager's existing portfolio continue over time, will any seeming past outperformance of individual managers continue. There is however, one case when past performance may indicate future performance. Poor past performance may be consistent with increased volatility of manager future performance, as poor managers "go for the gold" to obtain high performance.

The fact that past manager performance alone does not provide a means to obtain a forecast of those managers who may be expected to outperform in the near future, does not mean that superior performance does not exist. Unfortunately, evaluation of superior performance requires more data and more analysis to provide better decisions. There is never enough data to determine superior performance, so we are left with the analysis of other factors (e.g., depth of investment team, back office and front office support, etc.). The classic retort to the question, "If you are so smart, why are you not rich" is "If you are rich, why are you not smart," which reflects the timeworn evidence that success may be more in the hands of the gods than in people.

Myth 2.7: Given the Efficiency of the Stock and Bond Markets, Managers Provide No Useful Service

The inability of managers to consistently outperform passive indices is one reason for concerns over the benefits of manager-based security selection. The failure to find a method that determines only the best managers, however, does not mean that managers do not matter. First, managers do provide many investor services (e.g., accounting and tax reporting) that would be costly, if not impossible, for individual investors to perform. In addition, managers may provide one service that most simple passive benchmark-based investments cannot, that is, an option to be discretionary. When one purchases an index, one simply rides the index up and down. Managers provide a security or asset allocation function, in that they can rebalance in markets or securities as needed. Managers who provide such skills result in a type of downside risk protection similar to put protection. In short, the fees paid to a manager should be considered as an alternative to a simple put or option protection. The real question to be considered is, are the manager's fees worth the cost of that option? In considering this question, there is a serious argument that a substantial number of the large mutual fund complexes are "closet indexers." Here, senior management understands that it is marketing its performance against that of passive indices and that underperformance hinders the ability to raise additional capital and thus grow investment income or management fees. As a consequence, money managers are required to manage client monies within very specific asset allocation bands that mirror those of the corresponding passive index. Typically this scenario is cast as a risk management tool— however, the net effect is to ensure that money managers do not stray too far from the norm and to further ensure that the firm continues to have a marketable product. Here, from a business perspective, it is more important to show consistent performance against a given passive index than to risk underperformance by deviating from that index's parameters.

Myth 2.8: Superior Managers or Investment Ideas Do Not Exist

As stated earlier, superior managers may exist. The problem is that there is often not enough data to determine who those managers are, or the economic condition that allows us to see their unique contributions are so few that we only recognize them ex post. For example, there is the rare occasion in which a manager has an insight that is not currently shared by the market, and the execution of that insight results in outsized returns (e.g., those managers that shorted the ABX Index in 2007 and 2008). There is also the rare circumstance in which a manager creates a legitimate informational advantage and acts on it prior to the market knowing its value (e.g., finding information within Securities and Exchange Commission [SEC] filings that has been overlooked or not digested by the market). The fact that past manager performance alone does not provide a means to obtain superior future performance does not mean that superior performance does not exist, only that if a manager has consistent superior gross performance, he will most likely charge a fee for his or her services such that the net return across competitive funds would be similar to that of a "regular" manager.

Remember, individuals often need heroes even if they do not exist. If a Peter Lynch or the Sage of Omaha did not exist, we would have to invent one. Do we regard them as great because they were, or were they just lucky? As we have noted, the language of investment management often mirrors that of a casino. History and experience has taught us that it would be a mistake to discount luck as a factor in a manager's returns.

Myth 2.9: Stock and Bond Investment Means Investors Have No Derivatives Exposure

This is simply not true in today's market. In fact, almost every investment into an equity or bond is also an investment into a derivative either directly or indirectly. A financial derivative may be regarded as a secondary asset whose underlying value is based on the value of the portfolio of underlying primary financial assets. However, that primary financial asset may also be based on holdings that contain derivatives. It is most certainly a sure bet that every firm uses derivatives in the management of its daily operations (e.g., currency futures, treasury operations, and pension fund investment decisions). Many firms (e.g., oil exploration and refinery, gold and other precious metal mining companies, airlines, bottling companies, and food processing or manufacturing companies) use derivatives to offset fundamental risks in their business. In short, most investors are exposed to derivatives; they just do not know it.

Myth 2.10: Mutual Fund Investment Removes Investor Concerns as to Leverage

Regulation, as well as investor concerns, generally limit the amount of leverage used in a range of investment products (at least those targeted to retail mutual fund clients). As stated in the previous myth, however, most firms use derivatives in a wide range of activities both to increase and reduce a range of business risk exposures. In addition, since corporations borrow, the sensitivity of a firm's equity and debt valuations to certain changes in information is a function of the firm's leverage. Banks, for example, are often levered five to eight times equity, and from a historical perspective, investment banks were levered as much as 30 times equity. As a result, highly levered firms may try to reduce total risk by investing in less volatile products or ideas. The raw conclusion is that leverage is used in almost every investment in some way. As important, there may or may not be any relationship between a firm's or fund's leverage and its risk since firms or funds with high leverage may simply invest in less risky assets, and those firms with no or little leverage may invest in highly risky investments. The solution is to make sure you know the degree to which managers use leverage, the assets they invest in, and the degree to which they have the right and the ability to change leverage or asset-selection policy quickly without your knowledge. There is the real risk.

CHAPTER 3

Hedge Funds

An Absolute Return Answer?

In 1947, A.W. Jones began trading what is known today as a long/short equity fund. In the decades that followed, hedge funds continued to grow but were not a major part of the financial system. However, in the late 1980s, the interaction of advances in technology, the growth of derivative markets, and regulatory changes encouraged many financial trading firms and banks to sell all or part of their proprietary trading operations to outside legal entities. Banks and many trading houses simply found it more profitable to charge certain services (e.g., brokerage, lending, and back-office support) than to have to cover the new capital charges required by changing regulations.

Although many investors see hedge funds as unique animals, hedge funds are actually just one example of the privatization of the trading floor. Over the course of the 1990s, the growth of financial markets, both in the United States and globally, increased the availability of new security forms (e.g., mortgages), new markets (Europe and emerging), and new strategies (convertible arbitrage and fixed-income arbitrage). Hedge funds had matured, but unfortunately, the public perception of the industry had not. Even within the hedge fund industry, many managers continued to portray themselves, inaccurately, as absolute return managers—managers who could make money in every market. Academics and others, of course, were well aware that most hedge fund strategies provided investor opportunities not available in other long-only stock and bond strategies, covering a wide array of investment strategies, and that, just as with other investment strategies, each strategy had its own unique set of return factors. For many in the hedge fund industry at that time, considerable debate existed between those who wished to sell primarily to high-net-worth individuals or other retail type clients, and those who regarded the institutional market as the future for hedge funds. All a hedge fund had to do was transform itself from a small three- to five-person trading operation to an actual firm with the back-office, trading, and compliance personnel required to provide style- and strategy-consistent returns in a form suitable to mainline institutional clients.

In 2000, we were retained by Zurich Capital Markets (ZCM) to restructure and manage its hedge fund platform. Randall Kau, ZCM's CEO, had a vision of hedge funds becoming an integral part of his institutional business, but after a number of misfires with joint venture partners and internal personnel, he had become frustrated with the platform's progress and its inability to attract meaningful institutional investments.

The ZCM platform had approximately USD 80 million in total assets under management (AUM) as seed money and a few small outside investors. The platform had invested in 30 hedge fund managers across eight to nine different investment styles to create diversification of risks and returns. The size, investment sophistication, and institutional integrity of this grouping were at best uneven. Our initial review showed that the platform had no coherent economic structure, nor did it have a comprehensive operational and investment management due diligence program. This was pretty much consistent with the vast majority of the platforms of that era. For the most part, these earlier hedge fund businesses were built on referrals from friends and family, with the assumption that operational capabilities were in place. To a limited extent, this was a correct assumption. Typically, the funds had a prime brokerage relationship with a large institutional bank or investment bank, and this "prime broker" provided most if not all back-office functions and administration as well as trading and support. Although the ZCM platform was touted as a means of freeing the hedge fund manager to focus exclusively on money management, it's not unfair to say, with limited exception, that once you moved beyond the capabilities of the prime brokers, the common denominator among ZCM hedge fund investment managers was that they were people with dogs and computers operating out of their garages.

Once ZCM verified and recovered from the shock of our report, we began the process of creating a hedge fund platform in which institutional investors would be comfortable investing their funds. The first step was to close the platform to all non-ZCM investors and to liquidate all invest-ments in an orderly fashion. Next, we scheduled interviews with large institutional investors to gauge their view of hedge funds and whether they would invest in this upcoming asset class. More than half of the respon-dents of our initial survey stated that they would never invest in hedge funds. This sampling cited issues such as volatility, lack of transparency, fraud, and career risk. Those institutional investors who would consider an investment in hedge funds were remarkably consistent in their responses.

Collectively, they viewed an investment as an investment. In their world-view, the same criteria used to evaluate an investment in equities, bonds, real estate, or any other asset class should be used to determine whether to invest in hedge funds.

The potential investors went on to describe the characteristics of a hedge fund platform that would be consistent with an institutional framework. The first question to be asked and answered involves identifying the economic characteristics of the investment that permit an understanding of its behavior in different markets and within a diversified portfolio. Next, there must be sufficient transparency to conduct independent and meaningful investment due diligence, monitoring, and valuations. Third, given that investment performance and its execution cannot be separated from the business platform, the operational infrastructure must be sufficient to support a particular investment approach. The operational needs will of course change depending on the complexity of the investment program. Here they noted that most failures of asset management firms are not caused by direct fraud but by operational failures. Related to this concept is the belief that a great deal of consideration has to be given to the length of time a firm has been in business. In regard to hedge funds, typically star managers leave major firms to set up their own shops. Within that major firm they were in cocoons, surrounded by a collection of support staff, managed and paid by the firm, responsible for the day-to-day tasks of running the business. Now as both owners and money managers, they are responsible for all of the functions relating to both business management and investing. Quite simply, these are very different skill sets, and it takes time to determine whether these parts will come together and be successful. The core of the institutional model is that there must be sufficient transparency to independently and rigorously conduct both operational and investment due diligence, and the knowledge that these are separate lines of inquiry. Equally important, the institutional model suggests that if an investor cannot intuitively understand and verify all of the parts, it is probably a bad investment idea.

Using the institutional model as our map, we designed and implemented an investment approach based on a variation of factor analysis that explained the differing risk and reward characteristics of each of the sub-classes of hedge fund investments, as well as their sources of return. We then created a managed account platform in which ZCM owned, managed, and controlled all aspects of the day-to-day operations and directly employed all prime brokers, auditors, and lawyers associated with the platform. With this approach, we attained full and complete transparency, which permitted us to monitor and value both risk and performance on a daily basis. Next, we entered into sub-advisory agreements with managers who met our selection criteria, allowing them to trade or manage monies within exacting investment guidelines that ensured that they could not exceed agreed-on levels of risk. Along the way, we had to shatter some myths and misconceptions relating to hedge fund investing. In so doing, we learned that there are very few true wizards in the world. Most hedge fund managers are inextricably tied to the common economic characteristics of the underlying assets in their portfolios. We also learned that although sources of return and associated risks are different within each sub-strategy of hedge funds, the constant in determining the success or failure of a manager lies in the business model. Performance is simply an expression of that model and incorporates not only management and incentive fees but the invisible costs of items such as legal structure, research, borrowing, trading, audit, and other things tied to infrastructure. Each has the ability to negatively or positively impact performance, and each has the implicit ability to disguise malfeasance and fraud.

During our relationship with ZCM, we bought and managed the MAR Hedge Fund Database. Greg Newton, the CEO of Metal Bulletin Research in the United States at the time, had concluded that the cost of an information platform could not be justified within a noninvestment management firm. MAR was the oldest continuing collection of information on the performance of individual managers within the hedge fund industry going back some 17 years, and we believed that its purchase would provide an enhanced level of transparency that would better serve our clients. In addition, we decided that it would make an excellent marketing tool, because the monthly performance results were published in *Barron's* and also picked up by the wire services. Ernst & Young was retained to analyze the platform and concluded that at best, the database provided indicative insights yet certainly not the type of foundation that a firm could use to build investment products. The MAR Database, like all other databases since, relied on self-reporting information from managers and had no level of oversight verification. The self-reporting business model for hedge fund indices and databases is prevalent because investors have shown an unwillingness to pay for the increased costs of verification; and frankly, even if investors were willing to pay, it is highly doubtful that any firm would be able to gather the type of information required to conduct reliable analysis. Thus, for the most part, hedge fund indices are relegated to providing indicative guidance while serving as marketing tools for their owners.

As we began to implement our new strategy and platform, the catastrophe of September 11, 2001, occurred. One of the aftermaths of that tragedy was that a great deal of pressure was put on property and casualty insurance companies to justify their reserves and explain their liabilities. The major rating agencies (e.g., Standard & Poor's and Moody's) reluctantly admitted that they did not have the staff or resources to understand and rate ZCM's exposure to hedge funds in its differing business lines, and Rolf Hüppi, the CEO and chairman of Zurich Financial Services, made the decision to close ZCM despite the fact that the firm had been the single best division of profit for the year after September 11. This factual pattern seems to be a constant and persistent theme with the rating agencies based in the United States. As witnessed in the Senate hearings relating to the 2007–2008 financial crises, the major U.S. rating agencies failed to properly understand and rate the risks associated with alternative pooled investments. From recent conversations with senior officials of the Securities Investor Protection Corporation and the Securities and Exchange Commission, it is clear that investors tend to wholly rely on the due diligence of others and thus fully rely on ratings in purchasing pooled alternative investments, even when historical evidence leads to a different approach.

We ultimately purchased ZCM's hedge fund platform and built the business from a seed investment of just under USD 80 million to approximately USD 3.5 billion when we sold it to a European bank. In making our way through this industry, we have rebranded the MAR Hedge Fund Database as the Center for International Securities and Derivatives Markets (CISDM) Hedge Fund Database; created the Dow Jones Hedge Fund Benchmark Series; and built hedge fund products for distribution in Undertakings for Collective Investment in Transferable Securities (UCITS) wrappers.

In brief, over the past 10 years, the hedge fund industry has evolved from two people in a garage to a global industry that increasingly incorporates all the operational and risk-management principles required by large financial institutions for their traditional stock and fixed-income asset managers. Today, the market factors driving individual hedge funds strategies are well known, and most institutional investors require and can obtain daily valuations of their hedge fund holdings such that dynamic daily risk management and risk evaluation can be conducted. There even exist a number of hedge fund tracker products that provide passive index-based products that attempt to capture the general factor exposures of hedge fund strategies in a way similar to that of passive index-based products in the traditional equity and fixed-income areas. Against this background, hedge funds can now be analyzed using the same approaches investors use to understand the return and risk characteristics of traditional equity and fixed-income investment. With the good, however, comes the bad. Although some of the analytical tools and investment analyzers that work well for traditional assets also work in the hedge fund area, many do not transfer easily. The trick, of course, is to know which are which.

WHAT ARE HEDGE FUNDS?

Although some academics and practitioners would argue that hedge funds are merely variants of traditional stock and bond investments, we accept the argument that hedge funds reflect a unique and separate asset class that provides distinct risk and return opportunities not easily obtained in other investment vehicles. Moreover, given the knowledge of the return and risk characteristics of each strategy as well as which managers fit into each strategy, meaningful hedge fund indices and benchmarks have been developed to help in the application of traditional asset allocation decisions. We are also mindful that each hedge fund manager or platform is in fact a business product for which the individual business model ultimately determines performance and risk.

As previously discussed, hedge funds are generally regarded as investments that offer risk and return opportunities not easily obtained through traditional long-only stock and bond investment vehicles. Such unique investment opportunities are made possible primarily through the ability to participate in a wide variety of financial instruments and global markets not typically available to the traditional investor. The ability to take both long and short positions in a wide variety of securities markets further defines this investment approach. Next, hedge funds are often portrayed as absolute return vehicles. Contrary to popular belief, this nomenclature does not mean that hedge funds are designed to have positive returns irrespective of market conditions; it simply means that they are designed not to track directly any individual long-only investment benchmark (e.g., S&P 500 or MSCI World). The descriptive relief provides managers with greater flexibility in both internal asset allocation and investment strategy. At bottom, hedge funds are designed to benefit from a broad universe of profit opportunities within various economic environments. The hedge fund delivery platforms are often structured as privately pooled investment vehicles that employ varying degrees of leverage, and often charge a performance or incentive fee.

Our analysis concludes that a well-selected hedge fund or portfolio of hedge funds can provide return enhancement as well as risk reduction opportunities relative to stock and bond investments. In this chapter, we explore the potential benefits of hedge funds as stand-alone investments or as additions to portfolios of either traditional assets or a mix of various investments. First, we discuss approaches in which investors can gain exposure to hedge funds. Second, we explore sources of hedge fund returns. Third, we evaluate the performance of hedge funds on a stand-alone basis, as part of traditional stock and bond portfolios, and as part of portfolios including traditional and alternative investments. In each area, the facts surrounding the development of the hedge fund industry are well known; however, for many, a number of misconceptions about hedge funds, their performance, and their management still exist.

INVESTING IN HEDGE FUNDS

Under the current U.S. securities regulations, a "qualified" or "accredited" investor may directly invest with a hedge fund manager through fund-based investment pools, managed accounts, or managed segregated accounts. The key distinction among the three is that fund-based accounts and some managed accounts require a pooling of investor funds (in which case the exposure of one investor is identical to that of any other investor), whereas managed segregated accounts keep investor funds in separate accounts, which may offer unique risk-and-return objectives. The fees associated with these vehicles are typically a 1 to 2 percent management fee and a corresponding 10 to 20 percent incentive fee. The incentive fee is usually taken only when performance exceeds a predetermined benchmark. In addition, there are a number of silent fees associated with these vehicles. Fees such as audit, research, and trading are variable and can have a major effect on overall performance. There may also be unanticipated fees because of increased accounting costs, fees related to the vehicle's jurisdiction of incorporation, or fees tied to the costs of repatriating monies from offshore accounts.

HEDGE FUND STYLES AND BENCHMARKS

As in most investment strategies, hedge funds have been divided into the markets they trade (global macro) and some of their unique strategy approaches to trading (e.g., market neutral, equity long/short). For each of these forms of trading and markets traded, various firms have created manager based hedge fund indices similar to those that exist in equity and other investment asset classes (e.g., Morningstar and Lipper). Historically, the primary benchmarks are as follows.

Relative Value

Relative value strategies emphasize the purchase of undervalued securities and the sale of overvalued securities within the context of minimizing the market exposure inherent in the underlying security market traded (e.g., equity markets for equity market neutral and fixed-income markets for fixed-income arbitrage). It is important to note, however, that each relative value strategy leaves open exposure to certain market factors (e.g., industry and sector exposure) that provide, in part, the basis for expected return.

- **Market Neutral:** Represents strategies that take long equity positions and an approximately equal dollar amount of offsetting short positions in order to achieve a net exposure as close to zero as possible.
- **Fixed-Income Arbitrage:** Represents strategies that attempt to take advantage of mispricing opportunities between different types of fixed-income securities while neutralizing exposure to interest rate risk.
- **Convertible Arbitrage:** Represents strategies that take long positions in convertible securities (usually convertible bonds) and try to hedge those positions by selling short the underlying common stock.

Event Driven

Event-driven strategies emphasize the purchase of undervalued securities with appropriate risk-management techniques (e.g., shorting individual securities or sectors to reduce market or firm exposure) in the context of event-driven return opportunities (e.g., firm mergers and bankruptcies), which may be independent of general market movements.

- **Distressed:** Represents strategies that take positions in the securities of companies in which the securities' price has been, or is expected to be, affected by a distressed situation, such as an announcement of reorganization because of financial or business difficulties.
- **Event Driven:** Represents strategies that attempt to predict the outcome of corporate events and take the necessary position to make a profit. These trading managers invest in such events as liquidations, spin-offs, share buybacks, and other corporate transactions.
- **Merger Arbitrage:** Represents strategies that concentrate on companies that are the subject of a merger, tender offer, or exchange offer. Although there are a number of different trading-based approaches, merger arbitrage strategies often take a long position in the acquired company and a short position in the acquiring company.

Opportunistic

Opportunistic trading strategies emphasize the purchase of undervalued securities or markets (European versus U.S. fixed income, alternative energy sectors) and the sale of overvalued securities or markets without the constraint that the underlying market exposure will be systematically eliminated or minimized. Certain opportunistic strategies such as global macro are primarily trading strategies that do not emphasize long-term net-long or net-short investment positions. For these opportunistic strategies, the correlation between and among them as well as to other hedge fund strategies may be relatively low.

- **Equity Long/Short**: Represents strategies that take long and short equity positions varying from net-long to net-short, depending on whether the market is bullish or bearish. The short exposure can also be a put option on a stock index, which is used as a hedging technique for bear market conditions.
- **Global Macro**: Represents strategies that employ opportunistically long and short multiple financial or nonfinancial assets. Trading managers following global macro strategies might use systematic trend-following models or discretionary approaches. For systematic trend-following global macro managers who trade primarily in futures and option markets, returns are similar to those of commodity trading advisors.

In this chapter, the CISDM Equal Weighted Hedge Fund Index is used as the primary representative hedge fund index. As noted earlier, a number of larger investment firms, as well as other players in the hedge fund arena, offer a wide range of manager-based hedge fund indices. Each of these indices is unique in its own way. For example, Barclay and Hedge Fund Research (HFR) also provides active-manager-based hedge fund indices that are equal weighted and constructed using unverified information of "reporting managers" associated with each of the respective databases. These indices are not directly investable. In recent years, a number of manager-based hedge fund indices have been created that are designed to capture the returns of an investable set of active hedge fund managers (HFR, Lyxor, Dow Jones, and so on). Each of these indices differs slightly in its construction. Our past research has shown that the reported returns of the investable hedge fund indices are highly correlated with noninvestable manager-based hedge fund indices.

BASIC SOURCES OF RETURN AND RISK

Each of the foregoing hedge fund strategies reflect intrinsic economic and market risks, and an understanding of these risks is essential to asset allocation decisions. As discussed previously, hedge funds have been described as skill-based investment strategies, which obtain returns primarily as a result of a firm's unique trading abilities and infrastructure. Because these returns are a reflection of individual manager skill, they may not be correlated with the long-term return of the underlying traditional stock and bond markets. As a result, hedge funds have also been described as *absolute return* strategies, since their performance is not linked to any existing stock and bond index, and their trading strategies may offer positive returns across a wide variety of market conditions.

Over the years we have learned that industry shorthand can be misleading. Hedge funds are often presented as actively managed absolute return vehicles. Because they are actively managed, trader skill is important. However, trader skill cannot obviate the underlying economic realities of the assets traded. Traders work in a market in which the underlying assets they are trading have certain and finite properties. And no matter how skilled a trader may be, the essential nature of those underlying assets cannot be changed. Thus, the lack of direct index tracking does not mean that managers within a particular strategy do not have similar sensitivities to common market factors. In fact, research shows that various hedge fund strategy returns are driven largely by traditional market factors (i.e., S&P 500; Russell 2000; BarCap U.S. Government, U.S. Aggregate, and U.S. Corporate High Yield Bond indices). Previous research has shown that hedge fund strategies such as equity long/short are impacted primarily by equity factors and have the highest correlation with such indices as the S&P 500 and Russell 2000. In contrast, strategies such as convertible arbitrage and distressed securities have the highest exposure to changes in credit spreads and have a high positive correlation with corporate high-yield bond returns, as evidenced by such indices as the BarCap Corporate High Yield Bond Index. Merger arbitrages with the greatest ability to arbitrage out market factor exposures tend to have the lowest correlation with stock and bond factors.

On the risk side of the equation, strategies with the highest exposure (e.g., correlation) to market factors and with the highest volatility (e.g., equity or high-yield bond returns) are expected to have a relatively higher level of risk. The introduction of leverage to this risk analysis provides some interesting results. For the most part, leverage is associated with magnifying risk. Thus, the amount of leverage an individual strategy may take has a potential effect on its expected volatility and relative market sensitivity (e.g., beta). Some strategies, however, respond counter intuitively to leverage. By example, market neutral strategies tend to have the highest amount of leverage yet also tend to have the lowest level of volatility. Other strategies, such as distressed securities and emerging markets, usually employ no leverage and tend to have very high volatility. In sum, high volatility is not directly associated with high leverage; rather, it is associated with the inherent volatility of the underlying assets (e.g., sensitivity to informational change) and the degree to which additional leverage is taken.

In our experience, we have never encountered a distressed securities manager who uses leverage.

On the whole, hedge fund returns are a combination of manager skill and the underlying natural return to the strategy itself—no more, no less. As a result, similar to the equity and bond markets, indices can be created that capture the underlying return to the strategy. Within such a rules-based approach it is possible to measure a manager's alpha. A manager's performance is measured relative to a systematic passive hedge fund index, and as a consequence, the differential return may be viewed as that manager's alpha. In the absence of a rules-based approach, if a manager's performance is measured relative to an index of other active managers, then the relative performance simply measures the over- or underperformance to that index of manager returns. A rules-based approach also provides an opportunity to measure strategy performance and provides some insight into relative correlations among and between hedge fund strategies and traditional asset classes.

PERFORMANCE: FACT AND FICTION

Over the past decades, our understanding of how various hedge fund strategies perform across a wide range of market conditions has become more evident. Some of this new understanding (e.g., that hedge funds are not absolute return vehicles with the ability to make money in all markets) is now well-known fact; however there still remains a degree of fiction in how investors view hedge fund performance. In the following sections, we provide evidence not only on the standalone risks of various hedge fund investment, but also on the interrelationships of various hedge fund strategies within hedge funds and between hedge funds and various traditional (e.g., equity and fixed income market) and alternative asset classes. We have examined these markets over a broad time period, as well as on shorter time intervals (e.g., annual) as well as analyzed their relative performance in extreme market conditions. Results show that, as expected, (1) hedge funds often provide lower returns but at lower levels of risk than comparable traditional and alternative investments, and as such, they often provide superior standalone return to risk tradeoffs, and (2) hedge funds with low equity or credit spread exposure generally have a relatively low correlation with traditional and other alternative asset classes such that combining those hedge fund strategies (e.g., equity market neutral, merger arbitrage, event driven) with traditional and alternative asset-based portfolios may result in a superior return-to-risk tradeoff. Results also reflect that some of what was emphasized in the past (e.g., the ability of hedge funds to perform well in periods of extreme market stress and, the consistency of hedge fund returns over time) may be regarded as more fiction than fact. For example, (1) for certain hedge fund strategies, such as equity long/short, there is little evidence of diversification benefits when considered as additions to equity portfolios or portfolios of traditional and alternative assets with significant equity exposure; (2) in periods of extreme equity market movements, most hedge fund strategies (with the exception of relative-value-based strategies) have similar return patterns, that is, falling in down equity markets and providing positive returns in up equity markets; and (3) investors should not take risk-and-return performance from extended time frames as a basis for how various hedge fund strategies or hedge fund composite indices may perform over relatively shorter time periods (e.g., annual). Also, evidence derived over long investment periods as to the benefits of certain hedge fund strategies (e.g., equity long/short, distressed securities) may not reflect the relative performance when analyzed over shorter time intervals (e.g., annual). Finally, despite the potential differences among investment strategy approaches within a particular hedge fund strategy (e.g., equity long/short), most hedge funds within a particular hedge fund strategy (e.g., equity long/short) rise together in up strategy months and fall together in down strategy months such that diversification within a hedge fund strategy area may not provide the diversification benefits that most investors expect.

RETURN AND RISK CHARACTERISTICS

In this section, we review the relative performance of the CISDM Equal Weighted Hedge Fund Index (CISDM EW HF) with a range of traditional stock and bond indices as well as a number of alternative investment indices (real estate, private equity, commodities, and managed futures) over the period 1994–2011. In later sections, we focus on hedge fund composite and hedge fund strategy and market-based index trading performance in various subperiods. Again we wish to remind investors that the performance of any individual investment or investment strategy may not reflect current expected performance or the expected performance in periods that have economic conditions different from those of the period of analysis. For this period, as shown in Exhibit 3.1, the CISDM EW HF exhibited lower annualized standard deviation (7.7 percent) than that of the S&P 500 (15.7 percent). This may be surprising to most investors, who often regard hedge funds as being more risky than stocks.[1] Over the period of analysis, the CISDM EW HF also reported higher annualized total return (10.4 percent) than that of the S&P 500 (7.7 percent). However, stand-alone historical return and risk comparison may not reflect the potential for the benefits of a hedge

EXHIBIT 3.1   Hedge Fund and Asset Class Performance

Stock, Bond, and Hedge-Fund Performance	CISDM Equal Weighted Hedge Fund	S&P 500	BarCap U.S. Government	BarCap U.S. Aggregate	BarCap U.S. Corporate High Yield
Annualized total return	10.4%	7.7%	6.1%	6.3%	7.3%
Annualized standard deviation	7.7%	15.7%	4.4%	3.8%	9.4%
Information ratio	1.36	0.49	1.39	1.67	0.78
Maximum drawdown	−21.7%	−50.9%	−5.4%	−5.1%	−33.3%
Correlation with hedge funds	1.00	0.75	−0.17	0.03	0.63

Alternative Asset and Hedge-Fund Performance	CISDM Equal Weighted Hedge Fund	S&P GSCI	CISDM CTA Equal Weighted	FTSE NAREIT	Private Equity index
Annualized total return	10.4%	4.8%	8.1%	9.7%	8.0%
Annualized standard deviation	7.7%	22.5%	8.7%	19.9%	28.1%
Information ratio	1.36	0.21	0.94	0.49	0.28
Maximum drawdown	−21.7%	−67.6%	−8.7%	−67.9%	−80.4%
Correlation with hedge funds	1.00	0.40	0.05	0.45	0.77

Period of analysis: 1994 to 2011.

fund investment as additions to other traditional assets or other financial asset classes. For example, as shown in Exhibit 3.1, for the period analyzed, the CISDM EW HF has a relatively high correlation (0.75) with the S&P 500 and a low correlation (0.03) with the BarCap U.S. Aggregate. The relatively high correlation of the hedge fund index with stock returns may lead investors to question hedge funds as a primary means of diversification for equity-dominated portfolios.

Modern portfolio theory emphasizes that individual assets should be evaluated based on their performance alongside other assets in investors' portfolios. The diversification benefits of adding any individual investment

EXHIBIT 3.2 Hedge Fund and Multi-Asset Class Portfolio Performance

Portfolios	A	B	C	D
Annualized returns	7.3%	7.7%	7.9%	8.1%
Standard deviation	8.2%	7.9%	8.8%	8.5%
Information ratio	0.90	0.97	0.89	0.95
Maximum drawdown	−27.1%	−26.6%	−34.0%	−32.8%
Correlation with hedge funds	0.73		0.79	
Portfolio A	Equal weights S&P 500 and BarCap U.S. Aggregate			
Portfolio B	90% Portfolio A and 10% hedge funds			
Portfolio C	75% Portfolio A and 25% CTA/commodities/private equity/real estate			
Portfolio D	90% Portfolio C and 10% hedge funds			

to other assets or asset portfolios depend on the comparison stand-alone investment. As shown in Exhibit 3.1, the relatively high correlations between the CISDM EW HF and a range of financial assets (e.g., equity, real estate, private equity) may indicate that a portfolio of hedge funds provides only minimal reduction in the risk (standard deviation) of a stock or a multi-asset portfolio dominated by equity investment. As shown in Exhibit 3.2, for the period of analysis, adding a small portion of hedge funds (10 percent) to a stock and bond portfolio (Portfolio A) yields a Portfolio B with a similar annualized return (7.7 percent) and standard deviation (7.9 percent) as the pure stock and bond portfolio (Portfolio A, with an annualized return of 7.3 percent and a standard deviation of 8.2 percent). Similarly, adding hedge funds to Portfolio C that contains a range of traditional and alternative assets results in Portfolio D that exhibits a similar return (8.1 percent) and standard deviation (8.5 percent) to those of Portfolio C (7.9 percent and 8.8 percent, respectively), which does not contain hedge funds.

The ability of the CISDM EW HF to provide only marginally superior risk-and-return opportunities as additions to a sample portfolio is indicative of the potential of hedge funds to provide a positive return-to-risk trade-off to a multi-asset portfolio over a lengthy period of time, but the advantages of hedge fund investment may be concentrated in periods of market stress or in unique hedge fund strategies. Again, investors must be warned. First, as mentioned previously, performance in a single period is not indicative of relative performance in other periods. Second, the CISDM EW HF is only one of several composite hedge fund indices. Other hedge fund indices or sub-indices may provide different performance results. Third, there is no requirement that investors invest in a single composite hedge fund index.

EXHIBIT 3.3 Hedge Fund Index Performance

	CISDM Equal Weighted Hedge Fund	Equity Market Neutral	Convertible Arbitrage	Event-Driven Multi-Strategy	Merger Arbitrage	Distressed Securities	Equity Long/Short	Global Macro
Annualized return	10.4%	7.8%	8.7%	9.7%	8.1%	9.3%	9.9%	6.9%
Annualized standard deviation	7.7%	2.2%	5.1%	5.9%	3.5%	6.1%	7.8%	4.6%
Information ratio	1.36	3.62	1.70	1.63	2.31	1.54	1.28	1.49
Maximum drawdown	−21.7%	−2.8%	−22.5%	−20.2%	−5.7%	−21.2%	−17.2%	−8.2%
Correlation with S&P 500	0.75	0.45	0.45	0.72	0.61	0.62	0.75	0.39
Correlation with BarCap U.S. Aggregate	0.03	0.13	0.23	0.00	0.08	0.06	−0.01	0.23
Correlation with hedge funds	1.00	0.66	0.63	0.87	0.72	0.83	0.95	0.57

A composite hedge fund index covers a wide range of hedge fund trading strategies. Exhibit 3.3 shows risk-and-return performance over the 1994 to 2011 period for a range of hedge fund trading sub-indices. Their correlation with the S&P 500 (shown in Exhibit 3.3) illustrates that the correlation of some individual hedge fund strategies (equity market neutral, convertible arbitrage, global macro) is significantly less than that of the composite hedge fund index. However, two of the major hedge fund strategies (e.g., equity long/short, event driven) report a relatively high correlation (above .70) with the S&P 500. Clearly, there is no simple trick for determining if hedge funds will always result in superior performance when added to an equity-dominated portfolio.

In summary, there is much in the historical returns for the period 1994–2011 to support the view that the return-to-risk trade-off of hedge funds makes them suitable stand-alone investments and, more importantly, may make them beneficial as diversifiers to many financial asset-based portfolios. However, the relatively high correlation of both the CISDM EW HF and certain CISDM HF strategy sub-indices with the S&P 500 indicates that many hedge fund strategies may be better regarded as return enhancers than risk reducers. More important, simply reporting historical returns may not capture many of the risk-and-return characteristics of hedge funds over unique financial or economic conditions. Investors should be certain to check how a particular hedge fund index or individual hedge fund performs across a wide range of economic and financial markets and whether the program they wish to invest in has a strategy for taking those changes into consideration. Although the performance results illustrated in Exhibits 3.1 through 3.3 cover the entire period of analysis, they do not reflect the relative performance of hedge funds when stocks or bonds report extreme positive or negative returns.

THE MYTH OF AVERAGE: HEDGE FUND INDEX RETURN IN EXTREME MARKETS

The results in the previous section illustrate the performance of various hedge fund indices and how they compare to traditional and alternative investment indices over an 18-year period (1994 to 2011). The results indicate the potential return or risk benefits of hedge funds as a stand-alone investment or as an addition to an existing traditional investment portfolio or a portfolio of traditional and alternative investments. However, the relative stand-alone performance of the various hedge fund indices as well as the potential benefits when they are added to a portfolio of financial assets may differ in various subperiods in comparison to their performance over the entire period of analysis. This is especially true in periods of market stress, when certain hedge fund strategies may experience dramatic volatility consistent with the returns in the underlying markets of the securities they hold.

Exhibit 3.4 shows monthly hedge fund returns ranked on the S&P 500 and grouped into three segments (bottom, middle, and top) of 72 months each, with average returns for each hedge fund index presented. Results show that investment in the various hedge fund indices had less negative

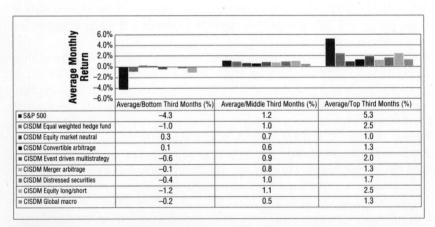

	Average/Bottom Third Months (%)	Average/Middle Third Months (%)	Average/Top Third Months (%)
■ S&P 500	−4.3	1.2	5.3
■ CISDM Equal weighted hedge fund	−1.0	1.0	2.5
■ CISDM Equity market neutral	0.3	0.7	1.0
■ CISDM Convertible arbitrage	0.1	0.6	1.3
■ CISDM Event driven multistrategy	−0.6	0.9	2.0
■ CISDM Merger arbitrage	−0.1	0.8	1.3
■ CISDM Distressed securities	−0.4	1.0	1.7
■ CISDM Equity long/short	−1.2	1.1	2.5
■ CISDM Global macro	−0.2	0.5	1.3

EXHIBIT 3.4 Hedge Fund Indices: Monthly Returns Ranked on the S&P 500 Period of analysis: 1994 to 2011.

returns than the S&P 500 in the worst S&P 500 return months, and provided somewhat less positive returns in the best S&P 500 return months. The positive performance in up markets may be partly caused by the positive economic conditions driving both stock market prices and financial securities in which hedge funds trade. The less negative return performance relative to the S&P 500 in down S&P 500 markets may primarily be a result of lower volatility in most hedge fund strategies as well as lower market sensitivity because of a combination of their hedging away market risk and holding non-equity-based securities. Notably, the results differ somewhat for fixed income. Exhibit 3.5 shows monthly hedge fund returns ranked on the BarCap U.S. Aggregate and grouped into three segments (bottom, middle, and top) of 72 months each, with average returns for each hedge fund index presented. Results show that the hedge fund indices had positive returns in the worst BarCap U.S. Aggregate return months and provided positive returns (although less positive than the BarCap U.S. Aggregate index) in the best BarCap U.S. Aggregate return months. In all cases, the return to hedge funds was positive across all market environments for the BarCap U.S. Aggregate. The superior performance in down BarCap U.S. Aggregate months and the participation in up markets may be partly caused by the ability of hedge funds to both participate in positive return opportunities in periods of low fixed-income returns and obtain positive returns even in periods of positive fixed-income return conditions.

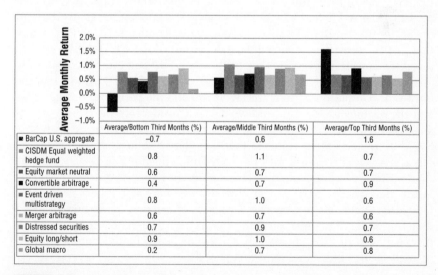

	Average/Bottom Third Months (%)	Average/Middle Third Months (%)	Average/Top Third Months (%)
■ BarCap U.S. aggregate	−0.7	0.6	1.6
■ CISDM Equal weighted hedge fund	0.8	1.1	0.7
■ Equity market neutral	0.6	0.7	0.7
■ Convertible arbitrage	0.4	0.7	0.9
■ Event driven multistrategy	0.8	1.0	0.6
■ Merger arbitrage	0.6	0.7	0.6
■ Distressed securities	0.7	0.9	0.7
■ Equity long/short	0.9	1.0	0.6
■ Global macro	0.2	0.7	0.8

EXHIBIT 3.5 Hedge Fund Indices: Monthly Returns Ranked on BarCap U.S. Aggregate
Period of analysis: 1994 to 2011.

HEDGE FUND ANNUAL PERFORMANCE

In the previous section, the average performance of the hedge fund index and sub-indices and their ranking compared to the best and worst performing equity and fixed-income environments was discussed. The representative hedge fund index (CISDM EW HF) was shown to provide potential diversification benefits in the worst months and positive returns in the best months of each index. In this section, we provide a review of the relative performance by year of the CISDM EW HF, the S&P 500, and the BarCap U.S. Aggregate. Results in Exhibit 3.6 show that over the entire period, the annual returns of these indices varied during many years. However, in 14 of the 18 years, the CISDM EW HF and the S&P 500 moved in the same direction. Three of the years in which the indices moved in opposite directions was the period surrounding the dot-com bubble. In those years, the CISDM EW HF had positive returns, while the S&P 500 reported negative returns. This is consistent with the ability of hedge funds to minimize equity market sensitivity. The CISDM EW HF and the BarCap U.S. Aggregate moved in the same direction in 14 of the 18 years. These results again indicate the importance of viewing hedge fund performance over short subperiods rather than viewing it based strictly on its performance over the whole 18-year period. In addition, results show the importance of hedge funds as part of an existing equity or fixed-income based portfolio.

Exhibits 3.7, 3.8, and 3.9 show standard deviations and correlations of the CISDM EW HF and CISDM HF strategy-based indices against those of the S&P 500 and the BarCap U.S. Aggregate. Results in Exhibit 3.7 show that, for the most part, the standard deviation of the CISDM EW HF has remained consistently below that of the S&P 500 and almost consistently above that of the BarCap U.S. Aggregate. Exhibits 3.8 and 3.9 show that the intra-year correlation between the S&P 500 and the BarCap U.S. Aggregate and the various hedge fund indices varies considerably over the years of analysis; however, the relationship between the hedge fund strategy and the S&P 500 remains fairly stable in that the relative value strategies generally report a lower correlation with the S&P 500, while the equity-biased hedge fund strategies report a higher correlation. In short, investors should be aware that results from longer time frames may not reflect results for individual years. We are surprised when we hear marketing presentations that emphasize the "inherent" absolute return benefits of hedge funds or their widespread diversification benefits. For hedge funds, lengthy periods of analysis may hide more than they reveal.

	1994	1995	1996	1997	1998	1999	2000	2001	2002	2003	2004	2005	2006	2007	2008	2009	2010	2011
S&P 500	1.3%	37.6%	23.0%	33.4%	28.6%	21.0%	-9.1%	-11.9%	-22.1%	28.7%	10.9%	4.9%	15.8%	5.5%	-37.0%	26.5%	15.1%	2.1%
BarCap U.S. aggregate	-2.9%	18.5%	3.6%	9.7%	8.7%	-0.8%	11.6%	8.4%	10.3%	4.1%	4.3%	2.4%	4.3%	7.0%	5.2%	5.9%	6.5%	7.8%
CISDM Equal weighted hedge fund	3.5%	21.2%	23.2%	21.8%	4.0%	36.8%	8.8%	5.7%	0.4%	20.6%	10.0%	9.8%	11.8%	10.5%	-19.2	26.1%	11.8%	-5.8%
Equity market neutral	5.1%	12.2%	13.7%	14.9%	11.2%	9.9%	13.9%	7.3%	2.0%	8.8%	5.0%	7.1%	7.6%	6.5%	0.6%	7.1%	5.3%	4.2%
Convertible arbitrage	2.2%	17.5%	14.7%	14.2%	7.5%	13.9%	15.2%	13.3%	8.9%	9.6%	2.5%	-1.1%	12.3%	4.0%	-19.1%	36.6%	12.3%	1.8%
Event driven multistrategy	3.6%	19.8%	22.3%	23.6%	3.9%	21.4%	12.1%	7.1%	1.2%	21.9%	12.1%	6.6%	14.0%	6.6%	-19.0%	20.0%	8.7%	-1.4%
Merger arbitrage	5.2%	16.6%	16.0%	18.2%	5.5%	15.8%	14.4%	4.3%	0.3%	7.4%	7.0%	5.8%	10.7%	3.7%	0.1%	7.9%	4.9%	4.2%
Distressed securities	-4.3%	22.0%	21.1%	18.7%	-4.8%	17.9%	5.9%	9.2%	6.9%	25.3%	16.6%	7.4%	15.9%	5.3%	-19.5%	24.0%	11.8%	0.2%
Equity long/short	3.4%	26.4%	22.3%	23.7%	9.6%	34.4%	7.8%	2.3%	-4.7%	18.9%	9.9%	8.9%	10.0%	8.5%	-14.4%	16.9%	9.2%	-3.0%
Global macro	-5.0%	11.2%	9.9%	16.0%	8.1%	8.5%	10.0%	5.6%	2.8%	11.8%	4.5%	6.7%	4.9%	12.0%	3.7%	5.5%	6.1%	3.3%

EXHIBIT 3.6 Hedge Fund Indices: Annual Returns

	1994	1995	1996	1997	1998	1999	2000	2001	2002	2003	2004	2005	2006	2007	2008	2009	2010	2011
■ S&P 500	10.6%	5.2%	10.9%	15.9%	21.5%	13.1%	17.2%	19.9%	20.6%	11.4%	7.3%	7.3%	5.6%	9.7%	21.0%	22.3%	19.3%	15.9%
■ BarCap U.S. aggregate	4.4%	3.5%	4.3%	3.6%	2.7%	2.7%	2.8%	3.8%	3.7%	5.3%	4.0%	3.1%	2.7%	2.6%	6.1%	3.3%	2.9%	2.4%
■ CISDM Equal weighted hedge fund	5.5%	3.4%	5.4%	7.7%	12.1%	9.3%	11.3%	6.8%	5.1%	3.4%	4.2%	4.7%	4.5%	5.1%	11.0%	7.6%	6.4%	7.3%
■ Equity market neutral	1.1%	0.9%	1.4%	1.3%	1.6%	2.9%	2.7%	1.3%	1.4%	1.5%	2.5%	1.3%	1.2%	2.1%	3.0%	1.7%	2.0%	3.2%
■ Convertible arbitrage	3.0%	1.4%	1.0%	1.4%	3.6%	1.5%	1.8%	2.5%	2.3%	2.8%	2.2%	3.9%	1.9%	3.2%	14.3%	5.1%	4.7%	3.1%
■ Event driven multistrategy	4.0%	2.1%	3.7%	4.4%	9.0%	5.6%	3.9%	4.9%	5.5%	3.7%	4.5%	4.1%	3.8%	4.5%	10.6%	3.3%	5.0%	7.5%
■ Merger arbitrage	3.6%	1.9%	1.9%	3.1%	7.2%	3.1%	1.7%	3.6%	2.2%	1.5%	2.7%	2.9%	1.9%	4.6%	5.6%	1.8%	1.9%	2.1%
■ Distressed securities	5.7%	3.6%	3.7%	4.9%	10.7%	4.7%	4.4%	3.4%	3.7%	3.4%	4.2%	3.4%	2.8%	3.7%	11.0%	5.2%	5.3%	4.3%
■ Equity long/short	4.9%	3.8%	7.3%	9.5%	13.6%	11.5%	10.4%	5.7%	5.3%	4.4%	4.5%	5.1%	4.9%	5.0%	8.6%	5.6%	7.3%	7.2%
■ Global macro	7.3%	7.4%	3.3%	6.8%	6.2%	4.0%	6.5%	3.0%	2.0%	3.4%	4.1%	4.7%	3.4%	3.0%	2.4%	2.2%	4.3%	3.6%

EXHIBIT 3.7 Hedge Fund Indices: Annual Standard Deviations

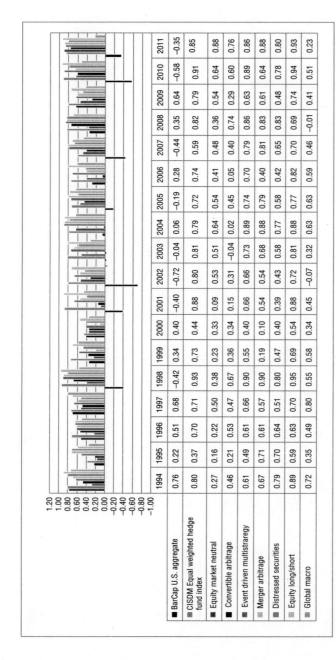

	1994	1995	1996	1997	1998	1999	2000	2001	2002	2003	2004	2005	2006	2007	2008	2009	2010	2011
■ BarCap U.S. aggregate	0.76	0.22	0.51	0.68	-0.42	0.34	0.40	-0.40	-0.72	-0.04	0.06	-0.19	0.28	-0.44	0.35	0.64	-0.58	-0.35
▨ CISDM Equal weighted hedge fund index	0.80	0.37	0.70	0.71	0.93	0.73	0.44	0.88	0.80	0.81	0.79	0.72	0.74	0.59	0.82	0.79	0.91	0.85
■ Equity market neutral	0.27	0.16	0.22	0.50	0.38	0.23	0.33	0.09	0.53	0.51	0.64	0.54	0.41	0.48	0.36	0.54	0.64	0.88
■ Convertible arbitrage	0.46	0.21	0.53	0.47	0.67	0.36	0.34	0.15	0.31	-0.04	0.02	0.45	0.05	0.40	0.74	0.29	0.60	0.76
▨ Event driven multistrategy	0.61	0.49	0.61	0.66	0.90	0.55	0.40	0.66	0.66	0.73	0.89	0.74	0.70	0.79	0.86	0.63	0.89	0.86
■ Merger arbitrage	0.67	0.71	0.61	0.57	0.90	0.19	0.10	0.54	0.54	0.68	0.88	0.79	0.40	0.81	0.83	0.61	0.64	0.88
■ Distressed securities	0.79	0.70	0.64	0.51	0.80	0.47	0.40	0.39	0.43	0.58	0.77	0.58	0.42	0.65	0.83	0.48	0.78	0.80
■ Equity long/short	0.89	0.59	0.63	0.70	0.95	0.69	0.54	0.88	0.72	0.81	0.88	0.77	0.82	0.70	0.69	0.74	0.94	0.93
▨ Global macro	0.72	0.35	0.49	0.80	0.55	0.58	0.34	0.45	-0.07	0.32	0.63	0.63	0.59	0.46	-0.01	0.41	0.51	0.23

EXHIBIT 3.8 Hedge Fund Indices: Annual Correlations with S&P 500

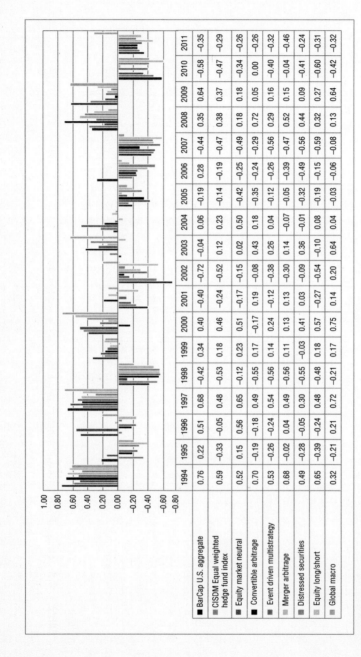

	1994	1995	1996	1997	1998	1999	2000	2001	2002	2003	2004	2005	2006	2007	2008	2009	2010	2011
■ BarCap U.S. aggregate	0.76	0.22	0.51	0.68	-0.42	0.34	0.40	-0.40	-0.72	-0.04	0.06	-0.19	0.28	-0.44	0.35	0.64	-0.58	-0.35
■ CISDM Equal weighted hedge fund index	0.59	-0.33	-0.05	0.48	-0.53	0.18	0.46	-0.24	-0.52	0.12	0.23	-0.14	-0.19	-0.47	0.38	0.37	-0.47	-0.29
■ Equity market neutral	0.52	0.15	0.56	0.65	-0.12	0.23	0.51	-0.17	-0.15	0.02	0.50	-0.42	-0.25	-0.49	0.18	0.18	-0.34	-0.26
■ Convertible arbitrage	0.70	-0.19	-0.18	0.49	-0.55	0.17	-0.17	0.19	-0.08	0.43	0.18	-0.35	-0.24	-0.29	0.72	0.05	0.00	-0.26
■ Event driven multistrategy	0.53	-0.26	-0.24	0.54	-0.56	0.14	0.24	-0.12	-0.38	0.26	0.04	-0.12	-0.26	-0.56	0.29	0.16	-0.40	-0.32
■ Merger arbitrage	0.68	-0.02	0.04	0.49	-0.56	0.11	0.13	0.13	-0.30	0.14	-0.07	-0.05	-0.39	-0.47	0.52	0.15	-0.04	-0.46
■ Distressed securities	0.49	-0.28	-0.05	0.30	-0.55	-0.03	0.41	0.03	-0.09	0.36	-0.01	-0.32	-0.49	-0.56	0.44	0.09	-0.41	-0.24
■ Equity long/short	0.65	-0.39	-0.24	0.48	-0.48	0.18	0.57	-0.27	-0.54	-0.10	0.08	-0.19	-0.15	-0.59	0.32	0.27	-0.60	-0.31
■ Global macro	0.32	-0.21	0.21	0.72	-0.21	0.17	0.75	0.14	0.20	0.64	0.04	-0.03	-0.06	-0.08	0.13	0.64	-0.42	-0.32

EXHIBIT 3.9 Hedge Fund Indices: Annual Correlations with BarCap U.S. Aggregate

PERFORMANCE IN 2008

In 2008, hedge funds experienced their lowest returns since major databases started tracking hedge fund data in 1994. When compared to the S&P 500, hedge funds reported higher returns and lower volatility. However, hedge funds reported a lower annualized return and higher volatility than the BarCap U.S. Aggregate Index. In 2008, the correlation between the CISDM EW HF and the S&P 500 was approximately 0.82, partially caused by the common decline in valuation in the fall of 2008. In short, in 2008, most hedge fund strategies, like traditional asset classes, were negatively impacted by the subprime crisis, by negative equity market performance, and by the rise in credit spreads (e.g., decline in high-yield bond returns). As shown in Exhibit 3.6, this was especially true for hedge fund strategies with exposure to equity markets (e.g., equity long/short) and credit markets (e.g., distressed securities, convertible arbitrage, and event-driven multi-strategies). In contrast, certain hedge fund strategies that were designed to have little market exposure (e.g., equity market neutral) or that were discretionary in nature (e.g., global macro) provided positive returns.

Summarizing the results of 2008, investors should be reminded that hedge funds encompass a number of strategies and that the performance of these strategies is based, in part, on their underlying exposure to the very markets in which they trade. In addition, there always exists a market condition in which a particular strategy or even, in fact, all strategies may perform poorly. An investor should always be aware of the unique conditions (e.g., lack of available credit, lack of secondary markets, or limits on exchange trading) to which even a strategy that has been profitable for years may be exposed. Over the years, there have been other "2008s," during which most investment strategies experienced similar common drawdowns. The actual participating event may have differed, but in each case, the result was a lack of liquidity and investor withdrawals.

MAKING SENSE OUT OF HEDGE FUND INDICES

There are currently a number of hedge fund manager-based indices that can be used as benchmarks for hedge fund performance. Investors should note that each hedge fund return index has its own approach to performance presentation, manager selection, and investment style classification. Hedge fund indices are products dependent on the business models and financing of their owners. As such, each has unique characteristics and should not be relied on at face value. This is similarly true for indices measuring traditional asset classes. Although an investor may disagree with the methodology, this transparency offers the ability to understand relative strengths and weaknesses and to make appropriate adjustments.

Again, it is important to remind investors that composite hedge fund indices may offer little as to the actual or expected performance of any individual investor. The hedge fund industry has evolved dramatically over the past 20 years. As discussed previously, focusing on the returns of a composite index for which the underlying strategies and investment in those strategies have changed dramatically offers little evidence as to the benefits of the universe of hedge funds over time, except under the most restrictive of assumptions as to investor behavior and investment. In short, most hedge fund indices reflect the performance of a noninvestable portfolio of hedge fund strategies. An equal-weighted index assumes that the investor holds a hedge fund portfolio that reflects the number of reporting funds and that the investor can rebalance consistent with the measurement period of the index (e.g., monthly). An asset-weighted index assumes that the investor holds a hedge fund portfolio weighted to reflect the AUM of the underlying managers and can adjust his or her portfolio to match incoming cash flows to each strategy. There is no single investor who can meet all of the above. What composite hedge fund indices do provide is an estimate of a composite return to a wide range of strategies within the hedge fund industry at a particular point in time. Individual funds of funds or individual funds will reflect the returns of the composite index only to the extent that the fund of funds or the manager's strategy reflect the composition of the historically derived hedge fund composite index.

Emphasis on individual strategy-based indices that more closely reflect the actual performance of a particular fund of funds or hedge fund manager may provide a more realistic portrayal of expected rates of return and risks across an array of market environments. However, even in this case, strategies do change over time. What is necessary is to understand the conditional factors driving individual hedge fund strategies and to ensure that particular hedge fund strategy returns are consistent with the historical factors (e.g., equity long/short managers generally make money in up equity markets, and distressed security hedge fund managers perform well in declining credit spread conditions).

An investor should not view the returns of a particular manager as reflecting the pros and cons of the entire industry or that of an average investor. A wide range of individuals/institutions hold a wide range of hedge fund strategies for a wide range of reasons (e.g., to lower risk or to enhance return). Investors should also not base the benefits of hedge funds solely on historical returns and risk. For example, looking over a past period of superior bond or stock returns (falling bond yields or low equity volatility) tells us nothing about how a portfolio of hedge funds may benefit bond or stock investors in a forecasted period of increasing interest rates or stock market volatility. Finally, given the varying risk exposures of any individual investor, determining the benefits of hedge funds in general, or of a strategy in particular, is investor specific.

The form of the return estimation should be consistent with the analysis conducted. If an investor is using monthly data to create a portfolio designed to reflect the actual historical conditions or to test the conditional impact of market factors on hedge fund return, then the use of monthly rates of return is generally recommended. If an investor attempts to estimate the return by which a \$1 investment grows to its final value over a period of time, then a geometric rate of return is often used. To reflect an individual investor's changing investment level over time, an internal rate of return (with a host of assumptions as to the reinvestment rate) is recommended (although the weighted risk assessment requires a different form of return measurement).

MAKING SENSE OUT OF ALTERNATIVE APPROACHES TO INVESTING IN HEDGE FUNDS

Investors can use five different methods for investing in hedge funds and related investment products: (1) direct investment, (2) fund of hedge funds, (3) structured products, (4) hedge fund replication products, and (5) hybrid mutual funds. This list of investment products requires a decreasing amount of resources and expertise on the part of an investor. For example, direct investment will be a suitable approach only for those investors who are allocating a significant amount to hedge funds and have the resources to evaluate individual managers. Conversely, hybrid mutual funds are rather transparent investment products that are accessible to retail investors. Of course, these products are unlikely to have the same risk-return profiles as fees, and restrictions on investment strategies will affect their performance profiles.

Individual Fund Investment

Individual funds across and within hedge fund strategies may differ on a wide range of qualitative factors and quantitative factors. Funds may differ in asset size, leverage, years since inception, level of incentive fees, management fees, lockups, redemption periods, high watermarks, investment structure (e.g., partnership or corporate entity), currency, and a number of other factors. Research[2] has indicated that some of these characteristics have little effect on fund performance (e.g., size), but other factors do seem to impact expected return and risk (e.g., lockups and years since inception).

Investors should be aware that the performance of a hedge fund index is in fact the performance of a portfolio of funds. Individual hedge funds within any individual strategy may have return and risk characteristics that differ from that reported for the hedge fund index.[3] Investors should also be aware that a single database does not represent all funds across the industry and that multiple databases are often required to adequately represent the investment strategy universe. Equally, investors should be made aware that the performances of funds currently reporting to major databases often do not reflect the average returns of funds that existed in the past but no longer report in the current database. The often higher historical returns to hedge funds listed in the current database in comparison to those in older databases is caused by several biases in database construction, including survivor and backfill bias: The historical returns of new funds reporting to the database are included in the new database but not in historical databases. Since, in most cases, only funds with superior historical returns report to databases, the returns prior to the database entry date may be biased upward relative to all those funds that do not report, or to funds that had been reporting for several years. In addition, funds that once existed in the database are removed from the database when they stop reporting. Often these funds stop reporting because of poor returns. The often-lower returns of these funds are not contained in the live portion of most databases. Therefore, investors must ask for the dead fund databases in order to measure the actual returns to investment in funds that may have existed in the past (e.g., survivorship bias).

Other biases may also exist in any single database, such as selection bias (databases differ on their requirements for reporting) and reporting bias (managers may be in one strategy but report as if they were in another). The extent of these biases may differ by strategy, time period, and database. A potential investor, therefore, must use proper due diligence in understanding the actual performance characteristics of a fund before considering investment in it. For example, research has shown that if the first year or so of performance is removed from a fund reporting to a database, the impact of backfill bias is reduced dramatically. An investor should also remember that most hedge fund indices do not contain survivorship bias or backfill bias, as all managers reporting to the database at any one time are used. Historical index returns are not changed when these managers are removed from the database and, therefore, do not reflect survivorship bias. Similarly, as new managers are added to the database, historical index returns are not changed to reflect those new managers and corresponding historical index returns. Hence, no backfill bias or survivor bias is contained in these indices. Various hedge fund indices may still differ because of differences in reporting managers or construction (e.g., median return or asset weighted), but these differences are similar to those existing in traditional asset indices.

Fund-of-Funds Investments

Most major hedge fund indices reflect the performance of a portfolio of hedge funds. However, the actual performance of a fund of funds differs somewhat from a portfolio of hedge funds. First, funds of funds often add on an extra layer of fees to reflect their additional asset management and oversight role. Additionally, fund-of-funds managers often engage in more active management of funds within their strategy and do not employ the current composition of the composite hedge fund index or the style purity of the individual strategy indices. Finally, it is important to point out that a composite hedge fund index is, in essence, a portfolio of hedge funds, whereas a composite hedge fund-of-funds index is, in essence, a portfolio of hedge fund portfolios (a fund of fund of funds).

Although the correlation between the two indices—composite hedge fund index and composite hedge fund fund-of-funds index—is high (for the CISDM EW HF and the CISDM Fund of Funds, the correlation was 0.89 for the period 1994 to 2011), the return and the standard deviation of the CISDM Fund of Funds are lower than those of the CISDM EW HF. This is expected, given the additional layer of fees existing on most hedge fund fund-of-funds products, and the tendency for hedge fund funds-of-funds products to create profiles that have lower risk and lower expected returns than the composite hedge fund index.

In addition to the issues involved in comparing traditional hedge fund performance indices with hedge fund fund-of-fund indices as well as the use of fund-of-funds indices to reflect the performance of individual fund of funds, another potential issue with funds of funds is the common use of indices based on risk classifications (e.g., HFR conservative, diversified, and strategic) rather than their primary strategy classifications (e.g., debt, equity long/short, and global macro). Rather than focusing on the risk level of a fund of funds, an investor should concentrate on the characteristics of the fund of funds that emphasize a particular strategy that may have return and risk characteristics that are more specific to the fund of funds' individual strategy. In short, use of generic hedge fund indices grouped by risk class may not be representative of individual fund of funds. As a result, a fund of funds' relative performance should be compared to a representative portfolio or another fund of funds that more accurately reflects the portfolio holdings of the individual fund of funds.

Investable Hedge Fund Indices

The growth in hedge fund investment has encouraged a number of firms to offer investable hedge fund index products. This group includes well-known index providers, such as Credit Suisse First Boston (CSFB) and firms that specialize in hedge fund investment, such as HFR. These manager-based investable index products reflect portfolios of hedge fund managers often created using systematic rules (e.g., size, time since inception, style purity). Since each active manager-based investable hedge fund index is based on a different set of investment rules, these hedge fund indices differ in many ways. As a result, seemingly similar hedge fund indices may have different return and risk performance over similar periods. However, previous studies show that despite differences in risk and return, the various hedge fund indices generally report similar correlations to one another as well as to major market factors, such as stock and bond indices.[4]

Hedge Fund Trackers

The growth in hedge fund investment has encouraged a number of firms to offer products called tracker/replication index/benchmark products. These products have the goal of providing returns that capture the underlying return of basic hedge fund strategies. The performance results for various replication indices have illustrated similar returns, risks, and correlations between the hedge fund tracker and corresponding non-investable hedge fund indices. For example, the correlations of the replication indices with the CISDM EW HF are fairly high. In addition, the Goldman Sachs Absolute Return Tracker Index showed correlations of 0.82 with the CISDM EW HF. To the degree that these hedge fund trackers are constructed with securities that can be shorted, investable products based on these trackers can be used both to provide liquid substitutes for relatively illiquid manager-based hedge funds and as a means to manage the risk (e.g., hedge) of hedge funds that cannot be sold in the short run.

Publicly Traded Exchange-Traded Funds or Mutual Funds

Publicly traded funds (mutual funds and UCITS) or investment securities (exchange-traded funds [ETFs] and exchange-traded notes [ETNs]) have recently come into existence, offering hedge fund-like products at both the mutual fund and the ETF or ETN level. Although there can be structural differences between private manager-based hedge fund products and publicly traded products, both offer access to the underlying returns embedded in an individual hedge fund strategy. These public investment vehicles include both manager-based hedge fund products (e.g., mutual funds) and more algorithmic-based public hedge fund-like vehicles. Algorithmic-based public hedge fund vehicles include both dynamic investment vehicles, which attempt to capture the returns of an active-manager trading approach (e.g., momentum trading processes), and hedge fund trackers, which generally follow a more prescribed set of investment rules (i.e., investment trackers use a variety of approaches, such as factor-based, security-based, and distribution-based replication, to track return streams of hedge funds). Both mutual fund- and ETF/ETN-based products offer relatively liquid access to both composite hedge fund returns and strategy-based hedge fund returns. Similar to private fund-of-funds investment vehicles, public investment vehicles exist, which invest in a number of hedge fund investment strategies and offer a diversified portfolio of hedge fund investment strategies to the typical nonqualified or non-accredited investor.

A PERSONAL VIEW: ISSUES IN HEDGE FUND INVESTMENT

Two areas of hedge fund investment have recently attracted the attention of the investment community: the risk-and-return profiles of fund-of-funds investments and the unique distributional characteristics of hedge fund managers. A primary reason that an investor chooses to invest in a fund of funds rather than directly in hedge fund managers is the ability of fund-of-funds managers to perform due diligence and select top tier managers. The Madoff fraud case showed that at least some fund-of-funds managers did not perform the most basic type of due diligence and made substantial allocations to Madoff. An analysis of the risk-return properties of hedge fund managers should examine whether there are common sources of risk and return among them and whether these properties are persistent through time.

Fund-of-Funds Investment

A qualified or accredited investor may also invest in a fund of hedge funds, which provides exposure to a basket of select hedge funds. Funds of funds may invest in a wide variety of underlying strategies or in a single strategy. If properly structured, such funds are deemed to be widely diversified and hence not exposed to serious losses of any individual fund. Funds of funds typically have lower minimum investment requirements, with their investors generally benefiting from the expertise of the fund manager and not having to conduct due diligence on the underlying funds, a process that requires a great deal of resources. The failure to conduct proper due diligence on

Madoff-based investments by several major fund-of-funds managers has raised questions about the processes they employ and the integrity of their due diligence and business models.

Fund-of-funds managers typically charge a fee in addition to the fees charged by the managers on their platform. In this regard, there may be a management fee as well as an incentive fee. The larger fund-of-funds platforms have negotiating power and can provide access to significantly lower management and incentive fees for the underlying managers, and can also negotiate lower silent fees. There is a small but growing trend of these firms charging a single flat fee for their services. Those fund-of-funds managers who do not have substantial due diligence teams and sufficient AUM to garner pricing power have been criticized for offering far too little for the fees charged. Also, there is a growing trend toward the larger fund-of-funds managers offering separately managed accounts and enhanced underlying liquidity for their clients.

Industry and academic research have often addressed the benefits of hedge-fund fund of funds and the effect of an additional layer of fees on product performance. Often research in the area has failed to consider the actual business model of a fund of funds. There are unique strategy emphases within individual funds of funds that are directly influenced by their underlying investors. In short, many of these investors have objectives that are not wholly performance oriented. Another factor has to do with when a fund of funds is created. Given lockups, due diligence, and other administrative costs, as well as the market sales environment, a fund of funds is often created with an emphasis on those hedge fund strategies that sell in the current market environment.

It is difficult to group differing funds of funds in a comparative performance analysis. As a consequence, due diligence must focus on such issues as the operational infrastructure, the length of time it has been in existence, and the abilities of the respective management teams. Many investors and academics seemingly believe that fund-of-funds managers have no or little costs and can easily reallocate across fund managers. They fail to realize the large costs involved in due diligence as well as the necessary banking relationships that enable these managers to obtain underlying lines of credit. In fact, one of the primary jobs of the internal risk-management process is to manage the lines of credit that permit the fund portfolio managers to make investor redemptions without fundamentally changing the risk characteristics of the fund.

Also, the distribution process of a fund of funds is often impacted by the ability of the fund to reach the proper investor audience. Many fund-of-funds vehicles have a relative value orientation, given the greater demand for low-risk hedge funds in periods of academic distress. Next, the entire area of fund-of-funds fees relative to a randomly selected portfolio of hedge funds must be considered in light of the costs of an investor to replicate the due diligence, accounting oversight functions. An additional factor in this market is that many hedge fund managers will only make a small portion of their overall investment available to these public pool vehicles (with the rest used primarily as managed-account investments, which may require less direct marketing efforts). Another element is that in this business model, money is often deployed to an underlying manager to lock up future capacity. Fund-of-funds managers also have the resources and technology to understand the underlying risk exposure of the overall portfolio and have the greater ability to micromanage factor exposure, providing an additional "implied option" benefit to their work.

Distributional Characteristics

The primary reason for hedge fund investment is the degree to which an individual hedge fund strategy provides unique risk and return characteristics not easily available in other investment vehicles. Various hedge fund strategies trade unique markets in proprietary forms. Moreover, these strategies have a dynamic element in that they are not restricted by law or custom to track a particular long-only strategy. That said, the expected distributional characteristics of an individual strategy simply reflect the security holdings of the hedge fund strategy and the degree to which individual managers can easily adjust the underlying risk of the portfolio (e.g., increase or decrease leverage). Unfortunately, the conditional nature of hedge fund strategies makes any cross-sectional or time series analysis of the historical distributional nature of a hedge fund strategy a simple "prisoner" of the data. For example, as shown in Exhibit 3.10, when the monthly returns of equity long/short hedge funds are ranked on the CISDM Equity Long/Short (ELS) Index, in periods of extreme monthly CISDM ELS Index returns, almost all the equity long/short managers have the same directional movement as the CISDM ELS Index. In brief, the expected returns of individual managers must be conditioned on the general movement of the underlying strategy. Removing a single day or a single month can dramatically change the reported distributional moments of a particular strategy. Simple descriptions of the risk characteristics of various hedge fund strategies based on monthly data should not be accepted by any academic or investor as the final statement on the risk characteristics of what is, by nature, a dynamic strategy.

Governance

The fundamental assumption of many analysts that a hedge fund is managed by the listed manager is fraught with error. No successful fund can rely

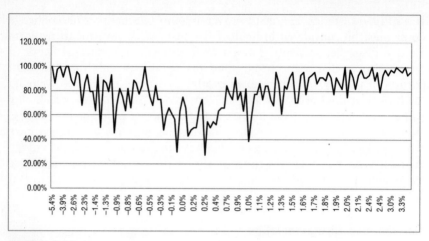

EXHIBIT 3.10   Percent Equity Short/Long (ELS) Hedge Funds with Same
Directional Return as CISDM ELS (Ranked on CISDM ELS Index)

on a single manager pulling the investment trigger. A similar concern
exists regarding the importance of boards of directors and their effect on
fund decisions: In addition to the legal structure of these entities, it is
also necessary to understand the internal operational and risk-management
structure. Issues such as (1) day-to-day investment decisions, (2) distribution
and accountability for the firm's reputation, (3) all-inclusive costs of the
fund's operations, (4) regulatory and internal compliance procedures, and
(5) conflicts of interest must all be addressed in a comprehensive manner.

Other Issues

A number of other issues have not been analyzed in a manner that adequately reflects the actual market structure. Many studies have analyzed
hedge fund flows to past performance for funds that have no public
marketing—whose sales flow is a function of the distributional agent.
Other issues include performance-fee analysis based on the reported current
fee structure but using a historical return (historical qualitative factors are
often not available in databases such that the qualitative factor used often
does not match the historical period used in return estimation); differences
between offshore and onshore vehicles in regard to investor redemption;
differences between UCITs and a managed account of the underlying
fund manager; how the use of ETFs today have fundamentally changed
the hedging approach; and how changes in regulation and availability of

credit have fundamentally changed the level of leverage available in many strategies.

WHAT EVERY INVESTOR SHOULD KNOW

In Chapter 3, the development of hedge funds, their strategies, their use as standalone investments, and their addition to stock and bond portfolios was explored. In brief, the evidence presented in this chapter shows that hedge funds, what they are, and how they perform, can be as easily understood and explained as most traditional stock and bond investments. At the same time, there are a few differences of which investors should be aware.

- **Hedge Funds Are Merely "Advanced" Traditional Assets.** Hedge funds are not black boxes where the average intelligent investor cannot understand the investment process and risks if properly detailed. Hedge funds as a class of investment strategies were unique in that they were historically available primarily to high net worth individuals because of certain regulatory restrictions. However, we know that they are not unique and that the sources of returns, their pricing, and their risks are often well understood at the strategy level. Investors should insist on full and complete disclosure and should not invest in funds or processes that do not provide the type of transparency required for an independent and objective analysis of risks and returns. Investors should not fall into the trap of proprietary information that cannot be disclosed, because it is vital to successful returns. As for any other investment, if a fund cannot or will not explain the sources of returns and risk when it makes or loses money, take your money and go somewhere else.
- **Hedge Funds, Like Other Assets, Have Benchmarks:** Some hedge fund managers may attempt to present themselves as so unique that it is impossible to compare their returns with others. Wrong. An active hedge fund manager's performance alpha is generally defined as the excess return to active management adjusted for risk; that is, the return adjusted for the return of a comparable investable "non-actively managed" risky asset position or portfolio. The only way of correctly analyzing an active manager's alpha is by measuring that manager's performance against a similar collection of risks. Therefore, deciding which tools and indices to use is paramount in performance measurement. Investors should ensure that their measurement proxies actually reflect the risk and rewards of a particular manager. In short, ask your potential manager for a set of comparable firms and a passive index benchmark that reflect the returns of its strategy.

- **Hedge Funds Offer Unique Opportunities but Not Absolute Returns.** Most regulatory agencies will tell you that investors always go wrong by believing in unrealistic returns or returns that are not consistent with a manager's stated strategy. This is a red flag that no investor should ignore. Do not let hope and greed trump what you know about the basic efficiencies of the market. With the exception of a very few, hedge fund managers are prisoners of the asset classes they trade, and abnormal returns do not occur. By example, John Paulson's returns were extraordinary during the subprime housing debacle, yet those returns were based on known facts and conditions that others participated in as well. Some lost money anticipating the burst of the housing bubble, and some, like Paulson, made a great deal of money. In sum, it was a known and verifiable "bet." When you invest, just know what the "bet" is.

MYTHS AND MISCONCEPTIONS OF HEDGE FUNDS

As discussed in previous chapters, a delay in investors' understanding, or even market awareness, of new research or market relationships often results in a delay in investors', corporate officials', and government regulators' appreciation of these changes and the creation of a series of myths about how financial products operate, as well as their effect on financial markets, domestically as well as globally. If a brief review of newspaper articles, books, and other public media is a basis for evaluation, hedge funds are one investment where both myths and misconception as to the costs and benefits are not in short supply. This may be caused both by hedge fund managers' desire to continue to exploit the allure of their uniqueness or the public press's desire to find a good story that draws readers' interest. Unfortunately, to paraphrase Mark Twain, "truth dies a quick death, but a lie well told lasts forever." Hopefully, the following may not bring the truth back to life but it may stop the life span of the lie.

Myth 3.1: Hedge Funds Are Absolute Return Vehicles

Hedge funds have often been described as absolute return vehicles both by hedge fund managers and by the financial press. So, in part, both are at fault. As discussed in this book, one of the reasons for the presentation of hedge funds as absolute return vehicles is that managers may maintain that since they do not try to track any specific benchmark, they have the opportunity to make positive returns in any market environment and that they attempt to search for "absolute" return rather than benchmark plus return. Some hedge fund managers may also use the risk-free rate as a "performance benchmark" since their strategy is designed to reduce or eliminate market risk. However, in truth, despite the fact that some hedge fund strategies have low equity betas or fixed income duration, as well as the lack of a regulatory requirement to track a particular passive index, it does not mean that hedge funds have the expectation of positive returns in all market environments. Unfortunately, many investors interpret the words "absolute return" as investment strategies that are not correlated with underlying traditional stock and bond markets. In fact, most hedge fund managers have correlations with stock and bond markets consistent with their underlying portfolio holdings such as equity for equity long/short managers and credit risk for distressed security managers. As a result, hedge fund returns, although partly caused by manager skill, are also based on a set of common market factors; thus, most hedge fund strategies have a common market factor benchmark component and so should not be regarded as absolute return vehicles but as investment strategies with their own unique expected return and risk exposures.

Myth 3.2: Hedge Funds Are Highly Levered Risky Investments

The risk and return attributes of hedge funds are determined solely by their investment strategy. Some hedge funds invest primarily in long-only cash instruments that employ little leverage, since the underlying asset itself has a high return-to-risk trade-off. Other hedge funds invest in low-risk strategies, such as security arbitrage. These funds use leverage positions in order to offer a reasonable expectation of return. The fact is that the typical portfolio of hedge fund returns has had low volatility (generally in the range of 6 to 12 percent annually, depending on the strategy), far less than the typical stock (approximately 25 to 40 percent) or stock mutual fund (approximately 10 to 20 percent). As discussed earlier, investors must also remember that leverage itself is not something to be avoided. According to recent data from the International Monetary Fund, European banks, for example, are levered about 20 to 1 (about 5 percent of assets are equity capital, 95 percent are loans and deposits). Residential real estate is typically levered 5 to 1 (a 20 percent down payment is common, with 80 percent borrowed). Corporations in risky businesses, such as technology stocks and automobile manufacturers, tend to be financed mostly with equity because of the unpredictability of the returns. In short, the more highly leveraged an investment or firm is, the more care one must take to ensure that the payment flows are more predictable or else large losses are possible.

Myth 3.3: Hedge Funds Are Black Box Trading Systems Unintelligible to Investors

For the most part, hedge funds protect their internal trading techniques from public scrutiny, but the same is true for mutual funds. For the most part, pre-trade transparency may have negative impacts on investor returns and market efficiency. Post-trade transparency, however, may provide investors with an understanding of the source of returns to various hedge fund strategies. In fact, today hedge fund trading approaches and sources of returns are well known. High-level risk-management tools are available to track the risk of individual hedge funds. Many investors have access to daily positions through managed accounts. Daily investable hedge fund indices are also available. In short, for the most part, hedge funds are not black boxes any more than traditional mutual funds or corporate firms are. Investors may not know the particulars of each trade or product creation pre-trade, but how and why they perform post-trade is well known within the industry. Investors should remember that for most hedge fund strategies, it is basically about buying and selling stocks, bonds, commodities, futures, and options, as well as other well-known exchange or over-the-counter (OTC)-based financial products. It is all basic blocking and tackling; it is not rocket scientist stuff despite how it is often pictured.

Myth 3.4: Hedge Fund Managers Fees Are Too High

One of the concerns placed on the back of the hedge fund industry is that poor average investor performance is caused partly by the high fees of hedge fund managers. Investors should be reminded that a hedge fund manager's gross profits and an investor's net profits are not comparable. Simply put, managers' gross profits do not reflect managers' net profits. One should not have to be reminded that the gross fees paid to managers does not equal net profits to them. In brief, a more extensive analysis, and not one based on hedge fund gross profit, is required to determine if hedge fund net profit can be regarded as exorbitant relative to the net return to the investor. An investor must ask and answer the question of what he is genuinely getting for the fees paid; and, whether those fees are in alignment with expected returns and other investment opportunities that provide similar results. If on an after-fee basis, the returns of an active manager are less than those of a passive benchmark, then the fees paid should be openly questioned.

Myth 3.5: Hedge Funds and Hedge Fund Strategies Are So Unique That They Cannot Be Replicated

Investable passive-index strategies have long been acknowledged as the cornerstone of an investor's core asset allocation methodology as well as an active manager's attribution analysis. In many ways this struggle between pure passive security-based benchmark replication and active manager-based investment has been resolved. While a tension still exists between the active and passive forms of direct security investment, they currently coexist within the stock and bond investment world. The new challenge is that today this tension also exists in the hedge fund world. As discussed previously, we now know the underlying sources of returns or processes by which most hedge fund strategies are conducted. If the underlying sources or processes of returns are known, it is not a large step to developing investable products that capture the underlying returns of the associated hedge fund strategy. Today, there exist a number of "tracker" funds that capture the market and alternative betas underlying the expected return and risk of a comparison investment. It should be noted that while tracker products may provide access to a major portion of fund manager returns (both alpha and beta), their primary advantage is to provide competitive after-fee returns along with superior liquidity, transparency, and a reduction in an investor's exposure to manager-specific risk (idiosyncratic or fraud). In short, a tracker-based fund may not provide the same level of "trading alpha" as a comparison actively managed fund but it does provide returns consistent with the underlying risk of that fund.

Myth 3.6: Database Biases Make Hedge Fund Index Returns of Little Use

As discussed previously, the use of any hedge fund index in any analysis must be done with care. There is plenty of academic research on problems in the use of hedge fund databases to reflect historical performance (e.g., many databases fill in the old returns of managers when they start reporting to databases and drop from their databases managers who no longer report). To the degree that the newly reporting managers' historic returns are better than the managers' historic returns who are leaving, the historical returns of the new database will be above that of the prior database. *Please note*: the primary hedge fund indices (HFR, CISDM [*not* HFRX], etc.) simply report the returns of reporting managers (some with restrictions). There may be backfill or survivor bias in the current database but not in the historically reported hedge fund index returns. Similar to the S&P 500, new firms come and go to the database from which the S&P 500 firms are selected, however, once a firm's return is included in the S&P 500, its return never leaves that index; if a firm is dropped from the S&P 500 because of poor performance, its old returns are not dropped from the historic S&P 500 and the S&P 500 index is not revised. Only for a new database for which a historical index is newly created from that database does an index have backfill bias. For the other indices (HFR, CISDM, Barclay, CSFB) used in this analysis, there is no basis for a backfill adjustment.

CHAPTER 4

Managed Futures

A Zero-Sum Game?

For many, managed futures remain somewhat on the border of asset management. In the past 20 years, managed futures have grown from less than 25 billion to approximately 300 billion assets under management (AUM). Although the growth has been substantial, managed futures have low AUM relative to other alternative asset classes such as hedge funds. There are various reasons for this. First, the name itself is somewhat confusing. Although the term *managed futures* brings to mind someone who manages futures contracts for profit, most managed futures traders have, for years, been referred to as *commodity trading advisors* (CTAs). This is somewhat unfortunate, because even though some managed futures traders do not even trade commodity-based futures contracts, many investors are reluctant to invest in a strategy that implies heavy concentration in commodity-based futures contracts, which they regard as inherently risky.

The nomenclature, commodity trading advisors, is partially caused by the fact that until the 1970s, active futures traders had to trade commodities, because financial futures contracts such as currency futures, financial futures, and equity futures did not exist. Currency futures began trading in the early 1970s, after the U.S. dollar went from fixed to floating. In the mid-1970s, interest rate futures began trading (primarily short-term instruments such as U.S. Treasury bills); and by the late 1970s, long-term U.S. government bond and note contracts began to trade. By the mid-1980s, various U.S.-based equity futures contracts began trading; and over the next decades, similar financial futures contracts started trading around the globe.

Other possible reasons for the slow growth of managed futures include the fact that for many in the investment community, futures markets were seen as a zero-sum game. That is, on any given day, gains to long positions in futures markets were, by design, offset by losses to those taking the opposite short positions, and vice versa. Investors questioned how active futures traders could make money in a market that had a zero balance at the end of the day. Of course, academics and practitioners had been looking at this same issue for decades. For some, the answer was relatively simple. Many firms want—or need—to hedge their exposures to various financial variables, including currencies, commodities, interest rates, and even equity prices. These firms use the futures markets to take long positions in futures contracts to offset the risk of future price increases, or take short positions in futures contracts to offset the risk of future price declines. When there is no natural buyer or seller on the other side of the transaction, they often have to price the contract to bring in a trader (e.g., CTA) who is not a natural hedger. This price benefit to the CTA may be one part of the potential return to the CTA. Other areas of potential profit include the fact that sometimes cash market participants just want to get out of a contract area, even if the commercial or financial firm believes prices will continue to rise or fall. CTAs can profit in just that market by taking the opposite side of the hedger's new short or long position, especially since they have the ability to take relatively large futures positions with relatively little cash. In brief, CTAs can profit from the needs of others to use futures markets as a primary risk-management tool.

As in any investment, "can make money" is not the same as "does make money." However, in 1983, John V. Lintner of Harvard University presented a paper, "The Potential Role of Managed Commodity-Financial Futures Accounts (and/or Funds) in Portfolios of Stocks and Bonds," to the Financial Analysts Federation.[1] The paper stated that "the improvements from holding an efficiently selected portfolio of managed accounts or funds are so large—and the correlation between returns on the futures portfolios and those on the stock and bond portfolio are so surprisingly low (sometimes even negative)—that the return/risk tradeoffs provided by augmented portfolios . . . clearly dominate the tradeoffs available from a portfolio of stocks alone or from portfolios of stocks and bonds." Not everyone, of course, agreed with Professor Lintner. During the 1980s, considerable research was published that attempted to address the issue of the benefits of managed futures.[2] It is somewhat sad, yet not surprising, that current views of many investors on the pros and cons of managed futures as an investment are still tied to that earlier research, which focused on a period when there were relatively few managed futures managers and when management and marketing expenses were greater than what exist today. By the mid-1990s, the managed futures industry had matured greatly. New futures markets had come into existence; CTA and marketing expenses (although high in current terms) were declining; and although many investors (institutional and private) were still leery of the image of active futures traders, professional organizations (e.g., Managed Futures

Association) and academic research centers (e.g., Center for International Securities and Derivatives Markets) had come into existence to promote and analyze the managed futures industry.

By the early 2000s, advances in technology and market structure, along with changes in regulation, had led to an increase in both the number of managed futures trading strategies and the AUM. On March 19, 2001, an article in *Business Week* brought the earlier research of Lintner and others on the benefits of futures funds up to date, concluding that

> [Futures funds] *have made money 17 of the past 20 years. Indeed, as long as you can stand the gyrations, putting a small part of your portfolio in these funds can't hurt.*[3]
>
> *Likewise for the period since 2001, managed futures have continued to provide positive returns over a number of market cycles. In 9 out of the past 10 years (2002–2011) the Center for International Securities and Derivatives Markets (CISDM) CTA Equal Weighted (EW) index has reported positive returns.*

For the past 15 years, we were fortunate to be part of the development of the managed futures industry both academically and professionally. Academically, we worked with various managed futures professional organizations on research focusing on the benefits of managed futures and sources of CTA returns. In the mid-to-late 1990s, we published a series of passive CTA trend-following indices and created one of the first academic research centers (i.e., CISDM) dedicated to derivative markets. We came to see that the process by which most managed futures traders conducted their operations provided the potential for gain as well as loss, as markets went into periods of non-trending range-bound prices. Although managed futures had continued to grow and by the early 2000s had become a major retail product, their potential gains were offset somewhat by fees charged by the firms marketing these funds. The high fees of some CTAs also encouraged the firms marketing CTAs to fund primarily those managers who had the highest volatility and greatest potential for gain—so much so that in 2003, we were asked by a major fund of funds firm to create a "tracker CTA," which could reflect the returns of a major CTA of the day. The idea was for the sponsor to keep offering the product at the high asset and performance fees charged by the previous manager but to keep the fees internal. That CTA trading program began trading in 2004 and runs to the current day. The program is based primarily on the theory that there exists a set of algorithmic trading processes that capture some of the fundamental return to CTA traders. During the past decade, the low equity returns of the post-dot-com bubble led to increased interest in the potential benefits of managed futures programs. In addition, the growth of financial firms capable of offering direct managed accounts reduced the cost of many managed futures programs to accredited investors. Note that regulatory rules permitted most financial firms to continue marketing various CTA programs directly through their marketing and sales effort, since sales personnel for CTA programs, for the most part, were not required to meet some of the licensing requirements of equity-based products.

If things had remained the same, managed futures would have continued as a small but profitable niche product for financial firms, marketed primarily to high-net-worth individuals and small institutions. But things did not remain the same. As new markets and forms of asset management in derivative products changed, so did managed futures. In addition to traditional systematic momentum-based CTA products, CTA products expanded into a larger set of investment forms, including trading products that emphasized volatility trading, short-term trading, and trading in specialty areas (e.g., energy). By the end of the first decade of the twenty-first century, managed futures products existed not only in their traditional form but also in mutual fund and exchange-traded fund (ETF) form. Despite these market product changes, managed futures growth has been limited relative to that of other alternative investments, such as hedge funds. This may be partially caused by competition from more traditional products and continued uncertainty as to the source of return to CTA programs. Given this headwind, managed futures (active trading of futures and option markets) have found their way into traditional investment products (e.g., global macro funds) through what we may say is the back door. Increasingly, investment firms are finding ways to use traditional managed futures trading processes within their business model and to explore other avenues to market this unique investment strategy.

WHAT ARE MANAGED FUTURES?

The term managed futures represents an industry composed of professional money managers known as CTAs or commodity pool operators (CPOs). CTAs and CPOs manage client assets on a discretionary basis, using forwards, futures, and options markets as the primary investment arena. Futures and options have long been used for both risk management and return enhancement. In fact, as discussed previously, producers and consumers of commodities have been using futures as hedging tools for many centuries. Managed futures funds have been available as an investment alternative since the 1970s and have experienced significant growth over the past several decades. As an active trading strategy, managed futures have the ability to take both long and short investment positions in international financial and nonfinancial asset sectors and to offer risk-and-return patterns not easily accessible through traditional (such as long-only stock and bond portfolios) or other financial assets (such as hedge funds, real estate, private equity, or commodities). Their additive potential value to a portfolio was highlighted in 2008, when most traditional and alternative assets performed poorly, but managed futures performed relatively well.

In the following sections, we first discuss various ways in which investors can gain exposure to managed futures. Second, we explore sources of managed futures returns. Third, we review managed futures as a stand-alone investment and as a means to provide additional return enhancement as well as risk reduction opportunities relative to those of stock and bond investments and other financial assets. Finally, we examine unique issues and myths in the area of managed futures.

INVESTING IN MANAGED FUTURES

There are four basic ways to invest in managed futures. Public futures funds offer investors the managed futures equivalent of a mutual fund. These public managed futures funds may have a fairly low minimum investor criterion, although some public funds may require investors to be of accredited investor status. The second way to invest in managed futures is through private funds (usually a $500,000 or higher minimum investment), which typically carry less expense than public funds. A drawback to this is that they often possess the characteristics of hedge funds and other private investment vehicles with regard to limited transparency and investor liquidity. The third method is that extremely high-net-worth investors can hire a futures manager directly. Although there are advantages to hiring a futures manager directly as part of a customized investment program, the cost of doing so usually requires a relatively high minimum investment. A fourth method includes a range of mutual fund or security-based investment vehicles (e.g., closed-end funds and ETFs) that offer a more direct means of capturing managed futures return opportunities in a public investment vehicle. The foregoing investment criteria relate to U.S. investors; institutional and individual investors under the regulatory oversight of global entities may have different investment opportunities than those just described. Investors should consider the unique investment opportunities and regulations related to their supervisory authority.

MANAGED FUTURES STYLES AND BENCHMARKS

As with most investment strategies, the managed futures arena can often be defined by the markets they trade and their unique approaches to trading (e.g., trend following and discretionary). For each of these markets and forms of trading, various firms have created CTA indices, similar to those that exist in equity and other investment asset classes. Historically, the primary benchmarks are as follows:

- **EW CTA Indices:** EW manager returns for all reporting managers in the particular database.
- **Systematic:** These trade primarily in the context of a predetermined systematic trading model. Most systematic CTAs follow a trend-following program, although some trade countertrend. In addition, trend-following CTAs may concentrate on short-term trends, midterm trends, long-term trends, or a combination thereof.
  - **Financial:** Trade financial futures/options, currency futures/options, and forward contracts.
  - **Currency:** Trade currency futures/options and forward contracts.
  - **Diversified:** Trade financial futures/options, currency futures/options, forward contracts, and commodity futures/options.
  - **Discretionary:** Trade financial, currency, and commodity futures/options based on a wide variety of trading models, including those founded on fundamental economic data or individual trader's beliefs. Traders often have the right to use a systematic model based on personal criteria in making trading decisions.

As in other investment areas, there exists in managed futures a variety of firms that provide a number of manager-based CTA indices. In this chapter, the CISDM EW CTA Index is used as the primary representative commodity index; however, when comparing certain CTA market or trading-based indices, Barclay CTA indices are also used. As noted earlier, a number of larger investment firms, as well as other players in the managed futures arena, offer a wide range of manager-based CTA indices. Each of these indices is unique in its own way. For example, the CISDM and Barclay active manager-based CTA indices are EW indices based on reporting managers to each of the respective databases. These indices are not directly investable. In recent years, a number of manager-based CTA indices have been designed to capture the returns of an investable set of active CTA managers (e.g., Barclay and Newedge). Each of these indices differs slightly in its construction; however, past research has indicated that the reported returns are highly correlated with noninvestable manager-based CTA indices.

BASIC SOURCES OF RETURN AND RISK

Each of the aforementioned managed futures strategies reflects certain market opportunities as well as economic and market risks, and understanding these risks is essential to comprehending managed futures returns and risks. In contrast to certain investment strategies for which the underlying return is systematically related to traditional market factors, the sources of managed futures returns are more often described as being based on the unique skill or strategy of the CTA trader. Because managed futures are actively managed, manager skill is important; however, academic research[4] demonstrates that many managed futures strategies are also driven systematically by algorithmic trading models or quantitative-based trading models. Therefore, an investor can think of managed futures returns as a combination of manager skill and an underlying return to the managed futures fund strategy or investment style itself. Similar to the equity and bond markets, passive security-based indices have been created to capture the underlying return to the managed futures fund. The performance of an individual manager can then be measured relative to that "strategy" return. If a manager's performance is measured relative to the passive security-based managed fund index or benchmark, then the differential return may be viewed as the manager's alpha (return in excess of a similar non-manager-based investable replicate portfolio). If a manager's performance is measured relative to an index of other active managers, then the manager's relative performance simply measures the over- or underperformance to that index of manager returns.

The sources of return to managed futures are uniquely different from those of traditional stocks, bonds, or even hedge funds. For example, although futures, swaps, and forward contracts can provide direct exposure to underlying financial and commodity markets (but often with greater liquidity and less market impact), as discussed earlier, futures and option traders may also easily take short positions or actively allocate assets between long and short positions within the futures and/or options market trading complex. In addition, options traders may also directly trade market and/or security characteristics that underlie the contract, such as price volatility. The unique return opportunities to managed futures may also stem from the global nature of futures and contracts available for trading and from the broader range of trading strategies. As a result, most CTA programs (e.g., discretionary, systematic, and so on) report a low correlation with most traditional market factors. At the same time, questions still exist as to the inherent long-term return for CTAs. Many managed futures strategies trade primarily in futures and/or options markets, which, as has been pointed out, are zero-sum games. If CTAs were only trading against other CTAs, then one might conclude that the returns to certain managed futures traders would be based primarily on the skill of their managers. However, some spot market players are willing to sell or hedge positions even if they expect spot positions to rise or fall in their favor (e.g., currency and interest rate futures may be traded over time due to government policy to smooth price movements). CTAs offer liquidity to such hedgers and obtain a positive convenience yield (i.e., return-to-risk trade-off) in return. In short, long-term positive expected returns may be consistent with the underlying instruments that CTAs trade.

Both academics and practitioners have often suggested that the return and risk opportunities of managed futures are available because the skill-based investment strategies employed by managers do not explicitly attempt to track a traditional stock or bond benchmark and/or index and have the opportunity to offer liquidity or informational trades, which offer managed futures traders the opportunity to maximize long-term returns independent of traditional asset benchmarks. However, as discussed previously, passive algorithm-based managed futures indices also exist, which represent the return process of active managed futures managers (at least systematic managed futures managers). Investors should understand that just because managed futures do not emphasize traditional stock and bond benchmark tracking does not mean that CTA return is based solely on manager skill. The performance of an individual manager can be measured relative to an active manager-based CTA benchmark or a passive algorithmic-based investable benchmark.

PERFORMANCE: FACT AND FICTION

For most investors, performance characteristics of equity and fixed-income markets and hedge fund strategies, which are based on their investments in equity and fixed-income markets, are easy to understand. As discussed in previous sections, managed futures or CTAs are a different animal. Managed futures are designed to have no consistent long or short bias equity or fixed-income exposure. As a result, for many investors it is expected that managed futures strategies will provide diversification benefits to long-only equity or fixed-income based investment portfolios in any market environment. In the following sections, we provide evidence not only on the stand-alone risks of various CTA investments, but on the interrelationships of various CTA strategies within the managed future area and between managed future and various traditional (e.g., equity and fixed-income market) and alternative asset classes. We examine these markets over a broad time period, and on shorter time intervals (e.g., annual), as well as their relative performance in extreme market conditions. The results support the fundamental basis for CTA investment, that is, as expected, CTAs are shown to have a low correlation with the comparison traditional and alternative investments and provide potential diversification benefits. Results also show, however, that certain investor beliefs about CTAs may be misplaced. Results show that individual CTAs may not be unusually risky and often have levels of risk similar to individual equities and that portfolios of CTAs often have levels of risk similar to portfolios of equities (Standard & Poor's [S&P] 500).[5] Results also show that (1) in periods of extreme equity market returns, most CTA strategies have similar return patterns, that is, marginal positive returns in down equity markets and positive returns in up equity markets; and (2) investors should not take return and risk performance from extended time frames as a basis for how various CTA strategies or a CTA composite may perform over relative shorter time periods (e.g., annual). Finally, despite the potential differences among investment strategy approaches within CTAs, most CTAs within a particular strategy rise together in up strategy months and fall together in down strategy months such that there is a commonality among CTA managers that is often overlooked by investors.

RETURN AND RISK CHARACTERISTICS

In this section, we review the relative performance of the CISDM EW CTA Index with a range of traditional stock and bond indices as well as a number of alternative investment indices (e.g., real estate, private equity, commodities, and hedge funds) over the period 1994–2011. In later sections, we focus on CTA trading performance using composite, strategy- and markets-based indices in various subperiods. Again we wish to remind investors that the performance of any individual investment or investment strategy may not reflect current expected performance or the expected performance in periods that have economic conditions different from those of the period of analysis. For this period, as shown in Exhibit 4.1, the CISDM EW CTA exhibited lower annualized standard deviation, or volatility (8.7 percent), than that of the S&P 500 (15.7 percent). This may be surprising to most investors, who often regard managed futures as considerably more risky than stocks. Over the period of analysis, the CISDM CTA EW reported higher annualized total return (8.1 percent) than that of the S&P 500 (7.7 percent). Moreover, stand-alone historical return and risk comparison reflect the potential for the benefits of managed futures as additions to other traditional assets or other alternative asset classes. For example, as shown in Exhibit 4.1, for the period analyzed, the CISDM EW CTA has a low correlation (−0.08) with the S&P 500 and a low correlation

EXHIBIT 4.1 Commodity Trading Advisor and Asset Class Performance

Stock, Bond, and CTA Performance	CISDM CTA EW	S&P 500	BarCap U.S. Government	BarCap U.S. Aggregate	BarCap U.S. Corporate High Yield
Annualized total return	8.1%	7.7%	6.1%	6.3%	7.3%
Annualized standard deviation	8.7%	15.7%	4.4%	3.8%	9.4%
Information ratio	0.94	0.49	1.39	1.67	0.78
Maximum drawdown	−8.7%	−50.9%	−5.4%	−5.1%	−33.3%
Correlation with CTA	1.00	−0.08	0.25	0.20	−0.11

Alternative Asset and CTA Performance	CISDM CTA EW	SP GSCI	CISDM EW Hedge Fund	FTSE NAREIT	Private Equity Index
Annualized total return	8.1%	4.8%	10.4%	9.7%	8.0%
Annualized standard deviation	8.7%	22.5%	7.7%	19.9%	28.1%
Information ratio	0.94	0.21	1.36	0.49	0.28
Maximum drawdown	−8.7%	−67.6%	−21.7%	−67.9%	−80.4%
Correlation with CTA	1.00	0.22	0.05	−0.02	−0.07

(0.20) with the BarCap U.S. Aggregate Bond Index. The relatively low correlation of CTAs with stock and bond returns is one of the prime sources of the belief in the diversification benefits of commodity trading advisors.

The relatively low correlations between the CISDM EW CTA and a range of financial assets as well as alternative assets shown in Exhibit 4.1 indicates that a portfolio of CTAs may reduce the stand-alone risk (standard deviation) of a stock or bond portfolio and a multi-asset portfolio. For the period of analysis, as shown in Exhibit 4.2, adding a small portion of CTAs (10 percent) to stock and bond Portfolio A yields Portfolio B with a similar annualized return (7.7 percent) and a lower standard deviation (7.4 percent) as the pure stock and bond portfolio (see Portfolio A, with an annualized return of 7.3 percent and a standard deviation of 8.2 percent). Similarly, adding managed futures to Portfolio C, which contains a range of traditional and alternative investments, results in Portfolio D that again exhibits a similar return (8.4 percent) but lower standard deviation (8.3 percent) to that of Portfolio C (8.3 percent and 9.1 percent, respectively), which does not contain managed futures.

EXHIBIT 4.2 Commodity Trading Advisor and Multi-Asset Class
Portfolio Performance

Portfolios	A	B	C	D
Annualized returns	7.3%	7.7%	8.3%	8.4%
Standard deviation	8.2%	7.4%	9.1%	8.3%
Information ratio	0.90	1.03	0.90	1.02
Maximum drawdown	−27.1%	−22.9%	−36.0%	−31.3%
Correlation with CTA	−0.03		−0.01	
Portfolio A	Equal Weights S&P 500 and BarCap U.S. Aggregate			
Portfolio B	90% Portfolio A and 10% CTA			
Portfolio C	75% Portfolio A and 25% HF/commodities/private equity/real estate			
Portfolio D	90% Portfolio C and 10% CTA			

The ability of the CISDM EW CTA to provide superior return and risk opportunities to other financial assets on a stand-alone basis or as additions to a sample portfolio is indicative of the ability of CTAs to provide a positive return-to-risk trade-off over a lengthy period of time. First, as mentioned previously and shown for other asset classes, performance in a single period is not indicative of the relative performance in other periods. Second, there is no requirement that investors invest in a single composite CTA index. A composite CTA index covers a wide range of CTA trading strategies. Exhibit 4.3 shows the return and risk performance over the 1994–2011 period for various Barclay CTA Trader Indices. As shown in Exhibit 4.3, none of the CTA strategy indices report a high correlation with the S&P 500 or the BarCap U.S. Aggregate High Yield Bond Index. However, there is also no simple trick for determining which CTA strategy index would perform best when considered as an addition to a non-CTA-based investment portfolio.

In summary, there is much in the historical returns for the period 1994–2011 to support the view that the return-to-risk trade-off of CTAs makes them suitable stand-alone investments and, more importantly, may make them beneficial as risk diversifiers to many traditional and alternative investment portfolios. Simply reporting historical returns, however, may not capture many of the return and risk characteristics of CTAs over unique financial or economic conditions. As in the previous chapters, investors should be certain to check how a particular CTA index or individual CTA performs across a wide range of economic and financial markets and whether the program they wish to invest in has a strategy for taking those changes into consideration.

EXHIBIT 4.3 Commodity Trading Advisor Index Performance

	CISDM EW CTA Index	Barclays CTA Index	Discretionary	Systematic	Diversified	Currency	Financial and Metals	Agriculture
Annualized return	8.1%	5.6%	4.2%	5.6%	6.9%	3.8%	4.7%	4.0%
Annualized standard deviation	8.7%	7.5%	4.3%	9.1%	10.9%	5.8%	6.4%	8.1%
Information ratio	0.94	0.74	0.99	0.62	0.63	0.67	0.74	0.49
Maximum drawdown	−8.7%	−7.7%	−10.7%	−10.1%	−12.0%	−7.0%	−11.1%	−19.9%
Correlation with S&P 500	−0.08	−0.07	0.04	−0.11	−0.13	0.03	−0.09	0.00
Correlation with BarCap U.S. Aggregate	0.20	0.23	0.01	0.24	0.19	0.12	0.31	−0.02
Correlation with CTA	1.00	0.97	0.55	0.96	0.96	0.59	0.85	0.18

*Subindices: Barclay CTA Trader Indices.

THE MYTH OF AVERAGE: COMMODITY TRADING ADVISOR INDEX RETURN IN EXTREME MARKETS

The results in the previous section illustrate the performance of various CTA indices and how they compare to traditional and alternative investment indices over an 18-year period (1994–2011). The results indicate the return or risk benefits of CTAs as a stand-alone investment or as an addition to an existing traditional investment portfolio or a portfolio of traditional and alternative investments. However, the relative stand-alone performance of the various CTA indices as well as the potential benefits when they are added to a portfolio of financial assets may differ in various subperiods in comparison to their performance over the entire period of analysis. This is especially true in periods of market stress, when certain CTA strategies may experience dramatic volatility in the underlying futures contract.

Exhibit 4.4 shows monthly CTA returns ranked on the S&P 500 and grouped into three segments (bottom, middle, and top) of 72 months each,

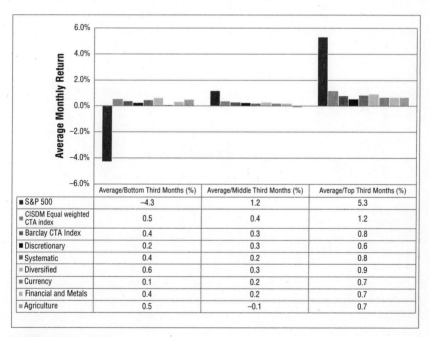

	Average/Bottom Third Months (%)	Average/Middle Third Months (%)	Average/Top Third Months (%)
■ S&P 500	−4.3	1.2	5.3
▥ CISDM Equal weighted CTA index	0.5	0.4	1.2
■ Barclay CTA Index	0.4	0.3	0.8
■ Discretionary	0.2	0.3	0.6
▥ Systematic	0.4	0.2	0.8
▥ Diversified	0.6	0.3	0.9
▥ Currency	0.1	0.2	0.7
▥ Financial and Metals	0.4	0.2	0.7
▥ Agriculture	0.5	−0.1	0.7

EXHIBIT 4.4 Commodity Trading Advisor Indices: Monthly Returns Ranked on S&P 500
Period of analysis: 1994 to 2011.
*Subindices: Barclay CTA Trader Indices.

with average returns for each CTA index presented. Results show that the CTA indices had positive returns on average in the worst S&P 500 markets and positive returns (although less than the S&P 500) in the best S&P 500 return months. The positive performance in up equity markets may be partially caused by the positive economic conditions driving both stock market prices and financial securities in which CTAs trade. The positive performance in down S&P 500 markets may be caused by a flight to safety for some financial assets (e.g., currency and interest rates), which might be beneficial to trend-following or discretionary CTAs. Notably, the results differ somewhat for fixed income. Exhibit 4.5 shows monthly CTA returns ranked on the BarCap U.S. Aggregate and grouped into three segments (bottom, middle, and top) of 72 months each, with average returns for each CTA index presented. Results show that the CTA indices had both positive (e.g., discretionary) as well as negative (systematic) returns in the worst BarCap U.S. Aggregate return months and provided positive returns (although less than the BarCap U.S. Aggregate bond index) in the best BarCap U.S. Aggregate return months. The positive performance in up markets may be somewhat due to the positive economic conditions driving both interest rate futures and other financial securities in which CTAs trade. Some academic research[6] has suggested that CTAs often trade in long-term

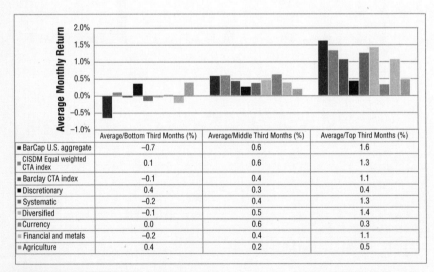

	Average/Bottom Third Months (%)	Average/Middle Third Months (%)	Average/Top Third Months (%)
■ BarCap U.S. aggregate	−0.7	0.6	1.6
■ CISDM Equal weighted CTA index	0.1	0.6	1.3
■ Barclay CTA index	−0.1	0.4	1.1
■ Discretionary	0.4	0.3	0.4
■ Systematic	−0.2	0.4	1.3
■ Diversified	−0.1	0.5	1.4
■ Currency	0.0	0.6	0.3
■ Financial and metals	−0.2	0.4	1.1
■ Agriculture	0.4	0.2	0.5

EXHIBIT 4.5 Commodity Trading Advisor Indices: Monthly Returns Ranked on BarCap U.S. Aggregate
*Subindices: Barclay CTA Trader Indices.
Period of analysis: 1994 to 2011.

U.S. Treasury bond futures contracts and that a large part of their performance often occurs in periods of high government bond yields or in periods in which yields drop from those high yields. These are the same periods (declining bond yields) that fixed income securities outperform. Its mixed performance in down BarCap U.S. Aggregate markets may be due simply to its ability to take short positions in markets with increases in interest rates (note the positive return to CTA discretionary traders in contrast to CTA trend followers in the worst return BarCap U.S. Aggregate month).

COMMODITY TRADING ADVISOR ANNUAL PERFORMANCE

In the previous section, the average performance of the CTA commodity index and subindices and their ranking compared to the best and worst performing equity and fixed-income environments was discussed. The representative CTA index (i.e., CISDM EW CTA), as well as many of the related CTA subindices, were shown to provide potential diversification benefits in the worst months and positive returns in the best months of each index. In this section, we provide a review of the relative performance by year of the CISDM EW CTA, Barclay CTA EW CTA and CTA strategy indices, the S&P 500, and the BarCap U.S. Aggregate. Results in Exhibit 4.6 show that over the entire period, the annual returns of these indices varied during many years. However, in 13 of the 18 years, the CISDM EW CTA and the S&P 500 moved in the same direction, and in 15 of the 18 years, the CTA EW CTA and the BarCap U.S. Aggregate moved in the same direction.

Exhibits 4.7, 4.8, and 4.9 show the standard deviations and correlations of the CISDM EW CTA and Barclay CTA EW CTA and Barclay CTA strategy indices against those of the S&P 500 and the BarCap U.S. Aggregate. Results in Exhibit 4.7 show that, for the most part, the standard deviation of the various CTA indices has remained consistently below that of the S&P 500 and consistently above that of the BarCap U.S. Aggregate. Exhibits 4.8 and 4.9 show that the intra-year correlation between CISDM EW CTA, Barclay CTA EW CTA and Barclay CTA strategy indices, the S&P 500, and the BarCap U.S. Aggregate varies considerably over the years of analysis. In short, investors should be aware that results from longer time frames may not reflect results for individual years. We are surprised when we hear marketing presentations that emphasize the inherent high risk of CTAs. For most periods of analysis, a portfolio of CTAs generally had lower stand-alone risk as well as low correlation to traditional stock and bond markets.

	1994	1995	1996	1997	1998	1999	2000	2001	2002	2003	2004	2005	2006	2007	2008	2009	2010	2011
S&P 500	1.3%	37.6%	23.0%	33.4%	28.6%	21.0%	-9.1%	-11.9	-22.1	28.7%	10.9%	4.9%	15.8%	5.5%	-37.0	26.5%	15.1%	2.1%
BarCap U.S. aggregate	-2.9%	18.5%	3.6%	9.7%	8.7%	-0.8%	11.6%	8.4%	10.3%	4.1%	4.3%	2.4%	4.3%	7.0%	5.2%	5.9%	6.5%	7.8%
CISDM Equal weighted CTA index	2.7%	12.5%	12.5%	13.2%	10.6%	1.3%	10.5%	4.9%	13.4%	11.1%	3.8%	2.4%	5.7%	11.6%	21.8%	0.6%	14.3%	-3.1%
Barclay trader index CTA	-0.7%	13.6%	9.1%	10.9%	7.0%	-1.2%	7.9%	0.8%	12.4%	8.7%	3.3%	1.7%	3.5%	7.6%	14.1%	-0.1%	7.0%	-3.1%
Discretionary	1.9%	4.2%	1.5%	2.6%	-6.2%	3.2%	2.1%	-0.1%	11.1%	5.2%	8.7%	7.5%	7.6%	6.2%	12.2%	1.9%	5.6%	2.7%
Systematic	-3.2%	15.3%	11.6%	12.8%	8.1%	-3.7%	9.9%	3.0%	12.1%	8.7%	0.5%	0.9%	2.1%	8.7%	18.2%	-3.4%	7.8%	-3.8%
Diversified	0.1%	14.3%	11.8%	14.7%	7.8%	-2.9%	10.9%	2.3%	14.2%	11.4%	1.1%	0.6%	5.3%	11.4%	26.6%	-3.6%	9.8%	-5.7%
Currency	-6.0%	11.5%	6.7%	11.3%	5.7%	3.1%	4.5%	2.7%	6.3%	11.1%	2.4%	-1.2%	-0.1%	2.6%	3.5%	0.9%	3.4%	2.2%
Financial and metals	-4.7%	12.9%	9.8%	5.6%	11.3%	-4.5%	3.4%	7.1%	12.6%	9.6%	-0.1%	1.7%	1.4%	7.2%	10.4%	0.6%	3.4%	0.4%
Agriculture	7.9%	26.0%	10.7%	-2.1%	2.2%	-2.1%	11.9%	-11.8%	0.0%	-7.6%	14.4%	-0.1%	3.6%	3.8%	9.9%	-1.4%	11.7%	1.1%

EXHIBIT 4.6 Commodity Trading Advisor Indices: Annual Returns
*Subindices: Barclay CTA Trader Indices.

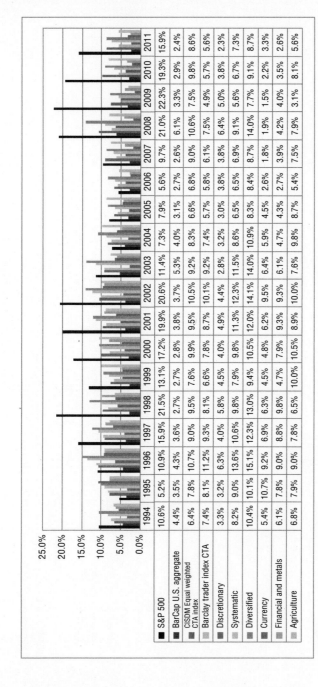

	1994	1995	1996	1997	1998	1999	2000	2001	2002	2003	2004	2005	2006	2007	2008	2009	2010	2011
S&P 500	10.6%	5.2%	10.9%	15.9%	21.5%	13.1%	17.2%	19.9%	20.6%	11.4%	7.3%	7.9%	5.6%	9.7%	21.0%	22.3%	19.3%	15.9%
BarCap U.S. aggregate	4.4%	3.5%	4.3%	3.6%	2.7%	2.7%	2.8%	3.8%	3.7%	5.3%	4.0%	3.1%	2.7%	2.6%	6.1%	3.3%	2.9%	2.4%
CISDM Equal weighted CTA index	6.4%	7.8%	10.7%	9.0%	9.5%	7.6%	9.9%	9.5%	10.5%	9.2%	8.3%	6.6%	6.8%	9.0%	10.6%	7.5%	9.8%	8.6%
Barclay trader index CTA	7.4%	8.1%	11.2%	9.3%	8.1%	6.6%	7.8%	8.7%	10.1%	9.2%	7.4%	5.7%	5.8%	6.1%	7.5%	4.9%	5.7%	5.6%
Discretionary	3.3%	3.2%	6.3%	4.0%	5.8%	4.5%	4.0%	4.9%	4.4%	2.8%	3.2%	3.0%	3.8%	3.8%	6.4%	5.0%	3.8%	2.3%
Systematic	8.2%	9.0%	13.6%	10.6%	9.8%	7.9%	9.8%	11.3%	12.3%	11.5%	8.6%	6.5%	6.5%	6.9%	9.1%	5.6%	6.7%	7.3%
Diversified	10.4%	10.1%	15.1%	12.3%	13.0%	9.4%	10.5%	12.0%	14.1%	14.0%	10.9%	8.3%	8.4%	8.7%	14.0%	7.7%	9.1%	8.7%
Currency	5.4%	10.7%	9.2%	6.9%	6.3%	4.5%	4.8%	6.2%	9.5%	6.4%	5.9%	4.5%	2.6%	1.8%	1.9%	1.5%	2.2%	3.3%
Financial and metals	6.1%	7.8%	9.0%	8.8%	9.8%	4.7%	7.9%	9.3%	9.3%	6.1%	4.7%	4.3%	2.7%	3.9%	4.2%	4.0%	3.5%	2.6%
Agriculture	6.8%	7.9%	9.0%	7.8%	6.5%	10.0%	10.5%	8.9%	10.0%	7.6%	9.8%	8.7%	5.4%	7.5%	7.9%	3.1%	8.1%	5.6%

EXHIBIT 4.7 Commodity Trading Advisor Indices: Annual Standard Deviation
*Subindices: Barclay CTA Trader Indices.

	1994	1995	1996	1997	1998	1999	2000	2001	2002	2003	2004	2005	2006	2007	2008	2009	2010	2011
BarCap U.S. Aggregate	0.76	0.22	0.51	0.68	-0.4	0.34	0.40	-0.4	-0.7	-0.0	0.06	-0.1	0.28	-0.4	0.35	0.64	-0.5	-0.3
CISDM Equal Weighted CTA index	-0.6	0.03	0.53	0.64	-0.5	-0.2	-0.0	-0.6	-0.6	0.18	0.44	0.69	0.40	0.43	-0.5	0.14	0.48	-0.0
Barclay CTA index	-0.6	0.01	0.49	0.63	-0.5	-0.2	-0.0	-0.6	-0.6	0.20	0.44	0.63	0.42	0.37	-0.4	0.16	0.56	-0.0
Discretionary	-0.3	-0.2	0.38	0.49	-0.0	-0.0	-0.0	0.71	0.10	0.48	0.05	-0.2	0.44	-0.2	-0.4	0.10	0.69	0.41
Systematic	-0.6	-0.0	0.51	0.64	-0.6	-0.2	-0.0	-0.6	-0.6	0.14	0.42	0.65	0.40	0.43	-0.5	0.10	0.57	-0.1
Diversified	-0.5	0.05	0.47	0.53	-0.6	-0.2	-0.0	-0.6	-0.6	0.12	0.37	0.65	0.39	0.36	-0.5	0.13	0.57	-0.1
Currency	-0.3	-0.2	0.27	0.43	-0.0	-0.1	-0.0	-0.2	-0.3	0.38	0.68	0.61	0.08	0.44	-0.3	0.11	0.53	-0.0
Financial and metals	-0.8	0.11	0.72	0.70	-0.4	-0.0	-0.1	-0.5	-0.6	0.35	0.66	0.20	0.50	0.39	-0.4	0.21	0.18	-0.1
Agriculture	0.23	0.02	-0.1	-0.2	-0.2	-0.1	-0.3	0.45	0.19	0.54	-0.1	-0.1	0.22	-0.2	-0.2	-0.0	0.09	0.35

EXHIBIT 4.8 Commodity Trading Advisor Indices: Annual Correlation with S&P 500

*Subindices: Barclay CTA Trader Indices.

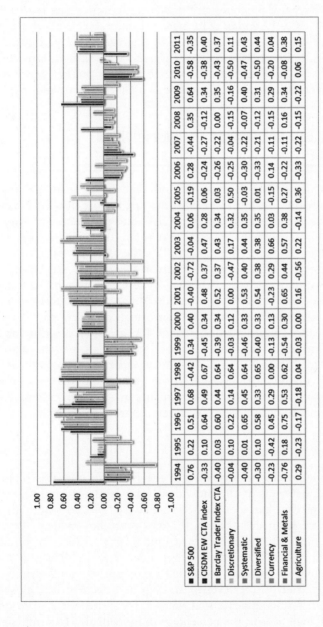

	1994	1995	1996	1997	1998	1999	2000	2001	2002	2003	2004	2005	2006	2007	2008	2009	2010	2011
■ S&P 500	0.76	0.22	0.51	0.68	-0.42	0.34	0.40	-0.40	-0.72	-0.04	0.06	-0.19	0.28	-0.44	0.35	0.64	-0.58	-0.35
■ CISDM EW CTA index	-0.33	0.10	0.64	0.49	0.67	-0.45	0.34	0.48	0.37	0.47	0.28	0.06	-0.24	-0.27	-0.12	0.34	-0.38	0.40
■ Barclay Trader Index CTA	-0.40	0.03	0.60	0.44	0.64	-0.39	0.34	0.52	0.37	0.43	0.34	0.03	-0.26	-0.22	0.00	0.35	-0.43	0.37
Discretionary	-0.04	0.10	0.22	0.14	0.64	-0.03	0.12	0.00	-0.47	0.17	0.32	0.50	-0.25	-0.04	-0.15	-0.16	-0.50	0.11
■ Systematic	-0.40	0.01	0.65	0.45	0.64	-0.46	0.33	0.53	0.40	0.44	0.35	-0.03	-0.30	-0.22	-0.07	0.40	-0.47	0.43
Diversified	-0.30	0.10	0.58	0.33	0.65	-0.40	0.33	0.54	0.38	0.38	0.35	0.01	-0.33	-0.21	-0.12	0.31	-0.50	0.44
■ Currency	-0.23	-0.42	0.45	0.29	0.00	-0.13	0.13	-0.23	0.29	0.66	0.03	-0.15	0.14	-0.11	-0.15	0.29	-0.20	0.04
■ Financial & Metals	-0.76	0.18	0.75	0.53	0.62	-0.54	0.30	0.65	0.44	0.57	0.38	0.27	-0.22	-0.11	0.16	0.34	-0.08	0.38
■ Agriculture	0.29	-0.23	-0.17	-0.18	0.04	-0.03	0.00	0.16	-0.56	0.22	-0.14	0.36	-0.33	-0.22	-0.15	-0.22	0.06	0.15

EXHIBIT 4.9 Commodity Trading Advisor Indices: Annual Correlation with BarCap U.S. Aggregate

*Subindices: Barclay CTA Trader Indices.

PERFORMANCE IN 2008

Results in Exhibits 4.6 through 4.9 show the risk and return performance of CTAs, traditional U.S. stocks and bonds, and asset classes for 2008. In 2008, CISDM EW CTA index (21.8 percent) outperformed both the S&P 500 (−37.0 percent) and the BarCap U.S. Aggregate (5.2 percent). Most CTA strategies, unlike traditional asset classes, were little affected by the subprime crisis in 2008, despite the negative equity market performance and the rise in credit spreads (e.g., decline in high-yield bond returns).

MAKING SENSE OF COMMODITY TRADING ADVISOR PERFORMANCE

In this section we provide commentary both on the performance characteristics of individual CTAs and issues surrounding the use of CTA indices or CTA databases in estimating expected CTA fund performance. Academic and practitioner research has shown that trend-following strategy is the dominant strategy among CTAs and CTA indices. While most systematic trend-following CTAs follow momentum strategies that are longer term in nature, it is important to realize that some CTAs may be regarded as short-term trend followers. This section also discusses CTA performance in markets with high volatility and CTA performance in periods of extreme equity performance (positive or negative). CTAs are often described as long volatility traders (e.g., make money in periods of high market volatility), and they provide a hedge to equity holdings especially in periods of high equity market volatility. While the debate continues, the following sections offer a contrasting view as to CTA performance in periods of extreme equity market performance or in periods of extreme market volatility.

Individual Fund Performance

CTA indices reflect the performance of the portfolio of CTAs reporting as that strategy. Results at the individual CTA level may not reflect the results of the relevant index to the degree that the CTA does not represent the underlying performance of the index (e.g., portfolio) strategy.[7] Previous research has shown that a portfolio of four to five CTAs is required for the portfolio to reflect that of the strategy index. Research has also shown that the relationship between individual funds and the underlying CTA strategy is impacted by the level of strategy returns. Further, as shown in Exhibit 4.10, results indicate that when CTA systematic returns are at their historical high or low, the percentage of individual CTAs with similar

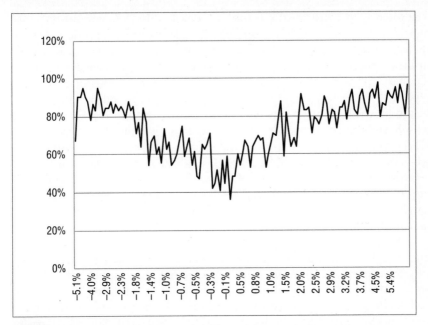

EXHIBIT 4.10 Percent of CTA Systematic with Same Directional Returns as CISDM CTA Systematic Index (Ranked on CISDM CTA Systematic Index) Period of analysis: 2001 to 2011.

directional return movement is high (often above 80 percent); however, when index or market returns are near zero, individual CTA returns are as likely to be positive as negative. In brief, individual CTAs may show little correlation with their underlying index when index returns are near zero, but are highly correlated with their underlying index when those returns are either highly positive or highly negative.

Individual CTAs across and within CTA strategies may differ on a wide range of qualitative and quantitative factors. CTAs may differ in asset size, leverage, years since inception, level of incentive fees, management fees, lockups, redemption periods, high watermarks, investment structure (e.g., partnership or corporate entity), currency, and a number of other factors. Investors should also be aware that a single database does not represent all funds across the industry and that multiple databases are often required to adequately represent the investment strategy universe. Equally important, investors should be made aware that the performances of CTAs currently reporting to major databases often do not reflect the average returns of CTAs that existed in the past but no longer report in the current database.

The often higher historical returns to CTAs listed in the current database are often a result of one or more biases in database construction. One of these is backfill bias, also called *incubation bias*, which occurs when the historical returns of new CTAs reporting to the database are included in the database. Since, in most cases, only CTAs with superior historical returns report to databases, the returns prior to the database entry date may be biased upward relative to the returns of those CTAs who do not report, or who have been reporting for several years. Survivorship bias occurs when CTAs who once existed in the database are removed from the database when they stop reporting. Often these CTAs stop reporting because of poor returns. The often lower returns of these CTAs are not contained in the live portion of most databases. Therefore, investors must ask for the dead CTA databases in order to measure the actual returns to investment in CTAs that may have existed in the past.

Other biases may also exist in any single database, such as selection bias (i.e., databases differ on their requirements for reporting) and reporting bias (i.e., managers may be in one strategy but report as if they were in another). The extent of these biases may differ by strategy, time period, and database. Investors must use proper due diligence in understanding the actual performance characteristics of a CTA before considering investment in it. For example, research has shown that if the first year of performance is removed from a CTA reporting to a database, the impact of backfill bias is mitigated dramatically. An investor should also remember that most CTA indices do not contain survivorship bias or backfill bias, as all managers reporting to the database at the time of the original return calculation are used. Historical index returns are not changed when these managers are removed from the database and, therefore, do not reflect survivorship bias. Similarly, as new managers are added to the database, historical index returns are not changed to reflect those new managers and corresponding historical index returns. Hence, no backfill bias is contained in the indices.[8] Various CTA indices may still differ because of differences in reporting managers or construction (e.g., median return or asset weight), but these differences are similar to those existing in traditional asset indices.

Trading Time Frame

In previous sections, we discussed CTA performance in terms of the markets (i.e., currency, financial, diversified) they trade on and the strategies (i.e., systematic and discretionary) they employ. In addition, CTAs often concentrate on different time frames regarding their trading process, that is, choosing short-term, midterm, or long-term historical data. Note there are no definitive definitions of these trading time frames. In general, for systematic trend followers, short term often emphasizes historical periods of less than a week; whereas for long-term trend followers, the period is often longer than 30 days. In this section, we review the relative performance of short-term and long-term discretionary and systematic CTAs. For both discretionary and systematic CTAs, those that emphasize shorter-term models report a lower standard deviation and a lower correlation with the underlying CTA index. This is not surprising. Given the higher volatility of longer-term time-frame traders, their volatility would be expected to dominate any EW index.

Market Volatility and Commodity Trading Advisor Performance

A common belief among traders and many CTA managers is that CTAs are long volatility—that is, they have the opportunity of making profits in markets in which return volatility is high. The basis for this belief is that in stock and bond markets, increases in standard deviation (volatility) are often consistent with decreases in return. At the same time, to the degree that CTAs are not strictly long or short markets, CTAs have shown the ability to have positive returns in down stock and bond markets—markets in which volatility is often high.

Although CTAs can profit in volatile markets, it is incorrect to say that they are long volatility.[9] In fact, increases in volatility often result in CTAs losing money, as the markets may find themselves in a tight trading range (prices rise and then fall, fall and then rise). Except for a few CTAs who might follow a contrarian methodology, most CTAs are systematic midterm to long-term trend followers—that is, they make money when prices trend slowly up or slowly down. That happens not in high volatility markets but in markets that (at least over the measured investment period) are relatively smooth.

Commodity Trading Advisors as a Hedge for Equity Investors

Academics and practitioners often refer to CTAs as a natural hedge for equity investors. One must be careful in using the term *hedge* when referring to the use of CTA investment as a means to diversify an equity biased portfolio. Many CTAs do not trade equity futures. One reason for this is that most research has shown that equities follow what is known as a random walk; that is, they do not follow a discernible trend. Certainly, CTAs can make money in periods in which the S&P 500 or other equity indices perform poorly, but that is not a hedge (a short or long position whose profits or losses are directly linked to the performance of the comparable asset). At best, CTAs who trade particular futures markets may be seen as investment programs that benefit from market conditions (e.g., falling interest rates), which may be consistent with a government program attempting to provide liquidity to a market following an equity market drop; that is, a particular CTA may trade a program in a fashion that is more likely to make money in economic markets that are consistent with equity declines, but that is a long way from calling a CTA a hedge against stock market declines.

MAKING SENSE OUT OF ALTERNATIVE APPROACHES TO INVESTING IN COMMODITY TRADING ADVISORS

Similar to hedge fund investment, investors have a range of choices for investing in CTAs, including direct investment in active manager-based individual CTA funds, individual CTA pool vehicles (e.g., fund of funds) or investable active CTA manager-based indices as well as hybrid mutual fund. In recent years, various algorithmic-based CTA trackers have been developed that attempt to provide return performance similar to that of an associated CTA benchmark. These CTA tracker approaches to capturing the fundamental returns of various CTA strategies are available both in ETF and mutual fund forms.

Commodity Trading Advisor Individual Fund and Pool Investment

CTA individual funds and CTA pools (similar to multi-CTA funds of funds) provide a direct means to access CTA performance. One of the investment concerns in CTA multi-CTA pools (e.g., funds of funds) is the extra layer of fees that the fund-of-fund manager requires for overseeing the construction of the fund of funds. Research shows that a portfolios of a CTA fund of funds (e.g., Eurekahedge Fund of Funds Index) underperforms a comparison EW CTA index (e.g., Eurekahedge Managed Futures Index) by almost 4 percent over the period 2001–2011 while showing similar correlation to a range of market factors (S&P 500, BarCap U.S. Government, U.S. Aggregate, and U.S. Corporate High Yield indices).[10] Investors should note, however, that results based on fund-of-funds indices include a wide range of CTA strategies such that the performance may not strictly reflect the strategy weights assumed in the EW composite CTA indices. Research also indicated that the standard deviation around a sample of trend-following CTA funds indicates that an investor in an individual CTA fund may not reflect the performance of a diversified fund of similar strategy CTAs. In short, investors should be aware that investing in a single CTA does not necessarily reflect the performance of a portfolio of similar CTAs.[11]

COMMODITY TRADING ADVISOR INVESTABLE INDICES

The growth in CTA investment has encouraged a number of firms to offer active manager-based investable CTA index products. This group includes global investment banks such as Credit Suisse First Boston (CSFB). Each of these CTA indices differs in unique ways. As a result, seemingly similar active manager-based investable CTA indices may have different return and risk performance over common time frames. However, studies show that despite differences in risk and return, the various investable and non-investible CTA indices generally report similar correlations to one another, as well as to major market factors, such as stock and bond indices.[12]

Passive Trackers

In addition, various futures-based passive CTA indices have been suggested as possible surrogates for active CTA investment. We recently examined the performance of various active manager-based CTA indices and passive futures-based CTA indices over the period 2004–2011. The results reflect that a managed futures securities-based passive index outperformed both the CSFB (which is an investable index of active managers) and the Mt. Lucas Management (MLM) Index (which is a passive index). In addition, high correlations (often above 0.50) were reported between the active manager-based CISDM CTA and the corresponding passive security-based index.[13]

Mutual Fund and Exchange-Traded Fund Products

In addition, CTA-based mutual fund products have been suggested as possible surrogates for active CTA investment. These mutual fund CTA-based products exist primarily in fund-of-fund form. Results of a recent analysis indicate that these mutual fund-based products have similar return and risk characteristics to the CISDM EW CTA index; however, for these funds, differences also exist such that investors should review the form and strategy emphasis of each mutual fund product. It is important to note that in recent months, an ETF-based CTA product has been created and is available. The CTA ETF is structured to follow a relatively simplistic trend-following approach. At this time, the historical time period does not permit a full analysis of the product. However, the existence of the ETF product is indicative of the continued interest in managed futures-based trading strategies.[14]

A PERSONAL VIEW: ISSUES IN MANAGED FUTURES INVESTMENT

The purpose of this section is to provide some insight into two areas of CTA investment that have recently been of interest to the investment community. They are the costs and benefits of CTA pool or fund-of-funds investment and the unique distributional characteristics of CTAs, such that CTAs may be viewed less as a long volatility investment than an investment whose performance is based on short-term or long-term momentum patterns in various U.S. and global financial and commodity markets. There are other issues in CTA analysis, including the degree to which other asset classes' passive investable index-based tracker products can be created.

- **CTA Pool (Fund-of-Funds) Analysis:** Academic research has often addressed the benefits of CTAs and the effect of an additional layer of fees on product performance, but little direct research has focused on pools of CTAs and the impact of an additional layer of performance. As for hedge funds, CTA pool research has failed to consider the unique strategy emphasis of individual funds of funds (i.e., funds of funds must be classified according to their underlying investor objective). What's more, when a fund of funds is created, given the lockup, due diligence, and other costs, as well as the market sales environment, a fund of funds (pool) is often created with an emphasis on those CTAs that have the highest potential for relatively high returns. Thus, the performance of CTA pools may represent investment in a unique set of CTAs, that is, CTAs who trade in financial and commodity futures contracts with the greatest potential volatility and expected return as well as those CTAs who are willing to take a higher degree of investment risk. Investors should not necessarily reject CTA pools as an investment form, but the underlying characteristics of the CTA pool (the managers and their historical return and risk patterns) should be thoroughly analyzed.
- **Distributional Characteristics:** The primary reason for managed futures and CTA investment is the degree to which an individual strategy provides unique risk and return characteristics not easily available in other investment vehicles. The very fact that CTAs trade in a dynamic fashion makes the historical distribution characteristics a prisoner of the analysis period. Several academic studies have analyzed the sensitivity of

various CTA strategies to both traditional market factors and systematic momentum or lookback straddles that are expected to capture the return patterns of active systematic CTAs.[15] This research has shown that in contrast to the view that the underlying return and risk characteristics of CTAs are not capable of replication, for systematic trend followers, simple algorithmic trend-following models may capture a significant portion of the return process.

WHAT EVERY INVESTOR SHOULD KNOW

As discussed in this chapter, managed futures are also known as CTAs. Since few investors feel comfortable trading in cash or spot markets, imagine how few are willing to invest in something called a futures or forward market, or even worse, something called a derivative market. If hedge funds are regarded as the bad boy on the block, managed futures are not even on the block but over near the railroad tracks. In this chapter we attempted to make it permissible to invite them over to dinner. As for most alternative investments, we showed that managed futures have a misunderstood past as well as a misunderstood present. This too is surprising, since forward markets have existed since the dawn of modern humanity (about 2500 BC), and futures markets have been around for more than 150 years. Still, despite their long history, there are still a few things that every investor should know.

- **Managed Futures Are Derivatives, but:** Futures markets (and prices) are well understood. Most futures market prices are merely derivatives of cash market prices. But for many futures contracts (e.g., stocks, bonds), the price of a futures contract is not the expected price of the cash. For equity and fixed income, if the cash market price moves, the futures price moves. So you can think of managed futures traders as simply cash market traders who can use futures as an easier way to go long and short the cash deliverable. Though it may seem sexy to try to make them sound like exotic gamblers (and since futures can trade with less advance money, they can have greater risk), investors should remember that managed futures traders are like other equity and fixed-income traders, but they often live in Chicago.
- **Zero-sum Games Do Not Mean Zero Profits:** There are many markets (poker, for one) that, in the short run, are zero-sum games in which some players leave with more money and some leave with less. There are other markets that are zero-sum games for the most part, in which some leave with a little more money (e.g., insurance companies) and

others (e.g., home owners who pay insurance) leave with a little less. Investors should know which game their CTAs are playing. If it is poker, they had better be very good. If they are insurance players, little money may be made in the long run. Note: There are many CTAs trading different strategies just as there are different types of poker and insurance programs. Know which game and in which market your CTA is trading. If your CTA cannot tell you which one he or she is in and why he or she makes money—go elsewhere.

- **CTAs Are Not Necessarily High Risk:** Many investors view CTAs as high-risk gamblers. Although CTAs have historically been regarded as high-risk investment products, data shows that at the individual CTA level, standard deviation is similar to that of individual stocks in the S&P 500, and that the standard deviation of a portfolio of CTAs is similar to that of various fixed-income corporate bond indices. However, 'most' CTAs does not mean 'all.' Investors should assure themselves that if they invest in a CTA, the CTA has a well-defined risk target (e.g., similar to the current S&P 500). Have your CTA give you a current update on his or her current historic volatility and how he or she monitors his or her positions to ensure that risk is monitored. If he or she says he or she cannot—he or she is either lazy or deceitful. In any event, go somewhere else.

MYTHS AND MISCONCEPTIONS OF MANAGED FUTURES

Even more so than hedge funds, managed futures investment is an area complete with myths and misconceptions. First, the trades are conducted in the mysterious area of derivatives outside of the normal investor's zone of comfort. Much of the trading is conducted by what many individuals see as gamblers or speculators for which no consistent form of trading is evident. Second, while managed futures or CTAs have existed as a well-known trading strategy for decades, it was primarily marketed to high-net-worth individuals and only recently has it become available to the more general retail public. Unfortunately, the myth and misconceptions on its use developed over the years are still with us.

Myth 4.1: Managed Futures Provide a Hedge for Equity Returns Especially in Down Markets

A common graph or chart seen in many CTA marketing documents shows that many CTA programs have offered positive returns in just those months when equity markets have had their poorest performance. While this may be empirically true, it is hard to say that managed futures can be viewed as a natural hedge. Many CTAs are momentum traders, and research has shown that equity markets often follow a random walk, such that many CTAs do not even trade equity futures. If CTAs have positive returns in down equity markets, it is more due to the fact that in periods of market stress the government may try to lower rates, and CTAs who may be long interest rate futures will profit in just that market environment.

Myth 4.2: Managed Futures Are Long Volatility

Historically, managed futures have often been described as being long volatility in that, as discussed above, they often seem to make money when equity market volatility is high (equity markets often fall when equity volatility rises). Calling managed futures "long volatility" is a poor choice of words. In fact, since most CTAs are trend followers, they profit primarily in market conditions in which prices move slowly up and slowly down, and they lose money in markets where futures contract prices are trendless and move up and down within a relatively small range.

Myth 4.3: Managed Futures Are Absolute Return Vehicles

Even more than hedge funds, managed futures have often been described as absolute return vehicles because of their low equity betas as well as the lack of a regulatory requirement to track a particular passive index. However, again even more so than hedge funds, many managed futures programs follow similar algorithmic-based systematic trading strategies, such that most managed-futures managers within a particular strategy often have similar exposure to fundamental market pricing patterns (e.g., momentum and short-term price reversal) and trading opportunities (e.g., liquidity risks). Thus most managed futures programs generally make money in similar market environments and lose money in similar market environments (e.g., markets within a trading range, low interest rate markets for which certain managed futures strategies have little positive carry interest on margin). As a result, managed futures returns, while caused partly by manager skill, are also based on a set of common trading approaches that make and lose money in common market environments and should not be regarded as absolute return vehicles.

Myth 4.4: Managed Futures Are Riskier Than Stock Investments

Many investors view CTAs as inherently more risky than more traditional equity investments, if for no other reason than that CTAs trade in exchange and off exchange derivatives markets and can easily increase risk. As discussed previously, while few investors would question if stocks are riskier than bonds (although in certain market environments such as high interest rate volatility, some bonds are expected to be riskier than some stocks), the question remains if investment in CTAs is by nature riskier than investment in stocks. While CTAs have often been regarded as a high-risk investment, research results show that the standard deviation of a single CTA is, on average, similar to that of a single S&P 500-listed security. In addition, as shown in this book, many portfolios of CTAs have volatility even lower than that reported for the S&P 500. As discussed for hedge funds, CTAs have the ability to increase their market exposure quickly because of the low required level of margin; however, most CTAs monitor markets such that they lower their exposure in risky market environments and increase it in low-risk environments. Thus many CTAs target their funds to a particular level of volatility. CTAs may have high levels of risk, but it is not inherent to the strategy. Similarly, while the recent MF Global and Peregrine Financial Group Best bankruptcies have highlighted operational risks, such risks are business model risks inherent in delivering any investment product to the market.

Myth 4.5: Managed Futures Require Their Own Unique Measures of Performance

Managed futures are often cited as requiring a unique set of performance measures that capture their ability to go long or short, as well as other specific managed futures attributes (e.g., low market factor sensitivity). While certain managed futures strategies (e.g., option based) that directly act to modify the return distribution or that focus on a set of additional measures of risk concerns (e.g., liquidity) may require forms of option-adjusted performance measures, most CTA specific recommended risk measures (e.g., semideviation, drawdown) provide little in additional information and rank funds similar to other traditional measures of risk (e.g., standard deviation). If an investment strategy is structured to have unique return and risk characteristics, those characteristics must be considered, but for CTAs, the expected probability distribution remains similar to that of traditional assets, and the traditional forms of performance measurement remain adequate.

Myth 4.6: Managed Futures Strategies Cannot Be Replicated?

Each managed futures manager is unique in its own way; however, as discussed above, many managed futures traders follow algorithmic-based systematic trading models often based on similar market patterns (e.g., momentum). As a result, there exists a number of style pure, investable managed futures strategy benchmarks, which track individual managed futures strategies or non-investable CTA-based benchmarks. Note that these replication products are often not designed to capture the risk factor or market sector exposures of their associated benchmark, but attempt to replicate the underlying exposure to certain pricing patterns (e.g., momentum, breakout patterns).

CHAPTER 5

Commodities

An Ever-Changing Balance

In the mid-1990s, we were asked by American International Group (AIG) to be part of a new advisory board that was to be involved in the creation of a new commodity index product, the AIG Commodity Index. Although commodities have been a central part of the economic landscape since the dawn of civilization (i.e., early examples exist in 3000 BC of forward contracts for the exchange of commodities for other basic goods), commodities came into existence as tradable assets with the introduction and development of commodity futures markets in the mid- to late 1800s. The growth of both financial markets and commodity markets in the twentieth century led to new ways of investing in commodities (options), including direct investment in the equity of commodity firms. Direct investments in firms that produce or consume commodities, however, do not offer the same return and risk opportunities of direct investment in commodities. Similarly, investment in a single commodity does not offer the same risk and return opportunities of investment in a basket of commodities. Fortunately, the continued growth of interest in commodities in the last century led to the creation of a number of commodity indices designed to reflect the performance of an index of commodity investments.

Commodity indices, which have been in existence since the 1860s (e.g., *The Economist* Commodity-Price Index), were popularized in the United States in the 1930s, when the Commodity Research Bureau (CRB) Index began publication. However it was not until the early 1990s that the first truly investor-friendly investable commodity index was introduced: the Goldman Sachs Commodity Index (GSCI). The index was later sold to Standard & Poor's (S&P) in 2007 and is known today as the S&P GSCI. What separates this index from earlier, relatively illiquid commodity indices is that it is an index of the performance of liquid futures contracts, with a set of rules for rolling from one commodity futures contract (when it expires) to the next. In addition, the weights on each commodity change over time, based on a formula that emphasizes the commodity's importance in global production (e.g., the volume of the commodity times its price).

The success of the GSCI was due not only to its connection to one of the premier trading firms in the United States but also to the uniqueness of the economic conditions surrounding its introduction. In the early 1990s, the first Iraq war had led to a short-term rise in oil prices. The GSCI offered a systematic means of investing in the energy complex. In addition, it offered historical evidence of its risk and return benefit relative to investment in traditional stock and bond investments. The information in the original marketing material showed the benefit of investment in the GSCI for approximately the past 20 years (since the mid-1970s). In fact, crude oil began trading in 1983 and was not part of the return composition of the GSCI in the 1970s. Absent crude oil futures, the historical returns of the GSCI in the 1970s were heavily dependent on agricultural prices. Fortunately, in the 1970s, agricultural prices had periods of rapid increase (e.g., Russia grain shortages), and in the late 1980s, when agricultural prices were stagnant, the index contained a healthy portion of oil futures. To the average investor, unaware of the unique construction of the index, the past performance provided a feeling of security that what had often seemed a risky, volatile asset had the assurance of a long-term positive rate of return. Although not necessarily a reason for its creation, the GSCI also permitted the firm to sell any excess commodity inventory.

In truth, the GSCI was not an immediate success with investors. First, stock and bond markets rebounded in the early and mid-1990s following the successful outcome of the first Iraq war. By the mid-1990s, the GSCI had started to become a recommended part of an investor's diversified portfolio. Second, individuals and firms had become familiar enough with the GSCI to know both how to trade against it and how to make money from such active trading. Third, competing firms had started to devise a new set of commodity indices that could benefit from some of the construction issues of the GSCI. Note that the GSCI was sold in part as a product that reflected global production and thus represented to the investor a proportional investment in global commodities. However, since it was production and price weighted, it also had a fatal flaw: It increased investment in a particular commodity as that commodity's price or trading volume (i.e., production) rose. It did not take long before traders realized that they could make considerable money trading against the index rather than with it; for commodities, the price of something often falls if it is priced too high or too much of it is produced, and likewise, the price of a commodity often rises if it is priced too low and there is little of it produced.

The simple idea behind the AIG Commodity Index was to create a new commodity index that minimized, in part, the natural mean reversion in commodity prices embedded in the GSCI (e.g., overinvestment in commodities with high prices and high production, and underinvestment in commodities with low prices and low production). Instead of using the most recent price and production to determine commodity weights, why not simply take an average of several past years' prices and production? By using the average of past years relative to the most recent year, an investor would have an increased weight to a commodity even as its price and production fell, and a reduced weight to a commodity even as its price and production increased. In terms of development, the AIG Commodity Index can be regarded as phase 2. The AIG Commodity Index was introduced in 1998. Soon after, a number of commodity indices came into existence. Each index was created to meet a unique concern or potential that did not exist in either of the existing indices. The Rogers International Commodity Index was introduced in 1997 and included a number of commodities traded in Japan but not elsewhere. (It is not surprising that the Rogers International Commodity Index is a favorite among certain Japanese trading firms, since if investors use it, they are the natural source for trading the contracts involved in its construction.) In 2003, the Deutsche Bank Commodity Index was created, which emphasized investment in only six commodities. Again, given the dominance of the GSCI and other passive commodity indices in the market, another simple production-and-price-based index was not likely to make a major effect on investors. Moreover, individuals were increasingly looking for phase 3 commodity products, which included some aspects of active trading.

This rush to create new investment products based on new commodity indices had many causes, one being the dramatic increase in commodity index assets in the late 1990s. During that time, we were also asked to be part of the development of the London Metal Exchange Metals Index. The hope was that metals, in contrast to other more generic commodities, had both a basis in global production and a limited supply pattern. As a result, it had a greater potential for price increases than did more generic commodities (e.g., agricultural) for which production could be easily increased. Commodity indices have grown from generic composites to specific commodity subindices. In the mid-2000s, Deutsche Bank and UBS introduced a commodity index that took advantage of roll yield (i.e., essentially the differential price between a near term and more distant commodity futures prices during the period of rolling from the contract maturity to a later contract). The hope was, of course, that the demand for commodities creating the roll opportunity would continue. Further attempts have been made to capture the changing economic and business cycle patterns implied in commodity prices.

In 2007, the Bache Commodity Index was introduced, which offered a more active element to commodity index creation. The Bache Commodity Index (now the Alternative Benchmark Commodity Index) was created to take advantage of the price momentum often seen in commodity prices. This index also introduced the ability to manage commodity price risk by adding cash to the portfolio in periods of historic commodity price decline.

It is not surprising that after 20 years of commodity index investing, the S&P GSCI remains the most popular investable commodity index, despite its known shortcomings. First, commodity products, as many other investment products, have what is called a *first-mover advantage*. The S&P GSCI became one of the first commodity indices to be part of larger multi-asset allocation portfolios. Because the index was in the set of benchmarks used to determine asset allocation as well as relative performance, the use of other non-S&P GSCI commodity indices could increase tracking error relative to the listed S&P GSCI. Second, the S&P GSCI, being first out of the gate, became the commodity index often used as the benchmark in programs used to promote the benefits of commodity investment. Equally important, the S&P GSCI, backed by the resources of Goldman Sachs, had the office and research support necessary for the successful promotion of the index. Moreover, although the S&P GSCI was composed of less than 50 percent energy investments at its creation, in the early 1990s, as energy prices and trading volume increased, the S&P GSCI became an increasingly energy-dependent index, with energy investments becoming well over 60 percent of the weighting.

Fortunately for the S&P GSCI, and commodity indices in general, economic and market conditions following the Internet bubble of the early 2000s led to increased demand for energy and other commodity-based products. Between 2000 and 2006, the rise of China and other emerging markets led to increased demand for commodities, while global tensions in the Middle East led to concerns over energy supplies and increased demand for gold as a safe haven investment. This increased demand for various commodities was also coincident with the development of new direct forms of commodity investment, such as exchange-traded funds (ETFs) and exchange-traded notes (ETNs). Although it took almost 20 years in the making, commodity investment became an overnight success, based both on new models of investment and on a new belief in commodities as a long-term source of return.

In the following sections, we review commodity investment as a stand-alone investment and as a means to provide additional return enhancement as well as risk-reduction opportunities relative to those of stock and bond investments and other financial assets. The potential benefits of commodities as stand-alone investments or as additions to existing asset portfolios are explored in different ways. First, we briefly discuss various ways in which investors can gain direct exposure to commodities. Second, we review the theoretical basis for commodity investment. Academic research suggests that commodity indices have sources of risk and return that are distinct from traditional assets such as stocks and bonds. We also report on the performance of direct commodity investment, at both the overall index level and the subsector level (e.g., energy, industrial metals, precious metals, agriculture, and livestock), and provide evidence on different aspects of direct commodity investment, including the impact of roll return, inflation protection, and relative performance of equity-based commodity investment. Finally, we explore unique issues involved in commodity investment, and discuss various myths in the area of commodity investment.

INVESTING IN COMMODITIES

Historically, direct commodity investment has been a minor part of an investor's asset allocation decision. In contrast, indirect investments (e.g., equity or debt ownership of firms specializing in direct commodity production) remain the principal means by which many investors obtain exposure to this asset class. However, as previously pointed out, in recent years, the number of investable commodity indices and commodity-linked investments has increased dramatically. Today, commodity investment, whether at the individual commodity level or through commodity-based portfolios, has become an increasingly important part of investors' diversified portfolios.

Private Investment in Commodities

Private direct investment includes investment in commodities either through direct spot markets or though futures markets. Investment in futures markets often requires an investor to select a futures commission merchant (FCM) and a broker or a brokerage house (or both) with which they will maintain their account. Individual firms may have different restrictions on the level of financial wealth required to invest through their operation. However, investors are cautioned that the choice of brokerage firm is a very important one. For starters, the firm must have the capacity to handle complex trades. The FCM generally has custody of the investors' funds and is responsible for furnishing investors with confirmations of all transactions, monthly statements showing information about trading activities in their account, and other account statements customarily furnished by the FCM to its customers. Private investment in commodities may also include direct investment through various private pools of investment in a wide range of commodity enterprises, including timber and other agricultural investment opportunities.

Investors may directly invest in commodities through spot markets or related futures markets. Although spot investment and futures investment are related through basic cost-of-carry arbitrage, investors must be warned that the underlying returns to each investment may differ because of a range of market factors (e.g., differential storage costs, carry costs, convenience yields). However, investors may be restricted to investment in spot markets (e.g., gold bullion) versus futures contracts (e.g., gold futures), depending on the regulatory rules governing the means of investment in the investor's country.

Public Investment in Commodities

Commodity exposure may also be gained through investment in public commodity funds. These funds offer commodity exposure to individual commodities or a basket of select commodity funds. These products capture the performance of active manager-based investments. A diversified commodity fund may invest in a wide variety of underlying commodities and, therefore, is not exposed to serious losses of any one commodity. As with any public fund, however, investors are advised to review the underlying objectives of the fund. Some public commodity funds stress a more active absolute return approach, while others are more benchmark focused.

Publicly traded equity firms, for whom commodity production and sale are a primary part of their business enterprise, and public equity based commodity funds, which attempt to provide commodity return opportunities based on investment in the equity of commodity-based firms, offer an additional means for retail and high-net-worth investors to obtain commodity-based returns. Investors are thus cautioned to determine if the funds they are investing in focus on direct commodity investing or indirect investment through investment in the equity of commodity-based firms. The performance of commodity funds that invest in the equity of firms specializing in commodities and those that invest directly in commodity-based products often provide different return-to-risk trade-offs.

Investable commodity products can also be accessed directly through ETF products. These products provide both long-only investment and the means to take short positions in select commodities. Most currently available commodity ETFs attempt to track the performance of existing commodity indices. However, as will be discussed, commodity indices may differ dramatically in terms of composition and return-to-risk trade-off. In addition, there are an increasing number of commodity ETF providers that are creating more active trading-based commodity ETFs. These commodity ETFs offer a systematic approach to commodity investing, which often includes a more active approach (e.g., dramatic changes in commodity weights) based on a well-defined trading methodology.

COMMODITY STYLES AND BENCHMARKS

As with most investment strategies, the commodity arena can often be defined by the markets the manager trades and the form of the trading that takes place. The primary commodity benchmark groupings follow. Each of these benchmarks can generally provide returns in total return form, excess return form (i.e., less the risk-free rate), and spot return form (i.e., return from investment solely in the futures contract with constant investment).

Sample Commodity Indices

Total Composite	Sub-Sector
Agriculture	Livestock Commodity
Agriculture and Livestock	Non-Energy
Energy and Metals	Non-Livestock
Energy Commodity	Non-Natural Gas
Enhanced Commodity Strategy	Non-Precious Metal
Ex-Gasoil Petroleum	Petroleum
Grains	Precious Metal Commodity
Industrial Metal Commodity	Reduced Energy
Light Energy	Ultra Light Energy

Indices also exist at the individual commodity level. As with more general composite commodity indices, individual commodity indices may differ based on the exact construction methodology.

Sample Individual Commodity-Based Indices

Aluminum	Crude	Heating oil	Silver
Brent	Feeder cattle	Lead	Soybean
Cocoa	Gas oil	Lean hog	Soybean oil
Coffee	Gasoline	Live cattle	Sugar
Copper	Gold	Natural gas	Wheat
Corn	Hard wheat	Nickel	Zinc

Similar to other investment areas (e.g., S&P 500, Russell 1000, and Dow Jones), there exist in the commodity area several firms that provide a number of futures-based commodity indices. In this chapter, the S&P GSCI is used as the primary representative commodity index; however, when comparing commodity index products, a number of large investment firms (e.g., Deutsche Bank, UBS, Merrill Lynch) as well as other players in the commodity area offer a wide range of commodity indices. Each of these indices is unique in its own way. For example, the S&P GSCI, the Dow Jones–UBS Commodity Index (DJ-UBSCI), and the Alternative Benchmark Commodity Index (ABCI) all differ slightly in their construction, with the S&P GSCI primarily following a production-weighted methodology. The DJ-UBSCI uses a combination of production, liquidity, and limits on sector and commodity weights. The ABCI is a bit more complex. It employs both upper and lower bounds on investment in each sector and each commodity, and includes a commodity momentum model, which results in a rebalance of individual commodities each day to maintain the desired exposure to each commodity market. Finally, investable commodity indices can also be created to meet a set of preselected filters (i.e., green commodity indices, metals indices) or to reflect a more active trading format (e.g., Morningstar Long/Short Commodity Index). As with many investment strategies, the form that investments can take is limited only by regulation, investor demand, and the trading firm's desire to create such a product.

BASIC SOURCES OF RETURN AND RISK

Commodity returns reflect price changes in the underlying commodity. These price changes are caused by changes in commodity supply and demand as well as changes in the unique factors directly impacting the commodity investment vehicle. For example, commodity futures contracts are impacted not only by the current spot price but also by a range of storage and cost-of-carry factors (such as interest rates, storage cost, and convenience yield). The equity of commodity firms is affected not only by the price of their underlying holdings but also by the extent to which they manage those resources (e.g., hedge current or expected output) and the efficiencies in their operational processes.

In this chapter, we concentrate on the performance of commodity investment through an analysis of public commodity indices. As discussed previously, commodity indices attempt to replicate the returns available to holding long positions in agricultural, metal, energy, or livestock investment. Since returns on a fully invested futures contract reflect those of an investment in the underlying deliverable, commodity indices based on the returns of futures contracts offer an efficient means to obtain commodity exposure. However, as discussed previously, these indices may differ in a number of ways, such as the commodities included in the index, the weights of the individual commodities, and a number of operational trading issues (e.g., roll period and rebalancing). The source of returns to commodity investment depends both on the underlying use of the commodity and on the investment vehicle used to capture a particular part of the commodity earnings stream. For many, commodities are seen as products to be consumed and that do not naturally provide investment returns, while for others, commodities are products that are a physical part of the production process with returns that are determined by their marginal value in the production process. For others, the debate as to the source and dynamics of commodity returns, as well as their place in an investor's strategic portfolio, lies primarily in a commodity's ability to offer return-to-risk trade-offs that cannot be easily replicated through other investment alternatives.

Research has examined the economic determinants of returns to commodity investment. As with any investment, returns are determined by the expected return on the deliverable and, for futures-related contracts, the expected cost-of-carry returns, as well as other storage and deliverable options. For example, there is a strong business-cycle component in industrial metals-based futures contracts, a finding that is consistent with the business-cycle variation of spot and futures prices of industrial metals. The theory of storage splits the difference between the futures price and the spot price into the forgone interest from purchasing and storing the commodity, storage costs, and the convenience yield on the inventory. Convenience yield reflects an embedded consumption timing option in holding a storable commodity. Further, the theory of storage predicts an inverse relationship between the level of inventories and convenience yield—namely, at low inventory levels, convenience yields are high, and vice versa. A related implication is that the term structure of forward price volatility generally declines over time until expiration of the futures contract—the so-called Samuelson effect. This is caused by the expectation that, although at shorter horizons, mismatched supply-and-demand forces for the underlying commodity increase the volatility of spot prices; these forces will fall into equilibrium at longer horizons.

Of course, there exist different approaches and research results on the ability to forecast various commodity prices. Forecasting the underlying risk process of various commodities is likewise a major aspect in managing the underlying risk embedded in commodities. Work is also being conducted on the price of volatility risk in various commodity products as well as the underlying pricing process of commodities. These studies focus on the underlying risk premiums for energy and the degree to which the underlying return-and-risk profile is time varying. Finally, research has explored the degree to which commodity prices follow various momentum patterns and for which more active systematic algorithmic-based trading approaches may be of value.

PERFORMANCE: FACT AND FICTION

Commodities differ from most investment vehicles since they are not directly related to corporate or global earnings growth captured by equity or fixed-income-based investment vehicles, or to investment strategies based on investment in derivative products (e.g., commodity trading advisors [CTAs]). Commodities may be regarded more as inputs to certain manufacturing processes and are related to certain measures of inflation. As a result, commodities returns, by their very nature, may respond to different informational factors than equity or fixed-income markets. While the level of long-term return is uncertain, it is generally expected that commodity investment will provide diversification benefits to long-only equity or fixed-income biased investment portfolios. In the following sections, we attempt to provide evidence not only on the stand-alone risks of various commodity investments, but on the interrelationships between various commodities and between commodities and various traditional (e.g. equity and fixed-income market) and alternative asset classes. As in previous chapters, we examine these markets over a broad time period, as well as over shorter time intervals (e.g., annual) including their relative performance in extreme market conditions. As expected, commodities are shown to have a low correlation with the comparison traditional and alternative investments and provide potential diversification benefits. The level of benefits partially depends on the level of commodity risk and expected returns. Results show that in periods of extreme equity or fixed-income market, most commodities strategies have similar return patterns, that is, falling in down equity markets and providing positive returns in up equity markets. To some, this is unexpected because commodities have been regarded primarily as sources of diversification, but for many commodities, underlying price movement is based on underlying demand that may fall in poor equity market conditions and rise in better equity market conditions. Given the changing nature of commodity demand, investors should not take return and risk performance from extended time frames as a basis for how various commodities or a composite commodity indices may perform over relatively shorter time periods (e.g., annual). Finally, while certain commodities have the potential for return patterns similar to comparison publicly traded commodity firms, the ability of many publicly traded commodity-based firms to directly manage the risk of commodity inputs and outputs often results in low correlation between long-bias commodity indices and publicly traded commodity returns.

RETURN AND RISK CHARACTERISTICS

In this section, we review the performance of the S&P GSCI with a range of traditional stock and bond indices as well as a number of alternative investment indices (e.g., real estate, private equity, CTAs, and hedge funds) over the period 1994–2011. In later sections, we focus on commodity performance in various subperiods. For this period, as shown in Exhibit 5.1, the S&P GSCI exhibited higher annualized standard deviation, or volatility (22.5 percent), than that of the S&P 500 (15.7 percent). This is consistent with most investors' expectations. Despite the higher volatility, the S&P GSCI reported lower annualized total return (4.8 percent) than that of the S&P 500 (7.7 percent). However, stand-alone historical return and risk comparison may not reflect the potential for the benefits of a commodity investment as additions to other traditional assets or other financial asset classes. As shown in Exhibit 5.1, for the period analyzed, the S&P GSCI has a relatively low correlation (0.25) with the S&P 500 and a low correlation (0.02) with the BarCap U.S. Aggregate Index. The relatively low correlation of commodities with stock and bond returns as well as the

EXHIBIT 5.1 Commodity and Asset Class Performance

Stock, Bond, and Commodity Performance	S&P GSCI	S&P 500	BarCap U.S. Government	BarCap U.S. Aggregate	BarCap U.S. Corporate High Yield
Annualized total return	4.8%	7.7%	6.1%	6.3%	7.3%
Annualized standard deviation	22.5%	15.7%	4.4%	3.8%	9.4%
Information ratio	0.2	0.5	1.4	1.7	0.8
Maximum drawdown	−67.6%	−50.9%	−5.4%	−5.1%	−33.3%
Correlation with commodity index	1.00	0.25	−0.06	0.02	0.26

Alternative Investments and Commodity Performance	S&P GSCI	CISDM Equal Weighted Hedge Fund	CISDM CTA Equal Weighted	FTSE NAREIT	Private Equity Index
Annualized total return	4.8%	10.4%	8.1%	9.7%	8.0%
Annualized standard deviation	22.5%	7.7%	8.7%	19.9%	28.1%
Information ratio	0.21	1.36	0.94	0.49	0.28
Maximum drawdown	−67.6%	−21.7%	−8.7%	−67.9%	−80.4%
Correlation with commodity index	1.00	0.40	0.22	0.21	0.34

Period of analysis: 1994 to 2011.

low correlation with other nontraditional asset classes is one of the prime sources of the belief in the diversification benefits of commodities.

The relatively low correlations between the S&P GSCI and a range of traditional and nontraditional assets indicate that a portfolio of commodities (e.g., S&P GSCI) may reduce the stand-alone risk (i.e., standard deviation) of a stock or bond portfolio or a multi-asset portfolio. As shown in Exhibit 5.2, adding a small portion of commodities (10 percent) to stock and bond Portfolio A yields Portfolio B with a similar annualized return (7.3 percent) and standard deviation (8.2 percent) as the pure stock and bond portfolio (see Portfolio A, with an annualized return of 7.3 percent and a standard deviation of 8.2 percent). Similarly, adding commodities to Portfolio C that contains a range of traditional and alternative assets, results in Portfolio D that again exhibits a similar return (8.0 percent) and standard deviation (8.7 percent) to those of Portfolio C (8.1 percent and 8.7 percent, respectively), which does not contain commodities.

If a composite commodity index such as the S&P GSCI fails to provide superior return and risk opportunities to other financial assets on a stand-alone basis or as an addition to a sample portfolio, what is the basis for investing in commodities? First, as mentioned previously and demonstrated later, performance in a single period is not indicative of the relative performance in other periods. Second, the S&P GSCI is only one of several composite commodity indices, and as will be shown later, other commodity indices may provide different performance results. Third, there is no requirement that investors invest in a single composite commodity index. A composite commodity index covers a wide range of commodity subgroups. Exhibit 5.3 shows return and risk performance over the 1994–2011

EXHIBIT 5.2   Commodity and Multi-Asset Class Portfolio Performance

Portfolios	A	B	C	D
Annualized returns	7.3%	7.3%	8.1%	8.0%
Standard deviation	8.2%	8.2%	8.7%	8.7%
Information ratio	0.90	0.89	0.93	0.91
Maximum drawdown	−27.1%	−30.1%	−32.1%	−34.3%
Correlation with commodity index	0.24		0.31	
Portfolio A	Equal weights S&P 500 and BarCap U.S. Aggregate			
Portfolio B	90% Portfolio A and 10% commodity			
Portfolio C	75% Portfolio A and 25% CTA/hedge funds/private equity/real estate			
Portfolio D	90% Portfolio C and 10% commodity			

Period of analysis: 1994 to 2011.

EXHIBIT 5.3 Commodity Index Performance

	S&P GSCI	Petroleum	Precious Metal	Livestock	Industrial Metal	Grains	Energy	Agriculture
Annualized return	4.8%	12.5%	8.7%	−2.9%	7.4%	−3.6%	7.5%	−1.4%
Annualized standard deviation	22.5%	31.8%	16.8%	14.4%	21.1%	23.8%	31.9%	20.0%
Information ratio	0.21	0.39	0.52	−0.20	0.35	−0.15	0.24	−0.07
Maximum drawdown	−67.64%	−74.93%	−30.30%	−53.75%	−61.73%	−74.09%	−74.57%	−66.40%
Correlation with SP 500	0.25	0.19	0.06	0.06	0.44	0.25	0.18	0.28
Correlation with BarCap U.S. Aggregate	0.02	−0.03	0.17	−0.02	−0.13	0.11	0.02	0.08
Correlation With S&P GSCI	1.00	0.93	0.28	0.15	0.45	0.36	0.97	0.38

Period of analysis: 1994 to 2011.

period for commodity subgroups, which differ from the composite S&P GSCI. Equally important, the relative standard deviations and correlation of the S&P GSCI sub-indices with the S&P 500 and BarCap U.S. Aggregate Bond Index (shown in Exhibit 5.3) illustrate that the correlation of the individual commodity subgroups with the exception of petroleum or energy are somewhat independent of the composite commodity index.

In summary, there is much in the historical returns for the period 1994–2011 to support traditional investors' view that the return-to-risk trade-off of commodities makes them poor stand-alone investments but may make them beneficial as diversifiers to many financial asset-based portfolios. Simply reporting historical returns, however, may not capture many of the return and risk characteristics of commodities over unique financial or economic conditions. Investors should be certain to check how a particular commodity index or individual commodity performs across a wide range of economic and financial markets and whether the program they wish to invest in has a strategy for taking those changes into consideration.

THE MYTH OF AVERAGE: COMMODITY INDEX RETURN IN EXTREME MARKETS

The results in the previous section illustrate the performance of the S&P GSCI and how it compares to traditional and alternative investment indices over an 18-year period (1994 to 2011). The results indicate little return or risk benefits of commodities as a stand-alone investment or as an addition to an existing traditional investment portfolio or a portfolio of traditional and alternative investments. However, the relative stand-alone performance of the S&P GSCI, as well as its potential benefits when added to a portfolio of financial assets may differ in various subperiods, in comparison to its performance over the entire period of analysis. This is especially true in periods of market stress, when certain commodity investments (e.g., gold) may be seen as flight to safety and when the period of market stress is caused by the price movement of underlying commodities.

Exhibit 5.4 shows monthly commodity returns ranked on the S&P 500 and grouped into three segments (bottom, middle, and top) of 72 months each, with average returns for each commodity segment presented. Results show that the S&P GSCI and the related sub-indices generally reported less negative returns than the S&P 500 in the worst S&P 500 return months and reported less positive returns than the S&P 500 in the best S&P 500 return months. The positive performance in up markets may be partially caused by the positive economic conditions driving both stock market prices and commodity demand. The relative superior performance in down S&P

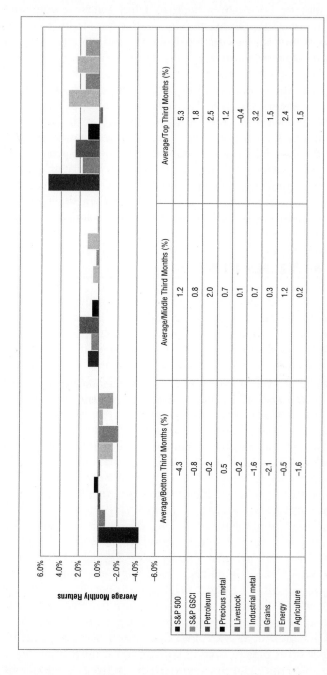

	Average/Bottom Third Months (%)	Average/Middle Third Months (%)	Average/Top Third Months (%)
S&P 500	-4.3	1.2	5.3
S&P GSCI	-0.8	0.8	1.8
Petroleum	-0.2	2.0	2.5
Precious metal	0.5	0.7	1.2
Livestock	-0.2	0.1	-0.4
Industrial metal	-1.6	0.7	3.2
Grains	-2.1	0.3	1.5
Energy	-0.5	1.2	2.4
Agriculture	-1.6	0.2	1.5

EXHIBIT 5.4 Commodity Indices: Monthly Returns Ranked on S&P 500 Period of analysis: 1994 to 2011.

500 markets may be caused by a flight to safety for some commodities. Notably, the results differ somewhat by commodity. Exhibit 5.4 shows that the precious metals index reported slightly positive returns when the S&P 500 had its worst performance. This return pattern is consistent with a flight to gold (i.e., safety) in periods of extreme market stress, which negatively impacts equity markets. Exhibit 5.5 shows monthly commodity returns ranked on the BarCap U.S. Aggregate Index and grouped into three segments (bottom, middle, and top) of 72 months each, with average returns for each commodity segment presented. Results show that the S&P GSCI and the related sub-indices reported mixed but generally positive returns (with one exception greater than that for the BarCap U.S. Aggregate Index) in the worst BarCap U.S. Aggregate months as well as mixed negative and positive returns (some greater and some less than the BarCap U.S. Aggregate) in the best BarCap U.S. Aggregate return months.

COMMODITY ANNUAL PERFORMANCE

In the previous section, the average performance of the S&P GSCI and sub-indices, and their ranking compared to the best- and worst-performing market environments, was discussed. The representative commodity index (i.e., S&P GSCI) was shown to provide potential diversification benefits in the worst months and positive returns in the best months of each index. In this section, we provide a review of the relative performance by year of the S&P GSCI, the S&P 500, and the BarCap U.S. Aggregate. Results in Exhibit 5.6 show that over the entire period, the annual returns of these indices varied during many years. However, in 12 of the 18 years, the S&P GSCI and S&P 500 moved in the same direction, and in 10 of the 18 years, the S&P GSCI and the BarCap U.S. Aggregate moved in the same direction. These results again indicate the importance of viewing commodity performance over short subperiods rather than viewing it based strictly on its performance over the whole 18-year period.

Similarly, as shown in Exhibits 5.7, 5.8, and 5.9, the standard deviation of the S&P GSCI and the S&P GSCI sub-indices, as well as the intra-year correlation of the S&P 500 and BarCap U.S. Aggregate with the S&P GSCI and the S&P GSCI sub-indices, vary significantly from year to year. However, the results also show that the intra-year correlation between the S&P 500 and the S&P GSCI has increased significantly since 2007. In short, investors should be aware that results from longer time frames may not reflect results for individual years, and that results from years before the recent economic crisis may not reflect current statistical relationships. The potential changing return and risk characteristics between commodities and

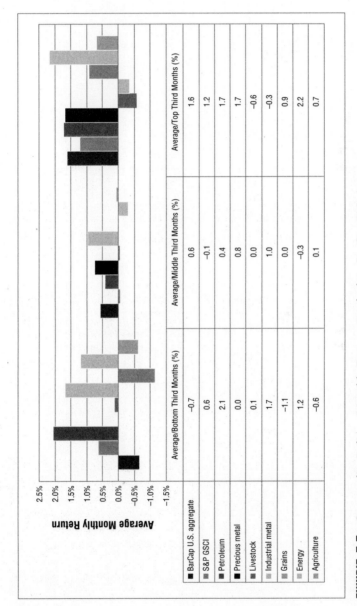

	Average/Bottom Third Months (%)	Average/Middle Third Months (%)	Average/Top Third Months (%)
■ BarCap U.S. aggregate	−0.7	0.6	1.6
■ S&P GSCI	0.6	−0.1	1.2
■ Petroleum	2.1	0.4	1.7
■ Precious metal	0.0	0.8	1.7
■ Livestock	0.1	0.0	−0.6
▒ Industrial metal	1.7	1.0	−0.3
▒ Grains	−1.1	0.0	0.9
▒ Energy	1.2	−0.3	2.2
▒ Agriculture	−0.6	0.1	0.7

EXHIBIT 5.5 Commodity Indices: Monthly Returns Ranked on BarCap U.S. Aggregate Period of analysis: 1994 to 2011.

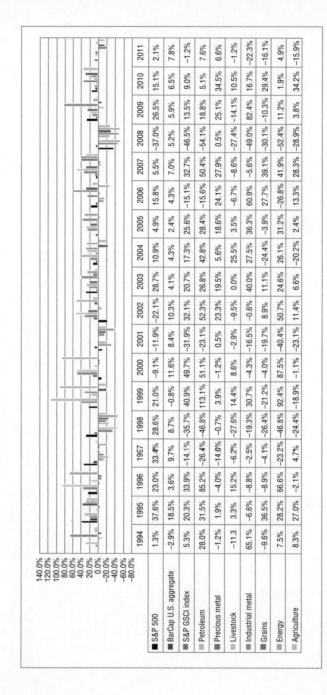

	1994	1995	1996	1997	1998	1999	2000	2001	2002	2003	2004	2005	2006	2007	2008	2009	2010	2011
S&P 500	1.3%	37.6%	23.0%	33.4%	28.6%	21.0%	-9.1%	-11.9%	-22.1%	28.7%	10.9%	4.9%	15.8%	5.5%	-37.0%	26.5%	15.1%	2.1%
BarCap U.S. aggregate	-2.9%	18.5%	3.6%	9.7%	8.7%	-0.8%	11.6%	8.4%	10.3%	4.1%	4.3%	2.4%	4.3%	7.0%	5.2%	5.9%	6.5%	7.8%
S&P GSCI index	5.3%	20.3%	33.9%	-14.1%	-35.7%	40.9%	49.7%	-31.9%	32.1%	20.7%	17.3%	25.6%	-15.1%	32.7%	-46.5%	13.5%	9.0%	-1.2%
Petroleum	28.0%	31.5%	85.2%	-26.4%	-46.8%	113.1%	51.1%	-23.1%	52.3%	26.8%	42.8%	28.4%	-15.6%	50.4%	-54.1%	18.8%	5.1%	7.6%
Precious metal	-1.2%	1.9%	-4.0%	-14.0%	-0.7%	3.9%	-1.2%	0.5%	23.3%	19.5%	5.6%	18.6%	24.1%	27.9%	0.5%	25.1%	34.5%	6.6%
Livestock	-11.3	3.3%	15.2%	-6.2%	-27.6%	14.4%	8.6%	-2.9%	-9.5%	0.0%	25.5%	3.5%	-6.7%	-8.6%	-27.4%	-14.1%	10.5%	-1.2%
Industrial metal	65.1%	-6.6%	-8.8%	-2.5%	-19.3%	30.7%	-4.3%	-16.5%	-0.6%	40.0%	27.5%	36.3%	60.9%	-5.6%	-49.0%	82.4%	16.7%	-22.3%
Grains	-9.6%	36.5%	-8.9%	-4.1%	-26.4%	-21.2%	-4.0%	-19.7%	8.9%	11.1%	-24.4%	-3.9%	27.7%	39.1%	-30.1%	-10.3%	29.4%	-16.1%
Energy	7.5%	28.2%	66.6%	-23.2%	-46.8%	92.4%	87.5%	-40.4%	50.7%	24.6%	26.1%	31.2%	-26.8%	41.9%	-52.4%	11.2%	1.9%	4.9%
Agriculture	8.3%	27.0%	-2.1%	4.7%	-24.4%	-18.9%	-1.1%	-23.1%	11.4%	6.6%	-20.2%	2.4%	13.3%	28.3%	-28.9%	3.8%	34.2%	-15.9%

EXHIBIT 5.6 Commodity Indices: Annual Returns

EXHIBIT 5.7 Commodity Indices: Annual Standard Deviation

	1994	1995	1996	1997	1998	1999	2000	2001	2002	2003	2004	2005	2006	2007	2008	2009	2010	2011
S&P 500	10.6%	5.2%	10.9%	15.9%	21.5%	13.1%	17.2%	19.9%	20.6%	11.4%	7.3%	7.9%	5.6%	9.7%	21.0%	22.3%	19.3%	15.9%
BarCap U.S. aggregate	4.4%	3.5%	4.3%	3.6%	2.7%	2.7%	2.8%	3.8%	3.7%	5.3%	4.0%	3.1%	2.7%	2.6%	6.1%	3.3%	2.9%	2.4%
S&P GSCI index	13.1%	11.2%	12.6%	16.6%	18.6%	21.7%	23.3%	14.7%	18.7%	25.8%	22.3%	25.4%	21.7%	17.0%	42.9%	24.5%	23.3%	20.8%
Petroleum	20.4%	16.2%	22.7%	20.8%	33.9%	43.0%	41.4%	25.9%	29.2%	31.7%	31.8%	32.1%	26.5%	24.3%	51.9%	32.7%	27.8%	24.5%
Precious metal	8.4%	6.5%	8.1%	13.7%	13.3%	18.2%	9.3%	11.1%	13.3%	14.6%	17.6%	13.3%	20.8%	14.4%	32.7%	22.5%	11.4%	30.8%
Livestock	18.0%	12.0%	12.4%	8.2%	16.5%	14.3%	11.3%	12.3%	17.4%	21.2%	12.4%	10.6%	16.8%	14.0%	16.6%	8.8%	10.5%	17.7%
Industrial metal	12.1%	16.1%	15.6%	12.6%	8.9%	19.5%	10.4%	19.4%	13.2%	20.0%	18.9%	14.1%	25.9%	19.6%	38.8%	19.0%	27.5%	24.5%
Grains	12.3%	13.6%	25.4%	24.4%	20.2%	16.8%	16.9%	15.9%	17.8%	17.8%	23.4%	22.3%	18.8%	24.9%	40.3%	30.2%	35.2%	33.2%
Energy	24.8%	22.3%	20.4%	27.3%	33.5%	39.7%	36.8%	20.8%	31.4%	36.4%	32.1%	33.5%	27.5%	22.7%	50.6%	31.9%	26.4%	23.9%
Agriculture	8.6%	8.5%	19.4%	18.9%	13.6%	13.9%	12.4%	14.0%	15.6%	11.7%	18.5%	18.3%	15.5%	21.7%	38.6%	22.9%	33.4%	27.2%

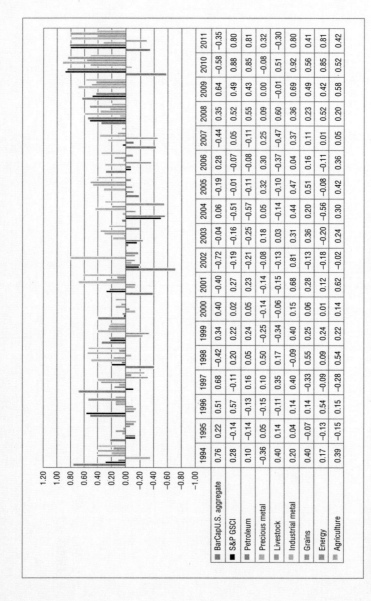

	1994	1995	1996	1997	1998	1999	2000	2001	2002	2003	2004	2005	2006	2007	2008	2009	2010	2011
BarCapU.S. aggregate	0.76	0.22	0.51	0.68	-0.42	0.34	0.40	-0.40	-0.72	-0.04	0.06	-0.19	0.28	-0.44	0.35	0.64	-0.58	-0.35
S&P GSCI	0.28	-0.14	0.57	-0.11	0.20	0.22	0.02	0.27	-0.19	-0.16	-0.51	-0.01	-0.07	0.05	0.52	0.49	0.88	0.80
Petroleum	0.10	-0.14	-0.13	0.16	0.05	0.24	0.05	0.23	-0.21	-0.25	-0.57	-0.11	-0.08	-0.11	0.55	0.43	0.85	0.81
Precious metal	-0.36	0.05	-0.15	0.10	0.50	-0.25	-0.14	-0.14	-0.08	0.18	0.05	0.32	0.30	0.25	0.09	0.00	-0.08	0.32
Livestock	0.40	0.14	-0.11	0.35	0.17	-0.34	-0.06	-0.15	-0.13	0.03	-0.14	-0.10	-0.37	-0.47	0.60	-0.01	0.51	-0.30
Industrial metal	0.20	0.04	0.14	0.40	-0.09	0.40	0.15	0.68	0.81	0.31	0.44	0.47	0.04	0.37	0.36	0.69	0.92	0.80
Grains	0.40	-0.07	0.14	-0.33	0.55	0.25	0.06	0.28	-0.13	0.36	0.20	0.51	0.16	0.11	0.23	0.49	0.56	0.41
Energy	0.17	-0.13	0.54	-0.09	0.09	0.24	0.01	0.12	-0.18	-0.20	-0.56	-0.08	-0.11	0.01	0.52	0.42	0.85	0.81
Agriculture	0.39	-0.15	0.15	-0.28	0.54	0.22	0.14	0.62	-0.02	0.24	0.30	0.42	0.36	0.05	0.20	0.58	0.52	0.42

EXHIBIT 5.8 Commodity Indices: Annual Correlation with S&P 500

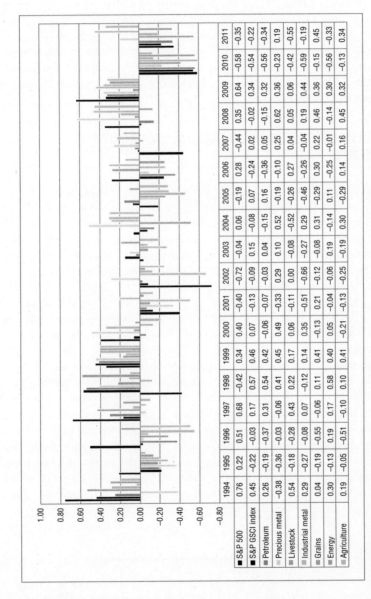

	1994	1995	1996	1997	1998	1999	2000	2001	2002	2003	2004	2005	2006	2007	2008	2009	2010	2011
■ S&P 500	0.76	0.22	0.51	0.68	-0.42	0.34	0.40	-0.40	-0.72	-0.04	0.06	-0.19	0.28	-0.44	0.35	0.64	-0.58	-0.35
■ S&P GSCI index	0.45	-0.22	-0.03	0.17	0.57	0.46	0.07	-0.13	-0.09	0.15	-0.08	0.07	-0.24	0.02	-0.02	0.34	-0.54	-0.22
■ Petroleum	0.26	-0.19	-0.37	0.31	0.54	0.42	-0.06	-0.07	-0.03	0.04	-0.15	0.16	-0.36	0.05	-0.15	0.32	-0.56	-0.34
■ Precious metal	-0.38	-0.36	-0.03	-0.06	0.41	0.45	0.49	-0.33	0.29	0.10	0.52	-0.19	-0.10	0.25	0.62	0.36	-0.23	0.19
■ Livestock	0.54	-0.18	-0.28	0.43	0.22	0.17	0.06	-0.11	0.00	-0.08	-0.52	-0.26	0.27	0.04	0.05	0.06	-0.42	-0.55
■ Industrial metal	0.29	-0.27	-0.08	0.07	-0.12	0.14	0.35	-0.51	-0.66	-0.27	0.29	-0.46	-0.26	-0.04	0.19	0.44	-0.59	-0.19
■ Grains	0.04	-0.19	-0.55	-0.06	0.11	0.41	-0.13	0.21	-0.12	-0.08	0.31	-0.29	0.30	0.22	0.46	0.36	-0.15	0.45
■ Energy	0.30	-0.13	0.19	0.17	0.58	0.40	0.05	-0.04	-0.06	0.19	-0.14	0.11	-0.25	-0.01	-0.14	0.30	-0.56	-0.33
■ Agriculture	0.19	-0.05	-0.51	-0.10	0.10	0.41	-0.21	-0.13	-0.25	-0.19	0.30	-0.29	0.14	0.16	0.45	0.32	-0.13	0.34

EXHIBIT 5.9 Commodity Indices: Annual Correlation with BarCap U.S. Aggregate

equity markets illustrated in Exhibit 5.8 are important. Recent global economic integration, the rise of China, and new financial products that emphasize commodities may have fundamentally changed historical relationships between equity and commodities. Marketing presentations that emphasize results based on 20, 30, or 40 years of historical data are inherently misleading. For commodities, such lengthy periods of analysis may hide more than they reveal. Investors must consider the relevance of historical data on corn before it became an energy substitute, on natural gas before the current supplies were discovered, and on many seasonal commodities before year-round production began. For commodities especially, investors are warned to be hypervigilant.

COMMODITY SUBSECTOR INDEX: ANNUAL COMMODITY PERFORMANCE

The results in Exhibit 5.3 show that the commodity indices that report the highest returns (i.e., energy and metals) often reported some of the highest standard deviations (i.e., volatilities) for the period 1994–2011. The relatively greater return for energy- and metals-based commodity investment is consistent with the economic argument that an underlying long-term positive return is more likely to exist for commodities for which supply may be constrained. The diversification potential of combining the various sector indices with the S&P 500 was also reflected in Exhibit 5.3. Although the annual returns of the S&P 500 and the S&P GSCI varied in many years, in recent years, they generally moved in the same direction. These results again indicate the importance of viewing commodity performance over short subperiods rather than basing it strictly on its performance over the past 18 years. The results in Exhibits 5.6 through 5.9 at the sub-index level reflect similar return patterns at the commodity index level—varying returns, standard deviation, and correlation over the 18 years of analysis—however, as indicated in Exhibit 5.8, in recent years there has been an increase in the relative correlation between many individual commodities and the S&P 500. Only the future will show if the increase in correlation between commodity and equity returns will continue; however, investors should be aware of which commodities are more closely linked with economic conditions and which may have a return process that is independent of global equity markets.

PERFORMANCE IN 2008

The relative performance of the S&P GSCI and comparison assets in 2008 requires special emphasis. In 2008, global investment markets underwent a severe correction that was experienced across most traditional and alternative investment markets. Results of previous exhibits show the risk and return performance of the S&P 500, the S&P GSCI, and S&P GSCI sub-indices for 2008. In this year, the S&P GSCI, similar to the S&P 500, was impacted by the subprime crisis. Although for commodities, cumulative return for the S&P 500 and the S&P GSCI was negative for the whole year, the real story lies in halves. Results differed between the first half and the latter half of the year. For the first six months of the year, the S&P GSCI had a positive return of 41.5 percent, while the S&P 500 reported a negative return (−11.9 percent); in the second six months, the S&P 500 had a negative return of −28.62 percent and the S&P GSCI had a negative return of −62.2 percent, as commodity markets responded to the declining drop in demand associated with declining global demand.

SPECIAL ISSUES IN COMMODITY INVESTMENT

While commodities remain a relatively small portion of most investors' portfolios, they have a demonstrated risk/return characteristic that shows that proper deployment can enhance overall returns. As with traditional investment opportunities, this asset class has continued to evolve. In the sections below, some of the more opportunistic developments are discussed.

Green Commodity Investment

There is currently a surge in investor interest in various green investment areas. Several approaches to investing in the green economy are available. The dominant green investment strategy involves buying equities. A number of indices track different sectors of the green equity markets. Similarly, there are various means of investing in green commodity products, from various biofuel-based investments to more specific carbon-related commodity products. (Biofuels are transportation fuels derived from non-fossilized biological sources.) Investment choices in the carbon economy include trading carbon credits, investment in carbon-reduction projects, and investment in corporations that are developing carbon-reduction and sequestration technology. The following is a brief overview of direct commodity investments in the biofuel area. In the commodity area, biofuel indices provide exposure to agricultural products used to create fuel in an environmentally friendly way. These indices include commodities, such as corn and sugar, which are used in the production of ethanol. There is a range of alternatives for investing in the green commodity. Following is a list of important green indices:

> **Bache Commodity Green Index (BCGI):** This index provides a benchmark for green commodity investments as well as diversified investment vehicles. It offers a multifaceted approach to holding

commodities and materials needed in the production of renewable energy and the reduction of carbon emissions. It is composed of 11 commodities that are traded on major exchanges and through over-the-counter markets located in the United States, Canada, the United Kingdom, France, and Malaysia. The commodities that comprise the index are primarily traded via futures contracts, with others being traded over-the-counter directly or through forward contracts.

Merrill Lynch Commodity Index (MLCX) Biofuels Index: This index applies the MLCX methodology to futures contracts on physical commodities. Futures contracts on physical commodities that are either biofuels themselves or feedstock commonly used in the production of biofuels are considered for eligibility in the index.

S&P GSCI Biofuel Index: This index reflects the total returns potentially available through an unleveraged investment in an index of five commodity contracts (i.e., corn, soybean oil, wheat, and sugar), with specific weights applied to each contract.

UBS Diapason Global Biofuel Index: This index covers a range of commodities used in the production of ethanol and biodiesel. Composed of various commodity futures, it is weighted to reflect the importance of each individual commodity used in the production of ethanol and biodiesel as well as the liquidity of the underlying futures.

S&P Global Clean Energy Index: This index includes 30 of the largest publicly traded stocks from companies around the world involved in clean energy. The index is composed of a diversified mix of companies focusing on clean energy production and clean energy equipment and technology.

WilderHill Clean Energy Index: This index is composed of approximately 54 companies that are publicly traded in the United States and engaged in a business or businesses that the Clean Energy Index Selection Committee believes stand to benefit substantially from a societal transition toward use of cleaner energy and conservation.

COMMODITIES AS AN INFLATION HEDGE

A significant part of the benefits that direct commodity investments provide is said to evolve from unique fluctuations of commodity values as a function of shifting economic forces. One such aspect of the commodity return pattern is that commodity cash prices may benefit from periods of unexpected inflation, whereas stocks and bonds may suffer. Results from a recent analysis, however, suggest that there is a slight positive correlation between the S&P GSCI and reported Consumer Price Index (CPI): All Items (due primarily to the inclusion of energy and food), but results also show that there is almost no correlation between inflation and the S&P GSCI when inflation is measured on CPI: All Items less food and energy. In short, within a given period there may be almost no relationship between inflation and a given commodity.[1]

Commodity Total Return Attribution

Most investors do not get into the specifics of breaking down a commodity index's total return into various sources of that return. Although the total return indicates the return that an investor can earn by holding a long-only, fully collateralized position in commodity futures, many commodity futures-based programs attempt to break the total return into three component parts: spot return, roll return, and collateral return. The spot return is simply the price appreciation in the spot price of the commodity, which is based on immediate delivery. Because investors in futures contracts have to roll contracts, they have to deal with contangos (i.e., longer-dated futures are more expensive than near-month contracts) and backwardation (i.e., longer-dated futures are cheaper). If the term structure is in backwardation, the roll yield is positive whereas it is negative when the term structure is in contango. (These concepts are discussed further in the next sections.) The final source of return is the collateral yield, which is the return accruing to any margin held against a futures position, and which is normally the U.S. Treasury bill rate.

Backwardation and Contango

When the front-month futures contract price is higher than the next futures contract price, the curve is said to be in *backwardation*. For investors, herein lies the problem. For many years, firms marketing the potential benefits of commodities cited positive roll return as a central return to commodity investors. Commodity indices were even created to maximize the potential roll return (i.e., overweight commodities in backwardation). However, as shown in Exhibit 5.10, although positive roll yield was evident primarily in the 1990s and into the first part of 2000, since then there has not been a consistent positive roll. The lack of consistent backwardation has also impacted the profitability of commodity indices designed to focus on the returns to roll. Investors may use the roll-return example as a case in point, in that some of the recently constructed commodity indices were

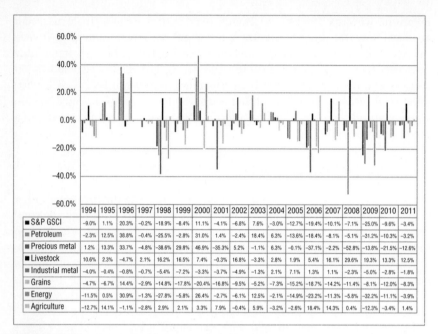

	1994	1995	1996	1997	1998	1999	2000	2001	2002	2003	2004	2005	2006	2007	2008	2009	2010	2011
■ S&P GSCI	-9.0%	1.1%	20.3%	-0.2%	-18.9%	-8.4%	11.1%	-4.1%	-6.8%	7.6%	-3.0%	-12.7%	-19.4%	-10.1%	-7.1%	-25.0%	-9.6%	-3.4%
■ Petroleum	-2.3%	12.5%	38.8%	-0.4%	-25.5%	-2.8%	31.0%	1.4%	-2.4%	18.4%	6.3%	-13.6%	-18.4%	-8.1%	-5.1%	-31.2%	-10.3%	-3.2%
■ Precious metal	1.2%	13.3%	33.7%	-4.8%	-38.6%	29.8%	46.9%	-35.3%	5.2%	-1.1%	6.3%	-0.1%	-37.1%	-2.2%	-52.8%	-13.8%	-21.5%	-12.6%
■ Livestock	10.6%	2.3%	-4.7%	2.1%	16.2%	16.5%	7.4%	-0.3%	16.8%	-3.3%	2.8%	1.9%	5.4%	16.1%	29.6%	19.3%	13.3%	12.5%
■ Industrial metal	-4.0%	-0.4%	-0.8%	-0.7%	-5.4%	-7.2%	-3.3%	-3.7%	-4.9%	-1.3%	2.1%	7.1%	1.3%	1.1%	-2.3%	-5.0%	-2.8%	-1.8%
■ Grains	-4.7%	-6.7%	14.4%	-2.9%	-14.8%	-17.8%	-20.4%	-16.8%	-9.5%	-5.2%	-7.3%	-15.2%	-18.7%	-14.2%	-11.4%	-8.1%	-12.0%	-8.3%
■ Energy	-11.5%	0.5%	30.9%	-1.3%	-27.8%	-5.8%	26.4%	-2.7%	-6.1%	12.5%	-2.1%	-14.9%	-23.2%	-11.3%	-5.8%	-32.2%	-11.1%	-3.9%
■ Agriculture	-12.7%	14.1%	-1.1%	-2.8%	2.9%	2.1%	3.3%	7.9%	-0.4%	5.9%	-3.2%	-2.6%	18.4%	14.3%	0.4%	-12.3%	-3.4%	1.4%

EXHIBIT 5.10 Commodity Indices: Annual Roll Return

marketed because of historical returns to a roll-based commodity index. However, soon after their construction and public sale, returns did not meet previous expectations. This was not caused by any problem in the construction or the theory, but because what happens in the past often stays in the past. Investors who concentrate on commodity indices that focus on a single source of return must be aware of the risks of such a concentrated strategy portfolio.

COMPARISON BETWEEN DIRECT AND EQUITY-BASED COMMODITY INVESTMENT

A number of commodity firms offer a means to access returns associated with commodity investment. Commodity firms' returns reflect, in part, their direct access to commodities (e.g., gold mining, agriculture, oil drilling) as well as their use of commodities in the production process (e.g. oil suppliers, farm machinery). To the degree to which corporate earnings are directly linked to holding long positions in agricultural, metal, energy, or livestock investment, the equity returns should reflect those of direct commodity investment. The return and risk opportunities of equity-based commodity-linked investment vehicles (and investment vehicles such as mutual funds, ETFs, and hedge funds, which are based on equity holdings) may also differ from their underlying commodity. For example, to the degree that corporations who use a commodity in their production process hold a number of real options based on the commodity, the value of the firm may change, with little change in the underlying commodity price. At the same time, if commodity price increases also increase future cash flows to a commodity-based firm or positively impact the value of its real options, equity returns of the firm may be positively related to increases in commodity prices. Stated another way, if corporate earnings are directly related to the production process that uses the underlying commodity as an input, then the degree to which price increases can be passed on to the consumer or the degree to which price decreases can be absorbed will impact equity returns. Conversely, for firms in which the underlying commodity is one part of the production process, on which the profit of the firm primarily relies, there may be little relationship between firm returns and direct commodity investment returns.

Research has shown that direct investment in equity securities of firms that specialize in particular commodity sectors have moderate correlation with the related commodity index. At the S&P GSCI level, the correlation between the S&P GSCI Energy Index and the S&P Energy subsector indices is 0.52. Similarly, the correlation between the S&P GSCI Precious Metals and Industrial Metals and the related S&P subsectors are all above 0.50. In contrast, the correlation between the S&P 500 Agricultural Products Index and the S&P GSCI Agricultural Index is only 0.18. Investors should also note that the positive correlation between energy futures-based commodity returns and energy equity-based commodity returns is partially caused by periods of extreme commodity price movement and the underlying management process of the associated equity firm. Some commodity-based equity firms hedge away the risk of unexpected changes in commodity prices. To the extent that the commodity-based equity firm in question has hedged unanticipated changes in the underlying commodity of the firm, one would expect a relatively weak relationship between commodity returns and the returns of the equity of the associated firm.

COMPARISON BETWEEN EQUITY-BASED MUTUAL FUND AND EXCHANGE-TRADED FUND COMMODITY INVESTMENT

For the period analyzed, the correlation between the S&P GSCI and the corresponding commodity-based mutual funds and commodity-based

ETF/ETNs is consistently above 0.90. Results indicate that, to the degree that the mutual fund or ETF/ETN is primarily a tracker of the underlying index (e.g., S&P GSCI), the return and risk are almost identical. The difference in return between the non-investable index and the S&P GSCI ETF is caused by the costs of implementing the investment strategy. However, investors must be aware of the fundamental differences in the construction of the ETF/ETN portfolios and the investment objective of the mutual fund.

A PERSONAL VIEW: ISSUES IN COMMODITY INVESTMENT

One of the central issues in commodity investment is the degree to which commodities offer a long-term positive expected return and the degree to which retail investment products (e.g., ETFs) are viable approaches for getting access to risk and return properties of commodities. There are other issues in commodity analysis including the degree to which historical commodity usage may not reflect current usage or that changing government policies (e.g., green investment, natural gas) may impact commodity return and risk patterns.

Distributional Characteristics

The primary reason for commodity investment is the degree to which an individual commodity provides unique risk and return characteristics not easily available in other investment vehicles. Various commodity vehicles trade in unique markets in unique forms. Moreover, these commodity vehicles have a dynamic element such that the instrument does not track a particular long-only strategy. That said, the expected distributional characteristics of an individual commodity vehicle reflect the holdings of the underlying product and the degree to which the commodity weights adjust to the driving factors of the portfolio (e.g., contango or backwardation). Several academic studies have addressed the additional higher moments of some commodities strategies, including yield-based products. Unfortunately, the conditional nature of various commodities makes any cross-sectional or time series analysis of the historical distributional nature of a commodity a simple "prisoner" of the data. Researchers and reviewers are often enticed by the "more data is better" syndrome; that is, five years of data is good, 10 years is better, 20 years is best. However, in a market partially driven by rapidly changing technological and distribution channels as well as regulatory rules, what is true of the 1980s may have little relevance for 2012. For example, many agricultural and livestock products have dramatically different seasonality characteristics in a global production market with low transportation costs. Many energy substitution products are driven more by changes in regulation than by changes in product consumption.

Governance and Micromarket Structure

In many analyses of commodity markets, it is often assumed that a commodity is just there and can be easily accessed by a number of potential suppliers. An investor rarely sees a detailed description of the various governance or structural holdups between the finding of a product and the delivery. We only note this because in our experience as part of a commodity index development team, we were surprised to find out, for example, that the amount of aluminum available for use is restricted to a limited monthly amount, regardless of the amount delivered to various warehouse sections—in short, controlled supply. There are numerous means by which supply and demand of commodities can be controlled; however, in our analysis, we found few if any academic studies that truly understand the management or trading process of any one commodity.

Other Issues

A number of other issues have not been analyzed in a manner that adequately reflects the actual commodity market structure. Many commodities are international in nature, but the effect of changing relative dollar value on demand has not found its way into most commodity analyses. Finally, the place of commodities in measuring worldwide inflation is a constant topic that has been a hit-and-miss affair, if for no other reason than that inflation is measured differently in every nation. In sum, what we call inflation in the United States is not inflation in China.

The increased energy weighting in the S&P GSCI in the last decade has made its return history somewhat problematic. Oil futures were not introduced until the mid-1980s, and the high returns to the GSCI when it was introduced were not due to an energy weighting but to the agricultural weighting. Since the introduction of the GSCI in 1991, the energy component of the index has increased while the agricultural component has fallen. This has unintended consequences for the current S&P GSCI. The increased demand for commodity index products as well as investor demand for new forms of financial products based on the S&P GSCI (e.g., S&P GSCI ETFs) has resulted in some elements (e.g., oil) of the S&P GSCI becoming more expensive in near-term contracts, and less expensive in far-term contracts. In short, historical prices and returns for commodity products may not provide an accurate picture of current expected risks and returns. Here is the good and bad news: Most new commodity products are designed (correctly) to meet current economic conditions and investor demand (e.g., green commodity indices and long/short commodity indices) as well as more dynamic modeling of portfolio construction. Unfortunately, these products are created not only with a view to the future but with a nod to the past. The backfill bias in any new commodity index requires the creation of an index that not only works for the present but has worked well in the past. In brief, the business model of the firm has to be aligned with the performance of the index and its potential customers. The dynamic element of new commodity indices and products results in investors being required to have a fuller understanding of the underlying return drivers of commodity returns as well as the business issues driving the creation of the product. Although we fully accept the argument that commodities reflect a unique and separate asset class, and as such, meaningful indices can be developed leading to more rational asset allocation decisions, we are also mindful that a commodity product or platform is in fact a structured product in which the individual business model ultimately determines performance and risks.

WHAT EVERY INVESTOR SHOULD KNOW

Today, commodities are hot. It is somewhat surprising that while the importance of commodities in the day-to-day consumer and corporate world is without question, its place in investors' portfolios remains a bit of a mystery. In this chapter we focused on the growth of commodities as an investment vehicle either as a stand-alone real investment or through an indirect investment via equity in publicly traded commodity-based corporations. Hopefully, we have removed some of the mystery of commodities by providing some historical context. But even so, the investor must come to realize that commodity markets are in a constant state of evolution.

- **For the Individual Investor: Stay Away.** Historically, direct commodity investment has been a minor part of an investor's asset allocation decision. In contrast, indirect investments (e.g., equity or debt ownership of firms specializing in direct commodity production) remain the principal means by which many investors obtain exposure to this asset class. However, in recent years the number of long-only investable commodity indices and commodity-linked investments has increased dramatically.

While certain market environments (e.g., commodity-based price inflation) may make direct commodity investment a worthwhile idea, for the most part individual investors should go elsewhere. Many futures-based commodities do not fit well into a long-run positive expected return environment. For institutional investors who have the resources to hire individuals to actively trade commodities both long and short, investment may make sense, but for everyone else we suggest a rethink.

- **Commodities Are Not *Automatic* Inflation Hedges.** Often we seek commodity investment as a means to protect against inflation. First an investor better get a fix on what they mean by inflation. Many commodities are not directly included in most published measures of inflation and often what we feel as inflation (food and energy) may or may not be included in the reported numbers. In short, commodities may protect an investor against certain types of price increases but not necessarily in price increases measures by government reports of CPI. If you want an inflation hedge, go elsewhere.

- **Don't Believe the Evening News:** According to the pundits, commodity investing is inherently evil and is akin to speculation, which for many is akin to gambling. Investors who wish to invest in a commodity-based product should realize that each product has its own unique characteristics, but there is little evidence that holding long-only futures contracts fundamentally distorts the markets. Remember, for every futures contract held long, there is one held short. For the most part, this sounds like offering an offset to investors who wants to go short for commercial reasons or for their own trading purposes. Investors have a lot of reasons not to invest in commodities, but feeling guilty for doing so is not one of them.

MYTHS AND MISCONCEPTIONS OF COMMODITY INVESTMENT

Perhaps since commodity investment has been historically available to investors through both direct ownership in cash as well as through equity ownership in commodity firms, there exists a large amount of potential confusion as to the risk and return characteristics of commodity investments and their place in investors' portfolios. Of course, in the world of the blind, the one-eyed person is king. In a world of uncertainty and confusion about the risk and returns of various commodity investments, acceptable myths may often outperform unacceptable facts.

Myth 5.1: One Commodity Index Is Like the Other

Today, commodity indices attempt to replicate the return available to holding long positions in agricultural, metal, energy, or livestock investment. Since returns on a fully invested contract reflect the investment in the underlying deliverable, commodity indices based on the returns of future contracts offer an efficient means to obtain commodity exposure. There are a number of commodity indices currently on the market, however, for the equity market where the S&P 500 is king, in the commodity index world the S&P GSCI rules. Yet, just because it rules does not mean it should reign or that other index-based commodity products may not offer alternative solutions. In recent years, a number of additional commodity indices have been introduced (e.g., Deutsche Bank), which have various degrees of a more active component in determining the allocation across various commodities. Commodity indices may differ in a number of ways as well, including the commodities that make up the index, the weightings of the individual commodities, and a number of operational trading issues (e.g., roll period, rebalancing, etc.). Whatever one says about one commodity-based index product may not be true about another. While there may be few myths about their relative performances, the fact that they all purport to offer commodity returns under different investing procedures will certainly lead to misconceptions.

Myth 5.2: Commodities Provide a Natural Diversifier to Traditional Assets (Stocks and Bonds)

Here is the good news and here is the bad news: The concept of a natural diversifier often refers to the idea that the return movement of a particular investment will consistently offer positive (or negative) returns when the other asset performs poorly (or well). The problem is that because many commodities do not have a long-term positive expected rate of return (except for certain commodities that have supply constraint, as discussed previously and for which returns move more randomly above and below zero) the natural return may be regarded as near zero. An analysis could reveal a low correlation between the commodity and a stock or bonds return simply because the commodity has no consistent return pattern. The commodity could be called a diversifier in the same way a U.S. Treasury bond would be identified—a low expected return and no correlation with risky assets. We recommend carefully considering a zero expected return asset as a natural diversifier to any other asset.

Myth 5.3: Commodities Do Not Have to Be Part of an Investor's Portfolio If One Holds Commodity Stocks

For many investors, holding equity in a commodity-based publicly traded firm is regarded as an alternative to direct commodity investment. Although the cash flows of commodity-linked firms are tied to the commodities they produce, research shows only moderate to low correlation of a commodity firm's equity returns and the stand-alone return of its underlying commodity. This is expected. Corporate earnings are impacted by a number of factors (e.g., hedging cash flows and operational risks) that do not directly impact the underlying commodity prices. Moreover, depending on the construction of the commodity index, each commodity-based index product may have sources of return (e.g., contango and backwardation) that are generally not directly accessible through equity investment in similar commodity-based publicly traded firms. In rare cases, when the commodity firm is a direct pass-through for the commodity and for which the commodity price is above the firms' breakeven, such that the increase in commodity prices leads to a direct increase in firm cash flow, equity in a commodity firm may be a substitute for the underlying commodity. In most cases, one thing is not like the other.

Myth 5.4: Commodity Indices Are Similar to Equity Indices

An index is an index is an index? Unfortunately, no. In fact, commodity indices may be regarded as derivative products to the extent that they are constructed from investment primarily in futures contracts. Futures contracts are a zero-sum game as discussed in the CTA section. So one may conclude that long-bias commodity indices, unlike equity indices, may not be expected to offer a unique positive expected return similar to investment in an equity index. In contrast, the return to investing in commodity indices may come from other return forms (e.g., roll return, active management in the contract design) as well as the maturity of the futures contracts held. To the degree that they are the same, long-dated-based (i.e., long maturity) commodity indices may have performance more similar to commodity-based equity firms, because for those contracts, the underlying supply is still waiting to be made available, such that future changes in price will affect both the index and a related firm. In contrast, the short-term maturity-based commodity indices may have performance more similar to firms that are involved in short-term shipping or storage.

Myth 5.5: Commodity Investment Is Speculation

In recent years, there have been concerns that certain financial investment in various commodity products was an improper use of commodities. In general, there is little evidence that the demand for commodities via various commodity financial products, including ETFs, have fundamentally impacted commodity markets. However, even more important is the fact that simple ownership of a commodity is not indicative of a pure speculator. *Speculation* is a loaded word. Although it is normally referred to in the context of individuals who trade futures contracts—not commercial hedgers—individuals or institutions who use commodity-based products as a means to diversify the risk of their asset portfolios may or may not be regarded as speculators.

CHAPTER **6**

Private Equity

Its True Value?

The first private equity (PE) transaction was probably initiated with the advancement of seed for some percentage of a crop to be grown, or some similar event. At its modern core, PE is a broad category that includes a range of direct investments that are made generally through structured general-partner and limited-partner governance vehicles. In past chapters, we have described the evolution of the modern investment management business and traced its origins to Markowitz and his work some 60 years ago. The inception of modern PE can be traced back to this period as well. While there is no single definition of PE, for many, modern PE began in the mid-1940s (e.g., American Research and Development Corporation and J.H. Whitney & Co.). However, it was not until the 1960s that PE began to be commonly formed as limited partnerships, consisting of a general managing partner and passive limited partners, who provide much of the capital. Also introduced was the compensation structure for the general partner (i.e., an annual management fee of 1 to 2 percent and a performance fee typically representing up to 20 percent of the profits).

As in any maturing asset class, the road to the current forms and use of PE has not been smooth. The 1980s gave rise to management and leverage buyouts and the terms *corporate raiders* and *hostile takeovers*. In the 1980s, it was estimated that there were nearly 2,000 leveraged buyouts valued in excess of USD 250 million. However, the leverage buyout form of PE was not destined to become the dominant form. The market crash of 1987 coupled with the collapse of Drexel Burnham Lambert—the leverage buyout model's primary architect—and the ensuing extraordinary rise in interest rates led to PE firms refocusing from early stage investments (e.g., venture capital) to more advanced, mature companies (e.g., PE).

Coincident with the growth of the U.S. economy following the economic slowdown in the late 1980s and early 1990s, the PE industry again began to grow, from approximately USD 20.8 billion of investor commitments in 1992 to USD 305.7 billion in 2000. However, just as the market crash in 1987 and the following economic slowdown hampered the then venture capital and PE industries, the collapse of the Internet bubble in early 2000 again forced retrenchment in the industry. It has been estimated that investment monies in the venture capital industry declined to about half of their all-time high by 2003.

In some ways, the 2000 dot-com bubble set the stage for the birth of the modern PE industry. For many PE firms, the collapse of certain parts of the industry resulted in new opportunities for those that survived. U.S. economic policy immediately changed, both to provide lower interest rates and to stimulate economic growth. Many PE and venture capital funds took advantage of these lower rates and improved economic conditions to increase buyout and initial investment. In addition, the changing regulatory environment forced increased costs on existing and developing firms. These changes encouraged some firms to go private and increased the need for mature management supervision of smaller nonpublic firms. The collapse of parts of the industry in the early part of the decade led to increased interest in the development of the secondary transaction market, as individuals sought to reduce their exposures in certain industries. Finally, the improved equity market of the mid-decade led to additional means for PE investors to capture the increased worth of their investments, including taking the private firm public through an initial public offering (IPO). The development of secondary and public markets also helped in the development of publicly listed PE firms and PE funds. Unfortunately, the development of these new investment and exit opportunities hit a wall similar to the one the industry hit in 1987. The worsening market conditions in 2007 and the credit freeze of October 2008 resulted in increased costs of financing, reduced expected cash flows to any new deal, and the collapse of the IPO market as an exit opportunity for existing deals.

The changing nature of PE, as well as the changing economic patterns that led to its historical rise and fall over the past 60 years, has led to a struggle with PE's place in differing portfolios. In large part this struggle is about the proper definition of PE and, as such, determining its true risk and reward properties. For PE, perhaps more than for any other investment asset class, past is not prologue. This is extremely difficult in an investment industry for which past performance is often a benchmark for how investors regard or determine future return and risk opportunities. As discussed in this chapter, PE occupies a very broad range of strategies and possible risk and return alternatives. In addition, if there is a common theme, that theme lies in the almost total lack of transparency in how holdings are valued and, as a consequence, what investors will receive and when. In a previous book,

The New Science of Asset Allocation, we pointed out that on a quarter-to-quarter and year-to-year basis, investors receive performance numbers based on the subjective valuation of the PE sponsor. We also discussed the fact that there is almost no way for an investor to conduct independent verification or analysis of these returns, and that the true economic value of this investment could not be known until a particular fund had made its final distribution. This final distribution is often five to seven years into the future. As a consequence, a PE investment requires a tremendous leap of faith by investors and, even more so than other strategies, a keen appreciation of the sponsor's business model and long-term track record.

More important, the asset allocation decision is by definition blurred because the subjective accounting returns during the course of the investment may differ wildly from the actual returns. Large U.S. public pension funds have witnessed their internal actuarial assumptions turned on their head because the expected return of venture capital investments within their portfolios did not live up to their billing. Yet this has not stopped these larger public funds from increasing their allocations to PE in what we perceive as a vain attempt to use the illusion of historical performance to offset the 7.5 to 8.0 percent actuarial assumption required to keep taxes from rising or benefits from decreasing. For the most part, public pension plans make asset allocation decisions based on the historical performance of asset classes. These pension plans then have actuarial assumptions that provide a basis for the expected growth of the pension plan. The state government's annual contributions and workers' benefits are tied to this assumption, irrespective of the actual return of the pension plan. Thus, there is a bias to move toward asset classes that have historically shown greater returns. Such an approach is completely counter to the Securities and Exchange Commission admonishment against using past performance as the basis for an investment decision.

The business model and long-term track record, however, are just the surface of the story. Many PE firms have multiple vehicles, often totaling 50 or more for the larger funds or institutions. It is not unusual for the performance of a successful fund to be put forward as representative of the firm's body of work while ignoring the less-than-stellar performance of others within the firm's family of funds. It is also not unusual to find that the professionals responsible for the returns of those outperforming funds are no longer associated with the firm and have moved on to start their own firms or to find more financially lucrative opportunities. This is particularly true within large financial institutions. Similarly, it is not unusual for firms that have done well in one area of the economy to move into the next hot area without a substantial grounding in the economics or business strategies of that area. By example, the economics of health care (a broad category with many subparts) and the economics of technology (again, with its different subparts) are fundamentally different and require different skill sets.

A recent meeting in London revealed that a number of the larger and more reputable firms share the concern that their industry is moving away from providing fair information, transparency, and returns to their investors into one of asset gathering. The chief concern is that more money is being raised because of the historical returns of this asset class than can be meaningfully deployed going forward. Moreover, there is concern that asset gatherers, rather than being true PE firms, behave like remoras—fish that attach themselves to larger hosts for safety and transport while feeding on the hosts' leftover fragments—and, as a result, are severely hurting the industry, as their primary business model is simply to buy the deals of others while charging fees that are inconsistent with their body of work. These firms are typically characterized as "lifestyle" firms, in that their true business is to support the current lifestyle of a few partners and not necessarily to provide significant returns for their clients. Typically, these firms rarely generate investment returns greater than two times the investment capital on any single investment and in most instances the total portfolio of investments after fees is breakeven at best; current assets under management rarely exceed USD 500 million; and there is a new set of limited partners within each successive fund, because limited partners exit as soon as they are able. In contrast, firms such as Pantheon Financial Ltd—a fee-based investment manager out of London—and Alternative Asset Risk Management (AARM)—a fee-based firm out of Boston specializing in the evaluation and measurement of PE risk—are working to bring transparency and structure to the business, yet they seem to be small voices against the screams of past performance, no matter how dicey that performance. Beyond attempting to interject additional transparency into this asset class, the common denominator of these firms is that they are fee based and thus have aligned their interests with those of their clients.

The issue of value added is particularly troublesome in the PE fund of funds business. The business model of charging a 2 percent management fee and an incentive fee is all but dead given the lack of returns that this model has provided clients over the past decade. At a recent trade seminar called PartnerConnect, participants estimated that of the 400 or so PE firms in existence today, 200 have dead business models, and the remaining are struggling to survive. Of particular interest is that, of those that are struggling, most are tied to banks or private wealth organizations in which the party responsible for due diligence and advising is also the money manager. This is not a prescription for impartial analysis, which probably explains why they have not joined their brethren in death. The future model for this group has to be one of the following: (1) managed accounts, a model that is more aligned to customizing to clients' risk and reward needs but requires a great deal of technical and professional support not heretofore required in this area; (2) specialized fund of funds with specialist alpha focus, which again requires a great deal of technical and professional support not previously seen in this segment of the industry; or (3) coinvestment funds, for which there is no additional layer of fees, but this requires work in deal negotiation and the ability to be something more than a remora to the host PE specialist.

As this chapter searches for transparency and fairness for the investor in PE, it first looks to definitions. What is PE, and what are its different subclasses? It then examines the different subclasses and their associated indices in determining sources of return and risk. Next, it provides certain observations relating to the performance of PE in different portfolios and how an investor could possibly use this asset class. Finally, it explores elements of due diligence and some of the myths and misconceptions surrounding investments in this area.

In this chapter, the risk and return characteristics of PE investments are reviewed, as well as the risk and return implications of adding PE to purely traditional stock and bond portfolios and portfolios composed of stocks, bonds, and various alternative investments. The results suggest that although PE investments differ widely, traditional PE indices may be better viewed as return-enhancement vehicles to traditional equity-biased portfolios. Although certain PE investments may provide diversification and return benefits, its general comovement with other asset classes suggests that the impact of adding PE to an existing stock and bond portfolio or to an existing mixed traditional (i.e., stock and bond) and alternative (i.e., hedge fund, commodity trading advisor [CTA], real estate, and commodity) portfolio must be considered carefully. It is also important to point out that the sector has undergone dramatic transformations in recent years. For example, several PE firms have undertaken public offerings, with their performance over time potentially reflecting the performance of other public equity-oriented vehicles.

INVESTING IN PRIVATE EQUITY

PE is often viewed as ownership in private or nonpublicly traded business. These ownership stakes may take various forms (e.g., proprietorship, partnership, and other corporate or legal entities). PE is viewed by some as including the entire range of nonpublic investments, from the early stage through the final stage of investment. For others, PE is limited to that section of the nonpublic investment process in which capital is soon to be raised via public offering. Often PE is discussed within various distinct stages or forms of investment. These include angel investors (generally seed capital), venture capital (i.e., start-up and first stage), leveraged buyouts, mezzanine investing, and distressed debt investing (i.e., late-stage investing). The long-term goal of many PE investments is to have the enterprise sold to other investors through private sales, mergers, or IPOs. Investors in PE should also be aware that the nonpublic nature of the PE holdings makes valuation of the underlying shares difficult. Valuations can be very subjective, with an investor having no means of comparison. Often the basis for valuation is either accounting (e.g., risk-adjusted cash flows) or various relative value assessments (e.g., comparisons to existing publicly traded firms). All of these approaches include a large discretionary factor on those providing the valuation assessments. In addition, the level of investor control has a direct effect on relative value among the various ownership groups. We will discuss each of these sectors as well as available indices and investment products.[1]

Angel Investors

Angel investing is often referred to as capital that is raised at the initial stage of company creation. This capital is often provided even before the initial product or organization structure is finalized. Given the lack of information as to the future profitability of such ventures, the expected risk and hence, expected return, on such angel investing is high. Moreover, future dilution issues, as additional capital is required, form a vital part of the initial operating agreements.

Venture Capital

Venture capital involves the financing of start-up companies that often do not have a sufficient historical track record to be able to raise capital from traditional outside sources. Often these companies lack tangible assets and may not be expected to generate positive earnings in the near term. Venture capitalists often finance these companies by acquiring senior equity stakes, with the expectation that these companies will ultimately be acquired by other PE firms that focus on late-stage opportunities, acquired by competitors, or acquired by public-offering candidates. Many investors and industry observers have expressed concern about the potential returns and risks relating to venture capital in the technology sector. These investors have noted a second Internet bubble, in which valuations are more in line with hopes and dreams than any real economic activity. In fact, it has recently come to light that venture capital investors in this area discourage firms from having or reporting revenues, because valuations then become tied to a tangible basis rather than to the expectations of their promoters.

Leveraged Buyouts

Leveraged buyouts (LBOs) are a way to take a publicly traded company private. Buyouts of companies in which control is concentrated in the hands of management are often called *management buyouts*. The purchase of the outstanding equity is usually financed with bonds issued by the corporation or loans from banks, which are often secured by the assets or cash flows of the acquired or the acquiring company.

Mezzanine and Distressed Debt Investing

Mezzanine and distressed debt investing can take various forms and serve various purposes. The distinctions between mezzanine and distressed debt can often become blurred. For example, mezzanine debt is often used in an LBO; however, the mezzanine debt can become distressed debt if the company's financial situation deteriorates following the LBO. Notwithstanding such a development, mezzanine debt can offer some portfolio enhancement features not found in other areas of PE (as suggested by the results in Exhibits 6.6 through 6.9). Mezzanine investors, such as Kohlberg Kravis Roberts, have shown that the standard deviation of private equity returns can be lowered by including this asset class within an overall allocation. This lowered risk experience is the result of three factors. First, mezzanine investing has been shown to have a lower loss ratio than other PE investments. Second, interest earned on mezzanine investing has historically been in the mid to high teens, higher than returns experienced by private equity over the past ten years or so. Finally, an indirect yet substantial benefit is that within mezzanine investing the "J" curve effect is mitigated because cash flows commence at the onset of an investment.

Private Investment in Public Equity

Although technically not a PE strategy in the strictest sense, it is worth mentioning private investment in public equity (PIPE). In PIPE investments, capital may be raised by direct placement of security issues. There are two forms of PIPE: traditional and structured. Traditional PIPEs use common or preferred equity, whereas structured PIPEs issue convertible debt. This type of financing gained some prominence during the financial crisis, as investment banking firms such as Morgan Stanley, Goldman Sachs, and Citigroup used structured preferred equity from investors Mitsubishi, Warren Buffett, and Prince Alwaleed bin Talal, respectively, to shore up their balance sheets.

As noted earlier, PE is a broad term for any type of equity investment in a company that is generally not listed on a stock exchange. Holders of PE investments will typically realize value in the form of capital gains through a sale to, or merger with, a competitor in the same sector, a sale to another PE investor, or an eventual flotation on the stock market.

PE is generally regarded as an investment that offers investors the opportunity to achieve superior long-term returns compared to those of traditional stock and bond investment vehicles. The long-term returns of PE are said to provide a premium over the performance of public equities. This premium is largely caused by PE's participation in privately held companies, which are inaccessible to traditional investors. The basis for returns to PE is similar to that for traditional stock and bond investment—that is, a claim on long-term earnings, a return premium for providing capital to an illiquid and risky investment, and a positive alpha generated from unique trading strategies or private information. However, private investment vehicles have a net asset value that is often determined as an internal appraisal value, not by a public market. Actual returns are often measured as an internal rate of return (IRR) or cash disbursements relative to capital investment. These cash flows may be lower at the initial stage than at later stages of the capital investment (known as the *J-curve effect*). It is also important to point out that private investors are often active participants in the management of their investments.

PRIVATE EQUITY STYLES AND BENCHMARKS

There is a range of additional PE indices available. Empirical results may differ based on which performance measures are used. An example of a non-investable PE index is one published by Cambridge Associates (CA). The CA U.S. Venture Capital Index is based on IRR data compiled on funds representing more than three-fourths of venture capital dollars raised since 1981, and nearly two-thirds of leveraged buyout, subordinated debt, and special-situation partnerships since 1986. Although this index provides information on how the PE sectors are performing, an investor cannot directly place monies in this index and realize the reported returns. An increasing number of investable PE indices are being published, including those by LPX GmbH (LPX) and Standard & Poor's (S&P).

The characteristics of the non-investable and investable PE indices used in this chapter are as follows:

- **CA LLC U.S. Private Equity Index:** An end-to-end calculation based on data compiled from 944 U.S. PE funds (i.e., buyout, growth equity, PE, and energy and mezzanine funds), including fully liquidated partnerships, formed between 1986 and 2011. Pooled end-to-end return, net of fees, expenses, and carried interest.

- **CA LLC U.S. Venture Capital Index:** Based on data compiled from 1,334 U.S. venture capital funds, including fully liquidated partnerships, formed between 1981 and 2010. Internal rates of return are net of fees, expenses, and carried interest. Vintage-year funds formed since 2009 are too young to have produced meaningful returns.
- **Private Equity Index (PE Index):** Based on monthly returns that are based on the S&P Private Equity Index from December 2003 onward. For the period prior to December 2003, firms which were listed in the June 2007 report were used to create an equal weighted monthly returns private equity index back to 1991.
- **LPX50:** The LPX50 is a global index consisting of the 50 largest liquid listed private equity (LPE) companies covered by LPX.
- **LPX Major Market:** The LPX Major Market represents the most actively traded LPE companies covered by LPX.
- **LPX Buyout:** The LPX Buyout represents the most actively traded LPE companies covered by LPX whose business model consists mainly in the appropriation of buyout capital or in the investment in such funds.
- **LPX Composite:** The LPX Composite is a broad global LPE index whose number of constituents is not limited.
- **LPX Europe:** The LPX Europe represents the most actively traded LPE companies covered by LPX that are listed on a European exchange.
- **LPX America:** The LPX America represents the most actively traded LPE companies covered by LPX that are listed on an exchange in North America.
- **LPX Venture:** The LPX Venture represents the most actively traded LPE companies covered by LPX whose core business lays mainly in the provision of venture capital or in the investment in venture capital funds.
- **LPX Direct:** The LPX Direct represents the largest liquid LPE companies covered by LPX that mainly pursue a direct PE investment strategy. An LPE company is not an eligible candidate for the LPX Direct if the sum of the indirect PE investment portfolio and the valuation of the PE fund management exceed 20 percent of the net assets of the company.
- **LPX Indirect:** The LPX Indirect represents the largest liquid LPE companies covered by LPX that mainly pursue an indirect PE investment strategy.
- **LPX UK:** The LPX UK represents the largest liquid LPE companies covered by LPX that are listed on an exchange in the United Kingdom.
- **LPX Mezzanine:** The LPX Mezzanine represents the most actively traded LPE companies covered by LPX whose business model consists mainly in the appropriation of mezzanine capital or in the investment in such funds.

BASIC SOURCES OF RISK AND RETURN

In recent years, traditional forms of PE investment (e.g., IPOs, secondary sales) have met resistance in the difficult global credit and equity markets. As a result, many PE firms are struggling to justify their existence against accepted benchmarks of performance—that is, cash flows on initial investment and measured internal rates of return. PE returns are often unique to the time of investment and the form of the investment vehicle. Once a firm puts investor money to work, it often does not have the ability to reallocate out of existing investments into new investments. If market conditions change and new investment opportunities are available, new funding is often required for a new investment vehicle. Two PE funds from the same family may perform differently over time based merely on their date of inception and the unique holdings of each fund based on the investment opportunities unique to that period.

PERFORMANCE: FACT AND FICTION

For some, the performance of PE is based primarily on the unique business opportunities corresponding to the ability of discretionary managers to select long-term investment opportunities whose performance may not be directly related to general market factors. For others, the underlying ability of PE to meet performance goals is partially dependent on the underlying strength of the economy as reflected in equity prices. To these latter investors, the important part of the term *private equity* is the equity and not the private. One of the principal problems in the analysis of PE is the quality of the data, which supposedly reflects the changing value of a PE investment. In the following sections, we provide evidence not only on the stand-alone risks of various public PE investments, but on the interrelationships of the public PE indices and various traditional (e.g., equity and fixed-income market) and alternative asset classes using an index of publicly traded equity firms. As in previous chapters, we examine these markets over a broad time period, shorter time intervals (e.g., annual), and their relative performance in extreme market conditions. Public PE indices are shown to have a high correlation with the comparison equity-based traditional and alternative investments and therefore may be regarded as more of a return enhancer than a risk diversifier to equity-based portfolios. The level of return enhancement, of course, partially depends on the level of PE risk and expected returns. Results show that in periods of extreme equity market returns most publicly traded PE firms have similar return patterns; that is, falling in down equity markets and providing positive returns in up equity markets. Again, to some this is expected, but investors may not wish take return and risk performance from extended time frames or from public PE performance as a basis for PE investment. There remains an unanswered question: the performance of publicly traded PE firms may not necessarily reflect the performance of *accounting*-based PE funds. At the end, PE should provide the potential for unique return opportunities based not on systematic return opportunities with the general equity market but on nonsystematic firm-based opportunities. Given the randomness of such firm success, it is not surprising that much of PE captures overall generic market returns patterns in contrast to the "black swan" of individual firm success. At the end, investors may have to live with some issues simply being unanswered.

RETURN AND RISK CHARACTERISTICS

In this section, we review the performance of a self-constructed PE index[2] with a range of traditional stock and bond indices as well as a number of alternative investment indices (e.g., real estate, commodities, CTAs, and hedge funds) over the period 1994–2011. In later sections, we focus on the index's performance in various subperiods. For this period, as shown in Exhibit 6.1, the PE index exhibited higher annualized standard deviation, or volatility (28.1 percent), than that of the S&P 500 (15.7 percent). Depending on the background of the investor, this may be surprising. Many investors who are familiar with IRR-based PE returns have become familiar with reported PE volatility near or below that of the S&P 500. For other investors, PE evokes feelings of high return expectations, as well as risk above that seen in the public equity markets. Even at the individual publicly traded PE firm, research[3] has shown that the volatility of the average publicly traded PE firm has volatility similar to that of the stocks in the Dow Jones Industrial Average. Over the period of analysis, the PE index also reported a higher annualized total return (8.0 percent) than that of the S&P 500 (7.7 percent). The lower information ratio (i.e., return-to-risk ratio) of the PE index relative to the S&P 500 may not reflect either the return-to-risk trade-off in other periods or the current expected return-to-risk trade-off. For example, as shown in Exhibit 6.1, for the period analyzed, the PE index has a relatively high correlation (0.74) with the S&P 500 and a low correlation (−0.03) with the BarCap U.S. Aggregate Index. The relatively high correlation of PE index with stock returns may lead investors to question PE as a primary means of diversification for equity-dominated portfolios.

The relatively high correlation between the PE index and a range of financial assets (e.g., real estate) may indicate that a portfolio of PE may

EXHIBIT 6.1 Private Equity and Asset Class Performance

Stock, U.S. and Private Equity Performance	Private Equity	S&P 500	BarCap U.S. Government	BarCap U.S. Aggregate	BarCap U.S. Corporate High Yield
Annualized total return	8.0%	7.7%	6.1%	6.3%	7.3%
Annualized standard deviation	28.1%	15.7%	4.4%	3.8%	9.4%
Information ratio	0.28	0.49	1.39	1.67	0.78
Maximum drawdown	−80.4%	−50.9%	−5.4%	−5.1%	−33.3%
Correlation with private equity index	1.00	0.74	−0.21	−0.03	0.64

Alternative Asset Performance and Private Equity	Private Equity	S&P GSCI	CISDM CTA Equal Weighted	FTSE NAREIT	CISDM Equal Weighted Hedge Fund
Annualized total return	8.0%	4.8%	8.1%	9.7%	10.4%
Annualized standard deviation	28.1%	22.5%	8.7%	19.9%	7.7%
Information ratio	0.28	0.21	0.94	0.49	1.36
Maximum drawdown	−80.4%	−67.6%	−8.7%	−67.9%	−21.7%
Correlation with private equity index	1.00	0.34	−0.07	0.56	0.77

Period of analysis: 1994 to 2011.

provide only minimal reduction in the risk (i.e., standard deviation) of a stock or a multi-asset portfolio whose volatility is dominated by equities. As shown in Exhibit 6.2, adding a small portion of the PE index (10.0 percent) to stock and bond Portfolio A yields Portfolio B with a similar annualized return (7.6 percent) and standard deviation (9.5 percent) as the pure stock and bond portfolio (see Portfolio A, with an annualized return of 7.3 percent and a standard deviation of 8.2 percent). Similarly, adding PE to a portfolio that contains a range of traditional and alternative assets results in Portfolio D that exhibits a somewhat higher return (8.1 percent) and somewhat higher standard deviation (9.3 percent) to those of Portfolio C (7.9 percent and 7.8 percent, respectively), which does not contain PE.

The ability of the PE index to provide superior return opportunities (albeit with higher risk) to other investment assets on a stand-alone basis or as additions to a sample portfolio is indicative of the ability of PE to

EXHIBIT 6.2 Private Equity and Multi-Asset Class Portfolio Performance

Portfolios	A	B	C	D
Annualized returns	7.3%	7.6%	7.9%	8.1%
Standard deviation	8.2%	9.5%	7.8%	9.3%
Information ratio	0.90	0.80	1.01	0.87
Maximum drawdown	−27.1%	−35.2%	−28.7%	−36.4%
Correlation with private equity	0.70		0.74	
Portfolio A	Equal weights S&P 500 and BarCap U.S. Aggregate			
Portfolio B	90% Portfolio A and 10% private equity			
Portfolio C	75% Portfolio A and 25% CTA/commodities/real estate/hedge funds			
Portfolio D	90% Portfolio C and 10% private equity			

Period of analysis: 1994 to 2011.

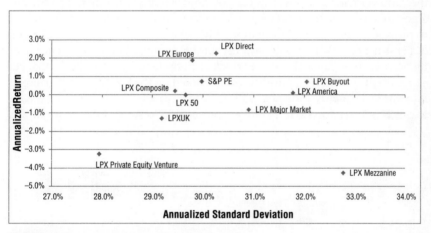

EXHIBIT 6.3 Private Equity Index Performance
Period of analysis: 2004 to 2011.

provide the potential for a positive return-to-risk trade-off over a lengthy period of time. However, the PE index used in this analysis is only one of several composite PE indices. Other PE indices may provide different performance results. Exhibit 6.3 shows the return and risk performance over the 2004–2011 period for various PE trading subindices, which differ from the composite PE index. Equally important, results in Exhibits 6.8 and 6.9 illustrate that individual PE indices report a relatively high correlation with the S&P 500, and a relatively low correlation with the BarCap U.S. Aggregate.

Simply reporting historical returns, however, may not capture many of the return and risk characteristics of PE over unique financial or economic conditions.

THE MYTH OF AVERAGE: PRIVATE EQUITY INDEX
RETURN IN EXTREME MARKETS

The results in the previous section illustrate the performance of various PE indices and how they compare to traditional and alternative investment indices over an eight-year period (2004–2011). The period since 2004 reflects more current PE investment approaches than those conducted in the 1990s or during the period of the dot-com bubble. The results indicate the return or risk benefits of PE as a stand-alone investment or as an addition to an existing traditional investment portfolio or a portfolio of traditional and alternative investments. However, the relative stand-alone performance of the various PE indices as well as the potential benefits when they are added to a portfolio of financial assets may differ in various subperiods in comparison to their performance over the entire period of analysis. This is especially true in periods of market stress, when certain PE strategies may experience dramatic volatility, particularly in periods of poor equity-market performance.

Exhibit 6.4 shows monthly returns ranked on the S&P 500 and grouped into three segments (bottom, middle, and top) of 32 months each, with average returns for each PE index presented. Results show that the PE

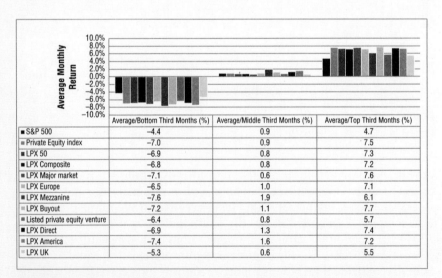

	Average/Bottom Third Months (%)	Average/Middle Third Months (%)	Average/Top Third Months (%)
■ S&P 500	−4.4	0.9	4.7
■ Private Equity index	−7.0	0.9	7.5
■ LPX 50	−6.9	0.8	7.3
■ LPX Composite	−6.8	0.8	7.2
■ LPX Major market	−7.1	0.6	7.6
■ LPX Europe	−6.5	1.0	7.1
■ LPX Mezzanine	−7.6	1.9	6.1
■ LPX Buyout	−7.2	1.1	7.7
■ Listed private equity venture	−6.4	0.8	5.7
■ LPX Direct	−6.9	1.3	7.4
■ LPX America	−7.4	1.6	7.2
■ LPX UK	−5.3	0.6	5.5

EXHIBIT 6.4   Private Equity Indices: Monthly Returns Ranked on S&P 500 Period of analysis: 2004 to 2011.

indices had more negative returns than the S&P 500 in the worst S&P 500 return months and provided higher positive returns than the S&P 500 in the best S&P 500 return months. The under-performance of PE relative to the S&P 500 in the worst S&P 500 return months and the outperformance of PE relative to the S&P 500 in the best S&P 500 return months may be caused in part by the use of public PE in this analysis. Public PE generally have betas above 1 such that they would be expected to underperform in negative equity market environments and outperform in periods in which the equity markets perform well. Notably, the results are not similar for fixed income. Exhibit 6.5 shows monthly PE returns ranked on the BarCap U.S. Aggregate Index and grouped into three segments (bottom, middle, and top) of 32 months each, with average returns for each PE index presented. Results show that the PE indices had negative returns greater than the negative BarCap U.S. Aggregate returns in the worst BarCap U.S. Aggregate return months, provided positive returns greater than the BarCap U.S. Aggregate return in the middle BarCap U.S. Aggregate months, and lower returns than the BarCap U.S. Aggregate in the top BarCap U.S. Aggregate return months. One reason for the results is the unique period of analysis; that is, 2004–2011 contains a significant period over which fixed income performed well (post 2008 crash) and in which financial based equities have not. Thus to the degree that PE is regarded by investors as a similar investment to various financial securities, its public trading vehicles may not reflect the performance of private investment vehicles.

PRIVATE EQUITY ANNUAL PERFORMANCE

In the previous section, the average performance of the PE index and sub-indices over the best and worst performing equity and fixed-income environments was discussed. The representative PE index was shown to provide for equities little potential diversification benefits in the worst months as well as in the best months of each index. In this section, we provide a review of the relative performance by year of the PE index and the LPX Composite indices and sub-indices, the S&P 500, and the BarCap U.S. Aggregate. Results in Exhibit 6.6 show that over the entire period, the annual returns of the S&P 500 and the various PE indices differed in many years. However, in six of the eight years, the PE index and the S&P 500 moved in the same direction. In contrast, the PE index and the BarCap U.S. Aggregate moved in the same direction in only five of the eight years. These results again indicate the importance of viewing PE performance over short subperiods rather than viewing it based strictly on its performance over the whole 8-year period.

Exhibits 6.7, 6.8, and 6.9 show the standard deviations and correlations of the PE index and the various LPX indices against those of the S&P 500 and

Average Monthly Return

4.0%
3.0%
2.0%
1.0%
0.0%
-1.0%
-2.0%
-3.0%
-4.0%

	Average/Bottom Third Months (%)	Average/Middle Third Months (%)	Average/Top Third Months (%)
■ BarCap U.S. aggregate	-0.6	0.5	1.5
■ Private equity index	-1.9	3.1	0.1
■ LPX50	-2.0	3.0	0.2
■ LPX Composite	-2.1	3.0	0.3
■ LPX Major market	-2.3	3.0	0.3
■ LPX Europe	-1.6	2.7	0.5
■ LPX Mezzanine	-3.2	2.7	1.0
■ LPX Buyout	-2.3	3.0	0.8
■ Listed private equity venture	-1.5	2.5	-0.8
■ LPX Direct	-1.8·	3.1	0.5
■ LPX America	-2.4	3.2	0.6
■ LPX UK	-1.7	2.6	-0.1

EXHIBIT 6.5 Private Equity Indices: Monthly Returns Ranked on BarCap U.S. Aggregate Period of analysis: 2004 to 2011.

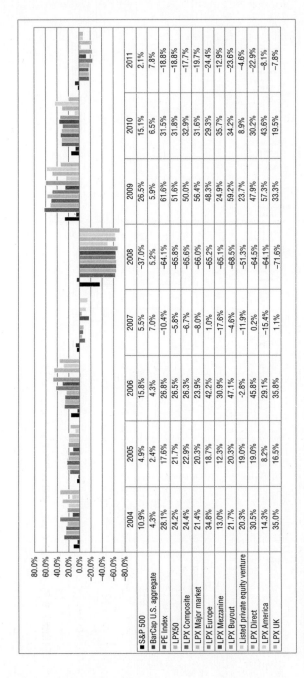

	2004	2005	2006	2007	2008	2009	2010	2011
S&P 500	10.9%	4.9%	15.8%	5.5%	-37.0%	26.5%	15.1%	2.1%
BarCap U.S. aggregate	4.3%	2.4%	4.3%	7.0%	5.2%	5.9%	6.5%	7.8%
PE Index	28.1%	17.6%	26.8%	-10.4%	-64.1%	61.6%	31.5%	-18.8%
LPX50	24.2%	21.7%	26.5%	-5.8%	-65.8%	51.6%	31.8%	-18.8%
LPX Composite	24.4%	22.9%	26.3%	-6.7%	-65.6%	50.0%	32.9%	-17.7%
LPX Major market	21.4%	20.3%	23.9%	-8.0%	-66.0%	56.4%	31.6%	-19.7%
LPX Europe	34.8%	18.7%	42.2%	1.0%	-65.2%	48.3%	29.3%	-24.4%
LPX Mezzanine	13.0%	12.3%	30.9%	-17.6%	-65.1%	24.9%	35.7%	-12.9%
LPX Buyout	21.7%	20.3%	47.1%	-4.6%	-68.5%	59.2%	34.2%	-23.6%
Listed private equity venture	20.3%	19.0%	-2.8%	-11.9%	-51.3%	23.7%	8.9%	-4.6%
LPX Direct	30.5%	19.0%	45.8%	0.2%	-64.5%	47.9%	30.2%	-22.9%
LPX America	14.3%	8.2%	29.1%	-15.4%	-64.1%	57.3%	43.6%	-8.1%
LPX UK	35.0%	16.5%	35.8%	1.1%	-71.6%	33.3%	19.5%	-7.8%

EXHIBIT 6.6 Private Equity Indices: Annual Returns

	2004	2005	2006	2007	2008	2009	2010	2011
S&P 500	7.3%	7.9%	5.6%	9.7%	21.0%	22.3%	19.3%	15.9%
BarCap U.S. aggregate	4.0%	3.1%	2.7%	2.6%	6.1%	3.3%	2.9%	2.4%
PE Index	18.3%	11.2%	9.5%	14.9%	38.1%	51.8%	28.1%	27.0%
LPX 50	14.8%	9.6%	10.7%	14.6%	41.1%	49.6%	27.5%	27.4%
LPX Composite	15.0%	9.5%	10.7%	14.5%	40.9%	49.4%	26.9%	26.9%
LPX Major market	15.5%	10.7%	11.4%	15.1%	42.1%	52.3%	29.4%	29.0%
LPX Europe	11.5%	9.7%	11.5%	14.3%	40.0%	50.7%	27.6%	28.6%
LPX Mezzanine	14.2%	9.1%	6.2%	16.3%	52.9%	61.1%	25.4%	21.6%
LPX Buyout	11.9%	7.1%	10.0%	15.9%	44.0%	56.5%	28.6%	28.2%
Listed private equity venture	21.4%	19.2%	19.2%	18.8%	35.5%	46.6%	23.2%	26.0%
LPX Direct	14.2%	8.7%	9.1%	15.8%	41.1%	52.2%	28.3%	27.8%
LPX America	18.5%	10.0%	8.2%	19.2%	50.6%	51.8%	27.7%	25.4%
LPX UK	11.8%	6.9%	9.7%	14.7%	41.4%	52.0%	22.1%	21.7%
LPX America	18.5%	10.0%	8.2%	19.2%	50.6%	51.8%	27.7%	25.4%

EXHIBIT 6.7 Private Equity Indices: Annual Standard Deviations

	2004	2005	2006	2007	2008	2009	2010	2011
BarCap U.S. aggregate	0.06	-0.19	0.28	-0.44	0.35	0.64	-0.58	-0.35
PE Index	0.80	0.71	0.90	0.72	0.84	0.94	0.95	0.98
LPX50 total return	0.83	0.71	0.90	0.69	0.88	0.92	0.93	0.96
LPX Composite total return	0.83	0.69	0.90	0.69	0.89	0.92	0.93	0.96
LPX Major market total return	0.79	0.63	0.89	0.69	0.88	0.93	0.94	0.96
LPX Europe total return	0.87	0.67	0.82	0.49	0.90	0.91	0.87	0.92
LPX Mezzanine total return	0.37	0.58	0.72	0.86	0.72	0.93	0.87	0.95
LPX Buyout total return	0.66	0.71	0.89	0.81	0.84	0.94	0.91	0.95
Listed private equity venture	0.82	0.55	0.82	0.47	0.85	0.85	0.87	0.86
LPX Direct total return	0.82	0.66	0.82	0.76	0.85	0.93	0.92	0.95
LPX America total return	0.53	0.77	0.85	0.87	0.74	0.92	0.93	0.96
LPX UK total return	0.72	0.15	0.59	0.49	0.72	0.79	0.74	0.90

EXHIBIT 6.8 Private Equity Indices: Annual Correlation with S&P 500

	2004	2005	2006	2007	2008	2009	2010	2011
■ S&P 500	0.06	−0.19	0.28	−0.44	0.35	0.64	−0.58	−0.35
■ PE Index	0.45	0.04	0.16	−0.25	0.00	0.53	−0.41	−0.34
■ LPX 50	0.41	0.01	0.14	−0.20	0.14	0.50	−0.38	−0.31
■ LPX Composite	0.45	0.06	0.14	−0.20	0.16	0.50	−0.37	−0.30
■ LPX Major market	0.47	0.13	0.15	−0.20	0.12	0.52	−0.38	−0.32
■ LPX Europe	0.21	−0.25	0.12	−0.11	0.22	0.52	−0.31	−0.27
■ LPX Mezzanine	0.80	0.23	0.34	−0.19	0.12	0.52	−0.31	−0.31
■ LPX Buyout	0.63	−0.04	0.26	−0.20	0.14	0.54	−0.36	−0.34
■ Listed private equity venture	0.14	−0.15	−0.11	−0.18	0.32	0.34	−0.42	−0.28
■ LPX Direct	0.48	−0.08	0.29	−0.25	0.09	0.52	−0.36	−0.34
■ LPX America	0.60	0.11	0.36	−0.24	0.10	0.52	−0.39	−0.36
■ LPX UK	0.20	−0.01	0.25	−0.03	−0.05	0.34	−0.17	−0.17

EXHIBIT 6.9 Private Equity Indices: Annual Correlation with BarCap U.S. Aggregate

the BarCap U.S. Aggregate. Results in Exhibit 6.7 show that the standard deviation of the PE index has remained consistently above that of the S&P 500 and consistently above that of the BarCap U.S. Aggregate. Exhibits 6.8 and 6.9 show that the intra-year correlation between the S&P 500 and the BarCap U.S. Aggregate varies considerably over the years of analysis; however, the relationship between the PE index and other PE indices and the S&P 500 remains fairly stable, especially in recent years. Investors should be aware that results from longer time frames may not reflect results for individual years. We are surprised when we hear marketing presentations that emphasize the widespread diversification benefits of PE. For PE, lengthy periods of analysis may hide more than they reveal. Although composite PE indices generally report consistently high volatility, their correlation with traditional stock and bond markets changes from year to year.

PERFORMANCE IN 2008

In 2008, PE experienced its lowest returns since major databases started tracking. When compared to the S&P 500, PE reported lower returns and higher volatility in 2008. PE also reported lower returns and higher volatility than the BarCap U.S. Aggregate. In 2008, the correlation between the PE index and the S&P 500 was approximately 0.84. This correlation was partially caused by the common decline in valuation in the fall of 2008. In 2008 most PE strategies, like those of traditional asset classes, were negatively impacted by the subprime crisis, the negative equity market performance, and the rise in credit spreads (e.g., decline in high-yield bond returns).

In summary, PE often is used as a term to encompass a number of strategies (e.g., venture capital, mezzanine financing), and the performance of those individual strategies is partially based on their underlying exposure to the markets in which they invest. In addition, there always exists a market condition in which a particular strategy or even, in fact, all strategies, may perform poorly. The actual precipitating event may differ, but in each case, the result is a lack of liquidity and investor demand.

ISSUES IN PRIVATE EQUITY INVESTMENT

As mentioned earlier, PE returns are typically measured from the perspective of an IRR or cash disbursements as a percentage of capital investment.

As shown below, these cash flows may be lower at the initial stage than at later stages of the capital investment (i.e., the J-curve effect):

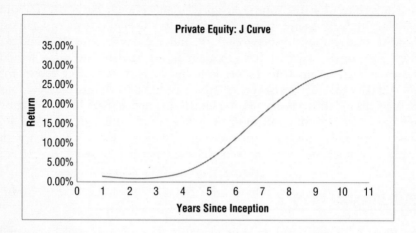

According to Venture Economics, the total investment in venture capital in U.S. companies increased from around $11 billion in 1996 to $102 billion in 2000, then declined to about $28 billion in 2010. In recent years, several forms of publicly traded PE vehicles have come into existence. These include publicly listed investment companies, business development companies, and special purpose acquisition vehicles, which we discuss in more detail in later sections. Our results show that the return streams of these vehicles closely track those of PE indices.

PRIVATE EQUITY INDICES

As we conducted research for this book, we wanted to understand the performance and risk differences, if any, between accounting-based indices and those based on reported market returns. All of our calculations in this section used quarterly data. The results in Exhibit 6.10 show significant deviation in both performance and risk using market-based returns versus accounting-based returns for the construction of PE indices. The CA PE Index (accounting based) realized a higher quarterly return over the period (3.9 percent), than the PE index (market based), at 3.5 percent. The difference in volatility is also evident, with the CA PE Index reporting an quarterly volatility of 5.6 percent, and the market equity-based PE index reporting a quarterly volatility of 18.3 percent. The results in Exhibit 6.10 also report a relatively high volatility for the CA Venture Capital Index.

EXHIBIT 6.10   Private Equity Indices: Comparison Market Price and Accounting Based Indices

	S&P 500	Private Equity Index	Cambridge Venture Capital (CVC)	Cambridge Private Equity (CPE)
Quarterly return	2.3%	3.5%	4.5%	3.9%
Quarterly standard deviation	8.7%	18.3%	13.6%	5.6%
Information ratio	0.13	0.10	0.17	0.34
Correlation with S&P 500	1.00	0.78	0.44	0.73
Correlation with Private Equity Index	0.78	1.00	0.59	0.66
Correlation with CVC	0.44	0.59	1.00	0.68
Correlation with CPE	0.73	0.66	0.68	1.00

The reason for the higher volatility of the CA Venture Capital Index in comparison to the CA PE Index is not evident unless one reviews the relative growth pattern of the two indices over the periods of analysis. As shown in Exhibit 6.11, the CA Venture Capital Index had a rapid rise and fall during the dot-com bubble, which is not evident in the more mature investments often represented in the CA PE Index. However, it

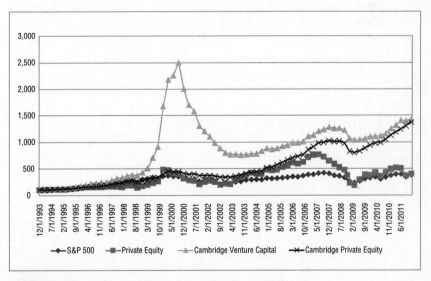

EXHIBIT 6.11   Private Equity Indices: Growth of $100
Period of analysis: 1994 to 2011.

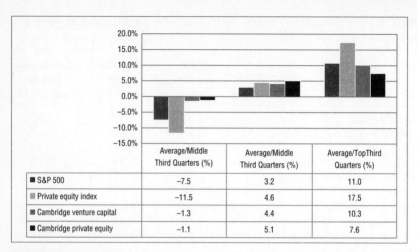

	Average/Middle Third Quarters (%)	Average/Middle Third Quarters (%)	Average/TopThird Quarters (%)
■ S&P 500	−7.5	3.2	11.0
▨ Private equity index	−11.5	4.6	17.5
▨ Cambridge venture capital	−1.3	4.4	10.3
■ Cambridge private equity	−1.1	5.1	7.6

EXHIBIT 6.12   Private Equity Indices: Quarterly Returns Ranked on S&P 500
Period of analysis: 1994 to 2011.

is unclear whether investors should remove those years when estimating
venture capital's future expected performance or if, in fact, it is exactly
those years that may reflect the true benefit of more risky PE investment. In
any event, as shown in Exhibit 6.12, when returns for the various public
private equities are ranked by the S&P 500, results show that the returns of
the public PE indices more closely reflects that of the S&P 500, whereas the
returns of the CA Venture Capital or PE indices have the same directional
returns. The magnitude of the reported returns in down and up S&P 500
markets are not as significant as those reported for the public PE indices.

ALTERNATIVES TO INVESTMENT IN PRIVATE EQUITY

In recent years, there have been numerous developments in the PE space. One
development that deserves special attention is the development of publicly
traded investment products that can be accessed by retail investors. These
typically consist of portfolios of PE firms whose shares are publicly traded.
In addition, there are other vehicles available, such as special-purpose
acquisition corporations (SPACs) and business development companies
(BDCs). Finally, there are investment approaches that attempt to capture
the current return opportunities available through previous PE investments
that have recently gone public by investing in firms represented in various
publicly available IPO indices. These public investment vehicles offer only

a lens by which one can ascertain the underlying profitability of various PE investments. Investors should be aware, as discussed in this chapter, that one of the challenging areas of PE investment is the lack of underlying transparency in most PE investments and in determining the real fair-value determination of PE investments.

Private Equity as Public Equity

Several large investment firms that have significant PE interests have either gone public or filed documents for an IPO. These include Fortress Investment Group, Blackstone Group, and Kohlberg Kravis Roberts & Co. Most recently, the Carlyle Group issued its own IPO. Although met with some degree of fanfare, each of these offerings has traded below its initial offering price for some time. At this point, there are several issues. First, as previously noted, when investors purchase an equity security, what they are really purchasing is a claim on future earnings of a company and not the possible outsized returns of an investor in a PE fund. Next, for the most part, PE firms—and *alternative asset management firms*, as they have sought to redefine themselves—offer a volatile and unpredictable earnings stream because a significant part of their earnings are related to incentive fees. Incentive fees can readily be defined as a percentage of positive returns over a pre-negotiated benchmark. Given this inherent volatility, the market has a tendency to discount their value. To offset this negative valuation, a number of firms within this sector are attempting to change their business models to emphasize and increase annual or management fees while simultaneously reducing or, in some cases, eliminating incentive fees. Whether this changed business model will help or hinder the future performance of the sector is a matter of debate. Finally, there is a strong cross-section of the financial community that believes these public offerings of PE firms are really for the benefit of their internal stakeholders and not the investing public. Although the jury remains out, it is difficult to see how this sector offers a realistic opportunity to participate in the "actual" returns of PE, or how it can be more than an indicative barometer of the sector's growth prospects. One aspect of their performance, however, does not seem open to question. As shown in Exhibit 6.13, the performance of public PE is highly impacted by the underlying movement of equity markets. When the S&P 500 has its worst and best performance, almost 100 percent of the firms in the S&P PE Index have the same directional return movement as the S&P 500. This degree of common comovement, especially in periods of extreme return movement, may make public PE more of a return enhancer to equity than its private market alternatives. Time will tell as to whether the sector can be viewed otherwise in the longer term. In the interim, an investor should

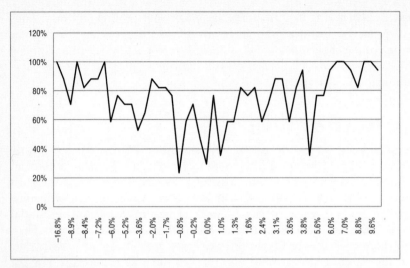

EXHIBIT 6.13 Percent of Public Private Equity Firms with Same Directional Return as S&P 500 (Ranked on S&P 500)
Period of analysis: 2008 to 2011.

be extremely wary of using an investment in this sector as a proxy for PE returns.

Special-Purpose Acquisition Corporations

A special-purpose acquisition corporation, commonly known as a *SPAC*, and formally known as a *development-stage company*, is a corporation formed to raise capital through an IPO of its securities for the funding of an acquisition of an existing operating company or companies. They are listed on various exchanges, such as the American Stock Exchange (AMEX) and the National Association of Securities Dealers Automated Quotations (NASDAQ), as well as on the Over-the-Counter Bulletin Board (OTCBB).

Business-Development Companies

BDCs are closed-end funds whose shares trade publicly on the open market. BDCs are specially regulated retail investment companies that typically make PE-type investments in small- and middle-market companies. Recent BDCs sponsored by PE groups have generally focused on mezzanine and debt investments. BDC managers may charge performance fees and have greater flexibility than do typical mutual funds to use leverage and to engage in certain affiliate transactions with portfolio companies. These companies, generally trade at a discount as do most closed-end mutual funds. In addition, the volatility of the revenue stream coupled with the inability to directly approve the management team—the fund has total discretion in this regard—provides a great deal of uncertainty as to the future return and risk profile. Although it is possible that a select few will provide significant returns for their investors, most simply will not. Investors should be hypersensitive in monitoring these investments, pay attention to changes in investment personnel, and measure the general investment process against historical norms and approaches. These funds are structured to provide the management team complete flexibility and control with little oversight. In this latter regard, an investor should closely review the governing structure and determine if there are sufficient independent directors to maintain the fund's integrity.

A PERSONAL VIEW: ISSUES IN PRIVATE EQUITY INVESTMENT

There is an overriding constant in investment management. Firms sell the product they have; whether it fits within an investor's portfolio or not is totally dependent on the investor. Most firms will not self-select out of making a sale. The corollary to this is that in investment, product development firms often create the product they can sell, not the product they should sell. As investors traverse the differing sectors of PE, they should be reminded that the vast majority of the institutions and people they will come across have only one goal: to sell the product they have. Against this truth, an investor must demand transparent and verifiable information, and examine such information closely prior to making any decision.

PE Analysis: Academic research has often addressed the benefits of PE from the viewpoint of a fundamental valuation of new product opportunities. Research in this area has often failed to consider the unique sources of return to current PE investments as well as the potential risk involved in the changing nature of regulatory and economic conditions driving PE valuation. In addition, this research has tended to treat all PE the same by providing comparative analysis on a vintage-year basis. In sum, the research that has also been adopted by the industry looks to the year of a fund's launch as the sole basis of comparison and makes no effort to understand the underlying assets or those assets' suitability for comparison across funds. Perhaps this approach worked when there were a limited number of PE opportunities and approaches. However, PE investment has undergone dramatic evolution over the past 30 years, from a long-term holding framework, to LBOs, to IPOs, and back to a fundamental cash flow IRR. Today, the changing nature of PE investment is such that comparing PE investments on a vintage-year basis simply does not inform, and investors must more directly consider the fundamental differences in portfolio investments and the sectors, accounting, and management teams associated with those returns. Simply put, vintage year comparisons do not advance a true understanding of a product's contribution to the asset allocation decision.

Distributional Characteristics: The primary reason for PE investment is the degree to which individual PE investments provide unique risk and return characteristics not easily available in other investment vehicles. Analysis of PE distributional characteristics, however, has been impacted by unique periods of investment as well as the form of the return estimation. PE return has been measured using market-based prices as well as vintage-year IRR processes. Depending on the form of the investment measurement as well as the use of comparable investments, the issue is the degree to which the performance reflects similar factors. The high sensitivity of PE to current economic variables requires a more dynamic investment model, which drives the distributional characteristics of most real estate investment. Researchers and reviewers are often enticed by the "more data is better" syndrome; that is, five years of data is good, 10 years is better, 20 years is best. However, in a market partially driven by rapidly changing technological and distribution channels as well as regulatory rules, what is true of the 1980s may have little relevance for 2012.

Micromarket Structure: Recent regulatory and market adjustments to the 2008 financial crisis have fundamentally changed many of the traditional approaches to PE investment. This is especially true in the structured product and debt area. Today, reduced availability of capital, as well as retractions on banking structure and risk exposure, have fundamentally impacted how and where PE capital is obtained.

WHAT EVERY INVESTOR SHOULD KNOW

PE is by its very nature a difficult subject to cover; that is, it is private. If we knew anything that we could talk about, we might be able to call it "just a little bit" private or "partly" PE. Moreover, it is so enticing for many investors. Who does not want to be invested into a private club? The question is, even if you are invited in, you have to ask why. Is it your good looks or your wit? In this chapter we pointed out that for much of the history of PE, the individuals running the game were very private. In addition, to the degree that they became public, their public image was a little questionable. In recent years, however, public equity has undergone a transformation. For the past decade, it has become more transparent and more available through multiple investment sources. Yet there is still much the typical investor does not know.

- **Trust the People, Do Not Trust the Returns:** Since most of the data on past performance is private, and since most of the investment opportunities (for certain types of direct fund investment) are unknown at the time of the investment, the question has to be: Who do you trust? As a result, the performance of any individual set of investment returns must be analyzed to see if they can be reproduced and to expose the framework for that belief. It reminds us of the old nuclear discussion, and it works here: Investors trust, but verify.
- **Do Not Be the Last One in the Pool:** With the exception of funds that only do direct coinvestment, investing in a PE fund of funds is a very bad idea. In addition to fees on top of fees and limited upside, fund-of-funds managers have no voice in decision making and are provided unverifiable information, on a quarterly basis, by the general partner they invest in. The historical performance for these vehicles has been abysmal and the value proposition on any diversification theme remote. As discussed above, when you enter a private club or you are invited to enter, you have to be pleased, but then ask why. Are they asking for new money to be added alongside theirs? Are they asking you to buy out their own holdings? Have all the good boat slots been rented out and all you have is the slip near the end of the dock? Maybe the real nice club is full and this private club is one mile down the road. Proximity and ease does not necessarily equate to competency.
- **PE Is More Equity Than Private:** PE investments may be better viewed as return-enhancement vehicles to traditional equity-biased portfolios. Although traditional PE investments may provide diversification and return benefits, the impact of their comovement with equity and equity-impacted assets, as well as their valuation difficulties, must be considered carefully. Finally, the PE sector has undergone significant changes in recent years. These include the listing of major PE firms on stock exchanges. Investors must distinguish between PE firms that are primarily asset gatherers or clubs and those that functionally add value.

If not publicly listed, ask for the firm's financials. Review performance numbers against equity and fixed-income indices. Examine the turnover of their limited partners. Investors should not assume that because a firm is registered with the Securities and Exchange Commission or some similar regulatory body that the regulators have approved the firm from a due diligence perspective. Many firms have been seemingly in regulatory compliance up to the day they close their doors due to misfeasance or malfeasance. While regulatory compliance can inform, a regulatory oversight scheme has a different objective than an investor searching for an appropriate opportunity—and at any given moment the investor's and the regulator's interest may not be in alignment. With the exception of a rare few, the value proposition for PE firms is remote, and historical data must be used or relied on with extreme care. Perhaps the most important point we can end this section with is to repeat that the return and risk characteristics of publicly traded PE firms differ from those of traditional accounting-based PE indices. Always remember that it is current market conditions that drive valuations, and projections offer little beyond hope.

MYTHS AND MISCONCEPTIONS OF PRIVATE EQUITY

There is a common phrase that says it is always dangerous to discuss the aims and intentions of others. This is especially true when the issues one is trying to divine are private and explicitly nontransparent. Any comment on the myths and misconceptions of PE is therefore more of a personal perspective than statements based on actual facts. There is myth in the following myths. Perhaps time will provide the answer.

Myth 6.1: Last Year's Private Equity Performance Is Indicative of Next Year's Private Equity Performance

Just as for those who invest in traditional stock and bond mutual funds, hedge funds, and CTAs, investment in publicly traded PE is often based on past performance. However, as with traditional stock and bond funds and various alternative investments, past performance provides little evidence as to near-term performance. For publicly traded equity, this is to be expected. Performance persistence does not exist for traditional assets, nor does it exist for PE. What of private market PE? Now the issues get more complex, but concern is that the historical return performance of any set of PE data reflects a historical event. For many PE firms, the past only reflects the fact that they were able to make and manage investments in the past. The unique skills that led to correct decisions in one market environment are not necessarily easily transferable into the next economic environment (e.g., technology to commodity investment). The seeming correlations between the performance in year one and year two for PE firms may simply reflect getting in at the right time. Since for the most part we only have quarterly data on most firms, we simply do not have enough data to know.

Myth 6.2: One Private Equity Benchmark Is As Good As Another

Indices are commonly used to provide a performance benchmark that reflects the particular style of an investment manager. Although benchmark indices are common in the areas of stock and bond investment, many investors are not familiar with the various benchmark indices in the PE area. As in the traditional asset area, there exists no one benchmark that reflects the performance of the asset class. Each PE index (e.g., S&P, LPX, CA) has unique weighting, composition, and structural issues (market based or accounting based), just as equity indices (e.g., S&P 500, Dow Jones) have their own unique weighting and asset composition. Nor does each index on its own capture the fundamental benchmark requirements of investability, systematic reproduction, and transparency.

Myth 6.3: A Single Private Equity Index Is Sufficient to Capture Private Equity Returns

In the first instance, an investor should question whether any PE index is capable of capturing the return profile of investable PE investments. For the most part, this cannot be accomplished. These indices tend to focus on vintage-year comparisons, which, as previously discussed, do little to inform the investor as to the underlying assets of any fund. Next, to the extent that they eschew the vintage-year concept, they are based on some methodology that includes publicly traded firms or some algorithmic mix of sources of return to provide a structured solution. For the most part, unless an investor has tasked someone with creating an index based on very specific criteria and designed to be used in a very specific manner in analyzing its portfolio, these PE indices provide little more than indicative results as to performance and associated risks. That said, the reliance on one index would be a mistake, and research has shown that two to three indices should provide sufficient information to gauge performance patterns.

Myth 6.4: There Exists a Single Proper Way to Measure Private Equity Performance

As discussed, the most well-known PE databases provide quarterly returns founded on IRR vintage year. In contrast, there are few public market examples of the *fair value* of current PE portfolios. For the past 20 years, publicly traded PE firms have existed. Research has shown a high correlation between generic equity market returns (e.g., S&P 500) and various equity market-based PE benchmarks. For certain years, there is evidence that the return patterns in various equity-based PE benchmarks reflect more reliable information than traditional consulting firm-based PE accounting-based returns. Of greater concern is the established fact that while the estimated returns may not differ dramatically, the estimated variance among the various indices does. The variance of publicly traded PE securities is often twice or three times that of accounting-based measures of PE performance. In sum, there is no established methodology to measure the performance of individual PE firms. Frankly, that is one of their advantages in raising capital from the uninformed.

CHAPTER 7

Real Estate

The New World

Real estate is perhaps the only asset class that evokes a visceral reaction in investors that at times transcends its monetary worth. There is something mystical here; something amorphous that reflects a magnified stability and sense of eternity. In ancient times, real estate was the defining symbol of wealth. The ownership of real property was the exclusive right of kings, and all others paid a toll for its use and enjoyment. In many ways, that theme is the undercurrent of today's trophy commercial properties, named office buildings, and homes. In the modern investment world, real estate investment exists in many forms. It is both public and private—both fixed income and equity—and both direct and indirect. Each has its own risk and return profile, and each has its own associated myths and misconceptions.

The types and forms of investment real estate are immense. Yet irrespective of form, there are a number of defining characteristics inherent in all such investments. First, investment real estate is relatively illiquid. As a result, it is difficult to market directly in its basic form. The cash flows or valuations must generally be in some structured security before being made available to investors. Second, real estate is subject to information asymmetries. By definition, investment real estate is not transportable. Thus, its risk and reward attributes are keenly influenced by local politics, sentiment, professional relationships, laws, regulations, tariffs, and growth patterns. An office park in Silicon Valley has significantly different valuation and return characteristics than does the same structure located in Chicago. Third, investment real estate is usually levered. Leverage can be a part of the initial transaction, when an investor places a down payment and finances the remainder of the purchase price, or it can be embedded in the various instruments and business models that sponsors employ to distribute this asset class. By example, a sponsor or developer may purchase raw land with the intent to build an office park. That land could be financed through a local bank, with the sponsor paying a modest-percent down payment and the bank financing the balance for a period of years. The sponsor could then obtain a construction loan to build the office park, again with financing. Finally, once completed, that office park could be folded into a securitized portfolio of similar properties to be redistributed as securitized partial interests in the larger portfolio. A degree of leverage and associated costs and fees exist at each level of this scenario, and all of the leverage and associated costs are eventually folded into the securitized transaction. As such, any analysis relating to risks, sources of return, valuations, and due diligence are inextricably linked to the business platform or model used to provide this asset class to investors.

Against these constants and despite the fact that real estate is considered a core allocation to most institutional portfolios, its intricacies require investors to spend considerable expense and effort to either conduct their own due diligence or find a suitable professional who can mitigate potential risks and understand the rewards. The office-park example is representative of most real estate transactions in the United States. Securitization is more the norm than the exception, even in the area of single-family homes. Local banks have essentially become toll takers, in that they originate loans and sell them off to others who repackage those loans as underlying assets for a vast array of product offerings. These offerings take many forms, such as real estate investment trusts (REITs) or variations of collateralized debt obligations.

The real estate structure of today actually began in the 1930s when, among other factors, a lack of liquidity and informational asymmetries led the U.S. government to create the Federal Housing Administration (FHA) and the Federal National Mortgage Association (FNMA, or Fannie Mae) to both insure loans and create secondary markets in home mortgages. These agencies were tasked with purchasing and securitizing mortgages from local banks, thus allowing local lenders to reinvest their assets into more lending. These securitizations were called *mortgage-backed securities* (MBSs). FHA and Fannie Mae were hugely successful in spurring growth, and by the 1960s, the U.S. housing market had grown to the point where the Government National Mortgage Association (GNMA, or Ginnie Mae) and the Federal Home Loan Mortgage Corporation (FHLMC, or Freddie Mac) were created as government-sponsored agencies to service the market for public and private real estate. This development provided the first active role of the government in securitization of commercial real estate. Up to this point, banks had created syndicates to diversify the risks associated with large development projects. Although somewhat efficient, this approach meant that the syndicating banks kept some portion of both the asset and the liability on their balance sheets, and as a consequence, their lending capacity was hampered. The ability to use government-sponsored securitization provided the mechanism to shift these liabilities off to an investing public and thus increase a bank's lending ability to the economy as a whole.

This implicit association with the U.S. government greatly opened the market for these types of securities, both as debt instruments and as proxies for direct real estate investment. As the major rating agencies (such as Moody's and Standard & Poor's [S&P]) began to rate these securities as investment grade, global demand increased significantly. Whether as a consequence of local laws or federally created mandates, and irrespective of their country of origin, most pension funds, banks, and insurance companies are required to have the bulk of their investments in rated investments. The thought is simply that given the infinite number of choices available, a standard associated with dispassionate ratings will assist those responsible with maintaining the financial integrity of these types of portfolios. Underlying this is also the legal fiction known as the "reasonable person" standard. A fiduciary overseeing a portfolio is tasked with the obligation of acting with care and objective intent in the management of another's monies. To the extent that a fiduciary is purchasing rated securities, it is most often said that the standard has been met and that the fiduciary has little to no liability in the event that monies are lost on the investment.

With the substitution of ratings for judgment, and with the implicit but unacknowledged backing of the U.S. government, came increased innovations in these basic structures and soaring demand within securitization. Products such as Ginnie Mae pass-through certificates and Freddie Mac participation certificates offered increasingly unique slices of the overall risk and reward profile of both residential and commercial MBSs. With greater innovation also came greater disintermediation. Interestingly, this disintermediation was on both the buy and the sell sides of the equation. We must keep in mind one of the basic tenets of real estate investing: All risk and associated returns are local. Investors were far removed from the underlying assets and, equally, so were the investment banks that created, marketed, and packaged these assets in more and more exotic fashions. Moreover, local risks became overlaid with unassociated economic, distribution, and political risks. Both the major rating agencies stood as Argus, the mythical guardian of reason; and as Argus, the rating agencies were found wanting.

In the United States, the advancements in the real estate fixed-income area during the 1960s were running parallel with the development of equity-based real estate investments. The Real Estate Investment Trust Act of 1960 created a framework for the first real estate investment trusts (REITs). Over the next 30 years, as the fixed-income investment forms were evolving, new regulation was changing the framework for REIT investment (e.g., REIT Modernization Act of 1999). Although there exist a number of regulatory restrictions related to their construction and sale, in the United States, a REIT is a company that owns, and in most cases operates, income-producing real estate. To be a REIT, a company must distribute at least 90 percent of its taxable income to shareholders annually in the form of dividends. The REIT structure is not unique to the United States, and each country has its own regulatory framework to protect investors and improve market efficiency.

As noted, real estate investment has generally been regarded as a primary part of individual and institutional investors' strategic asset allocation portfolios. In recent years, the sector has undergone a dramatic transformation both in investment structure and return opportunities. In the past, the physical real estate market has been characterized by a relative lack of liquidity, high transaction costs, high management costs, high information costs, and low transparency. Today, some of the costs of investing in real estate have been reduced, as initiatives to enhance liquidity and transparency in the property markets have been developed. Despite these changes, real estate investments remain relatively inefficient and substantially different from country to country, region to region, and property type to property type. As real estate investment opportunities differ widely, traditional real estate may better be viewed as return-enhancement vehicles to equity-biased and fixed-income investments. This is caused, in part, by the effect of interest rates on the present value of the fixed cash flows often generated by real estate. These cash flows are also impacted by dramatic changes in global economic conditions, which may change both the structure of financing and the demand of real estate investing.

In this chapter, the benefits, performance, and sources of return of real estate investment strategies are examined. We first present the different forms of private and public equity and debt investments available in the U.S. real estate market, as well as the primary corresponding indices that have been designed to track each of these markets. Second, we discuss and present a review of the literature on the determinants of real estate returns. Third, we review the data, methodology, and performance results related to real estate investments. Fourth, in presenting conclusions, we discuss a number of issues that are unique to real estate investment. As a final point, investment products are designed, marketed, and purchased within a regulatory and economic paradigm. With the exception of direct investments in real estate, for many, this has meant subjugating their judgment to ratings. History has shown that such an approach is wanting.

INVESTING IN REAL ESTATE

As discussed previously, with changes in regulation, variations in market structure, and advances in product creation, real estate investment now includes a wide range of investable forms in which investors can seek distinct return opportunities: (a) private commercial real estate equity, (b) public commercial real estate equity, (c) private commercial real estate debt, and (d) public commercial real estate debt.

The performance of each of these categories reflects a mix of equity and debt behaviors. This point is illustrated with the following two examples. First, consider the case of a private real estate equity asset that has been leased to a single high-quality tenant for a long period of time. The lease payments in this case will reflect the fixed payments usually associated with a bond, and the value of this property to the investor will also fluctuate in response to the same factors that affect the value of a bond (e.g., inflation, interest rate changes, and creditworthiness of the tenant). Now, consider the case of an equity position in an empty, speculative building. The value of this property will be determined in the market by the supply and demand for space—that is, by the forces that affect the price of an equity position. As the building is fully leased, this real estate investment changes from more of an equity investment to a debt-equity hybrid, in which the consistent cash flows offer debt-like payments, and the future options for alternative use of the building provide continued equity-like risk components.

Exposure to the equity side of the real estate market can be achieved via two principal modes of investment: private (also known as physical or direct) and public (also known as securitized, financial, or indirect). Private real estate investment involves the acquisition and management of actual physical properties. Public investment involves buying shares of REITs or other forms of indirect financial investment (e.g., futures or exchange-traded funds [ETFs] based on real estate). The real estate market is composed of several segments, which include housing, or residential real estate properties; commercial real estate properties; farmland; and timberland. We will discuss each of these segments and available indices and investable products in the following section.

HOUSING OR RESIDENTIAL REAL ESTATE PROPERTIES

The value of residential real estate properties has no single dominant market-based pricing service. One popular valuation index is the S&P/Case-Shiller Home Price Indices, which consist of 20 metropolitan regional indices, 2 composite indices, and a national index. The indices are constructed using a methodology known as *repeat sales pricing*, a process that involves recording sale prices of specific single-family homes in a particular region. When a home is resold months or years later, the new sale price is also recorded, and the two sale prices are referred to as a *sale pair*. The differences in the sale pairs of the region are measured and aggregated into one index.

Commercial Real Estate Properties

Currently, commercial property indices exist from a number of sources: The National Council of Real Estate Investment Fiduciaries (NCREIF) Property Index (NPI) is a quarterly total return index of a very large pool of individual commercial real estate properties acquired in the private market for investment purposes only. The NPI return provides an estimate of the quarterly internal rate of return (IRR), assuming that a property was purchased at the beginning of the quarter and sold at the end of the quarter, with the investor receiving all the corresponding net cash flows (i.e., net operating profits minus capital expenditures) during the quarter. The NPI is an appraisal-based index. Because of the methodology used in constructing the NCREIF, returns calculated solely on percentage changes in the index suffer from a number of deficiencies, such as smoothed or lagged price change estimates, which tend to cause downward-biased estimates of total return volatility. Another index that measures the performance of institutional commercial properties is the Massachusetts Institute of Technology (MIT) Center for Real Estate (CRE) Transactions-Based Index (TBI). The purpose of this index is to measure market movements and returns on investment based on transaction prices of properties sold from the NPI database.

Farmland

The NCREIF Farmland Index is a quarterly index that measures the investment performance of a large pool of individual agricultural properties acquired in the private market for investment purposes only. Only income-generating agricultural properties are included in the index. According to NCREIF, all properties in the Farmland Index have been acquired, at least partially, on behalf of tax-exempt institutional investors, the great majority being pension funds. As such, all properties are held in a fiduciary environment. This index is also an appraisal-based index.

Timberland

Timber is a unique investment, characterized by very long-term illiquid investments and particular risk and return determinants. The main factors impacting timber prices are the underlying demand and supply, however, timber demand and supply are very highly correlated to changes in the fundamental determinants of stocks and bonds. The NCREIF Timberland Index is a quarterly index that measures the investment performance of institutional timberland investments. To qualify for the index, a property must be held in a fiduciary environment and marked to market at least once per year. However, the lack of quarterly appraisals for many properties in the Timberland Index makes the annual return series more reflective of changes in the market than the quarterly series.

PRIVATE AND PUBLIC COMMERCIAL REAL ESTATE DEBT

Private commercial real estate debt can be held as directly issued whole loans, commercial mortgages held in funds, or commingled vehicles. Public commercial real estate debt is often composed of commercial mortgage-backed securities (CMBSs). CMBSs consist of many single-mortgage loans (of varying size, property type, and location) that are pooled and then transferred to a trust (see CRE Financial Council at www.crefc.org). The trust then issues a series of bonds that may vary in yield, duration, and payment priority. Interest received from all of the pooled loans is paid to the investors, starting with the highest rated bonds, until all accrued interest on those bonds is paid. Interest is then paid to the investors holding the next highest rated bonds, and so on. The same procedure is followed with principal as payments are received. Credit-rating agencies then assign ratings to the various bond classes. Investors choose which CMBS bonds to purchase based on the level of credit risk, yield, and duration that best suits their needs. Although CMBSs are a form of real estate debt, they also exhibit an equity-like behavior, given the nature of the CMBS market, in which cash flows from pools of mortgages are divided to produce high-grade cash flow characteristics in the senior tranches and more equity-like cash flow characteristics in the most subordinate pieces.

REAL ESTATE STYLES AND BENCHMARKS

As with most investment strategies, real estate investments can often be defined by the markets the manager trades in and the form of the trading that takes place. Similar to other traditional and alternative investment markets, real estate investing has been divided into the markets they trade (e.g., commercial and residential) and some of the unique approaches to trading (e.g., REITS). In addition to the different types of real estate property held, the primary difference between the various indices is the frequency of the reported returns and the methodology used to obtain the estimate for the current market value.

Name	Type	Available Data	Frequency	Methodology
1. Equity Private				
S&P/Case-Schiller Home Price Indices	Residential properties	1990	Monthly	Repeat sales
NPI	Commercial properties	1978	Quarterly	Appraisal-based
MIT/CRE Transaction-Based Index	Commercial properties	1994	Quarterly	Hedonic
NCREIF Farmland Index	Farmland	1992	Quarterly	Appraisal-based
NCREIF Timberland Index	Timberland	1987	Quarterly	Appraisal-based
2. Equity Public				
Financial Times and Stock Exchange (FTSE) National Association of Real Estate Investment Trusts (NAREIT) U.S. Real Estate Index	REITS	1979	Daily	Rule-based
S&P U.S. REIT Composite	REITS	1997	Daily	Rule-based
Dow Jones Wilshire Real Estate Securities Index (RESI)	REITS and real estate operating companies (REOCs)	1977	Daily	Market cap weighted
Real Estate Investment Trusts (REITS)	REITS	1977	Daily	Market cap weighted
MSCI U.S. REIT	REITS	1996	Daily	Market cap weighted

As shown, these indices exist not only for the United States as a whole but for regional equity and fixed-income markets. Each of these indices may have its own unique return-to-risk trade-off. Within any of the individual real estate reporting sectors, more detailed subsectors are available, which themselves have their own return and risk profiles. Samples of additional commercial real estate sub-indices include the following:

NPI	S&P Case
NCREIF Hotel	NCREIF Farmland
NCREIF Apartment	NCREIF Timber
NCREIF Retail	NCREIF Townsend
NCREIF Industry	NCREIF Value Added
NCREIF Office	NCREIF Opportunistic
MIT/TBI	MIT/TBI Industrial
MIT/TBI Office	MIT/TBI Retail

Each of these indices differs slightly in its construction. In addition, past research indicates that the reported returns of the investable Financial Times and Stock Exchange (FTSE) National Association of Real Estate Investment Trusts (NAREIT) indices often differ from those of similar market-based noninvestable accounting-based indices.

BASIC SOURCES OF RISK AND RETURN

The performance of various investment vehicles attached to each subsector reflects their underlying sources of cash flow as well as investors' perceptions of the current and future quality of that cash flow. Real estate debt and equity prices are determined both by overall market factors and by a myriad of real estate supply and demand factors, including: (a) long-term population growth affecting the demand for real estate housing; (b) government planning and regulations on the use of land playing a crucial role in the real estate market through their possible influence on real estate supply; (c) disposable income and availability of financing; (d) regional differences in insurance costs as well as maintenance and repair costs; and (e) differential tax treatment of real estate investments.

Real estate markets often follow economic cycles, and forecasting models accounting for these complex relationships are in development. For example, there has been substantial research in analyzing economic risk factors that are priced into real estate markets.[1] These researchers have identified growth in consumption, real interest rates, the term structure of interest rates, and unexpected inflation as systematic determinants of real estate returns. In exploring returns in global property markets and questioning their integration and relation to fundamental economic variables, researchers also found that a substantial amount of the correlation across global real estate markets is attributed to changes in economic growth. Thus, real estate can be considered a bet on internationally correlated fundamental economic variables.

Real estate cycles may operate at both international and local levels. The implication is that true international real estate diversification can only be achieved by investing on an intercontinental basis. Also, near-optimal diversification can be achieved by targeting one country from each continent. Some researchers,[2] however, warn that those investing internationally suffer from an information disadvantage over local investors. Research also concludes that high prices are not caused by shortages in space but by local zoning and land use regulations.[3] We have also seen that the risk of regulation speeds up the development of unregulated land.[4]

In general, empirical research has focused on REITs because of the availability of a series of monthly historical data for these investment vehicles as well as their liquidity and importance as a real estate investment alternative. REITs—corporations that invest in real estate markets and are required to distribute 90 percent of their income—can be thought of as the real estate equivalent of mutual funds. As mentioned previously, we also present a similar analysis on commercial and residential real estate toward the end of the chapter, as well as an analysis of the performance of other alternative real estate investment vehicles (e.g., mutual funds, closed-end funds, ETFs, and hedge funds that invest in real estate). We leave the consideration and analysis of data on private and public commercial real estate debt for another day.

PERFORMANCE: FACT AND FICTION

Real estate has been a major investment class for both retail and institutional investors. For decades, real estate investment across a wide range of real estate sectors has been promoted both by governmental policies as well as by changes in financial markets, which created additional investment vehicles that helped expand the demand for direct real estate investment. The question is whether, going forward, real estate investments will reflect a separate growth pattern as reflected in the period prior to the dot-com bubble or if real estate will continue to track traditional equity markets as it has for the period since the dot-com bubble. For some, the performance of real estate is based primarily on the unique business opportunities corresponding to the ability of investment managers to select real estate investment opportunities with performance that may not be directly related to general market factors. For others, the underlying ability of real estate to meet performance goals is partially dependent on the underlying strength of the economy as it impacts real estate demand on a U.S. or global basis. Thus what is an accepted fact for one real estate investor may be regarded as fiction for another. One of the principal problems in the analysis of real estate is the term *real*, in that there is little evidence on the quality of the data that supposedly reflects the changing value of a real estate investment. In the following sections, we provide evidence not only on the stand-alone risks of various real estate investments, but on the interrelationships between real estate and various traditional (e.g., equity and fixed-income market) and alternative asset classes using an index of publicly traded real estate firms. As in previous chapters, we examine these markets over both broad and short time intervals (e.g., annual) as well as their relative performance in extreme market conditions. Using the FTSE NAREIT indices as a basis for measuring the benefits of real estate investment, results demonstrate that real estate is shown to have a high correlation with the comparison equity-biased traditional and alternative investments and provides little potential diversification benefits especially in periods of extreme equity returns, that is, negative returns in down equity markets and positive returns in up equity markets. To some, this is expected, but investors should not take return and risk performance from extended time frames as a basis for how various certain real estate equity indices may perform over relatively shorter time periods (e.g., annual). Lastly, as discussed in Chapter 6, relative to investment in private equity, the performance of publicly traded REITS may not necessarily reflect the performance of accounting-based private real estate investment. In the end, real estate should provide the potential for unique return opportunities based not on systematic return opportunities with the general equity market but on nonsystematic firm-based opportunities. However, given the randomness of such individual REIT success, it is not surprising that since much of real estate is held in portfolio form, many real estate investments seem to capture overall generic equity market patterns in contrast to the "black swan" of an individual real estate investment success.

RETURN AND RISK CHARACTERISTICS

In this section, we review the performance of the FTSE NAREIT Composite Index with a range of traditional stock and bond indices as well as a number of alternative investment indices (i.e., private equity, real estate, commodities, commodity trading advisors [CTAs], and hedge funds) over the period 1994 to 2011. In later sections, we will focus on the performance of the FTSE NAREIT Composite and the FTSE NAREIT sector indices in various subperiods. For this period, as shown in Exhibit 7.1, the FTSE NAREIT exhibited higher annualized standard deviation, or volatility (19.9 percent), than that of the S&P 500 (15.7 percent). This may be surprising to most investors, who often regard REITS as diversifiers and as less risky than stocks. Over the period of analysis, the FTSE NAREIT also reported higher annualized total return (9.7 percent) than that of the S&P 500 (7.7 percent). The stand-alone historical risk-and-return comparison, however, may not reflect the potential for the benefits of a REIT investment as additions to other traditional assets or other nontraditional asset classes. For example, as shown in Exhibit 7.1, for the period analyzed, the FTSE NAREIT has a moderate correlation (0.57) with the S&P 500 and a low correlation (0.14) with the BarCap U.S. Aggregate Index. The relatively high correlation of

EXHIBIT 7.1   Real Estate and Asset Class Performance

Stock, Bond, and Real Estate Performance	FTSE NAREIT	S&P 500	BarCap U.S. Government	BarCap U.S. Aggregate	BarCap U.S. Corporate High Yield
Annualized total return	9.7%	7.7%	6.1%	6.3%	7.3%
Annualized standard deviation	19.9%	15.7%	4.4%	3.8%	9.4%
Information ratio	0.49	0.49	1.39	1.67	0.78
Maximum drawdown	−67.9%	−50.9%	−5.4%	−5.1%	−33.3%
Correlation with FTSE NAREIT	1.00	0.57	−0.05	0.14	0.63

Alternative Asset and Real Estate Performance	FTSE NAREIT	S&P GSCI	Private Equity	CISDM Equal Weighted Hedge Fund	CISDM CTA Equal Weighted
Annualized total return	9.7%	4.8%	8.0%	10.4%	8.1%
Annualized standard deviation	19.9%	22.5%	28.1%	7.7%	8.7%
Information ratio	0.49	0.21	0.28	1.36	0.94
Maximum drawdown	−67.9%	−67.6%	−80.4%	−21.7%	−8.7%
Correlation with FTSE NAREIT	1.00	0.21	0.56	0.45	−0.02

Period of analysis: 1994 to 2011.

the FTSE NAREIT with stock returns may lead investors to question a REIT-dominated portfolio as a primary means of diversification for equity-dominated portfolios but may result in its inclusion as an alternative equity investment in a fixed-income dominated portfolio. Investors who look to the low correlation between the FTSE NAREIT and low- to moderate-risk fixed-income securities are cautioned that, given the relative volatility for the BarCap U.S. Aggregate (3.8 percent) and the FTSE NAREIT (19.9 percent), even small additions of the FTSE NAREIT to a bond portfolio may tilt the portfolio to having a significantly higher correlation with equity markets.

Modern portfolio theory, however, emphasizes that individual assets should be evaluated based on their performance alongside other assets in investors' portfolios. The diversification benefits of adding any individual investment to other assets or asset portfolios depend on the comparison stand-alone investment. The moderate correlation between the FTSE NAREIT and a range of alternative investments (e.g., hedge funds [0.45], private equity [0.56]) with equity market exposures may indicate that a portfolio of REITs may provide only minimal reduction in the risk (i.e., standard deviation) of an equity, or an equity biased multi-asset portfolio. As shown in Exhibit 7.2, adding a small portion of real estate (10 percent) to stock and bond Portfolio A yields Portfolio B with a similar annualized return (7.7 percent) and standard deviation (8.7 percent) as the pure stock and bond portfolio (see Portfolio A with an annualized return of 7.3 percent and standard deviation of 8.2 percent). Similarly, adding real estate to a portfolio that contains a range of traditional and alternative assets results in Portfolio D that exhibits a similar return (8.1 percent) and standard

EXHIBIT 7.2 Real Estate and Multi-Asset Class Portfolio Performance

Portfolios	A	B	C	D
Annualized returns	7.3%	7.7%	8.0%	8.1%
Standard deviation	8.2%	8.7%	9.2%	9.6%
Information ratio	0.9	0.9	0.9	0.8
Maximum drawdown	−27.1%	−31.3%	−36.0%	−38.5%
Correlation with real estate	0.58		0.69	
Portfolio A	Equal weights S&P 500 and BarCap U.S. Aggregate			
Portfolio B	90% Portfolio A and 10% real estate			
Portfolio C	75% Portfolio A and 25% CTA/commodities/ private equity/hedge funds			
Portfolio D	90% Portfolio C and 10% real estate			

Period of analysis: 1994 to 2011.

deviation (9.6 percent) to those of Portfolio C (8.0 percent and 9.2 percent, respectively), which does not contain real estate.

As pointed out for other asset classes, the composite real estate index (i.e., FTSE NAREIT) reflects just one of several alternative REIT indices. Other REIT-based indices may provide different performance results. In addition, a composite REIT index covers a wide range of real estate sectors. Exhibit 7.3 shows risk-and-return performance over the 1994–2011 period for the FTSE NAREIT Composite Index and various FTSE NAREIT sector indices. The REIT sector indices report similar standard deviations and correlation with the S&P 500 and BarCap U.S. Aggregate, with all of the REIT sector indices reporting a moderate to high correlation (above 0.40) with the S&P 500 and a correlation generally below 0.20 with the BarCap U. S. Aggregate Index.

In summary, there is much in the historical returns for the period 1994–2011 to support the view that the relatively high correlation of the FTSE NAREIT with the S&P 500 and the relatively high correlation of the FTSE NAREIT sector indices with the S&P 500 is such that many REIT-based indices may be better regarded as return enhancers than as risk reducers.

THE MYTH OF AVERAGE: REAL ESTATE INVESTMENT TRUST INDEX RETURN IN EXTREME MARKETS

The results in the previous section illustrate the performance of the FTSE NAREIT and various sector indices and how they compare to traditional and alternative investment indices over an 18-year period (1994–2011). However, the relative stand-alone performance of the various REIT indices and their potential benefits when added to a portfolio of traditional assets may differ in various subperiods in comparison to their performance over the entire period of analysis. This is especially true in periods of equity and fixed-income market stress, when certain REIT strategies may experience significant return movement, similar to the markets in which they trade.

Exhibit 7.4 shows the FTSE NAREIT Index and sector indices monthly returns ranked on the S&P 500 and grouped into three segments (bottom, middle, and top) of 72 months each, with average returns for each NAREIT index and sector index presented. Results show that the NAREIT indices and sector indices would have had negative returns (but less negative than the S&P 500 except in one sector [see Lodging/Resorts]) in the worst S&P 500 return months and would have provided positive returns (but less positive than the S&P 500 except in one sector [see Lodging/Resorts]) in the best S&P 500 return months. The comparable performance in up and down S&P 500 markets may be partially caused by the economic conditions driving both

EXHIBIT 7.3 Real Estate Index Performance

	FTSE NAREIT	Equity Office	Equity Industrial/ Office	Equity Industrial	Equity Retail	Equity Shopping Centers	Equity Regional Malls	Equity Free Standing	Equity Residential	Equity Apartments	Equity Manufactured Homes	Equity Diversified	Equity Health Care	Equity Lodging/ Resorts	Equity Self Storage
Annualized return	9.7%	10.1%	11.2%	7.5%	11.0%	9.1%	12.9%	13.5%	12.1%	12.3%	9.2%	8.3%	13.2%	3.6%	16.0%
Annualized standard deviation	19.9%	23.9%	22.8%	32.7%	23.6%	23.0%	27.6%	17.7%	20.4%	20.8%	18.4%	22.3%	21.4%	32.9%	20.2%
Information ratio	0.49	0.42	0.49	0.23	0.47	0.39	0.47	0.76	0.59	0.59	0.50	0.37	0.62	0.11	0.79
Maximum drawdown	−67.9%	−74.8%	−70.9%	−85.4%	−75.3%	−72.9%	−82.0%	−37.9%	−67.0%	−67.7%	−47.5%	−68.8%	−48.1%	−83.9%	−51.6%
Correlation with S&P 500	0.57	0.56	0.56	0.48	0.49	0.50	0.46	0.42	0.53	0.52	0.45	0.54	0.43	0.58	0.40
Correlation with BarCap Aggregate	0.14	0.13	0.11	0.19	0.13	0.15	0.09	0.22	0.05	0.04	0.17	0.11	0.19	0.02	0.17
Correlation with real estate	1.00	0.97	0.95	0.86	0.96	0.95	0.91	0.81	0.90	0.90	0.76	0.93	0.84	0.83	0.84

Period of analysis: 1994 to 2011.

	Average/Bottom Third Months (%)	Average/Middle Third Months (%)	Average/Top Third Months (%)
■ S&P 500	-4.3	1.2	5.3
■ FTSE NAREIT	-2.7	2.0	3.6
■ Equity industrial/office	-3.2	2.4	3.9
■ Equity office	-3.1	2.4	4.1
■ Equity industrial	-3.7	2.9	4.1
■ Equity retail	-2.5	2.4	3.5
■ Equity shopping centers	-2.6	2.1	3.4
■ Equity regional malls	-2.6	2.7	3.9
■ Equity free standing	-1.6	2.3	2.9
■ Equity residential	-2.2	1.9	3.7
■ Equity apartments	-2.3	1.9	3.8
■ Equity manufactured homes	-1.7	1.4	2.9
■ Equity diversified	-2.9	1.7	3.8
■ Equity health care	-1.9	2.3	3.2
■ Equity lodging/resorts	-4.8	1.5	5.5
■ Equity self storage	-1.2	2.4	3.1

EXHIBIT 7.4 Real Estate Indices: Monthly Returns Ranked on S&P 500 Period of analysis: 1994 to 2011.

stock market prices and real estate holdings in which REITs trade. Notably, the results differ somewhat for fixed income. Exhibit 7.5 shows the FTSE NAREIT Index and sector indices monthly returns ranked on the BarCap U.S. Aggregate and grouped into three segments (bottom, middle, and top) of 72 months each, with average returns for each NAREIT Index and sector index presented. Results show that on average, the FTSE NAREIT and its related sector indices had mixed positive and negative returns (some greater than the BarCap U.S. Aggregate and some less than the BarCap U.S. Aggregate) in the worst BarCap U.S. Aggregate return months and provided positive returns (some greater than the BarCap U.S. Aggregate and some less than the BarCap U.S. Aggregate) in the best BarCap U.S. Aggregate return months. For all sector indices, the returns to REITs were considerable higher than the BarCap U.S. Aggregate returns in the mid-performing BarCap U.S. Aggregate months.

The results in Exhibits 7.4 and 7.5 are illustrative of the impact of extreme movements in the S&P 500 on the U.S.-based REIT market. The question remains to be asked: What is the relationship between extreme movements in the U.S. REIT market and REIT markets throughout the globe? Exhibit 7.6 shows the percentage of international REIT indices with the same directional return as the U.S. FTSE NAREIT Index when ranked on the U.S. FTSE NAREIT Index. Results show that in months of extreme

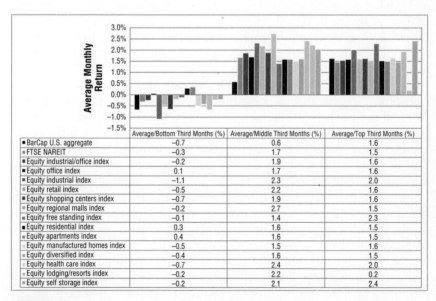

	Average/Bottom Third Months (%)	Average/Middle Third Months (%)	Average/Top Third Months (%)
■ BarCap U.S. aggregate	−0.7	0.6	1.6
■ FTSE NAREIT	−0.3	1.7	1.5
■ Equity industrial/office index	−0.2	1.9	1.6
■ Equity office index	0.1	1.7	1.6
■ Equity industrial index	−1.1	2.3	2.0
■ Equity retail index	−0.5	2.2	1.6
■ Equity shopping centers index	−0.7	1.9	1.6
■ Equity regional malls index	−0.2	2.7	1.5
■ Equity free standing index	−0.1	1.4	2.3
■ Equity residential index	0.3	1.6	1.5
■ Equity apartments index	0.4	1.6	1.5
■ Equity manufactured homes index	−0.5	1.5	1.6
■ Equity diversified index	−0.4	1.6	1.5
■ Equity health care index	−0.7	2.4	2.0
■ Equity lodging/resorts index	−0.2	2.2	0.2
■ Equity self storage index	−0.2	2.1	2.4

EXHIBIT 7.5 Real Estate Indices: Monthly Returns Ranked on BarCap U.S. Aggregate
Period of analysis: 1994 to 2011.

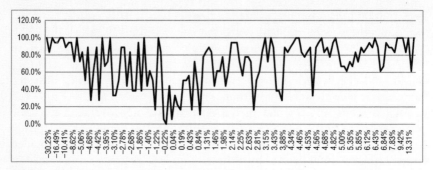

EXHIBIT 7.6 Percent of International REIT Indices with Same Directional Return as FTSE NAREIT Index (Ranked on FTSE NAREIT Index)
Period of analysis: 2001 to 2011.

positive or negative returns, the percentage of FTSE International REIT indices with the same directional return as the U.S. FTSE REIT Index is almost 100 percent.

REAL ESTATE ANNUAL PERFORMANCE

In the previous section, the average performance of the FTSE NAREIT index and sub-indices over the best and worst performing equity and fixed-income environments was discussed. The representative REIT indices were shown to provide little diversification benefits in the worst months as well as positive returns in the best months of the S&P 500. In this section, we provide a review of the relative performance by year of the FTSE NAREIT Index, FTSE NAREIT sub-indices, S&P 500, and BarCap U.S. Aggregate. Results in Exhibit 7.7 show that over the entire period, annual returns of the S&P 500 and the FTSE NAREIT, as well as its NAREIT sub-indices, varied in certain years but were generally in the same directional return. In 12 of the 18 years, the FTSE NAREIT and the S&P 500 moved in the same direction. The FTSE NAREIT and the BarCap U.S. Aggregate moved in the same direction in 14 of the 18 years. These results again indicate the importance of viewing REIT performance over short subperiods rather than viewing it based strictly on its performance over the whole 18-year period. In addition, results show the importance of having REITs as part of an existing equity or fixed-income-based portfolio. In addition, one must remember that a low correlation between a REIT index and a stock or bond index does not necessarily indicate the degree of market sensitivity of that REIT index to the equity or fixed-income index. The market sensitivity reflects both the correlation and the relative standard deviation of the respective indices.

Exhibits 7.8, 7.9, and 7.10 show the standard deviations and correlations of the FTSE NAREIT against those of the S&P 500 and the BarCap

	1994	1995	1996	1997	1998	1999	2000	2001	2002	2003	2004	2005	2006	2007	2008	2009	2010	2011
S&P 500	1.3%	37.6%	23.0%	33.4%	28.6%	21.0%	-9.1%	-11.9%	-22.1%	28.7%	10.9%	4.9%	15.8%	5.5%	-37.0%	26.5%	15.1%	2.1%
BarCap U.S. aggregate	-2.9%	18.5%	3.6%	9.7%	8.7%	-0.8%	11.6%	8.4%	10.3%	4.1%	4.3%	2.4%	4.3%	7.0%	5.2%	5.9%	6.5%	7.8%
FTSE NAREIT index	0.8%	18.3%	35.8%	18.9%	-18.8%	-6.5%	25.9%	15.5%	5.2%	38.5%	30.4%	8.3%	34.4%	17.8%	-37.3%	27.4%	27.6%	7.3%
Equity industrial/office	16.6%	25.8%	44.4%	27.5%	-14.4%	3.4%	33.4%	7.1%	0.9%	33.3%	25.2%	12.9%	39.4%	14.9%	-50.3%	29.2%	17.0%	-1.5%
Equity office	2.9%	38.8%	51.8%	29.0%	-17.4%	4.3%	35.5%	6.6%	-6.3%	34.0%	23.3%	13.1%	45.2%	19.0%	-41.1%	35.5%	18.4%	-0.8%
Equity industrial	18.7%	16.2%	37.2%	19.0%	-11.7%	3.9%	28.6%	7.4%	17.3%	33.1%	34.1%	15.4%	28.9%	0.4%	-67.5%	12.2%	18.9%	-5.2%
Equity retail	3.0%	5.1%	34.6%	16.9%	-4.7%	-11.8%	18.0%	30.4%	21.1%	46.8%	40.2%	11.8%	29.0%	-15.8%	-48.4%	27.2%	33.4%	12.2%
Equity shopping centers	1.3%	7.4%	33.5%	21.4%	-7.0%	-10.7%	15.1%	29.9%	17.7%	43.1%	36.3%	9.3%	34.9%	-17.7%	-38.8%	-1.7%	30.8%	-0.7%
Equity regional malls	8.8%	3.0%	45.3%	13.7%	-2.6%	-14.6%	23.5%	31.9%	24.6%	52.2%	45.0%	16.5%	23.8%	-15.9%	-60.6%	63.0%	34.6%	22.0%
Equity free standing	-5.5%	31.6%	30.9%	17.7%	-6.2%	-4.9%	8.9%	24.0%	21.8%	35.9%	32.9%	-0.5%	30.7%	-0.4%	-15.1%	25.9%	37.4%	0.4%
Equity residential	2.3%	12.0%	29.5%	16.3%	-8.1%	9.5%	34.3%	9.0%	-6.0%	25.9%	32.7%	13.7%	38.9%	-25.2%	-24.9%	30.8%	46.0%	15.4%
Equity apartments	2.2%	12.3%	28.9%	16.0%	-8.8%	10.7%	35.5%	8.7%	-6.1%	25.5%	34.7%	14.7%	39.9%	-25.4%	-25.1%	30.4%	47.0%	15.1%
Equity manufactured homes	3.3%	10.7%	34.9%	16.2%	-0.9%	-2.8%	20.9%	13.7%	-4.1%	30.0%	6.4%	-2.6%	15.3%	-19.3%	-20.2%	40.9%	27.0%	20.4%
Equity diversified	-6.0%	21.1%	34.0%	21.7%	-22.1%	-14.4%	24.1%	12.5%	4.2%	40.3%	32.4%	9.9%	38.0%	-22.3%	-28.2%	17.0%	23.8%	2.8%
Equity health care	4.1%	24.9%	20.4%	15.8%	-17.4%	-24.8%	25.8%	51.8%	4.8%	53.6%	21.0%	1.8%	44.5%	-2.1%	-12.0%	24.6%	19.2%	13.6%
Equity lodging/resorts	-8.9%	30.8%	49.2%	30.1%	-52.8%	-16.1%	45.8%	-6.6%	-1.5%	31.7%	32.7%	9.8%	28.2%	-22.4%	-59.7%	67.2%	42.8%	-14.3%
Equity self storage	8.9%	34.4%	42.8%	3.4%	-7.2%	-8.0%	14.7%	43.2%	0.6%	38.1%	29.7%	26.5%	40.9%	-24.8%	5.0%	8.4%	29.3%	35.2%

EXHIBIT 7.7 Real Estate Indices: Annual Returns

	1994	1995	1996	1997	1998	1999	2000	2001	2002	2003	2004	2005	2006	2007	2008	2009	2010	2011
S&P 500	10.6%	5.2%	10.9%	15.9%	21.5%	13.1%	17.2%	19.9%	20.6%	11.4%	7.3%	7.9%	5.6%	9.7%	21.0%	22.3%	19.3%	15.9%
BarCap U.S. aggregate	4.4%	3.5%	4.3%	3.6%	2.7%	2.7%	2.8%	3.8%	3.7%	5.3%	4.0%	3.1%	2.7%	2.6%	6.1%	3.3%	2.9%	2.4%
FTSE NAREIT index	11.2%	7.7%	9.5%	10.4%	14.6%	13.3%	14.1%	10.8%	12.0%	8.3%	21.0%	15.1%	11.8%	19.6%	43.4%	44.0%	18.7%	21.0%
Equity industrial/office	12.6%	9.0%	13.4%	16.3%	14.7%	14.9%	14.2%	13.0%	14.7%	8.0%	20.8%	15.5%	14.7%	19.7%	59.5%	52.3%	21.2%	25.8%
Equity office	13.0%	8.3%	14.7%	20.5%	15.5%	17.0%	14.5%	14.3%	16.2%	8.8%	19.5%	15.4%	14.7%	20.5%	48.9%	50.3%	20.8%	24.2%
Equity industrial	18.7%	10.1%	12.6%	10.8%	17.1%	10.4%	13.2%	12.6%	11.5%	8.6%	23.5%	18.3%	16.4%	20.2%	104.9%	63.8%	25.5%	35.0%
Equity retail	11.4%	8.8%	10.1%	8.0%	12.4%	12.1%	14.0%	11.2%	9.3%	7.7%	25.1%	18.2%	13.2%	24.9%	53.5%	58.3%	21.1%	22.7%
Equity shopping centers	11.4%	8.6%	10.1%	7.1%	14.2%	11.6%	13.2%	6.4%	7.8%	7.4%	22.8%	16.4%	14.9%	24.3%	53.6%	57.1%	22.7%	22.6%
Equity regional malls	8.9%	9.2%	11.9%	10.2%	10.4%	15.0%	17.7%	18.2%	11.4%	9.5%	28.5%	21.1%	13.7%	27.9%	58.1%	71.5%	23.3%	25.3%
Equity free standing	14.6%	12.7%	11.8%	15.5%	16.7%	15.5%	11.0%	8.5%	14.8%	8.2%	19.3%	13.7%	18.0%	19.2%	38.5%	30.8%	14.2%	11.7%
Equity residential	17.0%	10.4%	8.7%	10.4%	11.2%	13.0%	16.0%	12.5%	16.6%	9.4%	15.6%	17.5%	13.9%	24.9%	36.6%	46.3%	22.6%	23.7%
Equity apartments	17.0%	10.2%	8.4%	10.9%	11.6%	13.0%	16.5%	13.6%	17.2%	9.3%	16.0%	18.0%	14.1%	25.3%	36.8%	47.7%	22.8%	24.2%
Equity manufactured homes	18.8%	13.8%	13.0%	10.0%	11.3%	13.6%	16.3%	7.5%	15.3%	18.2%	17.1%	12.5%	14.1%	18.4%	39.0%	30.3%	23.0%	16.6%
Equity diversified	7.9%	6.1%	9.6%	9.7%	16.0%	14.3%	15.2%	9.5%	12.0%	11.4%	20.8%	16.0%	14.7%	19.9%	41.1%	60.5%	24.2%	22.3%
Equity health care	13.5%	8.5%	8.7%	9.6%	13.1%	15.6%	24.8%	11.9%	12.0%	16.4%	23.5%	16.4%	12.9%	26.7%	50.8%	38.0%	16.5%	18.5%
Equity lodging/resorts	14.1%	9.6%	15.1%	19.1%	22.5%	18.0%	22.2%	41.6%	23.3%	26.8%	16.8%	13.6%	13.5%	20.8%	47.6%	85.5%	36.8%	38.8%
Equity self storage	11.8%	7.9%	13.8%	14.8%	19.3%	16.2%	16.8%	13.0%	18.6%	14.8%	22.5%	12.5%	16.8%	23.8%	36.9%	38.5%	20.2%	21.8%

EXHIBIT 7.8   Real Estate Indices: Annual Standard Deviations

	1994	1995	1996	1997	1998	1999	2000	2001	2002	2003	2004	2005	2006	2007	2008	2009	2010	2011
▪ BarCap U.S. aggregate	0.76	0.22	0.51	0.68	-0.42	0.34	0.40	-0.40	-0.72	-0.04	0.06	-0.19	0.28	-0.44	0.35	0.64	-0.58	-0.35
■ FTSE NAREIT	0.44	0.33	-0.03	0.53	0.71	0.33	-0.12	0.43	0.28	0.58	0.44	0.69	0.56	0.76	0.83	0.89	0.88	0.95
▪ Equity industrial/office	0.43	0.09	-0.07	0.42	0.68	0.35	0.03	0.17	0.27	0.40	0.40	0.68	0.31	0.73	0.82	0.82	0.92	0.92
Equity office	0.61	0.00	0.01	0.40	0.76	0.29	0.00	0.05	0.32	0.57	0.39	0.62	0.25	0.74	0.87	0.79	0.87	0.88
▪ Equity industrial	0.09	-0.02	-0.15	0.52	0.54	0.57	0.13	0.44	0.02	-0.06	0.39	0.75	0.35	0.61	0.65	0.89	0.92	0.90
Equity retail	0.30	0.43	-0.17	0.42	0.74	-0.01	-0.30	0.52	-0.03	0.14	0.37	0.65	0.66	0.57	0.80	0.78	0.82	0.93
▪ Equity shopping centers	0.29	0.45	-0.21	0.36	0.81	0.13	-0.06	0.30	0.14	0.03	0.38	0.71	0.50	0.52	0.77	0.78	0.91	0.89
■ Equity regional malls	0.12	0.38	-0.11	0.44	0.59	-0.11	-0.42	0.59	-0.16	0.16	0.35	0.57	0.69	0.57	0.82	0.73	0.70	0.93
▪ Equity free-standing	0.44	0.17	0.07	0.57	0.45	-0.15	-0.44	0.30	0.04	0.50	0.46	0.81	0.67	0.57	0.64	0.86	0.71	0.50
Equity residential	0.32	0.31	-0.07	0.61	0.61	0.35	-0.11	0.13	0.39	0.55	0.48	0.56	0.40	0.78	0.73	0.91	0.67	0.79
▪ Equity apartments	0.31	0.31	-0.07	0.59	0.59	0.35	-0.10	0.14	0.42	0.52	0.46	0.56	0.40	0.78	0.73	0.91	0.65	0.79
▪ Equity manufactured homes	0.36	0.26	-0.05	0.64	0.55	0.40	-0.08	-0.19	-0.25	0.47	0.57	0.31	0.41	0.78	0.73	0.81	0.85	0.54
▪ Equity diversified	0.72	0.20	0.16	0.27	0.74	0.26	-0.23	0.46	0.28	0.49	0.46	0.60	0.60	0.74	0.84	0.84	0.79	0.90
▪ Equity health care	0.32	0.04	0.03	0.63	0.59	0.39	-0.07	0.05	0.28	0.69	0.29	0.57	0.57	0.51	0.65	0.89	0.65	0.88
▪ Equity lodging/resorts	0.05	0.43	0.32	0.29	0.51	0.43	-0.20	0.68	0.36	0.59	0.58	0.67	0.47	0.72	0.86	0.81	0.87	0.89
▪ Equity self storage	0.65	0.03	0.05	0.28	0.56	0.19	-0.04	0.04	-0.29	0.19	0.35	0.55	0.46	0.57	0.61	0.84	0.72	0.86

EXHIBIT 7.9 Real Estate Indices: Annual Correlation with S&P 500

	1994	1995	1996	1997	1998	1999	2000	2001	2002	2003	2004	2005	2006	2007	2008	2009	2010	2011
■ S&P 500	0.76	0.22	0.51	0.68	-0.42	0.34	0.40	-0.40	-0.72	-0.04	0.06	-0.19	0.28	-0.44	0.35	0.64	-0.58	-0.35
■ FTSE NAREIT	0.34	0.36	0.00	0.34	0.25	-0.03	-0.01	-0.68	-0.36	-0.03	0.74	-0.04	0.27	-0.12	0.32	0.43	-0.39	-0.08
■ Equity industrial/office	0.34	0.31	-0.11	0.26	0.29	-0.15	0.04	-0.72	-0.32	0.29	0.75	-0.18	0.25	-0.08	0.38	0.38	-0.45	-0.09
■ Equity office	0.41	0.42	-0.20	0.20	0.15	-0.20	0.00	-0.68	-0.33	0.14	0.78	-0.21	0.14	-0.16	0.32	0.37	-0.37	-0.01
■ Equity industrial	0.11	0.26	-0.05	0.55	0.47	0.02	0.18	-0.69	-0.25	0.56	0.69	-0.12	0.48	0.16	0.46	0.47	-0.61	-0.27
■ Equity retail	0.30	0.23	-0.13	0.27	0.22	-0.21	-0.23	-0.37	-0.17	-0.21	0.79	0.06	0.35	0.15	0.31	0.30	-0.39	-0.02
■ Equity shopping centers	0.30	0.21	0.01	0.28	0.13	-0.18	-0.08	-0.37	-0.28	-0.13	0.75	0.08	0.26	0.17	0.36	0.31	-0.41	0.04
■ Equity regional malls	0.22	0.24	-0.30	0.11	0.27	-0.29	-0.34	-0.35	-0.03	-0.26	0.80	0.06	0.38	0.11	0.24	0.25	-0.37	-0.08
■ Equity free-standing	0.12	0.63	0.25	0.39	0.56	0.02	-0.08	-0.28	-0.31	0.00	0.76	0.02	0.23	0.11	0.22	0.52	-0.07	0.29
■ Equity residential	0.20	0.12	-0.02	0.26	0.29	-0.08	0.12	-0.70	-0.39	-0.26	0.60	-0.20	0.21	-0.49	0.20	0.44	-0.27	0.16
■ Equity apartments	0.21	0.13	0.00	0.23	0.31	-0.08	0.12	-0.70	-0.42	-0.34	0.57	-0.21	0.21	-0.49	0.19	0.43	-0.27	0.16
■ Equity manufactured homes	0.10	0.06	-0.15	0.63	-0.05	-0.10	0.02	0.14	0.24	0.33	0.71	0.16	0.16	-0.18	0.26	0.49	-0.34	0.26
■ Equity diversified	0.41	0.59	0.06	0.11	-0.03	0.07	0.11	-0.68	-0.37	0.00	0.61	0.04	0.29	-0.26	0.24	0.36	-0.24	-0.03
■ Equity health care	0.06	-0.06	0.06	0.47	0.34	0.26	-0.20	0.21	-0.57	0.02	0.80	0.14	0.49	0.18	0.21	0.57	-0.18	0.01
■ Equity lodging/resorts	-0.04	0.04	0.01	0.26	0.01	0.19	-0.22	-0.45	-0.46	0.01	0.55	0.08	0.02	-0.30	0.30	0.28	-0.51	-0.33
■ Equity self storage	0.61	-0.37	0.02	0.17	0.38	-0.05	0.26	-0.20	-0.06	0.10	0.67	-0.06	0.39	0.07	0.28	0.46	-0.29	-0.05

EXHIBIT 7.10 Real Estate Indices: Annual Correlation with BarCap U.S. Aggregate

U.S. Aggregate. Results in Exhibit 7.8 show that the standard deviation of the FTSE NAREIT was generally below that of the S&P 500 prior to 2003, generally above that of the S&P 500 post-2003, and consistently above that of the BarCap U.S. Aggregate in all years. These results, however, show dramatic changes over the years in the volatility of the FTSE NAREIT. There are various reasons for this changing risk, including both increases in the underlying volatility of the markets in which REITs trade and the fact that the FTSE NAREIT itself has changed over time.

Exhibits 7.9 and 7.10 show the intra-year correlation between the FTSE NAREIT and its sub-indices and both the S&P 500 and the BarCap U.S. Aggregate. The correlation varies considerably over the years of analysis; however, the correlation with the S&P 500 remains fairly stable post-2003. In sum, investors should be aware that results from longer time frames may not reflect results for individual years. For REITs, lengthy periods of analysis may hide more than they reveal. Although composite REITs indices generally report relatively consistent correlation with the stock market over time, particularly post-2003, their volatility and correlation with fixed-income markets change from year to year. One example of the changing economic conditions on REIT investment, however, may be seen in the relative performance of one particular REIT sector—that is, the self-storage REIT. During the past four years, in those periods with negative REIT returns, the self-storage REIT has remained positive. When investors remark that they are currently invested in REITs or that they have recently added REITs to their portfolio, they must also detail the exact strategy invested in and, if they invested in the strategy based on these REIT indices, the degree to which their investment reflects the performance of the representative REIT index.

PERFORMANCE IN 2008

In 2008, REITs experienced their lowest return for the period analyzed. When compared to the returns (−37.0 percent) and volatility (21.0 percent) of the S&P 500, the FTSE NAREIT reported similar low returns (−37.3 percent) and higher volatility (43.4 percent). In 2008, the correlation between the FTSE NAREIT and the S&P 500 was 0.83. This correlation was partially caused by the common decline in valuation in the fall of 2008. In short, in 2008, most REIT indices, like those of traditional asset classes, were negatively impacted by the subprime crisis, the negative equity market performance, and the rise in credit spreads (e.g., decline in high-yield bond returns). As shown in Exhibit 7.7, this was especially true for REITs with exposure to equity markets (e.g., industrial). In contrast, certain real estate indices (e.g., health care) with less direct equity exposure provided smaller negative returns.

THE U.S. REAL ESTATE "BUBBLE" AND THE SUBPRIME MORTGAGE CRISIS OF 2007 TO 2010

Real estate valuations collapsed in 2007 when, according to the S&P/Case-Shiller Home Price Indices, home prices in the United States experienced an 8.9 percent decline through 2010, the first yearly drop in 16 years and the largest decline in home prices in at least the past 20 years. Was this really a real estate bubble that was bursting? Some researchers[5] argue that bubbles are more likely to develop in the housing market than in the stock market for the following reasons:

- Real estate markets lack a central exchange and are quite illiquid.
- Short selling is almost impossible in the underlying real estate market, especially in particular regions. Consequently, prices tend to be driven by individuals who overestimate potential value.
- Lenders whose primary business is real estate lending and who have the ability to off-load loans tend to increase lending as much as possible during real estate booms.
- Real estate supply tends to adapt slowly over time, and the supply seen at the time of construction may no longer reflect the demand of the day.
- Real estate markets with stricter planning and building regulations exhibit greater uncertainty as to supply adjustments, increasing volatility.

Some research also contends that there is evidence that property prices are "sticky downwards" in the declining phase of real estate cycles.[6] This research argues that prices do not tend to fall because owners set minimum reservation prices, below which they are unwilling to sell. As a result, the number of real estate transactions declines when property prices decline. Others, analyzing data from downtown Boston in the 1990s, argue that loss-aversion determines seller behavior in the housing market, and that there is a positive price-volume relationship in the real estate market.[7]

To complicate matters, a mortgage crisis erupted in 2007, related to a sharp decline in home prices. Some of the research during this era suggests that a rapid expansion in the supply of mortgages, which had been driven by disintermediation in the mortgage industry, can explain a large fraction of the initial U.S. house price appreciation.[8] The research also argues that the expansion in the mortgage supply was targeted at subprime loans, a sector of the market consisting of high-default-risk borrowers, who are traditionally unable to borrow in the mortgage market. The resulting sharp shift in mortgage supply caused a significant increase in the risk profile of borrowers and pressed housing prices upward. Subsequently, when default rates started to increase in 2007, they had the effect of depressing the housing market.

Demyanyk and van Hemert (2009) also attempted to determine the causes of the recent mortgage crisis. They document that the subprime mortgage market experienced a very rapid growth between 2001 and 2006, and that this growth was enhanced by the creation of private-label MBSs. Even though these MBSs do not offer credit risk protection by a government-sponsored enterprise, demand for these private-label MBSs kept increasing as investors searched for higher yields. The end result was a sharp increase in the subprime share of the mortgage market, from 8 percent in 2001 to 20 percent in 2006, and in the securitized share of the subprime mortgage market, from 54 percent in 2001 to 75 percent in 2006. Also important was the growth experienced within subprime loans by hybrid mortgages, which carry a fixed rate for an initial period (typically two or three years), after which the rate resets to a reference rate (often the 6-month London Interbank Offered Rate [LIBOR]) plus a margin.

Once real estate prices in the United States started to deteriorate in mid- to late 2006, the mortgage market began to fall. Interestingly, some researchers found that the poor performance of the mortgage loans originating in 2006 was not confined to a particular segment of the subprime mortgage market.[9] This is because fixed-rate, adjustable-rate, purchase-money, cash-out refinancing, low-documentation, and full-documentation loans originating in 2006 all showed substantially higher delinquency and foreclosure rates than loans made in the prior five years. This finding contradicts the widely held belief that the subprime mortgage crisis was mostly confined to either adjustable-rate or low-documentation mortgages.

SPECIAL ISSUES IN REAL ESTATE

Current research in real estate has focused on the study of the effects of the recent introduction of new real estate financial instruments. A related stream of research has focused on analyzing the supposed real estate bubble that burst in 2007 and its concomitant effects, unleashing the subprime mortgage crisis of 2007 to 2010.

Given the stellar performance of real estate investments during the period 2001 to 2007, the discrepancies between the suggested weights and the more modest weights of real estate investments in institutional portfolios that have been documented by some researchers represent a puzzle.[10] Attempting to understand this and other behavior exhibited by institutional investors' decisions to invest in real estate, Dhar and Goetzmann (2005) analyzed, using an online questionnaire, the factors influencing these decisions. They found that diversification potential and inflation hedging are the main reasons for investing in real estate. Conversely, the institutional investors surveyed suggest that the main risks of real estate investing are liquidity risk, lack of reliable valuation data, and the risk of poor management. Furthermore, institutional investors perceive the expected return and expected risk of real estate investments to be midway between U.S. stocks and bonds. This substantiates our own analysis, which suggests that institutional investors view real estate as an inflation protection asset class that must be widely diversified to mitigate against risks inherent in local markets.

Price smoothing (causing a lag effect and reduced volatility in valuation-based indices when compared with the underlying market) and using non-market-price-based returns in the real estate sector have an effect on asset allocation decisions because the estimation of risk and return profiles of various asset classes is critical to the construction of efficient portfolios. For example, following the mean-variance model of Markowitz, one would assign an optimal high weight to real estate because valuation-based real estate indices exhibit low risk levels. However, portfolios of institutional investors typically have a real estate weight of between only 5 and 10 percent. The difference between optimal and current real estate weights can be partially attributed to the underestimation of volatility in available real estate indices.

Commercial and Residential Real Estate Investments

Now we shift the analysis toward commercial and residential real estate investments. For commercial real estate, the NPI and the MIT TBI were used as proxies. Data for the NPI and the MIT TBI indices were obtained from the NCREIF website. For residential real estate, the S&P/Case-Shiller Home Price Indices were used as proxies. This index family consists of 23 indices: 20 metropolitan regional indices, 2 composite indices, and a national index. One composite index consists of 10 regions, while the other consists of all 20 regions.

An examination of the performance statistics of various real estate classes reveals that investments across these classes differ with regard to returns and volatility. In addition, the performance properties of direct versus securitized real estate investments differ. As shown in Exhibit 7.11, the return over the period 2002–2011 for the FTSE NAREIT was 12.6 percent, while that of the commercial NPI was 8.0 percent. The volatility, however, of the NPI (6.3 percent), was far lower than that of the FTSE NAREIT (25.5 percent). The extremely low volatility of NCREIF returns is indicative of the volatility-dampening biases associated with smoothing and lagging because of stale valuations. The different return movement between the equity market-based FTSE NAREIT and the NPI is illustrated in Exhibit 7.12. In Exhibit 7.12, the quarterly returns of the FTSE NAREIT

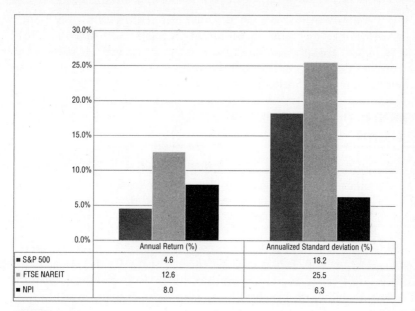

	Annual Return (%)	Annualized Standard deviation (%)
■ S&P 500	4.6	18.2
▣ FTSE NAREIT	12.6	25.5
■ NPI	8.0	6.3

EXHIBIT 7.11 Real Estate Indices: Comparison Market and Accounting Based Period of analysis: 2002 to 2011.

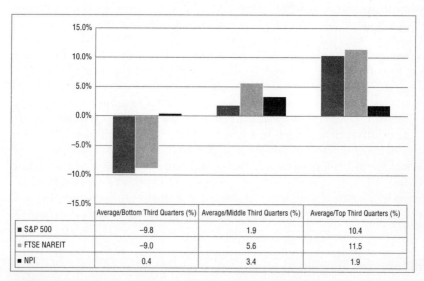

	Average/Bottom Third Quarters (%)	Average/Middle Third Quarters (%)	Average/Top Third Quarters (%)
■ S&P 500	−9.8	1.9	10.4
▣ FTSE NAREIT	−9.0	5.6	11.5
■ NPI	0.4	3.4	1.9

EXHIBIT 7.12 Real Estate Indices: Quarterly Returns Ranked on S&P 500 Period of analysis: 2002 to 2011.

index and the NPI are ranked on the quarterly returns of the S&P 500. Results show that the return patterns of the S&P 500 and the FTSE NAREIT indices are similar in both the worst and best months of the S&P 500; however the return patterns of the NPI seem unaffected by the worst and best months of the S&P 500.

A PERSONAL VIEW: ISSUES IN REAL ESTATE INVESTMENT

Academic research has often addressed the benefits of real estate from the viewpoint of a changing value reflecting changing supply and demand characteristics. Research in this area has often failed to consider the unique investment vehicle or real estate area or how that real estate investment must be classified. Recently, REITs have been classified into more specific real estate areas as well as geographic areas. Until each of these real estate areas is given its own factor model in which many of the impacts are considered, real estate analysis remains a "first-pass" attempt, with little real understanding of the benefits and costs of the underlying investment.

Distributional Characteristics

The primary reason for real estate investment is the degree to which individual real estate investments provide unique risk and return characteristics not easily available in other investment vehicles. Analysis of real estate distributional characteristics, however, has been impacted by unique periods of investment. In two years in the early 2000s, generic REITs outperformed many alternative equity investments. This performance may have been linked with the unique interest rate environment supported by the U.S. government and Treasury policy. In contrast, in the period since 2008, real estate was negatively impacted by the crash, only to rebound in 2009. The high sensitivity of real estate to current economic variables requires a more dynamic investment model, one which drives the distributional characteristics of most real estate investments. Researchers and reviewers are often enticed by the "more data is better" syndrome; that is, five years of data is good, 10 years is better, 20 years is best. However, in a market partially driven by rapidly changing technological and distribution channels as well as regulatory rules, what was true just a decade ago may have little relevance for 2012.

Micromarket Structure

Recent regulatory and market adjustments to the 2008 financial crisis have fundamentally changed many of the traditional approaches to real estate investment. This is especially true in the structured product and debt area. Today, reduced availability of capital, as well as retractions on banking structure and risk exposure, has fundamentally impacted how and where real estate capital is obtained. Future research may wish to concentrate less on what has happened in the developed and undeveloped real estate markets and more on what may or may not happen in the development of global real estate investments.

WHAT EVERY INVESTOR SHOULD KNOW

The world changes. For some, change is good, for others, not so much. Real estate remains, for most individual investors and many institutional investors, the bedrock of their investment portfolio. The forms and types of real estate investment are numerous and require an in-depth knowledge of the financial instrument as well as the cash flows or investments they provide access to. However, as for private equity, much of real estate is hidden from the public view. As a result, it requires, more than many other more transparent offerings, a more thorough knowledge of the *inside* nature of the investment. In this chapter, we provided a brief review of how old forms of real estate investment evolved over time and how new forms are currently being presented. We certainly do not have all the answers for how to best invest in real estate. Today's real estate is a new world.

- Before You Buy the House, Go in the Door and Look Around: With the exception of direct investments, real estate investment returns are completely dependent on the business model of the sponsor. The business model reflects items such as accounting practices, leverage used, distribution, and management cost. Each is highly volatile, and collectively, they will create return differentials from one product to the next, even within the same sector. Remember, real estate investment forms that are not valued in open-market exchange-traded environments but are valued primarily from appraisal or accounting-based approaches often have historical-based risk measures that underestimate the true market risk of the investment. Although historical data may show that real estate provides some diversification and return benefits to a traditional or mixed traditional and alternative investment, those benefits must be considered carefully because of potential problems in risk-and-return estimation.
- All Homes Look the Same from the Outside: Real estate investments require a commitment to rigorous due diligence and analysis. Real estate has become a securitized investment scheme, with each level of

the scheme containing elements of risk and return. Although reliance on rating agencies can protect an investor from lawsuits regarding negligence and violation of reasonable-person standards, such reliance cannot protect against deterioration of wealth.

- **Private or Public, There Is a Difference:** Although returns differ widely depending on sectors and timing, traditional public real estate may be better viewed as return enhancement vehicles to equity-biased portfolios. Investors should realize there is a lot of competition for quality investment. The question is what happens to the bad ones and how are they sold, especially in an illiquid risk-adverse world (see the section "Performance in 2008"). Not only should you know how much you own, you should know how much others own of what you own and who gets out the door first. Also know how big the door is in case of a fire. You cannot trust the promise.

MYTHS AND MISCONCEPTIONS OF REAL ESTATE

If any investment vehicle or asset class has undergone a reassessment in recent years, real estate investment must be near the top. A real estate firm called our offices several months ago looking for a new potential hire. We pointed out that we had many young analysts who might fit the need, but none of them had direct experience in the real estate area. He answered that they were exactly who he was looking for. His final comment struck home. He said he did not want analysts with experience in real estate since they would continue to do things the way they had been done before. His comment made it clear that individuals with experience in the field would bring with themselves all the historical myths and misconceptions. We list a few here.

Myth 7.1: Real Estate Investments Are a Natural Diversifier

For many investors, real estate seems like a natural diversifier to traditional stock and bond markets. While equity portfolios and bond portfolios seem to respond to national or global changes in basic economic factors (e.g., growth in gross domestic product [GDP], changes in credit spreads), real estate seems more affected by local or regional economic conditions that may seem separate from overall economic conditions. For many, real estate (at least if managed well) seems a natural diversifier. Not to overemphasize a point, but recent experience has indicated that in the current national and global economic scene, economic impacts seem to affect a broader set of regional and global markets. Even if local conditions dominate, many modern real estate-based products are based on a diversified set of cash flows where their final value is impacted more by general economic events than is assumed in historical models. This is not to say that certain regional or specialized real estate products do not act uniquely (e.g., storage-based REITS in 2008), but today most real estate investments should no longer be regarded as equity risk diversifiers but as equity return enhancers. More important, if any concept has been made clear in today's environment, it is that real estate is a highly illiquid asset class and that the outcome of the valuation processes is dependent on the strength of the credit markets.

Myth 7.2: Real Estate Benchmarks Reflect Reality

Most investors are comfortable with investment indices' (e.g., S&P 500, BarCap U.S. Aggregate) ability to provide a performance benchmark that reflects the particular style of an investment manager. Although benchmark indices are common in the areas of stock and bond investment, many investors are not familiar with the various benchmark indices in the real estate area. To the degree that a benchmark exists, many investors use what is easily available. In the case of real estate, real estate investment trust-based equity indices are often used to provide a measure of the returns to various real estate investments. Of course, as in the traditional asset area, there exists no one benchmark that reflects the performance of the asset class. Each real estate index (e.g., S&P/Case-Shiller, FTSE NAREIT, Dow Jones) has unique weighting, composition, and structural issues (market based or accounting based), just as equity indices (e.g., S&P 500, NASDAQ) have their own unique weighting and asset composition. In addition, none of the indices capture the fundamental benchmark requirements of investability, systematic reproduction, and transparency. Investors should take the time to ensure that they understand the investment characteristics of the index that they use in their investment management decisions and that the actual investments that they hold reflect the return and risk characteristics of the index they used in their analysis.

Myth 7.3: Local Commercial and Noncommercial Real Estate Investments Have Similar Performance Patterns

This is the problem: One would expect so, but we just do not know. In this book, we report on various measures of commercial and residential real estate performance. These performance measures now exist even for the regional or local area. In fact, the characteristics of the commercial properties may be so different, the source of valuations so unconnected except in rare economic conditions, that relying on historical performance data may simply offer no answer. The purpose of raising this myth or misconception is that the basis for determining if local commercial or noncommercial real estate have similar performance patterns cannot or should not be based on some historical set of data but based on a more direct analysis of economic cash flow determinants. In short, the data is so bad we cannot even tell if a myth is truly a myth or if a fact is truly a fact.

Myth 7.4: International Real Estate Offers Significant Diversification Potential

One would hope so; however, in recent years, the global slowdown has indicated a higher level of comovement among various global real estate products than historical data would have suggested prior to the financial market crash. While in relatively calm market environments, U.S. and international REIT returns may reflect relatively low correlation, in periods of global market stress, there seems to be a growing comovement. The reasons for this increased correlation may have less to do with the actual correlation in local economic conditions than with the increasing globalization in how funds are raised or fund portfolios are created. In periods of market stress, the lack of transparency of both local and global real estate results in a common discounting of all real estate-based investment products. There may be solutions to this generic discounting in the future as the differential means of evaluating local conditions are designed; but for the foreseeable future, the commonly held belief that global real estate offers (at least at the size required for major investors) inherent diversification benefits may have to be put on hold.

CHAPTER 8

Asset Allocation

The Simple Way and the Hard Way

For many, the central question of modern finance is where to invest in order to maximize return relative to risk. Over the past 60 years, advances in financial theory and the introduction of new financial products, as well as the growth of new financial markets, have added complexity to how best to answer that question. For most investors, modern finance remains focused on the original portfolio selection approach put forth by Harry Markowitz (modern portfolio theory [MPT]). At its core, MPT is an analytical approach through which knowledge of the expected returns and the return correlation among assets provides a means to find a set of assets, which, in turn, provides the highest expected return for a level of expected risk. At its inception, simple correlation-based asset diversification was the principal means of return and risk management. What it lacked, in part, was a simple mechanism to forecast assets' expected returns. As noted in Chapter 1, the capital asset pricing model (CAPM) attempts to link all assets into a single-factor approach in which all assets are priced relative to their common sensitivity to a single common market portfolio, but CAPM is completely useless as a forecasting tool because (a) we need a forecast of the expected return on the market and (b) the portion of the stock returns not explained by the return on the market is rather large. To be fair, CAPM was not meant to be a forecasting tool; rather it is an explanation of which stocks will earn a return higher than the market, and which will earn a return less than the market. In addition, these differences in returns were meant to be entirely due to differences to riskiness—no free lunches.

Other authors have attempted to design various multifactor approaches, each aimed at producing a manageable set of security groupings (e.g., asset classes), such that each group may be said to offer unique characteristics that separate it from other investments. For the most part, these multifactor models are of little use in forecasting the absolute returns on a given investment opportunity. They do a much better job of explaining differences in return, especially among various asset classes. Let us recall that according to the efficient market hypothesis (EMH), there is no point in forecasting returns because in a world of informational transparency and trading efficiency, investors could feel safe that the prices that existed in the market at any one time reflected the true expected return-to-risk trade-off embedded in current information.

The threshold question is what makes a security fit into a unique asset grouping? To get to the answer, there must be a determination as to whether the securities share some common feature or quality. Simple return and risk models fail to incorporate directly a host of qualitative risks (e.g., liquidity, counterparty risks, political risks, transparency) that may or may not be reflected in the price risk of a set of tradable assets. Moreover, most models of expected return and risk determination have failed to adequately measure the relative impacts of illiquid assets, including the investor's "personal value" in any applicable model of asset class determination.

There are unique features of some investment strategies (e.g., fixed-income and publicly traded equities) that have permitted them to be universally accepted as an asset class. Extrapolating from these conventions provides an aid to understanding the return and risk properties and the inherent trading patterns that can be said to establish the requisite behavior of an accepted asset class. We know that, in the case of hedge funds, there are sets of investment opportunities, which have a central focus and market risk exposure. In addition, they have well-defined trading processes that separate them from other potential asset classes. We also know that various hedge-fund strategies can be seen as an extension of the security markets in which they trade (e.g., equity long/short in the equity space and distressed debt in the fixed-income area). With this knowledge, it is also possible to create a taxonomy in which hedge funds (or at least equity-based hedge funds) are regarded as variants of the equity asset class rather than a separate asset class on their own.

As we find our way through new terrain, there are a range of issues in determining the taxonomy for asset class determination. The degree of difficulty must not be the stopping point of establishing a process by which we address asset allocation issues. The approach must be the creation of a map. In designing any map, we first look to its purpose and then gauge the level of detail required to make it useful. Here, usefulness is analogous to the risks involved with any particular investment path. Every path has its own risks, and every map its faults.

How do investors determine risk and benefits involved in various approaches to asset allocation? If more than 30 years in the investment management business has taught us anything, it is that for the most part, asset allocation services remain a seemingly free service with firms promoting a particular product as a solution to an investment problem and using their own investment products as a basis for asset recommendations. There are numerous examples of the conflict between business management and potential investor products. In the early 1980s, there existed disagreement in the consulting community about the benefit of new forms of investor mutual funds. At that time, investment firms often offered a limited number of investment products to its potential clients: an equity fund, a corporate and government bond fund, and a money market fund. With the growth of stock and bond markets, there was some investor demand for increasing the number of equity funds (U.S., international, and emerging markets), and increasing the number of bond funds (government, corporate, and high yield), as well as creating a series of multi-asset balanced stock and bond portfolios to provide access to mixed stock and bond portfolios that were conservative, moderate, and aggressive in focus. However, many firms considered the idea to be detrimental to their investors. The counter arguments were that too many choices would confuse the investor. These firms also argued that offering individuals high-risk/high-return products would encourage them to leave lower risk/lower return "safe" products in their search for higher return. It was their responsibility not to increase the number of choices to investors but, just the opposite, to control those choices in the best interests of the investor. For the next 30 years, the same battle was fought repeatedly. Each firm approached its investors as if they were small children. It was their purpose not to overburden their investors with the particulars of the investment, only to ensure that their approach (e.g., diversified stock, diversified bond, mixed portfolios, etc.) provided a complete or, at least, an important solution to the investor's investment concerns.

The parental approach offers simple solutions to one of the basic tenets of modern investment, that is, the trade-off between risk and return. However, if the asset allocation solution is free and simple, it probably offers a very low benefit to the investor and this is also consistent with the tenet of return for risk. Against this proposition, let us explore both the meaning and implementation of the asset allocation decision. MPT suggests that individuals can select a group of financial assets, which provides maximum return for a given level of risk (i.e., standard deviation). This theory is premised on (a) the financial assets to be considered, (b) the validity of the return and risk inputs into the model to represent the current and future financial conditions, and (c) the desired level of risk of the investor. As to the financial assets to be considered, most asset allocation services focus on a single set of assets or, at most, a limited set of asset classes. This approach assumes that an investor exists in a regional incubator. Further, it ignores the geographic, cultural, economic, and political risks of a global economy.

Genuine asset allocation is in every instance a risk-management tool. As such, it requires investors to view a multidimensional world that contains both known and hidden risks. And in so doing, it requires investors to seek an asset allocation approach that looks beyond particular products or institutional affiliations to asset strategies or opportunities presented within the context of a global economy that is at times fraught with as much anxiety as opportunity. This matrix recognizes that there are many unique and investable sources of returns in the market place. We use the term *sources of return* because the investable universe has significantly expanded beyond prior notions of auction-traded stocks and bonds or the purchase of land. For all intents and purposes, the investable universe is dominated by structured products (at least if the concept of structured products is taking individual assets and putting them together in a new product form). These structured products take the form of mutual funds, hedge funds, private equity, real estate, and commodities, to name a few. The returns associated with these investments are more a function of their business model than the underlying assets that they either trade or manage. Similarly, the risks are not a function of traditional research and analysis. There are no objective analysts covering these businesses. There is no rush to provide transparent information and guidance. There are no efficient frontiers here. There are no CAPMs that pierce the corporate veil and reveal that investment management is as much about luck as skill. And, there is no efficient market for the investor who is without significant resources.

In understanding the foregoing, our task is to provide the reader with as many functional tools as possible so as to make reasoned decisions. We realize that readers fall into differing categories of risk tolerance and the ability to assess risk. For the individual, risk has to take into account factors such as job security, family, and housing. For the institution, risks not only take into account the traditional mix, such as of time horizon and return goals, but must incorporate nontraditional aspects, such as immediate career risk and organizational failure. The behavioral science aspects of asset allocation are undoubtedly a strong subtext of investment decision making. However, these fall outside of our present analysis as we attempt to provide a set of universal tools capable of general application. The first tool is the understanding that there is no substitute for independent analysis and judgment. The language of finance can be intimidating. It can be used by some to forestall meaningful analysis and questions. There is one question that escapes embarrassment: "When does this investment lose money and when does it make money—*exactly*?" Absent a detailed answer that appeals to commonsensical notions of logic and just play, do not invest—ever. Second, investors must fundamentally understand that if an asset allocation process suggests that it can produce positive returns in any economic environment, the return it offers should be the risk-free rate.

Against these rather fundamental thoughts, in this chapter, we concentrate on the liquid financial part of an investor's portfolio. When looking at financial asset portfolios, however, every investor must keep in mind that it represents only a part of his or her asset portfolio, and financial asset portfolio decisions should not be made outside of understanding the other illiquid assets in the portfolio. In addition, in this chapter, we concentrate on the traditional Markowitz mean-variance asset allocation approach across multiple asset classes. We realize that concentrating on the mean-variance approach to asset allocation is, in the words of William Sharpe, "not an entirely happy state of affairs."[1] We understand that the mean-variance approach is really a special case of various approaches to asset allocation. However, as William Sharpe further explained, mean-variance-based asset allocation is a "special case with many practical advantages."[2] We attempt to put some constraints around the mean-variance approach by considering the impact of alternative means of portfolio risk management. In addition, we will briefly discuss volatility targeting, risk parity, and portfolio insurance as special cases of asset allocations.

THE WHY AND WHEREFORE OF MULTIPLE ASSET ALLOCATION APPROACHES

As noted, we are faced with the dilemma of providing universal tools. Here, we can provide simple solutions that will be of limited use given the changing economic environment and the fact that there are as many unique circumstances as there are investors. The simple solutions are easily understood by many investors, but actually pretty worthless. Alternatively, we can provide a more complex model that offers a greater appreciation for the dynamics of asset allocation. We offered such a view in our last book, *The New Science of Asset Allocation*, and discovered that the audience for that book was almost exclusively traders, academics, and policy wonks with mathematical backgrounds. Now, we have chosen a building-block approach. One designed to provide investors with the means to question and analyze the accepted models surrounding asset allocation and, in so doing, effectively protect themselves in a global multi-asset class environment. Our building blocks ask and answer the question of whether alternative investments provide investors with valuable return and risk opportunities beyond those easily available in the traditional equity and fixed-income markets. In addition, it explores the nature of individual assets and their corresponding benefits in a multi-asset universe and concludes, in relation to asset allocation, that perhaps more is, in fact, better than less. Finally, we explore results based on some common benchmarks for each suggested asset class. To the degree that an individual invests in a particular product that does not reflect the return and risk process of the benchmark, the results based on the benchmark approach are relatively meaningless.

OVERVIEW AND LIMITATIONS OF THE EXISTING ASSET ALLOCATION PROCESS

In a world of multiple markets and opportunities, investors are rarely faced with the choice of just two assets (unless one is investing along the capital market line). When several assets are held together, they behave quite differently from an average of the assets' individual behaviors. One general observation is that the more assets held in the portfolio, the lower the total risk of the portfolio as long as each new asset added to the portfolio has some unique risk-return characteristics not completely shared with assets already in the portfolio. Investors should note that the expected standard deviation of a portfolio comprised of equally weighted assets decreases as the number of assets increases. If the number of assets is large enough, the total portfolio variance does, in fact, stem more from the covariances than from the individual variances of the assets. It is, in other words, more important how the assets tend to move together than how much each individual asset fluctuates in value. However, even in the simple equal-asset-weighted portfolios, volatility estimation has its limitations. First, it assumes equal weighting of the assets. Second, it is an estimation of the expected standard deviation. In short, there is risk even in the estimation of risk.

There may be a reason that the MPT is not called the modern portfolio *fact*. While the theory of risk reduction in combining two assets that react differently to unexpected changes in economic information is sound, in practice, the result may be much different than expected. The word *expected* is important. The MPT is based on expectations; that is, expected returns, expected volatility, and expected correlations. The primary goal of many investors is to maximize the long-run rate of return. For some investors, this means concentrating in a few assets or asset classes, such as investing primarily in equity markets. Recent performance of traditional stock markets has illustrated the risks of such an allocation process. Research has shown that given two investment streams with roughly the same expected per period rate of return, the investment stream with the lower standard deviation has the higher long-term compounded rate of return. As a result, for many investors, one of the primary goals of multi-asset asset allocation is to hold a variety of investments to lower future expected return volatility.

The asset allocation process often starts with the following three steps:

1. **Description of available investment opportunities.** In this step, the relevant asset classes and their risk-to-return characteristics are analyzed. Considerable academic research exists detailing the unique risk and return attributes of stocks, bonds, private equity, and hedge funds.
2. **Investor's preference, assets, and liabilities.** This step begins with a description of the investor's financial condition (e.g., assets, liabilities, financial goals, taxes, etc.) and then proceeds with an estimation of the client's risk capacity and risk tolerance.
3. **Optimal asset mix.** In this final stage, the above information is employed to develop an investment policy statement and to recommend a strategic optimal asset mix. Recent studies have shown that asset classes should include investments that create alternative risk-to-return patterns through the use of investments such as private equity, which offer return enhancement to traditional stock and bond investments, and hedge funds, which also provide investment opportunities and exposure to economic factors that are not available through traditional asset classes.[3]

If alternative investments, such as private equity and hedge funds, are to be included in an investor's optimal portfolio allocation, investors need to determine if alternative investments, such as private equity and hedge funds, represent a distinct asset class and therefore, should be included in the analysis. The common denominator within each of these steps or scenarios is unbiased information and research. Neither risk and return characteristics, nor preferences, nor optimal asset mix can be determined without understanding the economics, liquidity, correlations, or regulatory structure of a particular asset class or its underlying components.

ASSET ALLOCATION IN TRADITIONAL AND ALTERNATIVE INVESTMENTS: A ROAD MAP

If a person is going to go on a journey, he needs a map. The details of the map, of course, depend on the distance of the journey and the terrain of the path. The map may also be affected by where the mapmaker wants you to go. In this section, we provide two maps covering the same geography. In the first, we construct the map with four primary forms of geography (i.e., traditional stock, traditional bond, traditional alternatives [i.e., real estate, commodities, and private equity] and modern alternatives [i.e., hedge funds, managed futures, etc.]). In this map, an equity class consists of various security groupings such as the Standard & Poor's (S&P) 500, MSCI Europe, Australasia, Far East (EAFE) and MSCI Emerging Markets indices. Fixed income may include government bonds, corporate bonds, and high-yield debt within an overall fixed-income asset class. Traditionally, other less liquid, less transparent, or nonequity-based investments have been grouped as "traditional alternative investments," since they are viewed primarily as alternatives to the traditional stock and bond asset classes. This group of traditional alternatives includes investments such as private equity, real estate (residential and commercial), and commodity investments. In recent years, an additional set of "modern alternative investments," such as hedge funds and managed futures, has become increasingly available for both retail and institutional investors. Of course, in each geographical area, different details are needed to understand the risks of travel in that area. Our map looks to proven market tools such as standard deviation, beta, and multiple risk dimensions (liquidity and transparency) for guidance.

The second map is based on a grouping of the assets founded primarily on the relative market factor correlations within each group, such that the groupings reflect an equity factor, an interest rate factor, and a high-yield factor, and a final grouping with a low correlation to each of the three market factors. It is important to note that the primary emphasis on these two approaches is partially due to the necessity of keeping it simple. Given the number of external personnel involved in the investment management process, the asset class structure may be, by necessity, designed to fit a required business model which, while academically flawed, is workable from an organizational viewpoint.

RETURN AND RISK ATTRIBUTES AND STRATEGY ALLOCATION

MPT emphasizes that the benefits of individual assets should be evaluated based on their performance alongside other assets in investor's portfolios. The diversification benefits of adding any individual investment to other securities within an asset class, or the benefits of adding any individual asset classes to other asset classes, depends on the comparison stand-alone investment. As discussed in the previous section, in the traditional asset class breakdown shown in Exhibit 8.1, stocks and bonds were regarded as separate asset classes due primarily to the assumed low correlation between stocks and bonds. Similarly, real estate, private equity, and commodities were assumed to, in many cases, be in a unique asset class due to opportunity for positive return in economic conditions for which stocks and bonds did poorly. In recent years, two additional investment areas, hedge funds

EXHIBIT 8.1   Traditional and Market Factor-Based Asset Groupings

Traditional Asset Class-Based	Market Factor-Based
Equity	**Equity**
U.S. investment (S&P 500)	U.S. investment (S&P 500)
Non-U.S. developed (MSCI EAFE)	Non-U.S. developed (MSCI EAFE)
Emerging markets (MSCI EEM)	Emerging markets (MSCI EEM)
	Real estate (Financial Times and Stock Exchange [FTSE])
	Real estate investment trusts [REITs])
	Hedge funds (Center for International Securities and Derivatives Markets [CISDM])
	Equal Weighted Hedge Fund Index (CISDM EW HF)
Fixed Income (FI)	**Fixed Income (Interest Rate)**
FI government (BarCap U.S. Government)	FI government (BarCap U.S. Government)
FI aggregate (BarCap U.S. Aggregate)	FI aggregate (BarCap U.S. Aggregate)
FI high yield (BarCap High Yield)	
FI emerging (BarCap EMBI)	
Alternative Investments	**Credit Quality - High Yield**
Private equity (PE)	FI high yield (BarCap High Yield)
Commodities (S&P Goldman Sachs Commodity Index [GSCI])	FI emerging (BarCap Emerging Markets Bond Index [EMBI])
Real estate (FTSE REITs)	
Modern Alternative Investments	**Low Market Sensitivity**
Hedge funds (CISDM EW HF)	Commodities (S&P GSCI)
Managed futures (CISDM commodity trading advisor [CTA])	Managed futures (CISDM CTA)

and managed futures, have been added to the list of investment classes and are assumed to provide skill-based manager returns, which are not correlated with traditional asset classes. Exhibit 8.2 shows the return and risk characteristics for the range of various investments depicted in the traditional asset class breakdown in Exhibit 8.1. There are, of course, alternative bases for grouping asset classes, both traditional and alternative. These groupings include measures of stand-alone risk, such as standard deviation, as well as their correlation to various common market factors

EXHIBIT 8.2 Asset Class Performance

Equity and Fixed-income Performance	S&P 500	MSCI EAFE	MSCI EEM	BarCap U.S. Government	BarCap U.S. Aggregate	BarCap U.S. Corporate High Yield
Annualized return	1.5%	2.0%	9.6%	5.7%	6.0%	8.5%
Annualized standard deviation	16.3%	18.7%	24.8%	4.5%	3.7%	11.3%
Information ratio	0.09	0.11	0.39	1.27	1.63	0.76
Maximum drawdown	−50.9%	−56.7%	−62.7%	−4.6%	−3.8%	−33.3%
Correlation with S&P 500	1.00	0.89	0.82	−0.35	−0.10	0.67
Correlation with BarCap U.S. Government	−0.35	−0.26	−0.27	1.00	0.91	−0.19
Correlation with BarCap U.S. Aggregate	−0.10	0.00	0.00	0.91	1.00	0.17
Correlation with U.S. Corporate High Yield	0.67	0.69	0.71	−0.19	0.17	1.00

Alternative Investment Performance	JPMorgan EMBI Global	FTSE NAREIT	S&P GSCI	Private Equity	CISDM EW HF	CISDM CTA EW
Annualized return	10.1%	10.1%	1.5%	2.3%	6.7%	7.6%
Annualized standard deviation	9.6%	23.5%	24.7%	29.9%	6.9%	8.7%
Information ratio	1.05	0.43	0.06	0.08	0.97	0.88
Maximum drawdown	−20.7%	−67.9%	−67.6%	−80.4%	−21.7%	−8.7%
Correlation with S&P 500	0.54	0.69	0.33	0.87	0.80	−0.12
Correlation with BarCap U.S. Government	0.21	−0.11	−0.15	−0.26	−0.31	0.21
Correlation with BarCap U.S. Aggregate	0.49	0.13	−0.04	−0.02	−0.02	0.14
Correlation with U.S. Corporate High Yield	0.70	0.65	0.32	0.72	0.74	−0.14

Period of analysis: 2001 to 2011.

(e.g., equity, interest rates, credit spreads). As shown in Exhibit 8.2, as additions to an equity portfolio, certain asset classes (e.g., real estate and private equity) reflect a higher standard deviation and a high correlation to the equity portfolio (e.g., S&P 500), and may be regarded as return enhancers (i.e., added potential return but with little reduction in expected risk), to an equity biased portfolio. As additions to an equity biased portfolio, a hedge fund portfolio reflects a relatively low standard deviation but with a relatively high correlation. Thus, a portfolio of hedge-fund strategies may be regarded primarily as a return enhancer to an equity-dominated portfolio. Other asset classes (e.g., managed futures) report a lower standard deviation and a low correlation with the S&P 500 and may be regarded as risk diversifiers (i.e., lower portfolio risk) to an equity biased portfolio. As shown in Exhibit 8.2, as additions to a fixed-income portfolio (e.g., BarCap U.S. Aggregate), most of the asset classes reflect both a higher standard deviation and a low correlation to fixed income. Thus, with the exception of fixed-income government, most assets may be regarded as risk diversifiers to a credit quality fixed-income portfolio. After reviewing these correlation and risk relationships, an alternative set of investment groupings based on the relative market factor correlations was created as shown in Exhibit 8.1.[4]

The results reflect the portfolios of the underlying asset classes. To the degree that any individual portfolio has return and risk characteristics that differ from the characteristics of the index, results may differ. For example, a hedge-fund strategy that emphasizes a relative value arbitrage strategy may have a relatively lower correlation with equity and may be regarded as an equity risk diversifier, rather than the portfolio represented by the hedge-fund index that may be driven by more volatile equity-based hedge-fund strategies. Thus, the actual return and risk characteristics of individual strategies must be evaluated separately.

The purpose of presenting each of the asset classes in alternative groupings (i.e., traditional and market factor sensitivity) is to illustrate the effect of alternative forms of asset class groupings on return and risk performance. As shown in Exhibit 8.3, the groupings by traditional risk class (i.e., equal weighted) and by market factor exposure (i.e., equal weighted) result in a set of portfolio groupings for which the market factor sensitive groupings show a similar or higher correlation to the comparison market factor. For example, the equity class (traditional [see Portfolio A] and market factor [see Portfolio A1]) has approximately the same correlation to the S&P 500 (0.93 and 0.93, respectively); however, the correlation of the fixed-income traditional asset class (see Portfolio B, 0.35) to the BarCap U.S. Government is considerably less than the correlation of the fixed-income market factor (see Portfolio B1) asset class (0.98) to the

EXHIBIT 8.3 Traditional and Market Factor-Based Multi-Asset Portfolios Performance

Traditional Asset Class-Based Portfolio	A	B	C	D	Portfolio Equal Weight (EW)
Annualized return	4.5%	7.8%	5.8%	7.3%	6.9%
Annualized standard deviation	19.0%	5.5%	20.9%	5.9%	11.3%
Information ratio	0.24	1.41	0.28	1.24	0.60
Maximum drawdown	−56.8%	−12.5%	−66.4%	−8.5%	−37.9%
Correlation with S&P 500	0.93	0.49	0.80	0.38	0.87
Correlation with BarCap U.S. Government	−0.30	0.35	−0.22	−0.03	−0.19
Correlation with BarCap U.S. Aggregate	−0.03	0.66	0.03	0.09	0.09
Correlation with U.S. Corporate High Yield	0.73	0.81	0.71	0.33	0.77

Portfolio A   Equal weight: S&P 500, MSCI EAFE, MSCI EEM
Portfolio B   Equal weight: BarCap U.S. Government, BarCap U.S. Aggregate and BarCap U.S. Corporate High Yield, JP Morgan EMBI
Portfolio C   Equal weight: FTSE Real Estate, S&P GSCI Commodity, Private Equity Index
Portfolio D   Equal weight: CISDM Hedge-Fund Index and CISDM CTA Index
Portfolio E   Equal weight: Portfolios A, B, C, D

Market Factor-Based Portfolio Performance	A1	B1	C1	D1	Portfolio EW E1
Annualized return	6.0%	5.9%	9.4%	5.3%	7.1%
Annualized standard deviation	18.1%	4.0%	9.6%	14.1%	8.4%
Information ratio	0.33	1.46	0.98	0.38	0.84
Maximum drawdown	−58.1%	−4.1%	−25.8%	−39.9%	−28.4%
Correlation with S&P 500	0.93	−0.24	0.66	0.25	0.76
Correlation with BarCap U.S. Government	−0.27	0.98	−0.01	−0.07	−0.06
Correlation with BarCap U.S. Aggregate	0.01	0.97	0.34	0.01	0.22
Correlation with U.S. Corporate High Yield	0.77	−0.03	0.93	0.23	0.77

Portfolio A1   Equal weight: S&P 500, MSCI EAFE, MSCI EEM, CISDM HF, real estate and private equity
Portfolio B1   Equal weight: BarCap U.S. Government and BarCap U.S. Aggregate
Portfolio C1   Equal weight: JP Morgan EMBI and BarCap U.S. Corporate High Yield
Portfolio D1   Equal weight: S&P GSCI and CISDM CTA Index
Portfolio E1   Equal weight: Portfolios A1, B1, C1, D1

Period of analysis: 2001 to 2011.

BarCap U.S. Government. Similarly, the traditional alternatives asset class (see Portfolio C) has a correlation (0.71) that is lower than the market factor class (see Portfolio C1) correlation (0.93) with BarCap U.S. Corporate High Yield. Lastly, the modern alternative traditional asset class (see Portfolio D) has higher correlations to the S&P 500 (0.38), BarCap U.S. Aggregate (0.09), and BarCap U.S. Corporate High Yield (0.33) than the market factor alternative asset group (see Portfolio D1) designed to have a low correlation to the same set of market factors (0.25, 0.01, and 0.23 respectively). Placing assets into groupings based on market factor sensitivity, rather than traditional asset groupings based primarily on risk and transparency, results in asset groupings that are more distinct relative to market factors and may differ in terms of overall risk exposure. For example, as shown in Exhibit 8.3, an equal weighted portfolio (see Portfolio E) formed by the traditional asset class grouping, reports higher volatility (11.3 percent) for the period of analysis than the volatility (8.4 percent) of an equal-weighted portfolio (see Portfolio E1) formed by the market factor sensitivity groupings. The reason for the lower volatility of Portfolio E1 is that the higher volatility equity-sensitive assets are grouped into one group, and therefore, receive a lower weight in the overall portfolio than when they are found across various risk classes as in Portfolio E.

THE MYTH OF AVERAGE: ASSET ALLOCATION IN EXTREME MARKETS

In past chapters, we emphasized the fundamental factors that drive returns in various asset classes. It should come as no surprise to investors, therefore, that in periods when the market factors (i.e., earnings, interest rates or changes in employment) are driving returns, that the returns of two asset classes affected by the same market factors will have a greater degree of comovement. Asset allocation models that do not permit the investor to evaluate the impact of that common market sensitivity fail to provide a true return and risk picture of the portfolio.

Traditional academic and practitioner research promotes the benefits of diversification within an asset class and between asset classes. Diversification of judgment, which is diversification within an asset class, depends on choosing individual securities. Diversification of style is diversification across asset classes to capture the response of different asset classes to different style factors. In truth, for both stocks and bonds, diversification provides risk benefits in periods in which portfolio returns reflect the differential sensitivity of these assets to changes in information. These benefits, however, are highest in asset groupings where the groups are formed to have the highest common factor sensitivity to that market factor. For example, as shown in Chapter 2, when stocks are ranked on the S&P 500, almost all of the stocks in the Dow Jones 30 Industrial Average lose money in the worst months and make money in the best months. Similarly, for a range of forms of fixed-income securities, most forms of risky debt (both domestic and international) move downward together in the worst months and move upward together in the best months. This is to be expected. The conditions driving a portfolio of stocks (e.g., S&P 500) are the common market factors driving stock returns. Similarly, the common factors (e.g., credit spreads) in a national and international market are the same factors driving all bonds.

The question remains, if the various asset classes that may be considered a part of a diversified portfolio are viewed on their performance over multiple time periods, does that representation reflect the true relative return movements of the asset classes in periods of extreme stress? Moreover, if portfolios are created based on their market factor sensitivity rather than simple traditional asset classifications, one would expect that the portfolio would better reflect the movements in market factors than the traditional asset groupings.

Results in Exhibit 8.4 show that portfolios (see Portfolio E1) formed from market factor-based groupings, in contrast to those formed from equal weight traditional asset class groupings (see Portfolio E), have less negative returns in the worst S&P months and less positive returns in the best S&P 500 months. In contrast, the results in Exhibit 8.5 show that portfolios formed from market factor-based groupings (see Portfolio E1), in contrast to

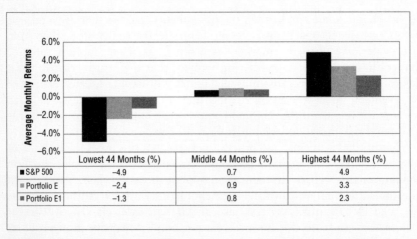

EXHIBIT 8.4 Traditional and Market Factor–Based Portfolios: Monthly Returns Ranked on S&P 500
Period of analysis: 2001 to 2011.

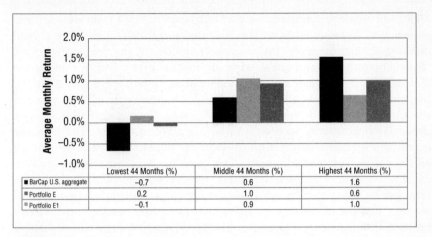

	Lowest 44 Months (%)	Middle 44 Months (%)	Highest 44 Months (%)
■ BarCap U.S. aggregate	−0.7	0.6	1.6
■ Portfolio E	0.2	1.0	0.6
▥ Portfolio E1	−0.1	0.9	1.0

EXHIBIT 8.5 Traditional and Market Factor–Based Portfolios: Monthly Returns Ranked on BarCap U.S. Aggregate
Period of analysis: 2001 to 2011.

those formed from equal weight traditional asset groupings (see Portfolio E), have greater negative returns in the worst BarCap U.S. Aggregate months and less positive returns in the best BarCap U.S. Aggregate months. This is as expected since, as shown in Exhibit 8.3, the market factor-weighted portfolios had higher correlation to the BarCap U.S. Aggregate Index than the traditional asset-weighted portfolios and had a lower correlation to the S&P 500 than the portfolio formed from the traditional asset class construction. But it also indicates if individuals wish to create portfolios that offer them the best opportunity to change asset allocations based on expected changes in market factors, that they should consider grouping assets based on market factor sensitivity rather than historically using the traditional equity, fixed-income, traditional alternatives, and modern alternatives asset classifications.

ALTERNATIVE ASSET ALLOCATION APPROACHES

A classic problem in many basic asset allocation models is that they are unintentionally structured to maximize parameter estimation error; that is, they are often designed to pick the asset with the highest ex post return and the lowest risk. These high-return, low-risk assets often have the highest estimation error (i.e., an overestimation of the true return and an underestimation of the true risk). As a result, the next period's returns are often less than expected, and the next period's risk is greater than expected. In brief, the problem with many of today's popular investor-based asset allocation models, especially as they relate to risk management, is their tendency to focus on what we can measure in contrast to what we should measure. Armies of consultants, computer specialists, and risk managers are focused on technical and quantitative approaches that are easily understood and accepted by the investing public and regulatory authorities. For example, many money managers are forced by regulatory rules or market practice to track a particular benchmark. Now, by limiting the manager to tracking a particular benchmark, both return and risk are constrained. The manager is not permitted to consider a much wider range of risks such as drawdown and changing-risk environments. This problem was expressly shown in 2008 when many fund managers lost over 30 percent because they were required by regulation or convention to track a benchmark that lost 40 percent. This occurred while volatility on the benchmark rose from 20 to 40 percent. If managers had been permitted to target volatility while tracking the benchmark, losses could have been dramatically reduced. In the future, managers must focus on the risks they want to control, not necessarily the risk embedded in the tools readily available to them.

Academics and practitioners have been aware of this important limitation of quantitative asset allocation models. When too many parameters (e.g., expected returns, volatilities, and correlations) have to be estimated, then there are more opportunities to make mistakes and increase allocations to assets that have provided abnormally high returns in the past. These assets are more than likely to provide abnormally low returns going forward. After all, competition is the great leveler of playing fields, and capital will flow to where profits have been the highest in the past, lowering the profits going forward. The problem with estimation risk has led investors to seek asset allocation models that rely less on past data.

While equally weighed asset allocation relies less on past data and is simple to implement, it may lead investors to leave some money on the table. As was indicated previously, some characteristics of assets can be estimated with less uncertainty than others. In particular, expected returns are notoriously difficult to estimate. Therefore, any asset allocation model that relies heavily on estimates of expected returns should be viewed skeptically. Conversely, estimates of volatility, especially if an investor has frequent observations (e.g., daily data) tend to suffer less from estimation error. This observation has led to four asset allocation models that rely heavily on estimates of volatility and ignore estimates of expected returns.

1. **Minimum Volatility:** This approach requires the investor to develop an asset allocation that has displayed minimal volatility in the past. If additional constraints are not imposed, the portfolio with minimal past

volatility is likely to be rather strange with large positive and negative allocations to various investments. Therefore, constraints should be imposed. Even when sensible constraints are imposed, the investors can still develop a portfolio with relatively low past volatility. The next step in this process is rather scary and strange to most investors: Use leverage to increase the volatility and hopefully the return of the portfolio. There are two reasons for this: First, the minimum volatility portfolio is likely to have a rather low rate of return going forward. Most investors would find both the risk and the return on this portfolio rather low. Leverage can be used to increase both. Second, academic research has shown that low volatility equities tend to outperform high volatility equities. Since the minimal volatility portfolio is likely to have large allocations to low volatility stocks, it is likely to perform rather well (of course, given its risk level). The last statement explains why we start with a low volatility portfolio and then lever it up rather than creating a moderate volatility portfolio to begin with. The minimal volatility portfolio has gained enough attention from the investment community that it has led MSCI to create a minimum volatility index.

2. **Volatility Ranked Equally Weighted Portfolio:** As noted above, research has shown that stocks that have displayed high volatility in the past are likely to underperform the stocks that have displayed low volatility in the past. Using this observation, an investor can rank stocks according to their past volatilities (e.g., previous 6–12 months) and then create an equally weighed portfolio of stocks that rank at the bottom of the ranking. To make this approach more sophisticated, the investor can create a more diversified portfolio by ensuring that most sectors of the economy are present in the portfolio. Clearly, this approach is suited for the construction of equity portfolios, and its effectiveness when applied to other asset classes has not been examined.

3. **Volatility (Estimated) Weighed Allocation:** This approach is a simplified version of the so-called risk parity approach and can be applied to equities and other asset classes. The process requires the investor to estimate the volatility of available asset classes. Then the share of each asset class will be proportional to the estimated volatility. For example, if the past volatility of the S&P GSCI has been twice as high as the volatility of BarCap Bond Index, then the weight of the S&P GSCI will be half the weight of the BarCap Bond Index. Here, as with the minimal volatility approach, the investor will need to employ some leverage to create a portfolio with an acceptable risk-to-return profile. This approach has been adopted by a number of large and small investors, and there are funds that offer risk-parity products. Because risk parity portfolios are likely to have large allocations to low risk

fixed-income instruments, their pro forma performance will be quite attractive. However, it is almost a certainty that going forward, fixed income cannot repeat the performance of the last several years. In fact, since late 1980s there has been a secular decline in interest rates, and given the current low levels of interest rates, it is reasonable to conclude that this once-in-a-generation secular decline has run its course.

4. **Portfolio Insurance:** This approach is a combination of risk management and asset allocation. It assumes that the investor has already developed an optimal portfolio of risky assets, and now the decision is how much of the investor's wealth should be allocated to this risky portfolio. Portfolio insurance can be implemented through the purchase of derivatives, such as put options, or through dynamic trading. The latter is rather easy to implement, and many investors may feel that it is a cheaper method of protecting the value of their investments. To implement this strategy, the investor must specify the minimum value of the portfolio that he or she is willing to accept. For example, the investor may state that any loss greater than 10 percent within the next 24 months will not be acceptable. The next step is to determine the amount that should be invested in safe fixed-income assets that can guarantee that minimum value. This amount will be the present value of the minimal value. For example, if the current value of a portfolio is $10 million, and the investor is not willing to accept a value lower than $9 million after 24 months, the amount needed to be invested in fixed-income assets when the two-year interest rate is 1 percent per year will be $8.82 million. This means the investor has a cushion of $1.18 million. The investor then allocates a multiple of this figure in the risky portfolio. For example, given a multiplier of 5, the investor would invest $5.9 million in the risky portfolio and the rest, $4.1 million, in the safe fixed-income asset. The level of the multiplier depends on the risk preference of the investor as well the riskiness of the investment environment. For example, with a multiplier of 5, the investor can be assured that the value of his or her portfolio will not go below the prescribed floor as long as there is no decline of more than 20 percent (that is, one-fifth) in the value of the risky portfolio between any rebalancing. Therefore, if an investor is willing to rebalance the portfolio more often, or the portfolio of risky assets has a low volatility, then a multiplier greater than 5 can be selected. Of course, there are a number of issues such as transaction costs, leverage, and changing interest rates that we have not touched on in this brief description of portfolio insurance. Interested investors should educate themselves about these and other aspects of this strategy before attempting to implement it.

Given the wide range of issues involved in asset allocation, a systematic approach to its use across traditional and alternative asset classes is important for client education, client marketing, and product creation and management. As discussed in previous chapters, the level of sophistication and detail may differ for each client. For more sophisticated investors, a wider range of asset allocation techniques and approaches is often introduced, if for no other reason, than to indicate that the firms' modeling processes are competitive in areas such as tracking error, capacity, and liquidity adjustments. At the basic investor level, the simple Markowitz mean-variance asset allocation is often used simply because of the clients' background with the methodology.

A PERSONAL VIEW: ISSUES IN ASSET ALLOCATION

A brief review of the academic literature on asset allocation stresses the algorithmic and mathematical models (e.g., mean-variance) that form the basis for asset allocation across multiple asset classes. In contrast, while the practitioner literature on asset allocation also provides various model-based approaches to asset allocation, this literature also attempts to focus on the art of asset allocation; that is, the required interaction between advisor and investor to determine the best set of approaches to ensure that the investor holds a portfolio that reflects that particular investor's true return and risk attitudes. This would be all well and good, if one could divine an investor's true risk appetite, evaluate that risk appetite over time, and constantly adjust one's investment portfolio (real and financial) to meet the changing needs of the investor.

A review of major asset allocation recommendations across major investment firms shows little if any difference in the recommended holdings for a range of investor types (e.g., conservative, moderate, aggressive). Of greater concern is that there is no means of determining any consistency of how those firms evaluate if an investor is conservative, moderate, or aggressive in nature, or if that determination is beneficial in determining the asset mix for a particular investor.

As discussed earlier, additional problems are inherent in the business model of the recommending firm. Most firms sell what they know. If an individual is not conversant with commodities, how could any individual expect that firm to recommend commodities? If a firm has little background in hedge funds, hedge funds will not be recommended. Similarly, in almost any area of investment, one generally requires a background in the asset before recommending its use. This problem exists not only in the individual investor area but at the institutional level as well. Increasingly, the boards of large pension plans are requiring that they have their own investment representative rather than solely accepting the recommendations of the advising investment firms or their own internal staffs. These boards know that the advising firms have their own set of preanalyzed, compliance-based firms that have passed certain screening tests. A different firm would offer a different set of firms, not because one is better or worse than another but simply because it is costly to analyze firms, and these are the firms that the consultant believes would be accepted by the investor.

An even greater problem is that once a firm or asset allocation process has been recommended and accepted (i.e., benchmarks agreed to, risk allocations determined), it is difficult to change the process despite changing product and market conditions. Individuals have made decisions and have placed capital based on recommendations and educational material produced by the firm. If firms are fundamentally going to change an investment balance or a particular benchmark, they generally have to contact all individuals currently using the product to ensure that each and every individual is assessed of the reason for the change and the potential effect of the change on the underlying portfolio. It is simply not worth the time, cost, and legal exposure.

For most firms, staying with the tried and true trumps change. For many firms, it is safer to be consistently wrong than sometimes right. In addition, the crux of asset allocation is reliable and independently verifiable information. The creation of asset classes for which the fundamental return process cannot be monitored or managed may be of little use. Asset allocation selection models are often little more than black boxes, whether in the form of investment processes or in the form of assets provided for selection. Do investors using these models appreciate that the results are dependent on the data provided or that historical returns for stocks and bonds may have little to do with expected returns and risk for the future? The historical return for the S&P 500 and historical returns for the Barclays bond indices may have little to do with current or expected returns to either index. Past historical measures of correlation are a function of the data period used and may not represent risks under a wide range of economic environments of greater concern to the investor. With technological and information advances, the character and definition of assets have changed. Therefore, most investors do not realize that returns associated with real estate and private equity are, for the most part, accounting returns based on the business model of the investment vehicle or management firm. For example, every investor should ensure that the benchmarks or asset indices used in his analysis reflects the return performance of actual investable assets. As shown in Exhibit 8.6, for each of the asset class benchmarks often

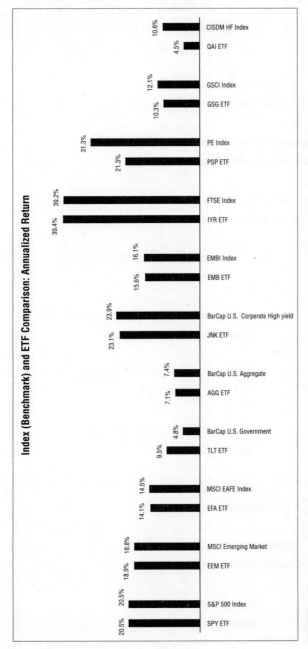

Index (Benchmark) and ETF Comparison: Annualized Return

CISDM HF Index	10.6%
QAI ETF	4.5%
GSCI Index	12.1%
GSG ETF	10.3%
PE Index	31.3%
PSP ETF	21.3%
FTSE Index	39.2%
IYR ETF	39.4%
EMBI Index	16.1%
EMB ETF	15.6%
BarCap U.S. Corperate High yield	23.9%
JNK ETF	23.1%
BarCap U.S. Aggregate	7.4%
AGG ETF	7.1%
BarCap U.S. Government	4.8%
TLT ETF	9.5%
MSCI EAFE Index	14.5%
EFA ETF	14.1%
MSCI Emerging Market	18.8%
EEM ETF	18.9%
S&P 500 Index	20.5%
SPY ETF	20.5%

EXHIBIT 8.6 Noninvestable Benchmark and Investable Exchange-Traded Fund Comparison: Annual Return 8.6 and Standard Deviation

251

Index (Benchmark) and ETF Comparison: Standard Deviation

CISDM HF Index	7.9%
QAI ETF	5.5%
GSCI Index	22.0%
GSG ETF	22.9%
PE Index	32.6%
PSP ETF	29.1%
FTSE Index	25.1%
IYR ETF	26.2%
EMBI Index	7.1%
EMB ETF	8.6%
BarCap U.S. corperate high yield	11.0%
JNK ETF	13.5%
BarCap U.S. Aggregate	2.7%
AGG ETF	3.0%
BarCap U.S. Goverment	3.8%
TLT ETF	15.6%
MSCI EAFE Index	21.5%
EFA ETF	22.3%
MSCI Emerging Market	25.2%
EEM ETF	27.6%
S&P 500 Index	16.8%
SPY ETF	16.9%

EXHIBIT 8.6 (continued)

used in this analysis, there exists a number of exchange-traded funds (ETFs) that have performance (annualized returns and standard deviations) similar, but not identical, to the comparison benchmark. Similar analysis should be done at the mutual fund or manager level to ensure that the results implied by the use of commonly used benchmarks can be replicated in the real world. Similarly, one should ensure that individual products created to meet unique investor needs, are not impacted or conditioned by the balance sheet of the provider or his or her prime broker and other borrowing relationships. Very little of this information is in the public domain, and rarely, if ever, do financial consultants or brokers incorporate these facts into their analyses for clients or prospects.

WHAT EVERY INVESTOR SHOULD KNOW

In this chapter we showed that the asset allocation decision lies at the heart of successful investing. At the same time, we showed that there is no single simple, all-accepted approach to making this most important decision. The approach you use is often founded on your list of acceptable assets and known risk tolerance. With so much at stake, there is simply too much to know. Perhaps the following list may help.

- **There Is NO Wizard.** The financial disturbances of 2007 and 2008 have forced the discipline of asset allocation, and those who profess to practice it, to enter into this new reality phase. Many asset allocators, before (and unfortunately after) continue to use equity and fixed-income markets as the primary investment vehicles in any asset allocation solution. They continue to use historical data from benchmarks that no longer exist or have changed so fundamentally that the historical results are meaningless. Of even greater significance, if you start using their system: how significantly different are their results from others'? It amazes us how all the major firms seem to advocate the same basic holdings. This seems strange. Either they all have the truth or they are all hoping not to be the odd person out. Investors should use different asset allocation models (e.g., traditional asset classes, factor based, risk parity).
- **Do Not Expect or Accept the Impossible, but Also Do Not Accept Just the Possible.** Asset allocation is a risk-management tool and, although not as commonly accepted, a return-enhancement vehicle. Investors must fundamentally understand that if an asset allocation process suggests that it can produce positive returns in any economic environment, the return it offers should be the risk-free rate. In short,

asset allocation should not be viewed as merely low-cost insurance. If it is, then as with any other low-cost insurance, it will fail to meet the needs of the investor at the most critical times. Rather, at its core, asset allocation permits a meaningful discussion of the risk-to-return trade-offs within a portfolio.

- **Accept Tension:** We know that the human condition is a constant trade-off between the comfort of constancy and the necessity for change. It is this tension that creates innovation. One of the major challenges facing an educator or manager is how to get others to change or revise heartfelt views that may have once proved useful but no longer fit reality. Often, our advisors become almost like friends. They want it that way. Investors (retail, institutional) should encourage and accept a healthy tension between themselves and their advisors. Losing money is never easy; it should be painful but within a boundary you, your advisor, and your asset allocation model understand. Remember, an asset allocation model is not set up to solve a problem (although that is how they are often marketed), it simply puts the problem in perspective.

MYTHS AND MISCONCEPTIONS IN ASSET ALLOCATION

Change is a common part of the investment world as well as academic research. Research in the areas of stock and bond investment, and all other asset classes, evolves. New theories and information come into existence, which better explain past relationships. Over time, we have developed a host of proposed asset allocation methods, models, and recommended procedures. Some of them are simple, some of them are hard, but all of them are established on a set of assumptions. At one time many of these assumptions may have correctly represented reality, but as in any field, as time changes, the conditions that supported these model approaches change. Today we have a set of simple models of asset allocation and asset allocation approaches, which, for the average as well as the experienced investor, are difficult to discern. But one thing is certain, they all contain myths and misperceptions.

Myth 8.1: Diversification across Equity Issues or Countries Is Sufficient

MPT, advanced originally by Markowitz in the 1950s, centers on the correlation relationships and risk reduction opportunities of adding together securities that respond differently to changing economic conditions. By combining securities, an investor can reduce a portfolio's variance. Recent experience, however, shows that especially during periods of market stress, such as unexpected increases in credit risk, combining securities may have a negative effect on both stocks and bonds. The market effect on stocks and bonds domestically and globally dominates returns, such that simple stock or international diversification may not reduce volatility in such market environments. As a result, diversification into alternative investments, which respond to different market factors than stocks or bonds, is required for an investor to most benefit from asset diversification. Even in this case, investors should be warned. As discussed in this book, many traditionally classified alternative investments (e.g., private equity, real estate, hedge funds) often react to extreme equity and credit movements as traditional equity and fixed-income securities. Asset allocation models that attempt to provide downside risk management can generally only be provided with targeted risk solutions (e.g., options). Diversification within or across assets may offer some reduction in asset or country-specific risk but is not often a solution to generic market risks.

Myth 8.2: Algorithmic Approaches to Asset Allocation Are Superior to Discretionary Asset Allocation

There is an increasing desire for asset allocation programs to be run using a set of decision rules based on a systematic algorithmic-based asset allocation model. These model-based approaches may cover not only strategic asset allocation (e.g., long-term weights) but also tactical (e.g., short-term rebalancing among asset classes) and dynamic (i.e., changes in the underlying risk distribution). One of the most well-known of these algorithmic asset allocation programs is Target Date funds, each with its own asset allocation model (e.g., glide path) that adjusts stock and bond investments over time. The issue really is in the degree to which these models have internal adjustments for changing market environments. The earliest forms of target date programs often put individuals in stocks when young, and bonds when old, even if current market conditions call for bonds now and stocks later. (Who wants to be in bonds when yields are 2.0 percent?) Algorithmic models may reduce the risk of certain discretionary manager-based decisions, but often replace it with poor, fixed, nondiscretionary asset allocation choices. One is simply replacing manager risk with model risk. Investors should be clear what those risks are.

Myth 8.3: Alpha Is Alpha

Asset allocation models are often driven by not only the desire to lower risk but to increase expected return. For many programs, those securities with higher alpha (i.e., excess return above that reflected in the securities' sensitivity to the market) are often selected over similar risk securities with lower alpha. However, the measured alpha may not be the *true* alpha. If there is a low estimate of true risk, then the program model also reports a higher estimated alpha than its true alpha. Of course, the asset allocation model picks all the assets with the high *false* alpha. It is even possible to regress A on B, and A will show an excess return (i.e., positive alpha). Similarly, we can run B on A with B showing an excess return (i.e., positive alpha). Both cannot be right. Simple models of alpha often give incorrect answers—one should know when or at least that alpha is often *not* true alpha.

Myth 8.4: Low Volatility Portfolios Provide a Solution to Investors Desiring Low Market Exposure

The relatively poor equity performance commensurate with high equity volatility have led to an increased desire for risk-managed products. Many of these products are aimed at creating a set of portfolios that capture the low volatility end of the traditional MPT efficient frontier. These products are created using a range of asset allocation techniques. Some attempt to find the lowest volatility portfolio by assuming certain historical correlation relationships between the securities in the sample. Of course, when market stress increases, and correlation increases, the correlation between securities increases, and the low volatility portfolio becomes a high volatility portfolio. Other techniques, such as raising cash or going short on certain futures contracts to try to keep the portfolio's risk level relatively constant, may not capture sudden moves in the market such that volatility-controlled portfolios are sensitive to market dynamics. One additional aspect should be considered: Low volatility programs are also low expected return programs. Many investors attempting to capture low risk may also simply be guaranteeing low returns.

CHAPTER 9

Risk Management

An Oxymoron

In Chapter 8, we noted that for many investors, portfolio creation is based primarily on the well-known and often used mean-variance asset allocation model. We also pointed out that over the past 30 years, there have been major advancements in financial products (e.g., options and futures) and product design (e.g., portfolio insurance, option-based risk management, targeted mutual funds), which have attempted to directly manage a portfolio's expected volatility.

It is a truism in investments that it is easier to forecast risk than it is to forecast return. Unfortunately, it is also a truism that individual investors target return as their goal rather than risk. In our years as investment advisors, most individuals have come to us with an expected return in mind. Few individuals have come to us with the idea of working the other way, which means finding a level of return volatility the investor was willing to live with and living with the accompanying expected return.

In fact, few individuals have a clear idea of the concept of risk. In our experience, it seems that what investors want is an investment professional to both protect their assets on the downside and offer them the potential for gains on the upside. They may be willing to lose a little on the downside, but that loss has to be well defined. From the investment manager's perspective, our hope lies only in helping to determine what the investor's expectations are and how to define them. If we cannot control the future, then we can attempt to control how our investors evaluate us in those various future states of the world. We work with the knowledge that if we cannot control future return, perhaps, at least, we can control the risk of how investors view our efforts in achieving that return.

Even when we discuss the concept of risk management with investors, we have to make sure that investors realize the risk in risk management. Many investors believe risk management should protect them against loss. In fact, in terms of mean-variance asset allocation, managing a portfolio's standard deviation does not protect against loss, it only provides a scale of the probability of potential losses using estimates of variance from the sample period and believing that it is likely to reflect that of the future investment period. Of even greater importance is the fact that price volatility is not the only definition of risk. In fact, there are states of the world in which we have little ability to assess the risk of an event (i.e., the probability that the event will occur), and we are often left with simple assessments of certainty or uncertainty (i.e., what one thinks might or might not happen). Thus, asset risk remains in the view of the beholder, and if the previous chapters are any guide, the truth is that almost 60 years after the introduction of modern portfolio theory, we are still struggling to find ways to precisely define and measure the individual factors that affect the expected risk of individual assets and to determine how best to manage the risk of those assets. In the previous chapters, we explained that the basic message of modern finance has been evolving. In modern portfolio theory, risk was initially viewed as the *measured price* risk. In fact, risk is multidimensional, whereas the often-used standard deviation of the historical return of an asset is merely one possible representation of price risk.

In this chapter, we do not explore the history of risk or even present a complete framework for its presentation. The typical measures recommended for review are risk measures that identify various market risks such as beta, and absolute risks, such as standard deviation. While concentrating on relatively simple approaches to risk analysis, market-only based risk measure may seem to miss more subtle risk exposures. They do not take into account many types of risk (e.g., uncertain changes in inflation or regulatory environment, changing correlations between and among assets, new assets, or the vagaries of herd instincts of investors). Often our most basic models of risk management assume an efficient market in ideas, intellect, information, process, company structure, and delivery systems as well as regulatory design. More damning, they are right just enough to be seductive, but not enough to protect against the event that can genuinely destroy wealth. They appeal to our central hope that the world is fair, all information is understandable, and all asset allocation models exist in an efficient market of ideas in which each model is well reviewed and tested, such that while differing in emphasis, each approach stands on the solid ground of academic theory and practitioner experience.

It is not that more advanced or complete risk-management models, which go beyond simple variance-based bonds of risk assessment, do not try to consider imperfections in market information and market structure, only that it is our belief that a unique definition of risk is almost unattainable and is surely impossible to measure completely. For example, even if the probability that particularly negative news (e.g., a company missing on its earnings) could arrive can be estimated with a high degree of accuracy, it still does not mean that we can measure the risk associated with that negative news. The information would have different implications for different investors. Consider the case of an investor who has substantial investments in the equity of the firm that may report the negative news, and works for the same firm as well. The risk is clearly far more substantial to this investor than to an investor who works for a competing firm and has a fully diversified portfolio of assets. Risk depends on context, and therefore, it is simply too multidimensional to measure by a single number. Yet, the more daunting the task, often the more worthy the venture. In this chapter, some of the most basic approaches to investment risk measurement and management are reviewed. One reason for the emphasis on examples of relatively simple risk estimation is that, for many, risk is simply any factor that may lead to the possibility of losing some or all of an investment. Risk measurement is the means by which one attempts to assess that likelihood of loss, its magnitude and duration, and to, perhaps, design investment policies aimed at managing that risk.

The typical measures recommended for review are risk measures that identify various relative market risks, such as beta, and absolute risks, such as standard deviation. While concentration on relatively simple approaches to risk analysis may seem to miss more subtle risk exposures, basic asset and portfolio risks are the foundation of any risk analysis. In addition to basic models of risk assessment and management, we do provide a brief review of what some investors may regard as more advanced forms of risk management. These approaches are partially based on the development of various derivatives such as futures and options. However, while introducing these advances to the reader, for more complex approaches to risk estimation at the individual asset or portfolio level, investors are directed to more complete presentations.[1] The reason we do not concentrate on more complex models is that for most investments discussed in this book, the less complex methods of risk assessment apply. In short, if you need a sledgehammer to knock in a nail, either you have the wrong hammer or you are trying to knock in the wrong nail.

RISK MANAGEMENT VERSUS RISK MEASUREMENT

Measuring and managing risk is the center of the activities undertaken by financial institutions. In fact, some institutions exist only because they provide a service to the investor in the risk-management area. Take a commercial bank. It provides a number of services to its clients, but one of the most important ones is to help them manage liquidity risk. A typical commercial bank takes liquid deposits and invests them in illiquid investments, such as commercial and real estate loans, and in the process earns a spread. Its clients have access to liquid investments that offer some minimal returns. Mutual funds are another example of how a financial institution provides risk-management services to investors. Mutual funds allow investors to diversify their portfolios even when the size of their investments are rather small. There are investment products that exist mostly because of their abilities to manage risk. Portfolio insurance and covered call strategies are two well-known examples of these products. To evaluate the services provided by these financial institutions and these investment products, investors need to be able to measure risk. In some instances, measuring a particular risk is rather elusive, while managing that particular risk could be within reach. For example, operational risk is one such risk that is extremely difficult, if not impossible, to measure, but relatively speaking, it can be managed by instituting enough checks and balances within an organization such that this immeasurable risk is mitigated. Therefore, it is important to understand that while certain risks can be measured, they may not be the most important ones. The financial industry has developed a whole set of risk measures not because they measure the most important risks, but because they are the easiest ones to develop and implement.

To develop useful models of risk measure, we must first decide on the types of risks that are important to investors. Once a list of relevant risks is provided, we can examine various ways that the risk can be measured. Next, we may want to look back at historical records of these measures to see if they would have been effective in informing investors of the risks that they were exposed to. Investors can learn a great deal from past financial disasters about how various risk measures should be used and implemented.

In general, risk measures can be put into two broad buckets. *Absolute measures of risk* refer to those measures that examine risk characteristics of assets as stand-alone investments. Standard deviation and value at risk are, for example, prominent measures of an investment's stand-alone portfolio risk. These measures are most useful for institutional investors or individual investors who have well-diversified portfolios and who may apply these measures to the entire portfolio rather than the individual securities that comprise the portfolio. In this context, absolute measures of risk do provide some valuable information. The same cannot be said when they are applied to single securities, because such investments do not have stable properties (e.g., standard deviation), and therefore, historically based risk measures are often not useful indicators of the future risks associated with these investments. Conversely, *relative measures of risk*, as the name implies, measure risk characteristics of an investment either in the context of a portfolio or relative to a benchmark. Examples of these measures are beta and marginal value at risk. These risk measures are widely used by institutional investors as they typically have well-diversified portfolios. While there is some ambiguity and uncertainty about absolute measures of risk, the relative measures are far less reliable measures of risk. The reason is that they tend to be more complex and they rely not only on the past behavior of the investment but also on the behavior of a whole set of other assets. Beta of an investment depends on both the volatility of the investment and its correlation with respects to other assets, and potential instabilities in these relationships could make measured beta a poor indicator of future risk.

Once we have a measure of risk, whether absolute or relative, we can go further and obtain a measure of risk-adjusted return. For example, the capital asset pricing model (CAPM) is simply a measure of risk-adjusted return, where beta is used to measure risk, while Sharpe ratio (discussed below) is a measure of risk-adjusted return where standard deviation is used as a measure of risk. Since the 2007–2008 financial crisis, the term *systemic risk* has come to dominate conversations related to risk. Systemic risk refers to events or breakdowns in established economic relationships that affect a wide set of investments. These are macro risks and generally anonymous with distress and turbulence in financial markets. While investors should be concerned with systemic and idiosyncratic risks of portfolios, systemic risk is generally of paramount importance to regulators and institutions that have many counterparties in the financial system. From an investor's point of view, there is very little that the investor can do to avoid or manage systemic risk of a portfolio, and any meaningful lowering of exposure to systemic risk is typically associated with lower return. Finally, while there are many quantitative and qualitative models of idiosyncratic risk of an investment, there are no generally accepted measures of the systemic risk that may be present in a portfolio. For example, beta is supposed to measure the exposure of an investment's return to changes in a diversified portfolio of securities (e.g., market portfolio), but it is not a measure of the systemic risk embedded in that security. In the presence of systemic risk, most of old economic and statistical relationships will cease to work. Security dealers refuse to submit a bid for securities in which they are supposed to make a market, and all but the most liquid assets can be sold only at deep discounts. In this case, knowing that your asset used to have a low beta is not a useful measure of its risk.

Every finance textbook contains a list of risks that investors face. They typically include the following:

- Market risk: This is related to random behavior of traded securities that are included in an investor's portfolio. Since we have long histories of prices of liquid equity and fixed-income securities, this has been an active area of quantitative risk measures. Beta, duration, value at risk (VaR), and other measures of volatility or exposures to market risk factors are primarily used in this area. Market risk itself can be further refined by examining the source of market risk:

- Equity risk: This is the most well-known and best understood source of risk. It results from unexpected changes in global economic prices. Since equity prices should have a positive return in the long run, higher exposure to this risk should lead to higher return.
- Interest risk: This is also a fairly well understood source of risk, and it mostly affects fixed-income instruments and equity prices of financial institutions.
- Currency risk: Positions denominated in foreign currencies have direct exposure to this source of risk. However, currency risk is not one of those risks that would contribute to a higher return on a portfolio. This means that if the hedging cost is zero, one may consider eliminating this risk.
- Commodity risk: Investment in commodities has become an increasingly important asset class in recent years. A portfolio may have exposure to unexpected changes in commodity prices even if it does not have direct investment in commodities; for example, an unexpected increase in oil price will significantly affect several sectors of the economy.
- Inflation risk: This risk will manifest itself through changes in interest rates and commodity prices. Further, this is an unappreciated risk for those portfolios where the total return is supposed to fund operations of an entity, cover the cost of living of a family, or pay for the replacement of real assets.
- Credit risk: This is associated with the failure of a company or counterparty to fulfill its obligations. Unlike market risk, which arises from unexpected changes in economy-wide risk factors, such as interest rates, equity prices, and currency rates, credit risk is primarily related to the nonperformance of one or more counterparties. Also in contrast to market risk, which may lead to symmetrical returns (e.g., a bell-curve shape for return distribution), credit risk generally leads to return distributions that are substantially skewed to the left. The upside performance of a position exposed to credit risk is limited to the recovery of the original investment plus the promised yield, while the downside performance could lead to the loss of the entire investment. Credit risk models are far more complex than market models, and this is an area where academic and industry research is trying to catch up with events on the ground. In its simplest form, credit risk can be measured by the probability of default or credit downgrade of an investment. This can be further

expanded by taking into account the potential recovery rate of the claim in the case of default and the systemic component of the credit event. The latter requires the investor to determine the degree to which default by counterparty could trigger defaults by other parties.

■ Liquidity risk: This is an important and equally difficult risk to deal with. This risk can be broken into two types: funding risk and asset liquidity risk. The first type arises when an investor needs to fund long-term assets through short-term funding. The risk arises because there are market conditions under which an investor may not have access to any source of short-term or long-term funding, and this typically leads to forced selling of assets. Some commercial banks, investment banks, hedge funds, and endowments learned painful lessons during the 2007–2008 financial crisis when short-term credit markets froze, and they were forced to sell assets to reduce their funding requirements. The forced selling in itself does not have to be costly to investors unless the assets lack sufficient liquidity, especially in times of crisis. This brings us to the second type of liquidity risk: illiquidity of assets. Forced selling of illiquid assets requires the seller to accept deep discounted prices for the assets. The potential size of the discount is a measure of the risk faced by the investor. Academic and industry practitioners have grappled with liquidity risk for many years, and we have yet to see a workable and reliable measure of this risk.

■ Operational risk: This is by far the most difficult, and some would argue the most significant, risk that financial institutions could face. In other words, this is a risk for an investor who delegates managing and monitoring of an investment portfolio to a money management firm. Financial press is quick to point out the spectacular losses that investors have experienced because of operational risk, meaning risk due to fraud, rogue traders, or poor risk management. The most recent examples of these were losses experienced by investors with Madoff, Amaranth Advisors, and Bayou Hedge Fund. As much as operational risk is important, it is the most difficult risk to measure quantitatively. Even qualitative models employed by auditors and compliance officers are not capable of providing a measure of operational risk. Finally, while exposures to market, credit, and liquidity risks can be justified because they may lead to higher returns, there is simply no reason to believe that increased exposure to operational risk will somehow lead to higher return. In other words, operational risk is the one risk that has to be avoided all together.

■ Political and regulatory risk: This risk was at center stage during the 1960s and 1970s when a number of emerging economies decided to nationalize some major industries previously owned by multinational companies. While the risk of nationalization has been reduced in recent years, the risks posed by changes in regulations have increased. The most recent example of this risk was the ban on short-selling that was instituted by some of the major industrialized countries at the height of the 2007 to 2008 financial crisis. The financial industry is the most regulated industry and thus investments in equity and fixed income are especially susceptible to this risk. In addition, investments where tax treatment of the income is important have exposures to this risk. For example, high-dividend stocks could be hurt if favorable tax treatment of dividends is changed. There are some quantitative models of political risk, but there are no well-accepted measures of regulatory risk. More recently, sovereign bond traders are learning that quantitative models are inadequate in dealing with risk and volatility that is created by uncertain outcomes of the political process.

MEASURES OF RISK

There are numerous quantitative measures of risk, and a discussion of all these measures is beyond the scope of this book and, in our opinion, not a useful exercise. In addition, there is a great deal of commonality among various measures of risk. For example, all else being equal, the higher a security's standard deviation, the higher its beta. In other words, after looking at less than a handful of measures of absolute and relative risk, estimating additional measures will contribute very little to our understanding of the risk characteristic of an investment.

Standard Deviation or Variance

This is the most well-known and accessible measure of risk. Basically, it measures the degree of dispersion or variation that exists from the average or mean return. Academic research has made much progress during the last 30 years in obtaining more accurate and robust estimates of volatility, which has been fueled by the expansion of derivative markets where volatility typically plays a crucial role in price determination. Similar to other estimates of an investment's characteristics, historical data is used to obtain estimates of volatility. Therefore, it is subject to various forms of estimation error, and if the estimate is obtained during normal market conditions, it is likely to prove highly inadequate during periods of financial distress. An important development during the past 10 years is that the volatility itself has become the basis of investment products. Whether it is futures contracts on volatility index (VIX) or volatility swaps, investors are now able to use these products to make directional bets on the market volatility or manage their volatility exposures.

Value at Risk

As discussed in previous chapters, many of the recommended asset allocation or asset class-based investment programs were often as much a function of investor needs as the business needs of the product provider. The promotion of a security's beta as the sole measure of its riskiness was partially the result of early 1960s-era computers requiring a simple means to determine an asset's expected return and risk; a security's beta gave them just that tool. The advancement of technology, market structure, and government regulation brought about major changes in risk management by forcing restrictions on what risks we managed and how we managed them. For example, regulations that encouraged asset managers to track *established* benchmarks for their strategy focused them on reducing a fund's tracking error relative to the cited benchmark. The change in regulations in the mid-1970s, which partially led to the rapid increase in defined pension fund assets, also led to the rise in firms providing risk-management services that attempted to insure that the asset returns tracked liability forecasts (e.g., asset liability-managed or liability-driven investment). In the latter half of the 1980s, partially because of increased pressures on financial institutions, central bankers from around the world met in Basel, Switzerland, and they published a set of minimum capital requirements for banks. In time, these efforts led to the development and adoption of the Basel Accords I through III, which were attempts to find better ways to come to grips with changing financial markets and financial products. This effort, in part, led to new, more structured approaches to determining the potential risk or value exposure of banks, including one of the most commonly used risk-evaluation measures known today: VaR.

The development of VaR was partially due to advances in computer technology and market structure, which led major investment banks to consider new methods of determining their overall risk exposure. In the early 1990s, two large money center banks, J.P. Morgan and Bankers Trust, generated two approaches to portfolio risk measurement known as RiskMetrics and risk-adjusted return on capital (RAROC). For many, these two models were the birth of modern risk management. While multifactor models of return estimation had long been part of the financial world, these models took a more structured approach to determining how the potential changes in the measured risk factors affected portfolio value. By assuming different future scenarios for each risk factor, the changes in a portfolio's value for changing market conditions could be estimated.

Again, the statistical concepts and risk measures used in both RiskMetrics and RAROC were not new to the academic or practitioner communities. What both approaches did was provide an impetus and a benchmark by which additional approaches to measuring the effect of changing market conditions on portfolios could be evaluated. The programs permitted firms to evaluate their portfolios over a range of risk measures.

The concept of VaR is highly connected to the concept of standard deviation. In fact, in its most common form, there is a one-to-one relationship between standard deviation and VaR. Given this fact, it is rather surprising how much attention is paid to VaR. One reason, as was mentioned, is that certain regulations require financial institutions to estimate and report their VaR to regulatory bodies. The other reason is that VaR makes standard deviation more intuitive. For a given portfolio, probability, and time horizon, VaR is defined as the loss that is expected to be exceeded with the given probability, over the given time horizon, under normal market conditions, assuming that there is no portfolio rebalancing. For example, if a portfolio of stocks has a one-day VaR of $1 million at the 95 percent confidence level, then there is 5 percent chance that the one-day loss of the portfolio could exceed $1 million, assuming normal market conditions and no intraday rebalancing.

The VaR has well-known shortcomings, including:

- The return distribution of the portfolio is assumed to be normal. This means that mean and standard deviation are enough to adequately describe the probability of bad outcome. If the return distribution is not normal, then knowledge of the form of the distribution is required before further analysis can be made. In most applications of VaR, the mean of the distribution is ignored because (a) the mean return is a rather small figure over short periods (e.g., one day) and (b) the mean of the distribution is notoriously difficult to estimate.
- Even if the distribution is normal, the problem then becomes how to measure standard deviation and whether the measured standard deviation is specific to the interval used or to the historical period of analysis. Thus, one of the principal decisions to be made when measuring risk or any return-based statistical parameter is the return interval to be employed and the period of analysis. For example, research has shown that if one day in 2008 is left out, the estimate of annualized standard deviation based on daily data can differ dramatically from weekly or monthly data. In brief, how are past observations that may not be relevant in future risk environments handled?
- VaR assumes that the investment is liquid enough so that, if desired, the portfolio can be liquidated at the assumed loss. For example, stating that

the daily VaR of a portfolio of illiquid assets is $1 million provides very little useful information because the investor will have a difficult time liquidating the portfolio if a loss greater than $1 million is supposed to trigger some type of sell signal.

■ VaR measures only one type of risk, and measures that risk rather imprecisely. VaR has little to say about credit risk, operational risk, political and regulatory risk, and risks that have not been observed in the past (the so-called black swan).

There are numerous books on the measurement and use of VaR. Despite its known limitations, it remains a principal means by which various regulatory agencies and firms track the potential downside risk of a current or anticipated portfolio. In recent months, J.P. Morgan's use of VaR or, more importantly, its alleged misuse of VaR, has been at the core of concerns over the trading loss of one of its divisions. Investors again are warned that passive or active risk-based models are susceptible to errors of omission or commission. Given the above concerns, investors should not use VaR as a sole or primary means of evaluating the risk of a portfolio.

Maximum Drawdown

While the relationship between VaR and standard deviation is in most cases highly predictable, the relationship between standard deviation and maximum drawdown (MDD) is not so well known. This measure of risk, which is rather popular in the alternative investment area, measures the maximum loss of an investment from peak to trough over a given period. It is argued that MDD can capture the risk-management skills of an investment manager and his ability to cut the losses resulting from a given investment strategy. Related to MDD is *time under high water mark*, which is also believed to measure the risk-management skills of a fund manager. Basically, high water marks measure the maximum value that an investment had achieved over an earlier given period. Therefore, time under high water mark measures the ability of a fund manager to recover losses and recapture the old maximum value for the fund. Of course, analyzing only those fund managers who recover from loses may reflect a high degree of backfill bias in that only the strong or the lucky survive.

Beta

As we have tried to emphasize throughout this book, asset allocation is the process of creating a portfolio with a proper risk-to-return balance. Further, as we have also argued, the performance of a diversified portfolio is mostly determined by its exposures to various sources of risk. In a multifactor model approach to risk estimation, one may wish to evaluate how the volatility of a security can be decomposed to determine how allocation to each asset class contributes to the total risk of the portfolio. In this way, the portfolio manager can balance the potential return from each allocation by the contribution of the allocation to the total risk of the portfolio.

It is essential that a portfolio manager be fully aware of how much risk each asset class or investment contributes to the total risk of the portfolio (i.e., its incremental risk). For a portfolio that is properly balanced in terms of risk and return, the expected return from each asset class should be directly related to the marginal contribution of that asset class to the risk of the portfolio. Therefore, if the contribution of an asset class to the total risk of a portfolio is twice as high as the marginal contribution of another asset, then the expected contribution of the first asset to the portfolio's performance should be about twice as high as that of the second asset. Investors should realize that there is not just one measure of the marginal impact of an asset to the risk of a portfolio. It partially depends on how that risk is measured.

Beta is the most well-known measure of relative risk. In a single-factor framework, beta measures the sensitivity of the return on an equity investment to the return on a well-diversified portfolio (e.g., the market portfolio). Also, beta offers an assessment of the marginal effect of a security on the variance of the benchmark. While in theory one can calculate the beta of any investment, beta is not typically used for fixed-income investments. The primary reason for this is that we know the beta of a fixed income will change through its life; that is, a 10-year bond will be a 9-year bond next year, an 8-year bond the following year, and so on. How do you measure the beta of a bond and how does that historical beta relate to the future beta of the bond?

In a multifactor framework, beta measures the exposure of an investment to some important economy-wide source of risk. For example, the exposure of investments to inflation can be measured through its beta with respect to inflation or even better to an investment whose return is highly correlated with unexpected inflation. There have been many books and articles written about beta, and a detailed discussion of this concept is beyond the scope of our book.

Marginal Value at Risk

The same way that beta measures the contribution of an investment to the total risk (i.e., standard deviation) of a portfolio, marginal VaR measures the marginal contribution of an investment to the total VaR of a portfolio.

It is important to note that marginal VaR of an investment is almost always less than its own VaR. The reason is diversification. Some of the risk embedded in VaR is diversified away in the context of a portfolio, and therefore the margin VaR of the investment could be substantially lower than its own VaR. The concept of risk budgeting is partly based on the measure of marginal VaR. In this approach to portfolio management, the investor establishes a risk budget for each asset class and then finds the *best* investments that can be put into that bucket.

Duration

Duration of a fixed-income asset is similar to the beta of an equity investment. For plain vanilla fixed-income instruments, duration provides an adequate measure of the exposure of the investment to changes in the general level of interest rates over a short period of time. Over long periods, duration is of little use because the duration of a bond changes as it approaches maturity. Further, the duration of a bond changes as interest rates change. For this reason, duration works reasonably well only when there are small changes in interest rates. Generally speaking, longer maturity and lower coupon rate means longer duration. Intuitively, when a bond is said to have a duration of, say, five years, it means that it behaves similar to a five-year zero-coupon bond.

Tracking Error

This measure of relative risk is applied when there is proper benchmark for the investment, and the investment manager's performance is measured relative to that benchmark. Tracking error is basically the standard deviation of the differences between periodic returns on an investment product and periodic returns on the benchmark. Generally speaking, investors are willing to accept some degree of tracking error if there is a chance that the manager could outperform the benchmark. For certain asset classes (e.g., large-cap U.S. equities), money managers rarely display skills needed to outperform their benchmark (e.g., Standard & Poor's [S&P] 500) on a consistent basis. Therefore, one could argue that there are likely to be no rewards to bearing tracking-error risk for this asset class.

Each of the measures of risk may be based on a range of estimated values. These values may be estimated using a range of estimation techniques including historical simulation as well as Monte Carlo simulation. Each of these methodologies has their own set of assumptions. One of the issues in the use of prepackaged methods of risk assessment is that a particular portfolio or asset may not fit well into the preprocessed risk package.

For example, the assets in a given portfolio may not be tracked by the pricing systems incorporated into the generic risk program.

For the average investor, both the cost and the level of detail offered by the current versions of these risk-management models make their use prohibitive. In addition, the systems are usually ex post in that they help in measuring the risk of an existing portfolio rather than helping to determine the potential impacts of programs aimed at directly managing the risk target of a defined program.

RISK-ADJUSTED MODELS

In many cases the risk measures discussed in the above sections are used to obtain risk-adjusted estimates of an investment's performance. Below, we discuss a few of these measures of risk-adjusted performance.

Sharpe Ratio

Among the primary forms of risk assessment, an asset's standard deviation remains the industry's primary benchmark for risk evaluation. While we understand the wide range of choices in risk evaluation, for many, when the choice is between two (or more) assets, one way of ranking investments is to simplify risk into a single parameter (e.g., standard deviation). The Sharpe ratio essentially divides the return of the asset or security (after first subtracting the risk-free rate of return from the return) by the risk (i.e., standard deviation) of the asset or security. The higher the ratio, the more favorable the assumed risk-to-return characteristics of the investment. The Sharpe ratio is computed as:

$$\frac{\text{Expected return} - \text{Riskless rate}}{\text{Standard deviation of return}}$$

This measure can be taken to show return obtained per unit of risk.

While the Sharpe ratio does offer the ability to rank assets with different return and risk characteristics (measured as standard deviation), its use may be limited to comparing portfolios that may realistically be viewed as alternatives to one another. First, the Sharpe ratio has little to say about the relative return-to-risk trade-off of individual securities. There is simply too much randomness of the price movement of individual securities to make the Sharpe ratio any real use at the individual asset level. Moreover, the Sharpe ratio does not take into account that the individual assets may themselves be formed to create a portfolio. The risk of a portfolio stems more from the covariance of the assets in the portfolio than from the stand-alone risk of the individual assets.

The Sharpe ratio has other well-known shortcomings, including:

- **In periods of historical negative returns, the strict Sharpe comparisons have little value.** The Sharpe ratio should be based on expected return and risk. However, in practice, actual performance over a particular period of time is often used. In periods of negative mean return, an asset may have a lower negative return and a lower standard deviation, yet report a lower Sharpe ratio (e.g., more negative) than an alternative asset with a more negative return and with a higher relative standard deviation.
- **Gaming the Sharpe ratio.** A manager with a high Sharpe ratio will get a close look from institutional investors even if the absolute returns are less than stellar. Investment managers employ a number of tactics to improve their measured Sharpe ratio. For many asset classes, increasing the time interval used to measure standard deviation will typically result in a lower estimate of volatility. For example, the annualized standard deviation using daily returns is generally higher than when weekly returns are used, which is again higher than when monthly returns are used. Lengthening the measurement interval will not alter return, but will generally lower the standard deviation. Another trick involves the way returns are reported. If the annual return measure is an arithmetic average of monthly returns, and the standard deviation is calculated from the monthly returns, the Sharpe ratio will be upwardly biased.
- **Options change the return distribution.** Rather than approximating a normal distribution, options produce nonnormal return distributions, depending on the choice of option types and strikes. For example, writing a 10 percent out-of-the-money put on a portfolio indexed to the S&P 500 each month generates annual premiums. If the manager is lucky, this strategy will show a significantly higher Sharpe ratio, as the premiums flow directly to the bottom line with no apparent increase in volatility. Strategies that involve taking on default risk, liquidity risk, or other forms of catastrophe risk have the same ability to report an upwardly biased Sharpe ratio. Purchasing a put or constructing a collar has other impacts, both in the return and the probability of extreme values. In both of these cases (i.e., purchasing put or active collar), the impact of measured volatility may be greater than the negative effect on expected return.
- **Smoothing is also a source of potential bias.** Smoothing is also a potential problem when the assets in a portfolio are difficult to price or for which the investment manager has a role in estimating an asset's

current price. The investment manager (or the pricing model employed by the manager or outside pricing service) may bias returns in ways that understate monthly gains or losses, thereby reducing reported volatility.

Investors are trained to ask for a portfolio's Sharpe ratio despite concerns as to how it is measured and what it measures. Other simple single factor measures (e.g., skewness or kurtosis), are often used to describe risk differences between assets with little or no knowledge as to their use, investor understanding, or problems in their construction. For example, we constantly see investment reports of a security's skewness with no information as to its meaning (e.g., for two assets with the same standard deviation, the one with the high level of positive [negative] skewness supposedly has a higher probability of very high [low] returns) or its level of significance (e.g., it is possible that while a security may report a historical measure of positive or negative skewness, the security's true expected skewness going forward may be zero).

Treynor Ratio

One potential disadvantage of the Sharpe ratio measure is that even if it is used solely at the portfolio level, if it exists within a multi-asset class environment, it may not provide a reasonable base for comparing portfolios of alternative assets (e.g., commodities, hedge funds, private equity, etc.) since it is based on a portfolio's stand-alone variance, and not its covariance with other assets that are included in a multi-asset portfolio. Another measure suggested in the literature is the Treynor measure. This measure flows from an understanding of CAPM. The Treynor model states that performance of an investment can be measured as the ratio of return in excess of a safe investment divided by the beta of that investment. That is,

$$\text{Treynor ratio} = \frac{\text{Expected return} - \text{Riskless rate}}{\text{Beta of the investment}}$$

As a consequence, the Treynor measure addresses one of the drawbacks mentioned earlier regarding the Sharpe ratio. The Treynor measure works well when adding assets to a multi-asset portfolio because the betas of the assets can be used as surrogates for the marginal risk of adding the asset to the multi-asset portfolio.

Other well-known shortcomings of the Treynor measure include:

■ **Market Portfolio and Benchmark Measurements:** As discussed in Chapter 1, the CAPM is not as generally accepted today as it was at its inception nearly 40 years ago. Finding the market portfolio is a more difficult task than was initially believed. It is not clear what that proxy should be.

- **Correlation or Beta:** Beta is often used as a measure of relative movement between two assets. However, beta is determined by its correlation with a proxy index and the relative standard deviations of the security and the proxy index. A security can have a high beta and a low correlation with the proxy index if its relative standard deviation is high, or it can have a low beta and a high correlation with the proxy index if its standard deviation is relatively low. In short, beta does not equal correlation.
- **Time Period of Analysis:** There is no single way to determine how many data points, or the time interval, to be used to capture a security's beta. If too long a period is used, you average over periods in which the *true* beta is not the same; if too short a period is used, you fail to capture the relative sensitivity of the security and the proxy index.

In almost any investment security report, a security's beta is presented. Almost no information is presented as to the benchmark used, the time period of estimation, the return interval used, or the significance of the beta in terms of the certainty of the level of the beta. The use of beta without this critical information is a useless exercise in understanding risk.

Information Ratio

There are various definitions of the information ratio. Therefore, investors need to be careful when they see reports containing this ratio. The simplest version of the information ratio is to divide the estimated mean return by the estimated standard deviation. In this case, the information ratio would be identical to the Sharpe ratio when the riskless rate is zero. The disadvantage of the information ratio, when compared to the Sharpe ratio, is that a portfolio manager could increase the reported information ratio by using more leverage. This does not apply to the Sharpe ratio, which is mostly fixed for different degrees of leverage. Another version of the information ratio requires dividing the alpha of an active portfolio by the tracking error of the portfolio. To apply this definition, the investor needs a well-defined benchmark, where it is used to estimate both the alpha of a portfolio, which is the difference between the return on the portfolio and the return on the benchmark, and the tracking error, which is the volatility of the differences in returns. In this form, the information ratio is a measure of active management risk and reward. Clearly, an investor should prefer a manager who can generate consistent alpha, which would lead to a very high information ratio.

WHAT A DIFFERENCE A DAY, WEEK, OR MONTH MAKES

Considerable research has been done in which differences in empirical results based on the use of daily, weekly or monthly data have been analyzed. Initial research in the 1960s and 1970s was founded primarily on monthly data partly driven by the availability of monthly stock and corporate data (e.g., obtained through the Compustat database). The increased analysis of daily data in the 1980s was driven by the availability of comprehensive daily data through the Center for Research in Security Prices (CRSP) at the University of Chicago. In the 1990s, increased availability of tick data led to a number of research projects on intraday pricing modes. Research on the performance of investment funds are mostly conducted on monthly data. Daily data is also increasingly available from real-time data providers (e.g., Bloomberg) as well as certain mutual fund and hedge fund data providers.

In Exhibits 9.1 and 9.2, we simply take a step back and remind investors and researchers alike, that there is no simple answer to the data, time horizon, or analytic program dependency. In this analysis, we use common data sources with available daily data, which is then used

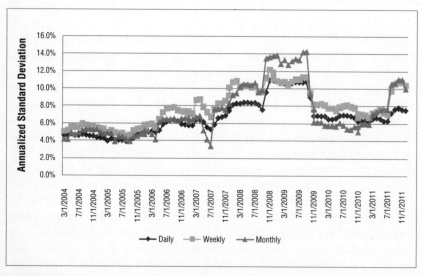

EXHIBIT 9.1 Hedge Fund Annualized Standard Deviation: Daily, Weekly, Monthly
Based on daily, 5-day, and 20-day intervals—one year rolling.
HFRXEH: Hedge Fund Research Equity Hedge.

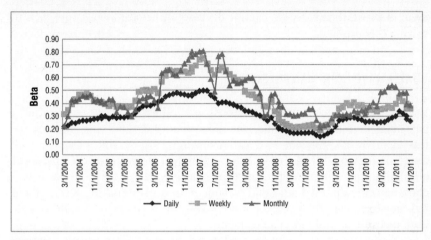

EXHIBIT 9.2 Hedge Fund Beta: Daily, Weekly, Monthly
Based on daily, 5-day, and 20-day intervals—one year rolling.
HFRXEH: Hedge Fund Research Equity Hedge.

to create different return series using various time intervals (e.g., daily, 5 day, 20 day). Over a common time frame, the various return intervals form the basis for a series of empirical comparisons. These empirical comparisons include analysis of (a) common measures of distributional characteristics (e.g., standard deviation) and (b) simple measures of market beta. Results indicate the effect on risk measures for the use of daily, 5-day, and 20-day return intervals, which indicate that the estimated values of standard deviation (see Exhibit 9.1) and beta (see Exhibit 9.2) are affected by whether the return is estimated on a daily, weekly, or monthly basis.[2]

In previous sections we discussed how risk estimated during periods of normalcy may not offer reasonable forecasts of risk during periods of market stress. In fact, investors should also be aware of the opposite set of events. That is, risk estimated during periods of market stress may not offer reasonable forecasts of risk during periods of normalcy. What role these extreme events play, and how they should be handled when estimating risk and return remains an open question. If October 2008 is assumed to be a rare event and a similar event may be observed only once every 20 years, then to obtain reasonable estimates of an investment product's volatility during periods of market normalcy, should October 2008 be excluded from the estimation process? Unfortunately, we do not have a good answer to this question because we do not really know how rare October 2008 was. In addition, the importance of this observation is different to different investors and, therefore, we cannot develop a one-size-fits-all approach to solving this problem.

QUALITATIVE RISK MANAGEMENT

We recommend that investors choose a number of managers within a particular investment to reduce the risks of an individual manager. While this chapter has concentrated on reviewing various risk processes and concerns regarding their implementation, for most investors, the process of evaluating and monitoring investment risk selection begins and ends with choosing an individual who will provide both portfolio asset selection and risk management. In short, for most investors the manager would handle both investment and risk management.

The decision begins and ends with the choice of an investor's personal investment and risk advisor. It is impossible in this brief section to detail all of the various due diligence aspects required for an in-depth analysis. The following points simply reflect some of the principal points involved in a due diligence review:

Financial Advisor or Consultant: For the most part separate yourself, at least emotionally, from your advisor. This may be a strange statement especially after pointing out the importance of investment advisors, but this is a business decision. Investors have to (a) verify education and certification, (b) understand the depth and breadth of the investment and support teams, (c) understand and test the fundamental investment methodology and investment process, (d) be aware of risk presentation bias, and (e) understand and test systems and procedures (including disaster recovery, back office and compliance practices).

Trading Process: If the manager has direct investing control, ensure that you know (a) who has authority to trade the portfolio and what their backgrounds are; (b) who are the counterparties and what is the due diligence regimen for their selection; (c) who are the auditors and whether they are independent; (d) who is responsible for risk management and what are the day-to-day procedures for tracking risks, portfolio composition, and allocations, as well as liquidity, and if risk management has the authority to stop unauthorized trades or the authority to demand that the portfolio be brought back into compliance with investment guidelines; and (e) who the internal and outside legal teams employed by the firm are.

Strategy: The manager must provide (a) investment style characterization; (b) instruments used for investment; (c) description of fund strategy and its principles; (d) trading philosophy; (e) information as to when the strategy will make money and when it will lose money; (f) strengths and weaknesses of the fund's investment strategy; (g) number of investments in the fund's portfolio; (h) breakdown of instruments traded (by percentage); (i) current long, short, and cash positions; (j) firm administration; (k) investment vehicles offered; and (l) brokerage firms and prime brokers used.

No matter how an investor arrives at managers or which vehicles are chosen for implementation, monitoring the strategy over time is key. Just as market fluctuations will gradually move the initial asset allocation decision, manager and/or product goals and objectives should be periodically reviewed.

A PERSONAL VIEW: ISSUES IN RISK MANAGEMENT

Simply put, economic and financial change is difficult for all of us. Moreover, the dynamics of the ultimate winners and losers is not an easy forecast. For much of the past, larger-fund firms with all their financial resources would have seemed easily positioned to defeat smaller rivals; however, new technology and regulatory freedoms have permitted smaller specialized firms to compete directly with larger rivals. Technology, globalization in trade and investment, and the ease of knowledge transfer enables many smaller firms to provide specialized local financial products with a comparative advantage as they take advantage of global risk-management tools. Just as this technology has arrived to permit a more level playing field, the worry is, of course, that government regulation will tilt the game back in favor of larger financial firms that can meet the cost and oversight needs of new regulatory controls. It would also be negligent of us not to point out that simple reliance on technology is not the answer.

As mentioned earlier, a quick click on a web search engine for asset allocation brings up millions and millions of hits. A multitude of models exist, each with their own unique twist on pricing and risk management. Complex problems are not solved with simple solutions. Risk-management models are mostly based on historical data that either does not reflect today's markets or fails to capture the probability of potential events. In any case, the dynamics have changed. Recent events in the United States have confirmed the failure of a rule-based-only approach to risk management. Even if it works in general, it may fail in the particular.

Is there a simple one-size-fits-all regulatory, technological, and financial framework that provides markets with both the financial needs and the competitive environment required for long-term market survival? It would have to protect the existing system from the impacts of that change while taking into consideration the competing interests of government, firms, and investors, who are the partners and the players in the modern global world of financial change. Even more so, how we proceed with this change will certainly affect the outcome. Given the dynamics of the competing interests and competing economic reality, how best can investors deal with future uncertainty? For those who manage funds, the concepts of option pricing should be familiar. Firms or funds that succeed must be flexible enough to react to any new reality. Firms must hold, if possible, a number of costless *real* call options that may not provide them with success in this current economic environment, but which can be easily turned on in the next. Funds are able to have the characteristics (costless real options) that allow them to mutate and enable firms, funds, or countries to meet those changes. It does not require much time in thinking of past examples of firms, funds, countries, or species that were dominant, only to fail as they were unable to adapt to new conditions and reality. Maybe the best thing we can learn from the past is that it is just that, the past. The future remains open to those who are prepared to meet the new realities of the present and are not constrained to constantly attempt to correct past shortcomings.

For many of the reasons provided above, risk management has had an increasing reliance on quantitative models that provide one-size-fits-all solutions to complex problems. If finance theory has provided any perspective on the investment world, it is that expected return is a function of risk (i.e., there are no free solutions without return and risk impact), and one can adjust the normal return and risk profile only through the use of options or their synthetic alternatives. In short, financial theory provides us with a limited framework that quantitative models, however neutral, generic, or evolutionary can fundamentally change. As a result, discretion in the asset allocation process is a necessity. It is an additional factor in a multidimensional equation. For much of this book, we have centered our discussions on the concept of risk management (e.g., a process for determining the probabilistic impacts of various investor choices). However, we also emphasized very early in our discussions, that in fact, most of our actions exist not in the world of risk, but in the galaxy of uncertainty. Again, we know what we know, we know what we do not know, we do not know what we do not know. To borrow a concept from the efficient markets, the known is a random variable with drift. The use of discretion adds an evolutionary control variable on both the changing risk postures of the asset allocation process as well as adding an additional factor to potential risk. For many, market-sensitive risk models only work if they are used by most participants such that there is an agreement as to the meaning of the outcomes of the model. At the same time, the fact that numerous individuals are using the model makes the system sensitive to the assumptions of the model being used. Both the failure in the assumptions behind the use of the copula model in measuring credit risks, or the current failure of the federal macroeconomic model to adequately forecast gross domestic product (GDP) growth, are but two examples of the failure of quantitative models in providing guidance for risk management.

Finally, in this chapter we have attempted to discuss various aspects of risk management. For various approaches to risk management, one of the assumptions is the existence of systemic risk and non-systemic risk. Investors diversify across multiple assets to reduce non-systemic risk, but systemic risk (i.e., the exposure to certain common risk factors) cannot be removed. One of the reasons for multiple assets is that not every asset has the same sensitivity to the same risk factors. Risks in various market environments can be managed by adjusting portfolio holdings to the various expected states of the world. But what happens if all the states of the world go to one—the advantages of asset diversification vanish. This is simply the truth of the matter. There is a substantial body of research regarding the causes of such risks. Yet researching and identifying causes such as market concentration, liquidity, and leverage cannot provide escape from the inevitable: It is virtually impossible to steel a portfolio against systemic risks. Hence, the need and requirement for discretion and flexibility in portfolio risk management.

WHAT EVERY INVESTOR SHOULD KNOW

Oxymoron is often viewed as a contradiction in terms. In truth, a better choice of subtitle for this chapter would have been *OXI*-moron (OXI is the Greek word for "No"). The idea that an investor can honestly and completely manage risk is a level of hubris that no one should approach. In this chapter, we attempted to provide a brief history of the development of risk management and discuss some of the current approaches. The very fact that we are constantly changing how we approach risk management should leave every investor with the understanding that there is risk in risk management.

- **Risk Management Is an Approximation:** Risk is almost impossible to define and is surely impossible to measure completely. It is simply too multidimensional in nature. Moreover, given the multidimensional nature of the investing public (i.e., individual versus institutional, private versus public), it is impossible to come up with a single one-size-fits-all asset allocation model. For every investor, the question really is how much risk do you want in your risk-management system? What is the time frame in which you are willing to hold that risk? What risks do you really want managed (e.g., standard deviation or shortfall risk)? There is simply no single all-inclusive risk-management system. Certain systems are fit for one type of investment (e.g., liquid equity) but not for others (e.g., portfolios of tradable and nontradable assets). We generally advise following risk-management systems that provide actionable results.

■ **Beware of Model Risk:** The problem remains that if asset allocation is the primary means by which investors attempt to reach the highest expected return at the lowest level of risk, then investors are simply exposed to too much risk from many of the more simplified methods of asset allocation. Most current asset allocation models use long-term return, historical volatility, and correlation when attempting to evaluate potential return and risk alternatives. The shortcomings of such models in current global markets in which the dynamics of technology, regulation, and economics make historic data of little use and require a more dynamic means of tracking changing risk relationships, is obvious. Finally, beware of accepting the common approach. Bond ratings remain a primary way for individuals to assess bond risk, even though we know the shortcomings of the ratings. In today's world, VaR remains one of the primary approaches to measure exposure to loss, but we also know its dramatic limitations. There is risk in any risk model—ask your advisor what they are and how he or she hopes to manage it.

■ **Beware of Simple Solutions to Hard Problems:** Within the past year, various firms have offered relatively simple solutions to managing portfolio risk. These methods include volatility targeting, minimum variance portfolios, and risk-based investment vehicles. They often offer historical evidence of the benefits they offered in periods of crisis. Of course they do; who would ever offer a new product that did not show evidence of solving a past problem (known as backfitting the model)? A typical example is a portfolio that uses historical low correlations between assets to create a low volatility portfolio that becomes a high volatility portfolio in periods of market stress when correlations go to 1. It sounded so simple to the investor; the risk-management guaranteed return seemed so enticing. Simple products that offer seemingly simple answers are generally too good to be true. No free lunch here. As for any product, know the cost of the insurance.

MYTHS AND MISCONCEPTIONS OF RISK MANAGEMENT

Recent market performance, which found many investors faced with large losses across a range of investment vehicles, has drawn into question many of the most strongly held beliefs about the benefits of a range of risk-management products and approaches. The financial disturbances of 2007 and 2008 have forced the discipline of asset allocation, and those who profess to practice it, to enter into this new reality phase. This is a difficult endeavor because it may very well be that mistakes were made that, on reflection, could have been prevented. The issue remains to what degree was the failure of many risk-management tools caused primarily by myths and/or misconceptions as to their use and supposed benefits.

Myth 9.1: Risk Can Be Quantified

Eighty years ago, Frank Knight attempted to distinguish *risk* from *uncertainty*. For Knight, risk meant the probability of an event that could be estimated and quantified. At the other extreme was the concept of uncertainty under which the probability of an outcome could not be estimated. In this case, one generally talked in generalities, such as: this could happen or might happen or is expected to happen. One reason for the failure of many risk- (i.e., probability) based models of risk management is that perhaps risk cannot be quantified in that fashion. Perhaps, the best we can do is to say something is *most likely* to happen or *most likely* to fail. Unfortunately, the use of the concept of uncertainty leaves many risk-management decisions in the eye of the beholder and not in the actual probability of the event succeeding or failing. However, investors must be aware that many models are based on the concept of risk (probability based on a set of accepted data), not because it is right, only that risk models have difficulty if based on the eye of the beholder.

Myth 9.2: Futures Contracts Provide Risk Control through Their Ability to Forecast the Future

Often individuals think of futures contracts as potential risk-control vehicles, since they maintain that futures forecast future prices. In fact, many futures contracts may be useful risk-control vehicles, not because they forecast the future (in many cases they do not), but because they track the return of the current cash price. Most futures contract prices are based on a cash-to-carry model in which the change in futures prices often reflect the change in the current spot price. If the cash price changes, the futures price changes. It is not necessarily the other way around.

Myth 9.3: Simple Measures of Risk Measurement Work

In this book we have discussed various simple measures of security risk estimation. Each of them, such as Sharpe ratio and implied volatility, has its own inherent problems. One measure that remains in common use to measure equity risk is a security's beta. However, beta, by itself, is not a measure of a security's total risk (i.e., variance) or even its systemic risk. In addition it may not even indicate how two securities move together. An asset can have a high correlation with another asset but a low beta simply if its standard deviation is low, or an asset can have a low correlation with another asset but a high beta if its relative standard deviation is high. In short, beta does not equal correlation.

Myth 9.4: Risk Minimization Ensures Reduced Risk

Just as the promise of returns attracts certain investors, the promise of risk minimization also attracts a set of investors. The problem is, of course, that risk reduction has its costs. Some of those costs are explicit (e.g., limited upside gain for downside protection), others of them are less transparent (e.g., the use of target funds with a specific glide path that may result in an investor holding bonds just when they are the riskiest). Investors should know that (1) seemingly cheap risk-management programs would not be expected to produce risk-free solutions and (2) seemingly riskless solutions by definition should be expensive. For example, current risk targeted funds have their place, but remember it is only a risk target.

Myth 9.5: Masters of Risk Assessment Exist

Like the wizard in *The Wizard of Oz*, most risk-management wizards are good people, not necessarily good wizards. While most investors have come to accept the fact that superior outperforming investment managers generally do not exist, somehow we continue to believe that there exists someone, somewhere, who somehow has come up with a foolproof method to measure and manage investment risk. The problem is if they focus on algorithmic solutions, those approaches are subject to model error (e.g., the use of the copula model of correlation, which led to individuals misrepresenting the risks of various tranches of collateralized debt obligation [CDO] of mortgage-backed securities, etc.). If you believe in discretionary approaches to override algorithmic models, you are faced with the problem that people make mistakes. In May of 2012 JPMorgan Chase, announced that one of its trading divisions lost a minimum of USD 2 billion while trading synthetic credit products. Senior management of the bank described this loss as an "egregious" failure of its risk management policies.

Myth 9.6: Regulation Reduces Risk

Regulation is often presented as a part of the risk-management process. Since regulation comes with a cost, it is often assumed that it must also come with a matched benefit. Examples of regulation directly aimed at managing risk are the Basel Accord recommendation of VaR and the Dodd-Frank rules on speculative limits. While government regulations have their anticipated benefits, they may also have secondary effects that may overwhelm the anticipated benefits. The use of VaR may force certain banks to reduce certain types of loan and trading activities beneficial to economic growth. Restrictions on speculation or a one-size-fits-all definition may reduce liquidity of futures markets and increase the cost of hedging for true hedgers. In short, regulations may reduce one risk while increasing others.

Myth 9.7: We Know How to Measure Systemic Risk

Whenever we hear that there is a set of measures that provides answers to the current level of systemic risk, we are reminded of *The Black Swan: The Impact of the Highly Improbable* written by Nassim Nicholas Taleb, or the classic statement: "We know what we know, we know what we do not know, we do not know what we do not know." Personally, we favor the statement: "We monitor what we measure." There are constantly new suggestions as to methods of testing market liquidity and transparency, but by its very nature, systemic risk cannot be controlled or it would not *be* systemic risk.

Myth 9.8: The Most Important Investor Risk Is Financial

As discussed in the preceding myth, we manage what we measure; however, financial risk is only one part of an investor's overall asset portfolio risk. The average person's total asset wealth, real estate, and private equity (i.e., a person's job), often add up to over 75 percent of total wealth (e.g., house, current discounted value of job, etc.). Equally important, the correlation between an investor's house, job, and the rest of his or her financial portfolio could be relatively high. When the plant closes, the house falls in value, equity in the IRA drops, and his or her job is on the line. We have not even added the liability stream into the picture. To sum it up, everyone's investment model should be a liability-driven model of asset risk management. But that is a book for a different time.

CHAPTER 10

In Conclusion

Throughout this book, we have consciously made no distinction between individuals and institutions when using the term *investor*. We saw no need to make a distinction since they confront the same issues and challenges as they navigate differing investment opportunities and associated risks. Furthermore, while at times we are seemingly harsh on managers and their institutions, we are reminded that this is a harsh business. It is a business where retirements, basic comforts of life, and careers are at stake. It is also a business where people are paid vast sums of money to produce very specific results. These vast sums also have, at times, the ability to compromise moral and intellectual compasses. We have no doubt that investment banks were not designed simply to relieve investors of their money. These institutions play a valuable role in the efficient movement and disbursement of monies and the building of opportunities. Similarly, there is no doubt that the vast majority of people in the investment and money management industry are just trying to do their jobs on a day-to-day basis. However, like all industries as large and complex as this, the level of competence, service, and expertise is at best uneven. At times, the lack of competence is forgivable, if not understandable. Far too often in the recent past, it has not been. The Financial Crisis Inquiry Commission (FCIC), a United States government commission tasked with the goal of investigating the causes of the 2007–2010 financial crisis, concluded in its January 2011 final report that dramatic failures in corporate governance and risk management, excessive household borrowing, systemic breakdowns in accountability and ethics, failure of financial regulation and supervision, and failure of rating agencies to properly inform, all contributed to the financial collapse. In short, a collective euphoria of unchecked greed and the suspension of well-tested norms created a contagion of doubt that led to the destabilization of the global economy.

The people in the United States who designed and wrote the securities laws of 1933 and 1934 pretty much followed the lead of their predecessors who wrote the U.S. Constitution. In each case, there was an unflattering but accurate view of human nature. They knew that if given the opportunity, most of us would try to get something for nothing. They also knew that people would gladly trade off long-term security for immediate gains. As a consequence, both designed systems of checks and balances meant to temper the desire for immediate gratification and to force introspection. In the case of financial regulatory oversight, the drafters of those laws and regulations assumed that information transparency and the elimination of insider self-dealing would ensure a level playing field and thus efficient and unbiased markets. Generally, given the monetary and penal sanctions surrounding violations of basic securities laws, the system worked and still works. The model breaks down, both for the institutional and individual investor, where a sense of restraint and responsibility is lost, and where incentives are not properly aligned. Institutions and their professionals are responsible for providing clients with transparent investable programs that tell investors when they will most likely make money and when they will most likely lose money. Investors, conversely, have to view these product offerings with skepticism. The regulators can neither change human nature nor save us from ourselves.

The greatest threat to an investor's wealth and to the financial system as a whole is not overt fraud. Ponzi, Madoff, and Stanford, in some form or another, will always exist and the effect of their schemes on the overall market will always be de minimis. The greatest threat is average people who work in a model of entitlement and have no idea of how very fragile the balance between dynamic capitalism and personal security truly is. At the writing of this book, it has become clear that one of the key global benchmarks—LIBOR—that affects the price of over USD 350 trillion of consumer and business borrowings—has been manipulated by a consortium of traders in the employ of varying international banks. One result of this manipulation was to present a positive but false picture of each bank's ability to borrow in an uncertain lending environment and to increase the traders' bonus pools. The more consequential result has been the introduction of additional uncertainty and suspicion into global capital markets by making borrowers question whether they are paying fair interest rates on homes, automobiles, credit cards and business loans.

Embedded in this affair is whether and to what extent each bank's senior management was involved in the scheme and whether the scheme was tacitly blessed by key governmental oversight authorities. Given the complexity of the issues, it will take years to fully unravel and begin to understand the design and impact of this fraud. Yet, even in its infancy there is a constant. Perhaps the most unsettling aspect of this scandal is how familiar it has all become—the subprime mortgage fraud, the J.P. Morgan hedging mess and the all but constant insider trading indictments appear to be more the norm than the exception. Moreover, regulators as well as their political overlords seem intent upon proving themselves at best indifferent and at worse ineffective in managing the infrastructure of global economies. It is all kind of human, pathetic and sad.

Over the years, both investors and those who would serve them have come to expect outsized gains and great lifestyles without the risk of failure. This very real sense of entitlement and expectation leads to a reliance on what we want to hear rather than what is plausible. In a meeting with senior officials at the Securities Investor Protection Corporation (SIPC), a U.S. agency tasked with protecting investor assets in the event of a brokerage firm's failure, we learned that even after the events of 2007 and 2008, investors still rely on historical and hypothetical returns when making investment decisions; they are genuinely surprised when these returns do not pan out, and the values of their holdings are substantially less than anticipated.

A central thesis of this book is that investors must be aware of the risks involved in modern asset management, including the simple fact that they work *without* all the facts. Within each chapter, we sought to explain both the history and the effect of selected asset classes on the market and on investors' ability to appreciate their contribution to their portfolio. We started with a brief overview of the financial markets and their evolution. We traced the development of the central features of financial models. We noted the strengths and weaknesses of these models, and the fact that some have become the bases for even more complex investment products and risk and return solutions. While acknowledging the value of some of these approaches, we cautioned the reader to understand that financial models have underlying assumptions and thus limitations, and that when the limitations are exceeded, the model simply fails. We then examined the traditional equity and fixed-income markets, recognizing that for most investors, the investment world around them is dominated by two asset classes: stocks and bonds. The reasons for their dominance are many, the first being their fundamental sources of risk (e.g., price change) and return (e.g., firm earnings: fixed income gets them first, and the residual goes to the equity owner). They are generally the easiest to trade, the most liquid, and the most transparent; even more importantly, they often differ in their sensitivity to changes in economic factors. For many investors, stocks and bonds make a perfect pair, and since they have been married for such a long time, there is a long history of how they act together.

From the expansion of models, and to investments beyond the traditional, we examined the unique aspects of certain alternative investments. Our analysis of hedge funds, private equity, managed futures, commodities, and various forms of real estate led us to the conclusion that the performances of these asset classes are determined by the business models used to provide investable opportunities. The cost of capital, accounting methods, and infrastructure costs all are a part of an investor's ultimate return. We also noted the limitations of some alternative indices, reminding the reader that indices are, in fact, the product of businesses and have embedded and explicit biases. Within this analysis, we also touched on the fact that governmental regulations play a key role in returns. Tax policy, lending constraints, and fiduciary mandates all contribute to the growth and type of transparency required for certain markets to grow, and these regulatory mandates also contribute to the failure of some products. We also reviewed the role of professionals and institutions in providing advice. Overall, our message to the reader has been to be wary and cautious.

Finally, we return to where we began. We have a simple story. As authors, we are torn between the simple, easy-to-act-on, yet incorrect answer, and the more complex, costly, often-misunderstood, and, in the authors' view, correct one. If truth comes at a price, it ought to be an expensive one. Much of the financial community believes that it offers investors investment product, asset allocation, or risk management based on the perceived needs of the client and the expressed demands of the client; and, within their ability to provide products and services that fulfill these needs within the context of a given firm's overall business operation and regulatory oversight. Within this genuine belief system, mistakes happen. Critical points are misunderstood. Wealth is lost. Some believe that the financial industry is to blame and that it did not protect the investors. While convenient, there is a strong argument that the onus of protection extends beyond these institutions and to the investor.

George Orwell has often been quoted as saying, "We sleep soundly in our beds because rough men stand ready in the night to visit violence on those who would do us harm." Perhaps, just perhaps, it is the investor who must stand ready.

Notes

CHAPTER 1

1. Credit should go to a group of academics and practitioners, including Jack Treynor, John Lintner, and Jan Mossin, for developing this CAPM relationship. $E(R_i) = R_f + [E(R_m) - R_f]\beta_i$, where $\beta_i = Corr(R_i, R_m) \times \frac{\sigma_i}{\sigma_m}$, R_f = return on the riskless asset; $E(R_m)$ and $E(R_i)$ = expected returns on the market portfolio and a security, σ_m and σ_i = standard deviations of the market portfolio and the security, and $Corr(R_i, R_m)$ = correlation between the market portfolio and the security. The βi is often determined using what is called the *market model*, which is derived from measuring the systematic relationship between the return on security $E(R_i)$ and the market portfolio $E(R_m)$: $E(R_m) = \text{alpha} + \beta_i * E(R_m)$.
2. Standard & Poor's Indices Versus Active (SPIVA) Scorecard, 2011 http://www.standardandpoors.com/indices/spiva/en/us.
3. "Poking Holes in a Theory on Markets," *New York Times*, June 2009.
4. R. Ball, "The Global Financial Crisis and the Efficient Market Hypothesis: What Have We Learned?" *Journal of Applied Corporate Finance* 21, no. 4 (Fall 2009): 8–16.

CHAPTER 2

1. J. A. Boquist, G. A. Racette, and G. G. Schlarbaum, *The Journal of Finance* 30, no. 5 (December 1975): 1360–65.
2. T. Schneeweis and C. Schweser, "A Note on the Usefulness of Bond Ratings as Measures of Systematic Risk," *Nebraska Journal of Economics and Business* (Winter 1980): 62–71.
3. For example, during this period there was an increase in the sale of junk bonds, which while they had high coupons, may have had lower duration than similar maturity high-rated bonds.
4. W. F. Sharpe, *Investors and Markets: Portfolio Choices, Asset Prices, and Investment Advice, Princeton Lectures in Finance* (Princeton, NJ: Princeton University Press, 2007), 185–212.
5. Z. Bodie, A. Kane, and A. J. Marcus, *Investments*, 9th ed. (New York: Irwin/McGraw-Hill, 2010 356–368.

CHAPTER 3

1. In fact, research (Schneeweis 2012b) has shown that for the period 2001–2011, the average standard deviation (20.4 percent) of equity long/short hedge funds with full data for the period (from the Morningstar database) was less than the

average standard deviation (27.8 percent) of the stocks in the Dow Jones 30 Industrial Average.

2. T. Schneeweis, H. Kazemi, and G. Martin, "Understanding Hedge Fund Performance: Research Issues Revisited—Part I," *The Journal of Alternative Investments 5* (2002): 6–22.

3. For example, as reported in Schneeweis (2012b), the average correlation between the reporting equity long/short (ELS) hedge-fund managers (reporting to the Morningstar database and with full data for the period 2001–2011) was 0.70. This may be regarded as high, but the average correlation had a standard deviation of 0.12. Similarly, the average standard deviation of the ELS managers was 20.4 percent, considerably above that of the CISDM ELS index (6.3 percent) for the period, and the average standard deviation was 8.3 percent, indicating a wide range of reported volatility for the individual managers.

4. For discussions of various hedge fund indices see Kat and Brooks (2001), Amenc and Martellini (2002), and Schneeweis (2012b).

CHAPTER 4

1. J. Lintner, "The Potential Role of Managed Commodity-Financial Futures Accounts (and/or Funds) in Portfolios of Stocks and Bonds." Presented at the Annual Conference of the Financial Analysts Federation, Toronto, Canada, May 1983.

2. D. Chance, *Managed Futures and Their Role in Investment Portfolios* (Charlottesville, VA: Research Foundation of the Institute of Chartered Financial Analysts, 1991); T. Schneeweis, R. Spurgin, and D. McCarthy, "Investment in CTAs: An Alternative Managed Futures Investment," *Journal of Derivatives* 3, no. 4 (Summer, 1996): 36–47.

3. P. Gogoi, "Futures Are Now," *BusinessWeek*, March 19, 2001.

4. T. Schneeweis, *The Benefits of Managed Futures* (INGARM, 2012c). www .ingarm.org/public/benefits

5. In fact, research (Schneeweis 2012c) has shown that for the period 2001–2011, the average standard deviation (19.6 percent) of systematic CTAs with full data for the period (from the Morningstar database) was less than the average standard deviation (27.8 percent) of the stocks in the Dow Jones 30 Industrial Average. http://www.ingarm.org/public/benefits

6. R. Spurgin, "A Benchmark for Commodity Trading Advisor Performance," *The Journal of Alternative Investments* 2, no. 1 (Summer 1999): 11–21.

7. For example, as reported in Schneeweis (2012c), the average correlation between the reporting systematic CTA (reporting to the Morningstar database and with full data for the period 2001–2011) was 0.60. This may be regarded as high, but the average correlation had a standard deviation of 0.25. Similarly the average standard deviation of the CTA managers was 19.64 percent, considerably above that of the CISDM systematic CTA index (9.73 percent) for the period. The average standard deviation was 9.73 percent indicating a wide range of reported volatility for the individual managers.

8. Note that the period before the data inception of a CTA may contain survivorship and backfill bias. For example, if a CTA started in 2002, returns pre 2002 would contain backfill bias and survivorship bias.
9. K. Black, D. Chambers, and H. Kazemi., eds., "Risk and Performance Analysis in Managed Futures Strategies," in *CAIA Level II: Advanced Core Topics in Alternative Investments*, 2nd ed. CAIA Knowledge Series. Hoboken, NJ: John Wiley & Sons, 2012, Chapter 31.
10. For a discussion of CTA and CPO performance see Thomas Schneeweis, Raj Gupta and, Jason Remillar (2011), Geetesh Bhardwaj, Gary B. Gorton and K. Geert Rouwenhorst (2008) and Schneeweis (2012c).
11. See Schneeweis (2012c) and Burghardt and Walls (2011).
12. See Greg N. Gregoriou and Joe Zhu (2005), Schneeweis (2012c), and Burghardt and Walls (2011).
13. See Black, Chambers, and Kazemi (2012); Schneeweis (2012c); and Spurgin (1998).
14. See George Comer (2006) and Schneeweis (2012b).
15. T. Schneeweis, R. Spurgin, and E. Szado, "Managed Futures Research: A Composite CTA Performance Review," *Journal of Alternative Investments* (forthcoming, 2012). W. Fung and D. A. Hsieh, "Empirical Characteristics of Dynamic Trading Strategies: The Case of Hedge Funds," *Review of Financial Studies*, 10 (1997): 275–302; W. Fung and D. A. Hsieh, "Asset-Based Style Factors for Hedge Funds," *Financial Analyst Journal* (September/October 2002); W. Fung, and D. A. Hsieh, "Hedge Funds: An Industry in Its Adolescence," Federal Reserve Bank of Atlanta (Fourth Quarter, 2006).

CHAPTER 5

1. Schneeweis, Crowder, and Kazemi (2011) and Anson et al. (2012).

CHAPTER 6

1. Investors are directed to organizations such as the European Private Equity and Venture Capital Association for detailed discussion of best practices in performance reporting of PE investments. Whatever the standards, investors should realize that *fair value* accounting, in which the underlying estimate value tracks actual market value at sale, is still in a process of evolution.
2. This PE index is based on monthly returns from the S&P PE Index (December 2003 onward). For the period prior to December 2003, firms that were listed in the June 2007 report were used to create an equal-weighted monthly returns PE index back to 1991. Other research has shown a high correlation between this constructed index and other PE indices (e.g., CA), which are based on nonpublic reported PE nonmarket-based returns published quarterly.
3. T. Schneeweis, *The Benefits of Private Equity*, INGARM, 2012e. www.ingarm.org/public/benefits

CHAPTER 7

1. D. Ling and A. Naranjo, "Economic Risk Factors and Commercial Real Estate Returns," *Journal of Real Estate Finance and Economics* 14 (1997): 283–307.
2. M. Hoesli, J. Lekander, and W. Witkiewicz, "Real Estate in the Institutional Portfolio: A Comparison of Suggested and Actual Weights," *The Journal of Alternative Investments* 6 (2003): 53–59; M. Hoesli and J. Lekander, "Suggested Versus Actual Institutional Allocations to Real Estate in Europe: A Matter of Size?" *The Journal of Alternative Investments* 8 (2005): 62–70.
3. E. Glaeser and J. G. Gyourko, "The Impact of Zoning on Housing Affordability," *Economic Policy Review*. Federal Reserve Bank New York 9, no. 2, 21–39.
4. G. Turnbull, "The Investment Incentive Effects of Land Use Regulations," *Journal of Real Estate Finance and Economics* 31 (2005): 357–77.
5. R. Herring and S. Wachter, "Real Estate Booms and Banking Busts: An International Perspective" (Working Paper No. 99–27, University of Pennsylvania, The Wharton School, 1999); R. Herring and S. Wachter, "Bubbles in Real Estate Markets" (Presented at the Federal Reserve Bank of Chicago and World Bank Group's Conference, "Asset Price Bubbles: Implications for Monetary, Regulatory and International Policies," 2003).
6. R. Shiller, "Understanding Recent Trends in Housing Prices and Home Ownership" (NBER Working Paper 13553, 2007).
7. D. Genovese and C. Mayer, "Loss Aversion and Seller Behaviour: Evidence from the Housing Market" (CEPR Discussion Paper No. 2813, 2001).
8. A. R. Mian and A. Sufi, "The Consequences of Mortgage Credit Expansion: Evidence from the 2007 Mortgage Default Crisis," January 1, 2010, http://ssrn.com/abstract=1072304.
9. Y. Demyanyk and O. van Hemert, "Understanding the Subprime Mortgage Crisis" (Working paper, last modified June 20, 2009), doi:102139/ssrn.1020396.
10. Hoesli et al., "Real Estate in the Institutional Portfolio," 53–59; Hoesli and Lekander, "Suggested Versus Actual Institutional Allocations to Real Estate in Europe," 62–70.

CHAPTER 8

1. Sharpe, *Investors and Markets*, 4.
2. Ibid.
3. See T. Schneeweis, *Benefits of Commodity Investments* (INGARM, 2012a); T. Schneeweis, *The Benefits of Hedge Funds* (INGARM, 2012b); T. Schneeweis, *The Benefits of Managed Futures* (INGARM, 2012c); T. Schneeweis, *Benefits of Real Estate* (INGARM, 2012d), and T. Schneeweis, *Benefits of Private Equity* (INGARM, 2012e), www.ingarm.org/public/benefits.
4. Each of the index components is readily investable, and there are multiple investment alternatives that closely reflect the performance of these indices.

CHAPTER 9

1. P. Jorion, *Financial Risk Managers Handbook*, 6th. ed. (Hoboken, NJ: John Wiley & Sons, 2003); P. Jorion, *Value at Risk: The New Benchmark for Managing Financial Risk*, 3rd. ed. (Hoboken, NJ: John Wiley & Sons, 2006).
2. For readers interested in the methodology for these exhibits, see H. Kazemi, T. Schneeweis, and E. Szado, "Issues in Hedge Fund Analysis: What A Difference a Day, Week, Month Makes," *Alternative Investment Analyst Review* (forthcoming, 2013).

Bibliography

Anson, Mark J. P., Donald R. Chambers, Keith H. Black, and Hossein Kazemi. *CAIA Level I: An Introduction to Core Topics in Alternative Investments*, 2nd ed. CAIA Knowledge Series. Hoboken, NJ: John Wiley & Sons, 2012.

Bhardwaj, Geetesh, Gary B. Gorton, and K. Geert Rouwenhorst. "Fooling Some of the People All of the Time: The Inefficient Performance and Persistence of Commodity Trading Advisors." NBER Working Paper No. 14424, October 2008, http://www.nber.org/papers/w14424.

Black, Keith H., Donald R. Chambers, and Hossein Kazemi, eds. *CAIA Level II: Advanced Core Topics in Alternative Investments*, 2nd ed. CAIA Knowledge Series. Hoboken, NJ: John Wiley & Sons, 2012.

Bodie, Zvi, Alex Kane, and Alan J. Marcus. *Investments*, 9th ed. New York: Irwin/McGraw-Hill, 2010.

Brueggeman, William, and Jeffrey Fisher. *Real Estate Finance and Investments*. New York: Irwin/McGraw-Hill, 2010.

Burghardt, Galen, and Brian Walls. *Managed Futures for Institutional Investors: Analysis and Portfolio Construction*. Bloomberg Financial. Hoboken, NJ: John Wiley & Sons, 2011.

Christoffersen, Peter. *Elements of Financial Risk Management*. Waltham, MA: Academic Press, 2003.

Comer, George. "Hybrid Mutual Funds and Market Timing Performance." *The Journal of Business* 79, no. 2 (March 2006): 771–798.

Darst, David. *The Art of Asset Allocation*. New York: McGraw Hill, 2008.

Demaria, Cyril. *Introduction to Private Equity*. Wiley Finance Series. Hoboken, NJ: John Wiley & Sons, 2010.

Demyanyk, Yuliya S., and Otto van Hemert. "Understanding the Subprime Mortgage Crisis." Working paper, last modified June 20, 2009. doi:10.2139/ssrn.1020396.

Derman, Emanuel. *Models. Behaving. Badly: Why Confusing Illusion with Reality Can Lead to Disaster, on Wall Street and in Life*. New York: Free Press, 2011.

Dhar, Ravi, and William N. Goetzmann. "Institutional Perspectives on Real Estate Investing: The Role of Risk and Uncertainty." Yale ICF Working Paper No. 05–20, June 2005, http://ssrn.com/abstract=739644.

Dunsby, Adam, John Eckstein, Jess Gaspar, and Sarah Mulholland. *Commodity Investing*. Hoboken, NJ: John Wiley & Sons, 2008.

Fabozzi, Frank J., Roland Füss, and Dieter G. Kaiser, eds. *The Handbook of Commodity Investing*. Frank J. Fabozzi Series. Hoboken, NJ: John Wiley & Sons, 2008.

Fabozzi, F. J., and Steven V. Mann. *The Handbook of Fixed Income Securities*, 8th ed. New York: McGraw-Hill, 2011.

Friedman, Jack P., Jack C. Harris, and J. Bruce Lindeman. *Dictionary of Real Estate Terms*. Barron's Business Guides. Hauppauge, NY: Barron's Educational Series, 2008.

Geltner, David. "Benchmarking Manager Performance within the Private Real Estate Investment Industry." *Real Estate Finance* 17, no. 1 (2000): 23–34.

Geltner, D., and David Ling. "Ideal Research and Benchmark Indexes in Private Real Estate: Some Conclusions from the REPI/PREA Technical Report." *Real Estate Finance* 17, no. 4 (2001): 17–28.

Geltner, D., Bryan D. MacGregor, and Gregory M. Schwann. "Appraisal Smoothing and Price Discovery in Real Estate Markets." *Urban Studies* 40, no. 5–6 (2003): 1047–1064.

Geltner, David M., Norman G. Miller, Jim Clayton, and Piet Eichholtz. *Commercial Real Estate Analysis and Investments*. Cincinnati, OH: South-Western, 2006.

Geman, Helyette, ed. *Risk Management in Commodity Markets*. Hoboken, NJ: John Wiley & Sons, 2008.

Gregoriou, Greg N., and Joe Zhu. *Evaluating Hedge Fund and CTA Performance: Data Envelopment Analysis Approach*. Hoboken, NJ: John Wiley & Sons, 2005.

Harris, Robert, Tim Jenkinson, and Steven N. Kaplan. "Private Equity Performance: What Do We Know?" Fama-Miller Working Paper; Chicago Booth Research Paper No. 11–44; Darden Business School Working Paper No. 1932316. doi:10.2139/ssrn.1932316.

Jorion, Philippe. *Financial Risk Managers Handbook*, 6th ed. Hoboken, NJ: John Wiley & Sons, 2012.

———. *Value at Risk: The New Benchmark for Managing Financial Risk*, 3rd ed. New York: McGraw-Hill, 2006.

Kazemi, Hossein, Thomas Schneeweis, and Edward Szado. "Issues in Hedge Fund Analysis: What a Difference a Day, Week, Month Makes." *Alternative Investment Analyst Review* (forthcoming, 2013).

Kritzman, Mark, Yuanzhen Li, Sebastien Page, and Roberto Rigobon. "Principal Components as Measure of Systemic Risk." *Journal of Portfolio Management* 37, no. 4 (Summer 2011): 112–126.

Lerner, Josh, Felda Hardymon, and Ann Leamon. *Venture Capital and Private Equity: A Casebook*. Hoboken, NJ: John Wiley & Sons, 2012.

Lerner, Josh, Ann Leamon, Felda Hardymon. *Venture Capital, Private Equity, and the Financing of Entrepreneurship*. Hoboken, NJ: John Wiley & Sons, 2012.

Lo, Andrew. *Hedge Funds: An Analytic Perspective*. Princeton, NJ: Princeton University Press, 2010.

Lo, Andrew. "Reading about the Financial Crisis: A 21 Book Review." *Journal of Economic Leadership* (forthcoming).

Lo, Andrew W., and A. Craig MacKinlay. *A Non-Random Walk Down Wall Street*. Princeton, NJ: Princeton University Press, 1999.

Malkiel, Burton. *A Random Walk Down Wall Street*, rev. ed. New York: W. W. Norton, 2012.

Schneeweis, Thomas, Raj Gupta, and Jason Remillard, "CTA/Managed Futures Strategy Benchmarks: Performance and Review." In *The Handbook of Commodity Investing*, edited by F. J. Fabozzi, R. Fuss, and D. G. Kaiser, Chapter 11. Hoboken, NJ: John Wiley & sons, 2008.

Schneeweis, Thomas. *Benefits of Commodity Investments*. INGARM, 2012a.

Schneeweis, Thomas. *The Benefits of Hedge Funds*. INGARM, 2012b.

Schneeweis, Thomas. *The Benefits of Managed Futures*. INGARM, 2012c.

Schneeweis, Thomas. *Benefits of Real Estate*. INGARM, 2012d.

Schneeweis, Thomas. *Benefits of Private Equity*. INGARM, 2012e.

Schneeweis, Thomas, Garry B. Crowder, and Hossein Kazemi. *The New Science of Asset Allocation: Risk Management in a Multi-Asset World*. Hoboken, NJ: John Wiley & Sons, 2011.

Sharpe, William F. *Investors and Markets: Portfolio Choices, Asset Prices, and Investment Advice*. Princeton Lectures in Finance. Princeton, NJ: Princeton University Press, 2007.

Swensen, David. *Pioneering Portfolio Management*. New York: Free Press, 2009.

About the Authors

Garry B. Crowder, JD, MBA, MS, is the managing partner of Cortland Advisory Group, LLC. He is a noted expert in the development and creation of multi-asset portfolio solutions and products. He has designed and implemented asset allocation solutions for leading multinational banks, insurance companies and family offices. Mr. Crowder created and was managing partner of one of the first and largest hedge fund managed account platforms. He is a co-founder of the Institute for Global Asset and Risk Management and a member of the editorial board of the *Journal of Alternative Investments*. With more than 25 years of experience in asset management, he has served as a managing director and member of the Executive Committee of Morgan Stanley Asset Management and chief executive officer of Credit Agricole Structured Asset Management Americas. In addition to consulting and angel investing, Mr. Crowder is currently a member of Northwestern University's Law School Board and the Board of Trustees of The New School.

    Thomas Schneeweis, PhD, is the Michael and Cheryl Philipp Professor of Finance and director of the Center for International Securities and Derivatives Markets at the Isenberg School of Management, University of Massachusetts-Amherst. He is the founding and current editor of *the Journal of Alternative Investments* and is co-founder of the Chartered Alternative Investment Analyst Association and the Chartered Alternative Investment Analyst Foundation. He is also a co-founder of the Institute for Global Asset and Risk Management. He has published widely in the area of investment management and has been widely quoted in the financial press. Professionally, he has more than 40 years' experience in investment management. He is currently a principal at S Capital Management, LLC, an investment management firm specializing in risk-based asset allocation and investment strategy replication/tracking programs.

    Hossein Kazemi, PhD, CFA, is Professor of Finance and associate director of the Center for International Securities and Derivatives Markets at the Isenberg School of Management, University of Massachusetts-Amherst. He has published more than 40 articles in academic and professional journals in the areas of asset management, valuation and international finance. He serves on the editorial boards of *Journal of Alternative Investments, Alternative Investment Analyst Review,* and *Journal of Risk and Financial*

Management. He is a managing director at Chartered Alternative Investment Association, the only global professional designation covering hedge funds, commodities, private equity, real assets and structured products. He has more than 20 years experience in the investment management industry and has worked with major financial institutions in asset allocation and risk management.

Index